THE COPYRIGHT BOOK

THE COPYRIGHT BOOK

A Practical Guide

Sixth Edition

William S. Strong

The MIT Press
Cambridge, Massachusetts
London, England

MIT Press books may be purchased at special quantity discounts for business or sales promotional use. For information, please email special_sales@mitpress.mit.edu.

This book was set in Palatino and Gotham by the MIT Press. Printed and bound in the United States of America.

Library of Congress Cataloging-in-Publication Data

Strong, William S.

The copyright book : a practical guide / William S. Strong. — Sixth Edition.

pages cm

Includes bibliographical references and index.

ISBN 978-0-262-02739-7 (hardcover : alk. paper)   1. Copyright— United States. I. Title.

KF2994.S75 2014

2013038918

10   9   8   7   6   5   4   3   2   1

In memory of my parents

CONTENTS

PREFACE

At their best, our laws embody our deepest assumptions about human beings and what proper relations among human beings ought to be. Copyright is such a law. It springs from the belief that those who try to contribute to our always inadequate store of information and inspiration ought to be paid for their pains. This seems a very creditable attitude.

My purpose in writing this book has been to make available to people whose lives and work are affected by the laws of copyright an understanding of their rights and responsibilities. However, I hope that in doing so I have also managed to communicate some of my own fascination with the subject.

I have found it useful to write much of this book as though from the standpoint of the creator of a work—be it a novel, a painting, a blueprint, a dance. But whatever is not kept safe for the artist is given to the public; if you are a would-be user of an artistic or other creative work, you will know your boundaries by the boundaries drawn for the creator of it.

I have tried to gather material and organize it in a way that will tell the story simply. This has not proved possible in all respects; parts of the law are so complex that no amount of pruning and rearranging could make them any less dense. Nor has it proved possible at every point to avoid technical language and terms whose legal definition differs from their ordinary meaning. In such places I have given examples to try to make clear what is being said.

Two further comments about organization are in order. First, because the copyright law that went into effect on January 1, 1978, governs all works created after 1977 and many aspects of works created earlier, I have used this law as my guide for most of the book. If you are concerned with pre-1978 works, you should be sure to read chapter 10, which deals with these works. Second, although many rules differ from one art form to another, it became apparent that to deal with various art forms individually would create a great deal of needless repetition. Instead, therefore, I have treated the various aspects of the law as units and within each unit discussed the exceptions pertaining to one art form or another.

Space does not permit me to acknowledge adequately the encouragement that family and friends have given me to write and later revise this book. In earlier editions I gave special thanks to two people, Evie Hanlon and Michelle Kincade, who had given new meaning to the word *secretary* and without whom all encouragement would have been in vain. But times change, and, like most people blessed with the curse of modern technology, I have become my own amanuensis. The focus of my gratitude therefore shifts to my wife Ann, who has put up with many a foregone evening and weekend to enable this sixth edition to see the light of day. I am grateful to her for so many things, though, that this (which would otherwise be enormous) is but a drop in the bucket.

THE SUBJECT MATTER OF COPYRIGHT

1

Copyright law is essentially a system of property. Like property in land, you can sell it, leave it to your heirs, donate it, or lease it under any sort of conditions; you can divide it into separate parts; you can protect it from almost every kind of trespass. Also like property in land, copyrights can be subjected to certain kinds of public use that are considered to be in the public interest. I shall explain these various aspects of copyright property through the course of this book.

The province of copyright is communication. It does not deal with machines or processes—those are governed by patent law—though it has been stretched, with a bit of sophistry, to cover computer software. It does not deal with titles, slogans, and the other symbols that businesses use to distinguish themselves in the public eye, for that is the stuff of trademark law. Works of art and literature are what copyright protects, no matter what the medium, and works whose purpose is to convey information or ideas. In the words of the statute, it protects "original works of authorship fixed in any tangible medium of expression, now known or later developed, from which they can be perceived, reproduced, or otherwise communicated, either directly or with the aid of a machine or device."[1]

This seemingly simple bit of language incorporates three of the fundamental concepts of the law, concepts whose meaning must be clearly grasped before all else: fixation, originality, and expression.

Fixation

Fixation is the act of rendering a creation in some tangible form in which, or by means of which, other people can perceive it. Even the word *perceive* has its own special legal meaning; in the law's definition one "perceives" a work of choreography, for example, or a work of music, by seeing on a piece of paper the notation that enables a performer to reproduce the work. Thus a musical work may be fixed in sheet music, as well as on tape. On the other hand performing the musical work, without taping it simultaneously, does not fix it because the performance is not tangible. It is heard and is gone.

The great importance of the act of fixation is that it marks the beginning of your federal copyright. You obtain copyright under the federal law as of the instant that you fix your work in tangible form. Fixation also draws the boundary line between federal copyright protection and so-called common law copyright, which is largely the prerogative of the individual states. (*Common law* is the term for law that is built up over the years by judicial opinions; in the copyright field there has not been a great deal of variation from one state to another.)

Until January 1, 1978, common law copyright protected all unpublished works except those that were registered with the U.S. Copyright Office; now it protects only works that have not been fixed in tangible form.[2] If, for example, you have developed a comedy routine in your head, but have not written any notes about it that would enable another performer to reproduce it, your unfixed work falls under the protection of common law copyright. You may perform it as often as you like, or you can let others perform it for a fee, and in theory no one else may copy it. Presumably also you can bequeath the right to perform it to your children, and they to their children, although the idea of an intangible right of indefinite duration seems to run counter to all our instincts and legal traditions of property.

Not much more of substance can be said at this point about common law copyright. Rights in works that have not been fixed are difficult to prove and difficult to protect; it is not even easy to prove what the work is if there is no tangible copy of it. Because the expanded federal law has so severely restricted the operation of the common law, this book is devoted to works that are fixed and thus governed by the federal law, except where I specifically state otherwise.

A work must be the product of your own mind in order to be copyrightable. Originality is not by itself sufficient; facts, even if they are facts that no one else has ever discovered, are regarded as the common property of all of us, as are scientific discoveries, mathematical equations, and historical theories.[3] Facts are not copyrightable because they are not human inventions; theories are not copyrightable because they are ideas, not expression. But although originality is not sufficient in itself, it is essential all the same.

Originality

The law follows a highly subjective theory of originality that often surprises, and sometimes shocks, those encountering it for the first time. If asked whether a person can get a copyright for something that has been created by someone else, most people would answer "no," but that answer would not always be correct. It is true that you cannot get a valid copyright in material that you have taken from someone else's work. But if you have recreated a preexisting work without having had access to it or knowledge of it, you are entitled to your own copyright. The logical extension of this is that you can enforce your copyright against anyone who has actually copied from you, regardless of the fact that that person might have copied with equal ease from the preexisting work. "If by some magic," one distinguished judge has observed, "a man who had never known it were to compose anew Keats's *Ode on a Grecian Urn*, he would be an 'author,' and . . . others might not copy that poem, though they might of course copy Keats's."[4] This is said to illustrate the difference between copyright and patent (which is based on objective originality), and indeed it does on a somewhat impractical level. The likelihood of someone's recreating Keats is vanishingly small, but lesser works—fabric designs, simple tunes, and the like—are often reinvented. Copyright's subjective approach to originality allows them all to flourish, in whatever soil they can find.

That elements of your work may be in the public domain does not invalidate your entire copyright. It only limits your copyright to what is original with you.

An original exposition of public domain material may take the form of arrangement. For example, *The Waste Land* is clearly a copyrightable poem, even though many of its lines are taken from works that are in the public domain. Eliot's originality lies (partly) in the juxtaposition of these public domain elements, and his copyright extends only to the limits of his originality. Similarly, a collage made of newspaper clippings is a copyrightable arrangement.

Derivative Works

Of a slightly different nature, but copyrightable on the same basic principle, are works the law calls "derivative works." Derivative works are those in which someone else's creation is "recast, transformed, or adapted."[5] Translations, sound recordings that transform musical or other works into digital notation, movie versions of plays or stories, orchestrations of melodies, and dolls based on cartoon characters are all obvious examples of derivative works. Others are less obvious but equally common, such as reproductions of artistic works in different media. A lithographic reproduction of a painting might seem to be a copy rather than a derivative work entitled to a protection in its own right, but in fact it is regarded as a derivative work. The reasoning behind this is that the manufacture of an art reproduction in a medium different from that of the original requires the reproducer to contribute some measure of his own special skill and artistic judgment, and that contribution is entitled to protection. There are limits on this, as I shall discuss shortly.

A derivative work may be made of a copyrighted work or of a work in the public domain. If it is of a copyrighted work, and if the artist or author has not authorized it, the work will constitute an infringement of the artist's or author's copyright. In any event the protection afforded to a derivative work extends only to the original contribution of the maker.[6]

Would Eliot's *The Waste Land* be regarded as a derivative work? Would *West Side Story* be regarded as a derivative work of *Romeo and Juliet?* Would Mussorgsky's *Pictures at an Exhibition* be regarded as a derivative work of the pictures that inspired him? The answer to all three of these questions is "no." It may be helpful to analyze why.

Partly the question is one of motive. Eliot's use of preexisting poems was intended not to recast those works in another medium but to use them, through parody and juxtaposition, as building blocks for a message uniquely his own. It was not Eliot's intent, nor was it his achievement, merely to create a new version of Marvell's *To His Coy Mistress* when he wrote

> But at my back from time to time I hear
> The sound of horns and motors which shall bring
> Sweeney to Mrs. Porter in the spring.

Similarly, *West Side Story* is not based on *Romeo and Juliet* in the way that the movie *Gone with the Wind* was based on Margaret Mitchell's novel; it attempts not to tell Shakespeare's story in another medium but to tell its own story, which resembles Shakespeare's play in many important respects. (If *Romeo and Juliet* were still under copyright, *West Side Story* might be an infringement, but that is another matter.)

Partly too the question is one of recognizability. Quite simply one does not recognize particular pictures in Mussorgsky's composition. Recognizability is not perhaps a firm and reassuring principle, but it is nonetheless an important one in determining derivativeness.

Another category of derivative works that deserves mention is that described in the statute as works "consisting of editorial revisions, annotations, elaborations, or other modifications which, as a whole, represent an original work of authorship." What the law protects here is the original contribution of the editor or annotator. The law will not protect trivial modifications, but it will protect modifications that are substantial enough to constitute a "new version" of the preexisting work. The protection given a revision would cover only the work of the editor's own creativity. If a scholar, on the basis of research, revises the text of, say, a poem by Spenser, he cannot get a copyright in the new text because what he has done is to restore Spenser's own words.[7]

The amount of originality required for a derivative work to be eligible for copyright is no different from that required for any other sort of work, but one must be careful to assess originality only in those elements that are new with the derivative work. The Seventh Circuit Court of Appeals summed it up well in these words: "the key inquiry is whether there is sufficient nontrivial expressive variation in the derivative work to make it distinguishable from the underlying work in some meaningful way."[8] Thus, the Second Circuit denied copyright to wind-up toy versions of Mickey Mouse, Donald Duck, and Pluto, because apart from the work involved in representing the characters in the form of small wind-up toys, the copyright claimant had added nothing original. (Indeed, Disney would probably have come down hard on the toy manufacturer if it had.) And as with any other sort of work, one must be careful not to give credit for things that are driven by considerations of function or materials. Thus, in another case, the Second Circuit struck down the copyright of an Uncle Sam mechanical bank that was a smaller-scale version of earlier, public domain models but with certain features altered, because (in part at least) it found that most of the variations from the public domain were dictated by plastic molding technology, which reduced the claimant's creativity to near zero.[9]

One court has held, in a questionable decision, that an exact reproduction of a piece of sculpture, substantially reduced in scale, can be copyrighted as a derivative work if the making of it requires great artistic skill and effort.[10] More recently, and correctly I believe, a court denied copyright to straightforward photographs of works of two-dimensional art, on the grounds that the photographer had not added sufficient original expression of his own.[11] Photographs of three-dimensional artworks, on the other hand, will almost always be copyrightable, for there is nearly always some exercise of judgment in how one photographs a three-dimensional object.

Authors should always bear in mind that the right to create derivative works is part of copyright. Thus, if an author transfers all rights in a work to someone else, this right goes with the rest. The author would no longer be able, for example, to create new versions of his own work. This is often an important negotiating point in copyright agreements.

Copyright in a derivative work is limited, like all other copyrights, to whatever material is original with the creator. An English translation of *Anna Karenina* is a derivative work, and it can be copyrighted, but the copyright will be narrowly defined to avoid giving the translator any kind of rights in what was actually created by Tolstoy. The translator will be protected against someone who copies his translation but not against someone who makes a similar translation by independent effort. Another example is the musical version of *Oliver Twist*. Without doubt the musical *Oliver* is copyrightable, but only to the extent that its characters, its plot, and its dialogue differ from Dickens's novel and are the original creation of its authors. You are at liberty, if it strikes your fancy, to write another musical based on *Oliver Twist*, but you cannot use the variations from Dickens's story that the authors of *Oliver* created, unless you can show that they are absolutely necessary to the task and unavoidable.

If the derivative work you make is of a work still subject to copyright, much the same rules apply. Your copyright in your derivative work covers only your own inventions, variations, and additions. You have no right to authorize someone else to use those parts of your derivative work that you have taken from the original, beyond whatever right your license agreement gives you.[12] Furthermore, when the copyright term of the original work runs out, everything in your work that you took from the original goes into the public domain, and only what you yourself have created will remain protected. The converse is also true: if a derivative work loses its copyright, the copyright of the original remains unaffected.

Tracing a work through its derivative forms can be like tagging migratory animals. Take the example of the movie *South Pacific*. It started out as a collection of short stories by James Michener. Next, several of the stories were combined and adapted into a musical by Rodgers and Hammerstein. Then the musical was rewritten as a screenplay, and the screenplay was made into a movie. There were thus three layers of derivative works, each cutting old material and adding new. And the movie producer had three different copyrights to worry about: the short stories, the musical, and the screenplay. The movie could not be made without derivative-work licenses covering all three previous forms.

The law regards an object code version of a computer program as a copy of the program, not a derivative work. (See below in this chapter.) The same rationale applies to the making of a computer-readable version of any work. For example, inputting an English-language directory into a computer database would be copying it, not "translating" it into a new language. Thus no one who makes a computer-readable version of any public domain work would have any copyright in it, unless some new elements are added. On the other hand, translating a computer program from one computer language to another *would* create a derivative work—assuming of course that anything survived the process other than the ideas or algorithms of the original.

Compilations   The other category of work in which copyrights can become layered is what the statute calls "compilations." This term covers two very different types of works: so-called "collective works," which are collections of things that could be copyrightable on their own, and databases, in which facts or other uncopyrightable things are collected. I use the computer-age term "databases" for convenience only; databases may in fact be fixed in print and other media as well as on computer tapes and disks.

The original authorship that the law protects in compilations is the selection, coordination, or arrangement of items. This is a separate copyright from any that may exist in the underlying material.

The author of a collective work may be the same, but need not be the same, as the author of the component parts. Anthologies are an example of the type of collective work that is made up of preexisting copyrightable works, often by many different authors. Magazines, newspapers, and encyclopedias are examples of collective works that pull together the fresh labors of numerous writers and photographers. The author of a collective work will often add new material of an editorial or descriptive nature. For example, a coffee table book of Monet's paintings might contain text supplied by the person who chose which paintings to include. Technically, the copyright in that editorial text is separate from the copyright in the collective work, although they are rarely separated in practice. The presence of some small embellishment of text would not affect the "compilation" nature of the work. By contrast, though, a scholarly study of Monet that happened to be illustrated with reproductions from his work would not be thought of as a collective work. Why the difference? The pictorial elements in the scholarly study are subservient to the text, whereas in the coffee table book the compiling of images, and their arrangement in the book, are what gives the book its shape.

The other kind of compilation is the database. Databases are all around us: telephone books, medical records, sports statistics, mailing lists. In all of these, facts or other data have been assembled, whether through careful thought or sheer drudgery. Not all of them are copyrightable.

It used to be that drudgery (if great enough) sufficed to secure copyright protection in some courts. Judges responded to the perceived unfairness of allowing people a free ride on other people's work, and upheld copyright in things as menial as the telephone white pages. In 1991, however, the Supreme Court put an end to this practice. In *Feist Publications, Inc. v. Rural Telephone Service Co.*,[13] the Court held that industrious labor by itself was not enough; some "spark of creativity" is needed. The Court even went so far as to say that it is constitutionally required. It held that the mere assemblage of people's names, addresses, and phone numbers, and their arrangement alphabetically by name, lacks that necessary spark.

By this long-overdue and potentially far-reaching opinion, the Supreme Court reasserted the importance of originality to copyright. But what kind of originality?

If selection, coordination, and arrangement are to rise to the level of originality, they must have some degree of arbitrariness. The very word "selection" implies a range of choices, all of which may be equally valid. No one, for example, could challenge the copyrightability of a listing of "America's Most Eligible Bachelors." But where a selection is either right or wrong—say, "America's 100 Largest Cities"—the necessary scope for originality is lacking.[14] It has been held that a book compiling the *complete* poems of Dorothy

Parker is not a copyrightable compilation, even though some of those poems had never been included in any previous such collection. A database that includes no selectivity cannot be copyrighted.[15]

What about mailing lists, which are the livelihood of much of America's retail commerce? They, too, present difficult issues. From one point of view, they are (unlike telephone directories) entirely random, consisting of the names and addresses of those who happen to order a company's products. But where is the spark of creativity?

These are issues certain to see a great deal of litigation, and perhaps legislation, in the future. Information has become critical to our economy, and the struggle between those who have it and those who want it is certain to intensify. It is easy to characterize one side as the hardworking, the diligent, and the other side as freeloaders. European countries, in this spirit, have enacted laws protecting databases that copyright cannot protect. The U.S. Congress has from time to time been pressed to follow suit. It should resist. The very premise of our copyright system is that what is not protected is free for all to use, and that society benefits by not forcing people to reinvent such things as the telephone book.

Expression The third requirement of copyrightability is that the work be "expression" and not "idea." It is an old truism in copyright law that you cannot copyright an idea but only your expression of it: ideas, like facts, are in the public domain. For example, a literary critic who publishes a new theory of the structure of the novel cannot obtain a copyright in that theory; he can copyright only his written expression of that theory. A thief may steal his theory with impunity if the thief expresses the theory in his own words, and the thief,

scurrilous though he may be, can obtain a new copyright in his own written work. Perhaps the first author
should have an action for unfair competition if no
attribution is made, given the nature of scholarly competition. But such a doctrine, which would be separate
from copyright, has yet to develop.

A simple example like this one of literary criticism
may make the rule itself seem simple. It is not. In fact it
is riddled with ambiguities. What, for example, is a
musical "idea" and how is it separable from musical
"expression"? How basic must a plot become, how
stripped of embellishment, before it ceases to be the
writer's own copyrightable expression and becomes
mere "idea"? No one really knows the answers to these
questions, though many a court has formulated an all-
embracing theory, only to see it discarded by the next
court. Judge Learned Hand, a man of legendary copyright jurisprudence, essentially threw up his hands:
decisions of where to draw the line between idea and
expression, he said, must "inevitably be ad hoc."[16]

Renderings of wildlife have led to some interesting
cases that turn on the idea-expression dichotomy. For
example, the Ninth Circuit found a very "thin" copyright in a glass-in-glass sculpture of a jellyfish. The
court said:

> The selection of the clear glass, oblong shroud,
> bright colors, proportion, vertical orientation, and
> stereotyped jellyfish form, considered together,
> lacks the quantum of originality needed to merit
> copyright protection. . . . These elements are so
> commonplace in glass-in-glass sculpture and so
> typical of jellyfish physiology that to recognize
> copyright protection in their combination effec-
> tively would give Satava a monopoly on lifelike
> glass-in-glass sculptures of single jellyfish with

> vertical tentacles. . . . Because the quantum of originality Satava added in combining these standard and stereotyped elements must be considered "trivial" under our case law, Satava cannot prevent other artists from combining them.

The court did, however, grant a copyright in the particular sculpture based on "the distinctive curls of particular tendrils; the arrangement of certain hues; the unique shape of jellyfishes' bells."[17]

Photographs of objects in nature are nearly always found copyrightable; courts are reluctant to find that a photograph lacks any sort of original expression. However, courts have denied copyright to photographs that are purely "descriptive" of natural objects—such as photographs of Chinese food for use on a menu—on the grounds of lack of originality.[18] And a court refused to find infringement when an artist created a sculpture that copied from a photograph the pose of a mountain lion holding a cub in her mouth. The pose, said the court, was something that had occurred in nature for which the photographer could not take credit.[19]

The rule that an idea cannot be copyrighted has an interesting corollary: copyright in the expression of an idea will not be enforced so as to prevent other people from putting the idea to practical use. This principle was first stated in the nineteenth century, in the case of *Baker v. Selden*, which involved a book on accounting techniques.[20] The book described a system of bookkeeping and, as illustration of it, contained a page ruled into columns appropriate for the system. When another publisher, impressed by the system, printed and sold copies of the ruled page—without any explanatory material—the original author brought suit.

In a decision that has continued to reverberate through the case law ever since, the Supreme Court would be "works fixed in letters or other symbols other than works intended for performance."

Although the law does not require that a work have artistic merit, certain works nonetheless do stand outside its shelter, in the cold drizzle of uncopyrightability. They are excluded for one of two reasons: either they are trivial, or they are utilitarian.

In the first category fall, for example, titles and slogans, simple designs, and minor variations on works already in the public domain.[26] Titles and slogans can be protected to some extent by federal trademark law and by state laws against unfair competition and misappropriation; a book title, for example, will be protected by those laws if it has acquired such a reputation in the public mind that the use of it by someone else would amount to taking a free ride on the first user's popularity.[27] This protection, though, exists entirely apart from copyright and is not available for most items that are excluded from copyright on the grounds of triviality. Ballroom or discotheque dance steps, for example, are not considered to rise to the level of choreographic works within the meaning of the copyright statute and are unlikely to find protection under any other legal doctrine.[28]

The exclusion of utilitarian works is considerably less simple a concept. The threshold question is what the term "utilitarian" means in a copyright context. Some answers to that will seem obvious, others less so. Toys and games have been found not to be utilitarian. They serve a function, it is true; they enable a child to play. But playing is not in essence a utilitarian thing to do, and toys and games are routinely given copyright provided they meet the other relevant standards. On the other hand, items of clothing—even strikingly original creations by great designers such as Chanel—are considered utilitarian in the United States (but, unsurprisingly, not in France), and their designs are not copyrightable. Between these two fairly obvious propositions lies a gray area that has caused some trouble. What is one to do, for example, with Halloween and masquerade costumes?

Courts have upheld copyright in slippers designed to look like bears' feet, and a "Rabbit in Hat" Halloween costume, in which the lower half depicted an inverted black satin top hat and the upper half a rabbit projecting above the brim. These perfectly rational decisions found that the artistic aspects of the slippers and the costume were conceptually separable from the utilitarian aspects of their use as garments. (See discussion a few paragraphs further on.) The Copyright Office takes the same position, refusing registration of fanciful costumes as such but allowing registration for any conceptually separable artwork in them. Yet a case decided by a normally reliable court held that masquerade costumes are useful articles not because they are garments, but because they enable the wearer to masquerade. This is clearly wrong. Granted, one cannot masquerade without a costume, but on what theory is masquerading a *useful* function? How is it any more useful than playing a game with a toy? Going from bad to worse, the court went on to say that the artistic elements of the costumes in question—the elaborate headpieces, the masks, and so on—were not separable from the utilitarian function of the costumes and therefore not protected. In the end, it threw out the entire copyright claim, and in the process appeared to set itself at odds with Copyright Office practice and common sense.[29]

Another interesting conundrum concerns typefaces. Digital fonts—the compilations of data that map the bit points of a letter in a computer font such as the one on this page—are considered copyrightable, on the theory that in data form they are not useful but merely descriptive. However, the designs of the letters themselves are not protectable; no typeface however fanciful has ever obtained copyright, because Congress regards typefaces as fundamentally utilitarian.

Defining a work as utilitarian does not necessarily end the discussion. The law holds that the design of a useful article may be protected as a pictorial, graphic, or sculptural work if the purely artistic elements of the article can be "identified separately from, and are capable of existing independently of, the utilitarian aspects of the article." The statutory history says that this language permits copyright to those design elements that are "physically or conceptually separable" from the utilitarian aspects—an explanation that has served to complicate, rather than simplify, the matter.[30] One almost needs training in Platonic philosophy to tell when a design element is "conceptually" separable from its utilitarian element. One is being asked, in essence, to discuss the lampness of a lamp, the tableness of a table. I bid you look up from this book for a moment at the lamp beneath which you are reading and identify those parts of its design that may clearly be segregated from its functional requirements. If your lamp is by Tiffany, your task will be relatively easy; if, on the other hand, it is made in the Scandinavian style, the problem is rather more challenging.

After a string of mutually inconsistent decisions in this area, the Second Circuit adopted the following test, focused on the design process. It seems to be the prevailing view and is the approach taken by the Copyright Office in assessing registration applications:

> [I]f design elements reflect a merger of aesthetic and functional considerations, the artistic aspects of a work cannot be said to be conceptually

separable from the utilitarian elements. Conversely, where design elements can be identified as reflecting the designer's artistic judgment exercised independently of functional influences, conceptual separability exists.

This is an effective way of separating wheat from chaff, even if its effect may occasionally be draconian.[31]

Does this mean that if a lamp cannot be copyrighted, a drawing of it cannot be either? Not so. Even a drawing by a lamp designer, made not as an end in itself but solely as a prelude to manufacture, is copyrightable as a pictorial work because it is not in itself a useful article but only teaches how to make one. No one may publish copies of the drawing without the designer's permission. However, the copyright does not prevent someone from actually making a lamp that embodies the functional parts portrayed in the drawing. (Here again you hear the echo of *Baker v. Selden*.) The designer's right to control manufacture based on his drawing extends only to those parts of his drawing that depict nonfunctional things.[32]

Architectural Works

Architectural works present special complications. An architect's plans, like any other drawings, have long been copyrightable as pictorial or graphic works. No one may copy or publish those drawings without the architect's permission. However, until July of 1991 U.S. law did not protect buildings from being copied, or prevent anyone from erecting a building from copyrighted plans, except insofar as an unauthorized building might copy "nonfunctional" or "monumental"—i.e., nonutilitarian—features.[33] (In practice this exception was rarely if ever invoked.) On the same basis, a landscape architect's drawings would be protected by copyright, but not the landscape created from them, and copyright in the drawings would not prevent anyone else from planting a garden that embodied those plans.

In July 1991, copyright was extended to the architectural design as such—but not to landscape design as such. The only court to have dealt with protection of an actual installed landscape found it uncopyrightable because the constant workings of nature deprive it of "fixation" and its creator of "authorship." This was a questionable holding, influenced perhaps by the fact that the plant materials had not remained constant over the years, and that the installation consisted simply of wildflowers arranged in two ellipses.[34] Surely there are landscape designs that qualify as pictorial or sculptural works? In Europe the copyrightability of landscape design is widely acknowledged. We shall have to await the appropriate case to establish this.

As a result of the 1991 change in the law, architectural plans are now protected against unauthorized construction, and buildings against unauthorized reproduction, to the extent that the plans or the building contain copyrightable elements. Of these two protections, the former is likely to be of greater significance. It gives architects a stick to wield against deadbeat or unscrupulous clients. Formerly, if a builder failed to pay his bill, the architect's sole remedy was to sue for breach of contract. Now, if the copyright license to build has been made contingent on payment in full, the architect can sue for copyright infringement, with the possibility of recovering attorney's fees. The same will apply if a builder tries—as many do—to reuse plans without paying the architect a new fee for the privilege.

The builder's principal defense to such suit will always be that the architectural design was dictated by functional considerations. For though the statute is silent on this point, the Congressional report on the bill states that copyright should be denied where form is dictated by function.[35] Technically, this is different from the "separability" analysis regarding designs of utilitarian objects, and it is clearly intended to be a looser standard. In practice it is probably just as difficult to apply.

The very definition of an "architectural work" presents some puzzles of its own. That definition is:

> . . . the design of a building as embodied in any tangible medium of expression, including a building, architectural plans, or drawings. The work includes the overall form as well as the arrangement and composition of spaces and elements in the design, but does not include individual standard features.[36]

According to the statutory history, the word "building" includes any "habitable structure."[37]

No sooner had this definition been enacted than the question arose whether it included habitable structures that are divorced from the real estate on which they sit, such as tents, recreational vehicles, and mobile homes. The Copyright Office has opined that it does not, because, in its view, a structure must be both permanent and stationary to qualify as a "building."[38] This view sounds comfortably definitive, and yet it may not prove so in practice. The permanence requirement, for example, is more subjective than it may at first appear. Presumably, it excludes any structure (such as a fair pavilion or a movie set) that is erected with the intent that it be dismantled shortly thereafter. And yet some famous movie sets from decades ago are still on the lots in Hollywood, more permanent probably than the houses of those who made them. The "stationary" requirement, too, while not subjective, is flawed in its own way. Things that their owners called "mobile homes" are probably just that, but what about the nearly identical things that other owners call "prefabricated housing"—built to be movable, but in practice never moved once installed? At what point, if at all, do they become architectural works? Or are they to be denied protection merely because at one point in their careers they drifted from one spot of earth to another?

The statutory history also says that "building" includes any structure "used by" human beings, and suggests that the term includes houses, office buildings, churches, gazebos, and garden pavilions, but excludes "purely functional structures" such as bridges, cloverleafs, dams, or walkways. But what does "used by" mean? Does copyright cover structures such as the Washington Monument (leaving aside the fact that that monument is now in the public domain) or the Vietnam War Memorial that serve no definable useful function? Is the presence of interior space enough to make a structure a "building"? The Hoover Dam has extensive habitable space inside its massive walls, but would that be copyrightable given that the exterior is an uncopyrightable dam?

What about "individual standard features"? Are we really excluding "standard designs of individual features"? If so, why was such an exclusion thought necessary, given that originality is a prerequisite of copyright and the word "standard" as good as presumes lack of originality? There is a general principle that statutes should not be interpreted so as to render them irrelevant. Yet that is precisely what the Copyright Office has done, and, given the Copyright Office's close involvement in developing the architectural work provision of the statute, its interpretation is probably definitive. In its final regulations on registration of architectural works, the Copyright Office has not only interpreted the phrase in question to mean "standard designs of individual features," but compounded the redundancy by adding solemnly that copyright does not extend to "standard configuration of spaces."[39] While engaged in these platitudes, it might have added that standard configuration of *features* (as distinct from spaces) is also not copyrightable. It did not do so, for whatever reason, but we should infer nothing from this silence. Whatever is standard, whether features, spaces, or arrangements of features and spaces, is no one's property, except in those rare cases where an original work by luck or genius becomes the standard that everyone must buy to stay in the game.

Does copyright extend to individual features of a building, provided they are not standard? Logically, the implication seems unavoidable that it does. This would mean, if true, that once a building design as a whole is protectable as an architectural work, that protection extends to the design of individual features, quite apart from the architectural work as a whole. Thus, if a house contained a window of particularly interesting and original design, the copyright would protect not only the house as such against piracy, but also the design of the window. Thus, no competitor could copy that window without permission, even if the window is the only feature copied from the architectural work.

This result, while perfectly logical, would create an odd tension. It would mean that we would apply one standard of copyrightability to features in an architectural context and a different standard to identical features that are developed independently. (For remember that a window or fountain standing alone is a "useful article," and only those elements that can be "identified separately" from its utilitarian features are copyrightable.) And the door, if you will, would thus open to abuse. The shrewd manufacturer would have its new line of faucets designed as part of a "dream house," copyright the dream house as an architectural work, and thus get a copyright in features it might otherwise not be able to protect. This is probably a *reductio ad absurdum*. The statute and its history seem to suggest that an architectural work arises from the selection and arrangement of features, not from any particular individual feature. If this is the case, then the design of those features is no more protected by the copyright in the architectural work than a scholarly article is protected by the copyright in the journal—the collective work—in which it appears. The individual feature should be judged on whether it has artistic merit that is "separable" from its utilitarian function, just as the individual scholarly article is judged on the originality of its own expression. And yet one wonders if courts will be able to keep this fine distinction always in their minds.

Must an architect be wary of too much success? What if a copyrighted feature becomes "standard" in the industry—does the statute intervene at that point to strip it of protection? Surely not, or we have stepped through the looking glass. Copyright exists to reward, not to punish, success.

Plots and Characters

In works that tell stories, copyright affords a broader coverage than one might think, primarily because more and more things that long ago were considered merely ideas have come to be regarded as expression. For example, the plot of a novel is covered by the novel's copyright, at least to the extent that it is original with the author. The courts have developed the ingenious theory that a plot is an "arrangement of ideas" and that an arrangement of ideas amounts, magically, to "expression."[40] From a philosophical or logical point of view, this is probably a falsehood, but nonetheless it is the law.

What about characters? Here again the law gives protection to what might at first seem to be an idea. Indeed similarity of characters is often the principal battleground when one author sues another for plagiarism. But there is one unusually perplexing problem with characters: who owns them? (You may as well resign yourself early to one of the facts of life of copyright law: no principle is fixed or firm, self-defining or self-limiting. If you are commonsensical, this will cause you frequent exasperation, but on the other hand common sense will also tend to get you out of the mazes into which pure logic leads.)

This problem of characters arose in a case involving *The Maltese Falcon*.[41] After selling the story to Warner Brothers, Dashiell Hammett wrote several more stories about his detective hero, Sam Spade. Warner Brothers took him to court, claiming that he had violated the terms of his contract of sale and that the character, Sam Spade, was their exclusive property.

It might have been enough for the court to construe the contract in Hammett's favor and to hold that he had not in fact sold Warner Brothers his rights in Sam Spade. The court did this, but it did not let the matter rest there. It went on to consider whether a character, as such, could even be copyrighted, and concluded that it could not, unless it constituted the story being told. (Emma in Jane Austen's novel might be an example of the latter case.) Its opinion was that characters like Sam Spade are a writer's stock-in-trade and that the activities or words of a character in a particular story are copyrightable but not the character as such. The court characterized an author's ownership of a character as property of a different sort—property that is protected by ordinary legal rules, not by copyright law.

This case has been nothing if not controversial. Commentators note that courts have often found (or denied) infringement of literary works by comparing their characters, thus suggesting that characters are indeed covered by copyright. It may be, though, that these characters simply fit the formula of the Spade case, as the story (or elements of the story) being told. The character who stands apart from the story, however, has an ancient lineage. From Genji to Sherlock Holmes, the world's literature is rich with heroes (and with villains like Professor Moriarty) whose identity builds over the span of many tales. Can there be any doubt that if Conan Doyle were our contemporary he could sue someone who created a detective with Holmes's characteristics, even if the new detective had a different name? And yet the character of Holmes does not reside in any one of Conan Doyle's stories. Assignment of copyright in any one of them would certainly not assign the rights to Holmes the character.

In the practical world people need not agonize over this issue. Publishers and movie producers who want the rights to characters usually include them specifically in their contracts. And conversely people who wish to retain the rights to their characters should specify as much in their contracts.

Nonetheless, if the Sam Spade case is still good law, its implications are far-reaching. How long does this unusual property right in characters last? Does it vanish when the author dies, or can he bequeath it to his children? Can he bequeath it to someone who has no connection at all with his copyrights? Could Hammett, for example, have bequeathed his rights in Sam Spade to Lillian Hellman, and would Hammett's children and publishers then have been powerless to stop her from writing books about Sam Spade? (The court never faced these problems; I would not venture to guess how a court might decide them in the future.)

The final problem of this case is that it may mean that a sale by an author of his "property" in a character is not protected by the provision in the copyright law that permits an author to terminate (revoke) a transfer of copyright. I shall deal with termination at length in chapter 3; I raise the point now only to underscore the dangers presented.

I should add that most of these issues do not arise where cartoon or other visual characters are concerned. Mickey Mouse and his colleagues are clearly protected by copyright as works of visual art. Furthermore, such visual characters can be protected separately from the particular works in which they appear.[42]

Layout and Graphic Design

Protecting the layout of a magazine or similar work creates obvious risks: there are only so many ways that a page can be designed, after all. Nevertheless, some layouts are so distinctive in their "selection and arrangement" of graphic elements that it would be unfair not to protect them, at least against the most flagrant knockoffs. In this spirit, for example, the distinctive layout of the cover of *Reader's Digest* magazine was found copyrightable.[43]

Computer Programs

Many principles of copyright have been put to the test as courts struggle with questions concerning computer programs. Programs are eligible for copyright, but there is considerable confusion about what such a copyright protects or should protect.

One important doctrine is that a computer program is protected not only in source code form but in object code form as well. This is true even if the object code is embedded in the computer, as is the case with operating system software.[44] (Source code is the version of a program that is written in any of the so-called computer languages, using words, letters, numbers, and symbols. The source code of a program is not intelligible to a layman, but can be easily read and understood by experts. Object code, on the other hand, is the machine-readable form of a program, whether on disk, or downloadable from the Internet, or in other form, and is intelligible for the most part only to the machine it is put into, not to humans. Operating system software is the set of instructions that governs the computer's thought processes, so to speak.) Though this doctrine is the cornerstone of practical copyright protection for software, it is by no means self-evident.

When the 1976 Copyright Act was nearing completion, Congress decided to duck this and several other technology-related issues that would have slowed or halted progress on the bill. Instead it appointed a commission—the National Commission on New Technological Uses of Copyrighted Works (CONTU)—to investigate these issues, including how copyright should protect computer programs. The Commission's report, released in 1978, was sharply divided on that question. Most Commission members felt that object code was merely a copy of the source code and should be protected by copyright. In a vigorous dissent, however, the novelist John Hersey and others protested that an object code, although it is an embodiment of the source code, functions solely as a part of the computer, is not intended to communicate to human beings, and should not be protected by copyright.[45] Thus the dispute centered on what the copyright law means when it defines a "copy" as "a material object in which a work is fixed by any method now known or later developed, and from which the work can be perceived, reproduced, or otherwise communicated, either directly or with the aid of a machine or device." The majority of the Commission took the view that the object code of a program was a copy because, theoretically, the source code could be printed out from it. The fact is, however, that that is not the purpose of object code, and indeed the last thing any program vendor wants is for his program to be deciphered; most try (however futilely) to encrypt or otherwise protect their object codes from being "read" and understood.

In my opinion the dissent held the higher ground, so far as logic is concerned. But logic was not the only force at work here; CONTU and later the courts acted, whether consciously or not, partly out of fear that not to extend copyright protection to object code would open the gates to the Japanese or Taiwanese invader. Many computer people will, if pressed, admit that copyright doesn't fit very well onto object code, but, they say, patent protection is expensive and time-consuming to obtain, and most programs have only a short commercial life.

The problem is that granting copyright protection to things like operating system software—to pick the most blatant example—in effect grants a long-term patentlike monopoly in the machine itself, without requiring the inventor to meet the standards of patentability. A better solution might have been to enact a special statute for software, combining elements of patent and copyright. So far the pace of "creative destruction" in the computer industry has been such that this super-patentlike protection has not had the negative effect it might have had on the economy—or if it has, the effect is difficult to measure.

Accepting, though, that copyright applies to software, we must somehow distinguish the "expression" in a program from the "idea." A program is fundamentally a series of instructions directing a computer to perform certain analytic or other functions. If the problem to be solved is a difficult one, writing the program requires great skill and creativity, and, we say at a gut level, this effort deserves protection. But how do we protect those instructions without actually protecting the process they embody? In the precomputer age instructions for doing something, even something as arbitrary as playing a game, were narrowly limited in their copyrights.[46] CONTU considered this question and decided that for any given data-processing problem there were a great number of possible programming solutions. At a certain level of specificity, they said, the choice of computer instructions constitutes the "expression" of the general solution or algorithm, which in turn constitutes the idea.[47]

If this strikes you as disingenuous, I am inclined to agree. A process is no less a process just because it is set out in more detail or is chosen from a group of processes that have the same end result. CONTU's analysis likens a program to the plot of a novel, in which the arrangement of ideas can constitute expression. But the specifics of a plot are themselves a commentary on human life and as such constitute part of the novel's end result; it cannot be said that two plots, in their details, are merely two ways of getting from A to B, because the author's choice of details helps define and describe the world he is writing about. Furthermore, the novelist's choices—including both A and B—are arbitrary, dictated only by imagination. A computer programmer, on the other hand, cannot choose details at random but must always have his eye on B, and his skill is judged by how quickly and efficiently he gets there. ("Efficiently"—is that a word compatible with copyright?) Still the CONTU theory has some validity, if only because there is no clear alternative.

Some courts in their eagerness to wed copyright to software have overlooked the more cautionary parts of the liturgy. An early and controversial case was *Whelan Associates, Inc. v. Jaslow Dental Laboratories, Inc.*,[48] in which it was held that the "overall structure" of a computer program could be protected by copyright. Addressing the idea-expression dichotomy, the court said that the "idea" concerned was the idea of running a dental laboratory by using a computer, thus implying that everything in the program more specific than that constituted copyrightable expression. But if copyright protects the "overall structure" of a program, is it not protecting the algorithm? Is it not protecting the process or method of the program, both of which are specifically excluded from copyright by statute?

Fortunately, later decisions have expressly rejected the teaching of *Whelan*. In a technically sophisticated and tightly reasoned opinion in the case of *Computer Associates International v. Altai, Inc.*,[49] the Second Circuit laid down principles for software copyright that have become the model throughout the country. Returning to a more traditional copyright analysis, and specifically citing *Baker v. Selden*, the court emphasized the need to draw the line between a program's idea and its expression so as not to prevent use of the processes embedded in the program. This, the court said, requires analyzing the various modules of a program and sifting out what is not copyrightable. It is in its analysis of what is not copyrightable that the *Altai* opinion gave its clearest and most desperately needed guidance. It reaffirmed that insofar as program structure is informed by concerns of "efficiency," the scope of expression is narrow and there is, in that narrow range, likely to be a merger of idea and expression, in which case the expression will not be protected. It thus reaffirmed what should have been obvious: that copyright must not protect program elements that are dictated by external factors, such as the demands of the task to be performed, or the compatibility requirements of other programs in conjunction with which a program is intended to run. Finally, it warned against inadvertent protection of programming that is common coin in the software industry. Having sifted out all these unprotectable elements we are left, in the court's colorful phase, with the program's "golden nugget" of copyrightable expression. Significantly, the court did not attempt to define what that is, though we may presume it is the programmer's own creative and somewhat arbitrary way of accomplishing the task before him. That nugget, like the gold in a prospector's pan, can only be arrived at by reduction, not assumed or defined a priori.

The effect of *Altai* has been a general narrowing of the scope of copyright protection for computer code, as opposed (perhaps) to the screen displays that it may generate. For the broader promise of protection held out earlier by *Whelan*, one should look to patent. Some software developers already have. In fact, many in the software industry believe that the only really valuable part of a program is its algorithm—and for that, only patent will suffice. The Supreme Court has upheld the issuance of a patent where a computer program is the key part—indeed the only novel part—of a mechanical process.[50] Patents of this type are now granted without much controversy. Patent thus appears well suited to robotics, expert systems, and the like. Furthermore there appears to be a trend in the U.S. Patent Office toward granting patents to algorithms, even where there is little if any connection to patent's traditional realm of processes, devices, and machines. For example, a patent has been granted to the algorithm developed at Bell Labs that can be used for optimal routing of everything from telephone calls to airline flights.[51] But patents are time-consuming to obtain and may turn out to have a high mortality rate in the courts. For many applications only copyright is appropriate.

Some who secure patents for their programs also secure copyright. The apparent conflict can perhaps be resolved by saying that patent protects the algorithm and structure of the program, whereas copyright protects the program at a more specific level. Thus when the 17-year patent term ends, copyright would continue to protect the specific instruction sequences of the program.

Yet for many software producers neither patent nor copyright is optimal. In fact, anyone planning to distribute software by one-on-one licensing would do well to follow common industry practice and rely primarily on trade-secret protection. This involves placing tight restrictions on the uses that the customer can make of the software, prohibiting disclosure to persons other than the licensee and its key employees, and requiring return or destruction of the software if for any reason the license is terminated. If you are marketing your software over the counter, trade-secret protection is of course not appropriate. In such a case copyright will be the underpinning of your user agreement.

Another area of controversy in the application of copyright to software is the protection of the "look and feel" of a program. At issue is the user interface of a program, which consists primarily of the menus and other displays that appear on the screen and the order of keystrokes by which a user inputs and manipulates data.

Popular software begets imitation, and clever imitators can copy the user interface of a program without copying any underlying code. Such was the case with Lotus Development Corporation's popular spreadsheet program 1-2-3, which had become the industry standard for financial spreadsheet software. In 1990 Lotus won a suit against a leading "clone" producer.[52]

Screen displays and the underlying code are considered to be parts of one unitary work.[53] Courts will nevertheless judge the copyrightability of screen displays separately from that of the code.[54] This means that a court may acknowledge copyright in the unitary work as a whole but still find that the screen display element is not copyrightable, just as it might find a novel to be copyrightable as a whole but deny copyright protection to various scenes or plot sequences. What sorts of screen displays, then, may be protected?

There can be little doubt that video game screens are copyrightable, provided they contain a minimal level of original expression. They are, in essence, animated cartoons. Even quite simple screen displays such as those in the popular computer game Tetris are protectable. As a court noted, there are "almost unlimited" options for the shape of the pieces, and their movement and rotation.[55]

But what about spreadsheet displays? Clone manufacturers argued that spreadsheets and accompanying menus, like the accounting sheets in *Baker v. Selden*, cannot be given copyright without granting a monopoly to Lotus in the financial planning techniques that the spreadsheets embody. The court disagreed, finding the screen displays to be copyrightable expression in most though not all respects.

A related issue raised in the Lotus and other look-and-feel cases is the copyrightability of the keystrokes required, menu structure, command hierarchy, and, in general, a program's user interface. The trial court had held that Lotus's copyright in its interface was valid. It found, moreover, that Borland International's Quattro Pro software, which copied none of Lotus's source code but was designed to be compatible with 1-2-3, using a so-called "Lotus Emulation Interface," infringed the copyright in 1-2-3 by copying such things as menu commands and macros.

The First Circuit reversed this finding on appeal. Contrary to most people's expectations, it did not engage in an "abstraction, filtration, comparison" analysis such as the Second Circuit (and many other circuits since) adopted for comparing one piece of software to another. It found that test not applicable to the fundamental question of whether a menu command hierarchy is copyrightable per se. Nor despite the urgings of Borland did it find *Baker v. Selden* especially helpful, although its analysis of that case strikes this observer as being rather oversimplified. Instead, the First Circuit found the menu command hierarchy at issue to be a mere "method of operation" and therefore ineligible for protection under the explicit wording of the Copyright Act, which denies copyright to any "method of operation."[56]

The Supreme Court, on appeal, was widely expected to use this case as a jumping-off point for a more far-reaching exploration of copyright as applied to computer software, as it had done for the "sweat of the brow" doctrine in *Feist Publications v. Rural Telephone Co.* But the smart money was disappointed, because one justice had to recuse himself and the remaining eight split down the middle. At the end of the day the First Circuit's decision was left undisturbed, but its value as precedent was seriously undermined because half of the Supreme Court evidently thought it was bad law and, for all anyone can tell, a 5–4 decision could well have gone against it.

Although the First Circuit got where it got by an uncharted route of its own making, its decision is sound. Granting copyright to the menu commands that a program user must employ to make the program run has always seemed overreaching. Certainly in past years, before this decision, it had a chilling effect on the development of products that could compete on efficiency and price for the loyalty of customers who have an investment in existing data files and staff training.

Is look-and-feel copyright dead? Where software is concerned, perhaps so. But other, equally questionable (to my thinking) claims to copyright for some nebulous overall impression of a work remain undisturbed. The *Lotus* decision has proved controversial among copyright scholars, suggesting that outside the easy cases there is no consensus on where the boundaries of copyright should be drawn. Recently, however, a District Court in California denied copyright to the application programming interface (API) of Oracle's Java programming language. Being in the Ninth Circuit, the court did not rely on *Lotus v. Borland*, but it arrived in much the same place, finding that a "long hierarchy of over six thousand commands to carry out pre-assigned functions" was a "command structure" and hence an uncopyrightable "method of operation."[57] Oracle did not rely on a look-and-feel theory but asserted that the "structure, sequence and organization" of its API should be protected. The court did not reject "structure, sequence and organization" as a theoretical basis for copyright, but decreed that on the facts before it, to allow copyright would in effect grant Oracle a monopoly on the underlying "commands" or functions. This was a welcome reaffirmation of the limits of copyright in software. Also welcome was the court's statement that *Baker v. Selden*, while "aged," is "not passé."

Works Created with the Aid of Computers

Can a work created by applying a computer program to a database receive a copyright? A typical work of this sort might be a biblical concordance, created by feeding the Bible into a computer bank and then applying to it a program designed to locate and arrange word correspondences. Although no reported case has yet raised the issue, there seems to be no reason why a work of this type should not be entitled to a copyright. Admittedly the computer is doing the bulk of the legwork, but this is only at the guidance of a human being. It is a tool, no matter how creative it may be. A certain degree of human will and intellectual labor is present in any computer product.[58]

As intellectual production of this type becomes more and more common, some unusual problems of ownership will emerge. I shall deal with these in greater detail in the next chapter.

Mask Works   By an amendment to the Copyright Act in 1984, Congress granted a truncated form of copyright protection to the masks, so called, that are used to create semiconductor chips.[59] It was felt that these masks, being essentially utilitarian works, would not receive protection without specific statutory language.

A mask lies somewhere between a design and a stencil, or perhaps more accurately it is both. In it the intricate circuitry of a semiconductor chip is cut, and through it laser light etches the circuitry design onto the chip's silicon. Because of their inherently utilitarian character, Congress has granted mask works a shorter term of protection and a narrower scope of rights than other works. And, interestingly, Congress has specifically authorized anyone to use the technology contained in a mask work, provided he obtains it by reverse engineering and does not merely copy the mask.[60]

Performances   Performances of works are not regarded as works themselves until they are fixed, on tape or film, as sound recordings or audiovisual works. They are therefore not protected by copyright law until that time. This does not mean that someone can film or record a performance without the performer's permission. That used to be forbidden by state law, if at all. Now, for musical performances, it is forbidden by federal law as well.

Federal law grants limited protection to unfixed live musical performances. Section 1101 of the Copyright Act makes it illegal to fix the sounds and images of a live musical performance in any medium, or to make, transport, or sell copies of phonorecords that duplicate any fixation, unless authorized by the performer(s). It is also illegal to "transmit or otherwise communicate to the public," by cable, broadcast, or otherwise, any live musical performance without the performer's permission. The remedies for a violation of this law are the same as for copyright infringement, but there is no requirement that anything be registered (indeed, what is there to register?) in order for the aggrieved performer to sue or to obtain any of the special benefits that timely registration confers on a copyright plaintiff. (See chapter 5.)[61] Furthermore, if the offender has acted with a motive of financial gain, he is guilty of a criminal offense and may be both fined heavily and imprisoned for up to 10 years.[62]

The sweep of this law is hard to overstate. It prohibits unauthorized distribution in this country even if the unauthorized fixation occurred outside the United States, and even, apparently, if the fixation occurred in a non-GATT country. It has no cutoff date. As far as anyone can tell, the performer's right continues to be protected indefinitely; there is no "life-plus-70" or other fixed term. This raises an interesting Constitutional problems, for the U.S. Constitution says that copyright may last only for "limited times." When the statute was challenged on that ground, however, the Second Circuit decided that while Congress did not have power to enact such a law under the Copyright

Clause, it had that power under the Commerce Clause (which gives Congress broad power to regulate interstate and international commerce).[63] But whether defensible or not on Constitutional grounds, the absence of a cutoff date will someday lead to trouble unless corrected.

Furthermore, the statute can be read as preventing distribution of (for example) bootlegged CDs even if the unauthorized fixation occurred before the statute was enacted. Nor is the performer's right subject to any third-party right of "fair use." The statutory history suggests that the statute may not be enforced in such a way as to conflict with First Amendment rights of free speech, but this is a narrower and even less clear limitation than fair use. (See chapter 9.) In the case just noted, the Second Circuit sent the matter back down to the trial court to determine if there were First Amendment problems with the law, but for reasons unknown to this writer the case never went any further.

Note that every performer has the right described here, no matter how insignificant his or her contribution to the performance. Every performer in a band or orchestra must consent or the fixation or broadcast is unlawful. In contrast to a copyright license, a license to fix a performance cannot be granted by just one of the group of right holders; it must be granted by all.

Nothing in the statute appears to prevent a performer from delegating his right of consent, so presumably orchestras and bands will obtain from their members the necessary authority to act for everyone in the group. What is less clear is whether the right can be assigned outright. The statute does not say. For example, what happens to the right of consent after a performer has died? If someone then starts selling copies of a bootleg recording of one of her concerts, who can sue the bootlegger? Is this right of consent a personal right, to be exercised only by a performer's family, or is it a commercial right that can be freely assigned? In contrast to copyright rights, the statute provides no rules or even guidelines for how the right can be transferred, and there is no registry where the right can be recorded. It is conceivable that the Copyright Office could record claims of ownership of this right, but its current procedures are not geared to do so and there are no implementing regulations in the offing. It is not even clear that the right survives the performer's death, although the failure to specify a cutoff date for the right probably implies, as I have said, that it does survive.

Another problem that the statute finesses is how "consent" is to be determined. There is no requirement that it be in writing. If the unauthorized fixation or transmission occurred in a foreign country with different legal customs as to what constitutes "consent," will U.S. courts defer to that law or judge the facts under American contract principles? There is no way to predict.

Just to make things more interesting, a treaty whose adoption is pending as this book goes to press would create a new set of economic and moral rights for performers of literary works, artistic works, and "expressions of folklore," including the right to prevent unauthorized fixation. The United States is a signatory to this Beijing Treaty on Audiovisual Performances, but of course the treaty must be ratified by Congress, and enabling legislation enacted, in order for these new rights to take effect. Since that process cannot be counted on to happen, and will be slow in any event, I will say no more about it in this edition.

Whether authorized fixation, when it occurs, will protect a performer's interpretation, voice, or style is a matter on which the courts have not agreed. In one case on the subject, Bette Midler was able to stop the use of television commercials in which another singer imitated her voice and style.[64] But in general, performers seeking to protect these elements should look to the "right of publicity" laws of the various states.

Interviews   People who grant interviews generally assume that somehow they own the words they utter. The situation is much murkier than that.

The first case to explore this involved Ernest Hemingway and the book *Papa Hemingway*, written by A. E. Hotchner. Hemingway's heirs sued for common law copyright infringement (this was back in the 1960s) when Hotchner included in the book several conversations (not real interviews) with Hemingway. The court decided the case against the heirs, on the grounds that Hemingway's "words and conduct . . . left no doubt of his willingness to permit Hotchner to draw freely on their conversation in writing about him and to publish such material."

The court did, however, observe that to claim a copyright Hemingway would at the least have had to indicate clearly that he "intended to mark off the utterance in question from the ordinary stream of speech, that he meant to adopt it as a unique statement and that he wished to exercise control over its publication." This is a fairly high bar.[65]

Some more recent cases have denied common law copyright to statements made in interviews, on the highly questionable grounds that the speakers' words were merely general ideas or spontaneous utterances. Another suggested that a televised interview should be the property of the television staff, who created the video and audio record of the interview—which of course is true as to the recording, as a derivative work, but does not solve the problem of who owns the underlying content.[66] One case has, however, granted copyright to persons who made their own fixation of the interviews they granted, even as those interviews were being fixed and broadcast by another party.[67]

And yet one wonders: would not the typical interview be the property of both parties? After all, a good interviewer contributes materially to the quality of an interview by the questions he or she chooses to put to the person being interviewed. A good interview—a dialogue—seems a perfect example of what is called a joint work, a concept I will discuss in the following chapter.

Vessel Hulls

Under pressure from industry, Congress in 1998 enacted statutory protection for the hull designs of yachts and ships. Contrary to good sense, and apparently for want of any better place to stick such protection, Congress inserted it into the Copyright Act, where it stands out in all its bizarre incongruity.

This is the first sort of industrial design protection the United States has ever enacted on the European model. European law has long protected the nonpatentable, noncopyrightable but original designs of ordinary commercial goods: a sleek new toaster, for example, or an aesthetically pleasing ball point pen would be given protection in most European countries for a decade or so against slavish copying. American industry has always resisted such doctrine. Whether vessel hull design protection will prove to have been the camel's nose in the tent, or will pass out of history unmourned, remains to be seen.

Essentially, the law protects vessel hull designs that are original and different from public domain designs in some significant way, and that are not staple, commonplace, or dictated solely by utilitarian function. To obtain it, one must apply for it within a year (or perhaps two years; the statute seems to contradict itself) after the design is made public. It is not available to designs already publicly known as of the date the law went into effect in late 1998.

Because the entire subject is so far removed from true copyright, I will say nothing more about it here. Interested persons should refer to Chapter 13 of the Copyright Act.

National Origin

The United States will honor the copyright of any unpublished work, regardless of the nationality of its author. Its protection for published works is only marginally less broad. It will protect any published work if, on the date of first publication, one or more of the authors is a national or domiciliary of the United States, or is a national, domiciliary, or sovereign authority of a foreign nation that is a party to any copyright treaty to which the United States is a party, or is a stateless person. The protection of works of foreign governments is worth noting, particularly inasmuch as the United States does not grant copyright to any work of its own federal government.

U.S. law will also protect any work first published in the United States or in any foreign country that is party to a copyright treaty, or is first published by the United Nations or any of its specialized agencies, or by the Organization of American States.

Given the ambiguity of whether buildings are "published," it is worth noting that U.S. copyright also extends to any pictorial, graphic, or sculptural work incorporated in a building or structure, and to any architectural work embodied in a building, if the building or structure is located in the United States or in the territory of one of its treaty partners.

There is also a special rule for sound recordings. Any sound recording first fixed in a foreign country that is party to a copyright treaty with the United States will be protected in the United States, regardless of whether it meets any of the other tests listed above. I should add that two of the copyright treaties in question are limited to sound recordings. If a country is party to one of these but not to any other copyright treaty, the protection extended to its works and those of its nationals, etc., is limited to sound recordings.

Finally, there is a provision for copyright to be extended to the works of a foreign country by Presidential proclamation. Given that most if not all countries now belong to one or more copyright treaties, this provision is no longer of much relevance.

In chapter 12, I discuss some of the interesting problems that arise in international copyright protection. What I have to say in the intervening chapters will be limited to U.S. law, and based on the assumption (largely but not wholly correct) that U.S. law will apply, within the borders of the United States, to any foreign work just as it applies to any native work.

OWNERSHIP

2

Copyright comes into existence at the moment of a work's creation, just as, in some theologies, the soul enters the body at birth. At that time ownership vests in the author or authors.

The word *author* has a special meaning in the copyright law. It is used regardless of the kind of work: writers, painters, sculptors, and composers are all authors. This usage indeed is almost universal—in other countries as a matter of convenience and in this country as a necessity. The Constitution, from which Congress derives its power to establish copyrights, speaks specifically of "authors" and "writings," and, to extend the law's protection to nonliterary works, the courts have had to interpret these words broadly. However, *author* is not synonymous with *creator*, for in certain circumstances a person, or company, will be considered an author without lifting a creative finger. So what seems at first almost a frivolous question—Who is the author?—is in fact both complex and important.

Authorship

Only in a work by one individual acting on his own behalf is the answer to the question obvious. In the case of, say, a poem written by one person and set to music by another, it is anything but obvious. Three different relationships can exist between that poet and that composer. The first, in which the words and music are considered separately, can hardly even be called a relationship. The poet is the author of the words and may do what she likes with her poem; the composer is the author of the music and may do with the music anything that he pleases. In the absence of some exclusive licensing arrangement, the first composer cannot prevent another from making a new musical setting for the poem, and the first poet cannot prevent another from writing new words to fit the music. A singer who wants to perform such a song would have to acquire the performance right in the poem from the poet and the performance right in the music from the composer.

Joint Authorship

It is also possible, and more common, for the poet and composer to be "joint authors," and for the song to be a "joint work." Joint authorship ranks among the more slippery principles of copyright law, and many courts and commentators have grappled with it without achieving a clear victory. Intuitively we all know what a joint work is; it is, just as the statute says, a work "prepared by two or more authors with the intention that their contributions be merged into inseparable or interdependent parts of a unitary whole."[1] But what do these words mean? Do they mean that for a work to be a joint work, all of the authors must agree among themselves before any of them begins creating any part of the work? That would violate good sense. As one court said in a case under the old law,

> Suppose, for example, that after Burnett had composed the music, expecting his wife to write the words, she had died or changed her mind about writing the lyrics, and Burnett had gone to [his publisher] and asked him to find someone to write

the words. We submit that no court would hold that the fact that when Burnett composed the music he expected his wife to write the words, would make the actual song any less a "joint work" of Burnett and the lyricist found by [his publishers].[2]

The force of this reasoning cannot be denied, and there seems no reason not to apply it to the statute that has superseded the old law. As the House Report accompanying that statute makes clear, the "intention" on which the law is focused is the intention with which the author's contribution was created.[3] And as the Burnett case holds, the intention need not be *mutual* among the authors; it is sufficient that each author have intended that his product be merged with others. Thus even if a lyricist dies before finding a composer, when a composer is finally found, the resulting work will be a joint work.

What is less clear is whether anything is gained by focusing on intention where the contributions are inseparable. Take, for example, the case of a mystery writer who, when she is halfway done, decides to bring in a collaborator to finish her newest work. Their contributions are inseparable, and the work is inescapably a joint work; no possible alternative designation exists. Now suppose instead that the first writer dies, leaving an unfinished manuscript. Her executor finds another writer willing to finish the book. Should not the resulting work be considered a joint work? The deceased author certainly intended that there be only one work, yet technically she did not intend that her efforts be merged with those of any other writer. The alternative is to consider the unfinished manuscript a completed work for copyright purposes and the finished product a derivative work with separate copyright. This seems absurd, but one cannot be sure it is incorrect.

Although the intention the statute requires is that the contributions be merged, court decisions have put a different spin on this language. Instead of asking what was the parties' creative intent, these decisions ask whether the parties intended to create the legal relationship of joint authorship. For example, the Second Circuit opined that while an editor at a publishing house may make substantial and inseparable contributions to a work, neither author nor editor intends to create a joint-authorship arrangement and thus the editor is not a joint author.[4] This reasoning is seductive, because the example is so compelling; to side with the author seems only common sense. The editor is a craftsperson, performing a function that editors have always performed, without ever expecting or being given any rights. An editor is an employee of the author's publisher, and the publisher, bound by age-old custom and needing to keep good relations with its authors, is never going to raise the issue. The fact that the publisher never has raised the issue may help explain why the court found it so easy to assume that the publisher has no legal interest. So a straw man was set up and knocked down.

But the precedent set in that case led to others less easy to justify. The same court subsequently had to deal with a case involving a dramaturg. Dramaturgs are typically brought into theatrical productions when it is clear that a script is not going to work. They are freelance "editors," so to speak, who sometimes become deeply involved in the plays they work on. One such person was responsible for extensive rewriting of the script for the Broadway musical *Rent*. Her role was so great that she was even given credit as "Dramaturg." But when she—breaking from the age-old custom of *her* industry—sought to establish joint ownership of the copyright, the original playwright refused. He said he had never intended that she be treated as a joint author—and indeed, in his dealings with third parties, he had acted as if he owned the whole play. The Second Circuit upheld his contention, based on evidence that he had never demonstrated any intent to share *authorship* with the dramaturg.[5]

Thus, on top of the test laid out in the statute, the court superimposed a further test rooted in commercial expectations. As the Seventh Circuit suggested in reaching a similar result, the real issue may be that giving joint-author status to someone brought in as an assistant could have a chilling effect on true authorship: "Those seeking copyrights would not seek further refinement that colleagues may offer if they risked losing their sole authorship."[6] This makes perfect sense from a practical standpoint, though there is nothing in the statute to support it. However, to its credit, the Seventh Circuit has not followed the lead of the Second Circuit in the dramaturg case; it has recently reaffirmed its belief that what counts is "the parties' intent to work together in the creation of a single product, not . . . the legal consequences of that collaboration."[7]

The Ninth Circuit has come up with yet a different approach. In a case involving a "consultant" who contributed substantial copyrightable expression to Spike Lee's movie about Malcolm X, the court asserted that three factors should be considered in determining whether joint authorship exists. The first two are fairly objective: whether the contributor exercised control over the final work, and whether the contributors objectively manifested their intent to be treated as coauthors. The third factor—whether the "audience appeal of the work" turns on both contributions such that "the share of each in its success cannot be appraised"—is hopelessly subjective and, curiously, focuses on the content of the work in a way that may yield a result exactly opposite to that of the first two factors.[8]

If "control" is really the critical factor, as the Ninth Circuit suggests, this approach may yield a more predictable result than inquiring whether the parties intended to be treated as joint authors. What it suggests is that a subordinate contributor to a work—whose contributions are used or not at the complete discretion of the true "author"—will never be considered a joint author unless the controlling party consents to that designation.

Regardless of which of these approaches one takes, some troubling questions remain unresolved. For if the dramaturg's or consultant's work is not a contribution to a joint work, what is it? If the court-endorsed "author" is lucky, it may be work made for hire (see below) of which he is the owner by dint of control. But if not, what is it? A separate work? A gift to the author? The Second Circuit overlooked the fact that unless the dramaturg is an employee for hire, the material he or she creates cannot be owned by the "author" in the absence of a written instrument.

We may not have heard the last of this problem.

An important but not always understood requirement of joint authorship is that there be authorship on all sides, i.e., that every contributor's input be copyrightable expression. Thus, the "idea person" cannot claim joint authorship simply on the basis of having contributed ideas, no matter how original or how critical to the work's success.[9] To hold otherwise, it is said, would impede the free exchange of ideas by creating fear that the use of those ideas would subject the author to claims upon his copyright.

Where joint authorship exists, it creates a hybrid sort of ownership. Joint authors are not like joint owners of a house, with the last survivor taking the whole title. Instead they are regarded as "tenants in common" (a term that also derives from real estate law). This means that each of them owns an undivided share of the entire work and can give or sell that interest, or bequeath it to his own heirs. This share is not necessarily equal to all the others, for the authors can slice the pie unevenly if they so choose.[10] However, unlike someone who owns land as a tenant in common, a joint author cannot force a division of the property as such. Instead, because ownership is theoretically undivided, each joint author can grant rights in the entire work without consulting the others. (If he does so, he will have to account to his fellow authors for their shares of the profits.) Yet by the same token a grant by any one joint author will not prevent any of the other joint authors from making an identical sale to someone else. For this reason purchasers generally insist on getting all of the authors to sign the contract.

Outside the United States the rule is stricter: to be effective, even a nonexclusive license must be signed by all joint authors. Anyone contemplating foreign distribution of a work should insist on obtaining all authors' signatures.[11]

I have discussed so far two possible relationships between persons whose creative efforts are in some manner connected. The first is that they are merely independent authors combining their independent creations; the second is that they are joint authors. A third possible relationship is that one of them is an employee of the other, in which case the resulting work is a "work made for hire." Works made for hire have a different copyright term from that of most other works, and they are the only works for which an author has no statutory right to terminate a transfer. (See the discussion of termination of rights in chapter 3.) The "author" of a work

Works Made for Hire

made for hire is the person who does the "hiring"; the creator has no rights whatever in the work.

The most obvious examples of works made for hire are newspapers, movies, dictionaries, and other works that we think of as created, in a sense, by the companies that publish them. These companies have staffs of full-time writers and artists who work specifically on these products.

The rule is broader, though. An employer is considered the author of anything written by an employee within the scope of his or her employment. Thus when a scientist in a research laboratory writes a report on her work for her supervisor, the laboratory is the author of the report.

Determining whether a person's authorship is within the scope of his employment is not as simple as it may sound. Courts look not only at the nature of the work but also at whether the work is done within the limits of time and space authorized by the employer. Where these factors do not yield an easy answer, they will inquire whether the authorship is motivated, at least in part, by a desire to advance the employer's interests. The outcome of this analysis can be surprising. Courts have even gone so far as to find that a company owned copyright in a scientific article written by its employee at home after hours.[12] On the other hand, for public policy reasons, courts have held that a teacher's own instructional materials are not work for hire under a so-called "teacher exception."[13] Of course, any express policy adopted by a school or university becomes part of the teacher's employment contract, and would overrule that presumption. Such policies have become increasingly common at least at the post-secondary level.

Even more open to argument than the "scope of employment" is the question of who is an "employee."

The clear-cut example is the full-time staff writer, who is an employee in every sense of the word. But what about someone who is commissioned to create a specific work, is paid by the job—or not paid at all—and then moves on? On this point there is a major difference between the law now in effect and the law that was in effect prior to 1978.

Under pre-1978 law it was generally held that one who commissioned a work became the "author" and copyright owner. This was largely a judge-made rule, based on what courts perceived as the legitimate expectations of the parties. For example, commissioned portraits were works for hire, and the copyright belonged to the purchaser instead of the painter.[14] Where a company paid someone to develop an advertisement, a court would attribute copyright to the company, believing that any other result would be unfair.[15] This was not an absolute rule; it was a presumption; and it could be overcome in particular circumstances depending on the intent of the parties.

The old statute gave little guidance on what constituted "for hire." By contrast, the current statute goes into it at some length. It sets up two categories of work for hire: on the one hand, work created by an employee "within the scope of his or her employment"; on the other hand, a specifically ordered or commissioned work *if* it falls within one of nine clearly defined categories and *if* the parties have agreed in writing to treat the work as made for hire.

Legal disputes quickly arose over the intent of this new language. The central question was whether Congress intended to limit the work-for-hire doctrine, in cases of commissioned materials, exclusively to works that fall within the nine defined categories and are the subject of written agreements. Or to put it another way, were there circumstances in which someone who was not strictly speaking an employee could still be treated as an employee for copyright purposes?

The first major case on this point came up from New York to the Second Circuit. It involved authorship of certain statuettes, and the evidence showed that the people who commissioned the work had actively participated in its creation, giving detailed instructions on various design issues. The Second Circuit held that even though the commissioned artisans were not employees in the legal sense, they had acted under the "direction and control" of the commissioning party and thus should be regarded as employees for work-for-hire purposes.[16] This rule was subsequently followed by a number of other courts and was extended to cases where a commissioning party had the *right* to supervise and control, even though the right might never have been exercised.[17]

All seemed tranquil, then, for a while; the Second Circuit had managed to establish continuity between the new statute and its own preexisting case law. But then the Fifth Circuit rejected this doctrine in the case of *Easter Seals Society for Crippled Children v. Playboy Enterprises*.[18] The facts are less titillating (and less one-sided) than the name of the case might suggest. At issue was ownership of some film footage of jazz musicians that had been made at the request of the Easter Seals Society for use in a promotional broadcast.

The Fifth Circuit carried out what might be termed archaeology on the statute, interpreting it in the light of the various drafts it had gone through, remarks of legislators, and the like. It decided that although "employee" did not mean only persons on a payroll, the term did exclude independent contractors who were merely subject to direction and control. An "employee" had to be either an employee in the strictest sense or at least someone so nearly like that as to be considered an "agent" of the other party. (At common law, contrary to popular usage, an "agent" is neither a spy nor a real estate broker but any person who acts on another's behalf, rather than his own.) To determine agency, the court suggested looking to the law of personal injury: if one would be held liable for a physical injury caused by a commissioned artist, one would be that artist's employer for copyright purposes.

Following this reasoning, the District of Columbia Circuit held, in the case that ultimately went on to the Supreme Court, that a statue belonged to the sculptor even though the charity that commissioned the sculpture had contributed portions of it and made far more than cursory stipulations about its design.[19] The D.C. Circuit went so far as to suggest that the commissioning charity and the sculptor might be joint authors—an idea neither party had suggested or, we may suppose, would happily endorse.

Not to be outdone, the Ninth Circuit, sitting in California, subsequently held that only works produced by actual salaried employees could be works made for hire, unless they fell within one of the nine special categories and were subject to written agreements.[20]

The end result of all this judicial activity was that, as of 1989, who owned copyright in a commissioned work depended on what circuit's jurisdiction you were under. At this point the Supreme Court stepped in and delivered a definitive ruling, endorsing the approach taken by the Fifth and District of Columbia Circuits.[21]

Though it may be idle now to complain, all sides in this dispute were guilty of the kind of entrail reading, known euphemistically as "statutory history," that other countries do not allow courts to indulge in when interpreting a law. All sides are victims of a Congress that seems incapable of saying what it means.

All sides have also overstated the virtues of their positions. The Fifth and D.C. Circuits, and now the Supreme Court, have claimed that their agency-based rule will promote certainty by adopting a "bright line" definition of employee. But nothing could be further from the truth. As I have noted, the D.C. Circuit and the Supreme Court suggested that joint ownership should apply where an artist is not an employee but the commissioning party makes substantial input into the work. Of what benefit is such a Solomonic decision? Neither the artist nor the patron can grant an exclusive license to a publisher, and no one in the real world will ever pay much for a nonexclusive license. The result is not certainty but stalemate. Perhaps parties who find themselves in such a situation will settle their differences and work out some *modus vivendi.* But perhaps they will not, and the work will never see the circulation it deserves. The law should avoid violently yoking together people who do not intend to be yoked.

Some groups representing the interests of authors hailed the Supreme Court's decision as a great victory. I am not convinced. It does unquestionably place on commissioning parties the burden of obtaining written agreements. An advertiser, for example, will need a written assignment of copyright to own the ads it commissions. Many deals that have traditionally been done on a handshake now require new legalisms, if the person paying the bill is to own what he thinks he has bought.

But if the commissioning parties have the bargaining power, they will usually manage to extract by contract what the old law gave them by right. The only right an author cannot contract away is the right of termination after 35 years (discussed in chapter 3); this right is meaningful only to the most significant works of art or letters. It has no relevance in those fields where the work-for-hire rules actually operate: commercial photography, computer software, and so forth. So what the new rule has accomplished is, where commissioning parties are alert, to stimulate a lot of paperwork, and where they are not alert, to create a trap into which they can stumble.

Even on its own terms the "bright line" rule adopted by the Supreme Court is anything but self-defining. As noted, it imports into copyright the law of agency, a strange new bedfellow. Treatises have been written about agency; treatises are not written about things that are neat and thoroughly predictable. In the income tax arena, Congress and the IRS have for years wrestled inconclusively with the problem of when A should be treated as an employee of B, and when as an independent contractor. The same issue has led to years of litigation over who can claim the benefits of collective bargaining. How then are we to know whether someone fits the employee/agent profile? The test, as described in older noncopyright cases cited by the Supreme Court, is whether the hiring party has the right to control not merely the result, but also the manner and means by which the result is accomplished, and the Court specifically invokes this language as the defining test. The Court then states that the following factors (and perhaps others as well) should be assessed when determining whether someone is *de facto* an employee and thus an agent of the hiring party in the creative process. I list these factors with some observations as to their application:

- *The skill required.* A highly skilled artisan is less likely to be an employee than a mere paper pusher.

- *The source of the tools and materials used to create the work.* This factor reflects the general truth that one in business for oneself has one's own tools; employees use their employers' tools.

• *The duration of the relationship.* A one-shot job is less likely to be a for-hire relationship than a job of long standing in which various works are created.

• *Whether the commissioning party has the right to assign additional projects to the creative party.* The right to say, "Hey, you, put down that paintbrush and shovel the driveway" (to give a perhaps extreme example), will clearly weigh for the hiring party. On the other hand, it has been held that a software designer is not an "employee" just by virtue of being the hiring party's "regular troubleshooter," called in whenever the hiring party has computer problems.[22]

• *Who determines when and how long the creative party works.* Control of one's own working hours tends to indicate independent contractor status.

• *The method of payment.* A flat fee (or better yet a royalty) will be most favorable to the creative party; payment by the hour will be most favorable to the commissioning party.

• *Who decides what assistants will be hired, and who pays them.* A creative person who can choose his own assistants is less likely to be considered "for hire" than one who must work with whomever the commissioning party assigns to the job.

• *Whether the work is in the ordinary line of business of the commissioning party.* The doll factory that commissions a new doll will fare better than the automobile dealership that commissions a music video.

• *Whether the creative party is in business on his own.*

• *Whether the creative party receives employee benefits such as health insurance from the commissioning party.* Employee benefits are obviously a very strong indicium of "for hire" status.

- *The tax treatment of the creative party.* For example, if the commissioning party pays FICA and withholding on an artist's earnings, it is more likely to be the copyright "author" than if the artist pays self-employment taxes.

The Supreme Court gave no indication of how these factors should be weighed. Should each be given equal weight, and whoever gets the most points wins, or are some of these more important than others?

It is somewhat in the nature of Supreme Court opinions to be Delphic; but some lower court attempts to fashion clear and useful rules out of this case have, by contrast, not been Delphic enough. A tendency has emerged to ignore the dynamic creative process and focus exclusively on the static relationship of the parties. Likewise, courts have given, in my judgment, far too much weight to the tax treatment of the hired party and whether the hired party receives employee benefits.

The Second Circuit, in a case following the Supreme Court's repudiation of its original approach, has ruled that different factors will be more or less important depending on the context, but that some are significant in nearly every case and are usually "highly probative" of the true nature of the relationship. Among these "highly probative" factors is the right to control the manner and means of creation. Here is a typical instance of doctrinal confusion in this field: what the Supreme Court described as the overarching inquiry is now described by the Second Circuit as just one of many questions. Other highly probative factors are: the skill required, whether the hired party receives employee benefits, the tax treatment of the hired party, and whether the hiring party has the right to assign other projects to the hired party.[23] The court went beyond this to state that failure to provide employee benefits or pay payroll taxes (Social Security, etc.) for the hired party will weigh heavily against the hiring party because they indicate that for purposes other than copyright the hiring party is treating the hired party as an independent contractor. The opinion seems to view a claim of work-for-hire in these circumstances as attempting to keep one's cake while eating it.

A major problem with the Second Circuit's analysis is that these tax and benefit arrangements are the standard indicia of ordinary, quotidian employment: the very sort of relationship that the Ninth Circuit had said the 1976 law requires and that the Supreme Court expressly said it does not. If we give too much weight to these factors, we will end up closing the door that the Supreme Court went to some pains to keep open. Of the two cases cited with approval by the Supreme Court in its discussion—both of which arose in the field of collective bargaining law—one found an employment relationship to exist even though the hired parties paid their own income taxes, and the other found no employment relationship even though the hired parties were on the hiring party's payroll. Thus, the Second Circuit's approach seems at odds with precedent.

Another problem with focusing too much on the static relationship of the parties is that we may fail to see "agency" in the truest sense of the word. One may imagine instances where the entire creative process is closely guided by the hiring party, or where the hiring party sketches the entire work and leaves the details to a hired draftsman. Fairness ought to favor the hiring party in such situations, but I would hesitate to say that the law will too. Fortunately, a decision in the Third Circuit seems to take a more flexible and realistic approach,[24] but it is still too early to tell which view of the law will prevail.

Whichever prevails, we cannot escape the fact that work-for-hire determinations are going to be to some degree ad hoc, and thus potentially unpredictable. This underscores the desirability of reducing every deal to writing, and specifically of allocating copyright owner-ship in writing. Indeed, at one level or another the par-ties' rights are always going to be ad hoc unless *everything* is written down. This is good for the legal profession but not the polity. An example may help to illustrate.

The example is unfortunately a common one. Sup-pose Green commissions Brown to create a work of some sort, and it does not qualify as a work made for hire. What rights do Green and Brown actually have in the work? If it is a portrait, for example, Green obvi-ously has ownership of the portrait itself and thus has a limited right to display it publicly.[25] Green does not own any other rights in it.

Suppose, though, that the work is something Green intends to use, such as software, advertising material, or architectural plans. Provided that Green pays the agreed-upon price, Green will presumptively have a nonexclusive license to use the work, to publish the work, to display or perform it, and (perhaps) to revise it as needed—and this license will be presumed to last for the life of the copyright unless the parties otherwise agreed. However, the circumstances must be such as to create an inference that the commissioned party intended to allow the client to use the work. Or at least, there must not be evidence strongly suggesting the con-trary, as a real estate development firm found to its (expensive) dismay. In that case, an architect provided preliminary design services, but repeatedly sent his client contracts (which the client never signed) stipulat-ing that his preliminary plans could not be used for final construction without use of the architect's services.

Those unsigned contracts destroyed the inference of an implied license, and the client was out of luck.[26]

As the holder of an implied license, a person in Green's shoes is at significant disadvantage in two respects. First, if some competitor of Green's infringes the copyright in the material, Green as a nonexclusive owner has no right to sue for copyright infringement (as will be discussed in chapter 8). Furthermore, as a nonexclusive licensee, Green will not be able to transfer his implied license to someone else, except perhaps as part of a sale of the business to which the license relates.

Does Brown have to give Green access to the source code of the software, or to the digital files used to print the advertising material? The statute does not say so, and neither does any reported case. The question is not a copyright question, strictly speaking, but a question of contract or of equity. A commissioning party in these circumstances might have some right of access, either expressly in its contract with the hired party or implied as a matter of equity. So might a joint author whose collaborator refuses to share possession of the work. So might an artist who has sold a painting and wants the collector to let her photograph it for reproduction. But if such rights exist—and it is not at all clear that they do—they exist outside copyright. Odd or counterintuitive as it may sound, copyright is the right to prevent others from copying, not an affirmative right to copy. In the case of the artist who has sold a painting, there may be an equitable answer, as I will discuss under the topic of "divisibility," later in this chapter.

Would Brown, the commissioned creator of the ad, be at liberty to revise the same software or advertising materials for the use of another client? As a matter of copyright law he ought to be, however much that violates the customer's expectations. Contract law might seek to imply a restriction on Brown's exercise of his rights, but this would be problematic, given the primacy of the copyright law over state law doctrines of equity.[27] So we are back to where we started, with an emphasis on the parties' states of mind—the very thing the bright liners claim to be avoiding.

Therefore it bears repeating: reduce your deals to writing. Try to be explicit about copyright ownership and about any uses or restrictions on use that might someday become important.

Can an "employee" and "employer"—whether of the formal sort, or considered such under agency law—opt out of the work-for-hire rules for a specific work? For example, if an employee of a software company wants to create a program that is within the scope of his work duties, but the employer does not wish to own it, can they agree that the work will not be made for hire? The answer is "yes and no." The statute does not provide any express opt-out provision, so if the parties want the employee to own copyright they have two alternatives. One is somehow to define the scope of employment so as to exclude the work or works concerned. This is not without perils for the employer, which must protect its more general interest in owning the work product of its employees. The other alternative is to execute a transfer of copyright. In that case the employer will be considered the author but the actual programmer becomes the assignee. The first type of agreement—defining the scope of employment—may be written or oral, but written is more reliable. The latter type must be in writing, and signed by at least the employer.[28]

Suppose, instead, that the employer and employee want an arrangement in which the employee gets certain rights in the work but the employer retains other rights. On this point the statute contains an odd anomaly. It says that an employer will own all rights in a work made for hire unless the employer and employee otherwise agree in a written instrument signed *by them*. In most circumstances, only the person giving up copyright rights need sign the relevant instrument. (See chapter 3.) But for whatever reason, in this particular context Congress decided that both signatures are required. In order to minimize the conflict between this and the general rules of copyright transfers and licenses, I am inclined to think that this special rule should apply only to agreements made in advance of the creation of a work, leaving the general rules to apply to any agreement made after the work has been created.

Thus far I have discussed only the "employment" sort of work made for hire. There is another type, created in the 1976 Copyright Act as a sort of safe harbor for various kinds of works that had traditionally been considered made for hire, but that might well not qualify under the new rules. Thanks to this safe harbor, certain types of commissioned works may be treated as works made for hire, regardless of the lack of supervision and control, if the parties so agree. These are:

- A contribution to a movie or other audiovisual work.

- A contribution to a periodical or other collective work.

- A translation.

- A supplementary work, that is, a work that is somehow auxiliary to the main work—for example, an illustration, an illustrative map or chart, editorial notes, a musical arrangement, a bibliography, a foreword, an index, and so forth—but only if it is subordinate to the main work. For example, illustrations that are of equivalent importance to the text will not qualify as subordinate works.

- A compilation, that is, a work created by collecting and assembling data or preexisting materials; an example would be an anthology, a hotel guide, or a racing chart.

- An instructional text.

- A test.

- Answer material for a test.

- An atlas.

For any of these commissioned works to be a work made for hire, the creator and whoever commissions the creator must agree that this will be so. The agreement must be in writing and signed by both of them. (Again note the requirement of both parties' signatures.) The law does not require in so many words that the contract has to say, "This work will be a work made for hire," but there is little doubt that that is what it means. A court is likely to interpret any language less explicit than this in the opposite way. Even if the contract says "A hires B to do such-and-such," a court may well believe that the word *hires* was used loosely as a synonym for *commissions*. The phrase "work made for hire" is a legal term and ought to be used wherever that is the intent.[29]

By the same token, if the hired party in these circumstances is to have any exclusive rights in that work, that understanding must also be in writing and signed by both parties.[30]

To be commissioned, a work must be done at the request of the person for whom it is done; the commission must have caused the work to be created. Nevertheless, people often try to get around this. For example, I have seen contracts sent to authors of unsolicited manuscripts, saying "This work will be a work made for hire." This is illogical and ineffective; at most, such a contract will be interpreted as a transfer of copyright ownership from the author to the magazine.[31]

Assuming that a work truly is commissioned, the question has arisen whether the written work-for-hire agreement may be signed after the work is done, or whether it must be signed in advance. Although the statute is not explicit on this point, the Seventh Circuit has held that the written agreement must precede creation of the work.[32] This is an impractical and needlessly rigid decision. The court said that its rule was necessary "to make ownership of property rights . . . clear and definite, so that such property will be readily marketable." Although it did not say so, the court may have been swayed by the fact that the commissioned party, a photographer, had already sold his business, including whatever copyright he owned, by the time he got around to signing a work-for-hire contract, so that validating the retroactive work-for-hire contract would have unfairly prejudiced the purchaser of his business. On its facts, the decision was clearly the only fair one. We can hope that future cases limit the advance-writing requirement to such circumstances. Indeed, the Second Circuit in a subsequent case specifically validated retroactive work-for-hire agreements, allowing them to be created by language included in the endorsement of the checks that paid for the work.[33] Only by referring to the very different situations involved can these two decisions be reconciled.

Another interesting question, which has not yet arisen in any reported case, is whether a work-for-hire agreement is invalid if the commissioned work ends up not being used for the originally intended purpose. For example, suppose that a drawing is commissioned to be used as a contribution to a periodical, but the publisher decides instead to use it as an illustration in a very different sort of book. Will the publisher still be considered the author? Since the ultimate use lies within the scope of commissioned works named in the statute, the commission should still count as a work-for-hire agreement. But what if the publisher decides to sell the illustration as a poster instead? A court could well find that the work-for-hire status of the drawing was invalid, and revise the relationship to one of author and assignee. It would probably not rescind the transaction, but, to be prudent, those who commission works of these specially listed types should always stipulate that if the work should not be eligible for work-for-hire status, the commissioned party assigns the copyright to the commissioning party.

Ownership of Works Created by Partnerships

Partnerships make each partner a co-owner, as a matter of law, of all property created to further the business of the partnership. This makes partners co-owners, but not coauthors, of any one partner's copyrightable works.[34] It is not clear whether the rights of a partner in partnership copyrights are quite the same as the rights of a normal co-owner. For example, the typical co-owner of a copyright—such as a child of an author who has inherited her father's copyrights in common with her siblings—cannot give anyone an exclusive license or transfer of the copyright. In a partnership, though, each partner is bound by the actions of the other partners. Does this mean that one partner can make an exclusive grant of copyright without the written consent of his partners, who may happen to be the authors? The answer is probably "yes," but there is simply no law on this point one way or the other.

U.S. Government Works

One special variant of the work-for-hire rule relates to works of the U.S. Government. The law denies copyright to works "prepared by an officer or employee of the United States Government as part of that person's official duties."[35] (These works may nonetheless receive copyright protection in other countries.)[36] By implication it seems possible that if a government officer or employee, working within the scope of his official duties, jointly authors a work with a private citizen, the private citizen could own the entire copyright and have no obligation beyond the terms of his contract to share any of the profits with the government.[37] Will the government or the public have any rights? It is impossible to say, for the issue has never been tried.

Authorship of Compilations

As discussed in chapter 1, compilations can be and derivative works always are layered works. The author of a compilation is the person who does the compiling, and copyright in a compilation covers only the arrangement and selection of material. The underlying material may be separately copyrightable, as in an anthology, in which case the copyright in the compilation is separate from each underlying copyright. Or the underlying material may be uncopyrightable facts, in which case the only copyright is that arising from the "selection, coordination, or arrangement" of those facts. In the same manner, a derivative work may be based on copyrighted material or on material in the public domain. In either case, the compilation or derivative work is owned separately from the underlying material.

If the underlying material has not been lawfully used, copyright will be denied to those parts of the compilation or derivative work in which the unlawful use occurs.[38] This acts, and was intended, as a severe penalty for unlawful use.

Divisibility

The principles of authorship determine who owns copyright at the time a work is first fixed in tangible form. At that point a property right comes into being and may be transferred to others. At that point also the principle of divisibility comes into play.

A copyright is in reality a bundle of rights, each of which may be exploited separately. These rights are to reproduce the work, to distribute it to the public, to perform it publicly, to display it publicly, and to create derivative works based on it. The author may transfer any one or more of them without transferring the others. The owner or exclusive licensee of any of these rights is, with respect to that right, a "copyright owner."

The divisibility principle goes further than this, though, for each of these five rights can in turn be carved up in a hundred ways. A novelist need not give a publisher the entire publication right to her novel. She may give her publisher hardcover and paperback rights but reserve electronic rights (although as a practical matter few authors have the bargaining power to do that). A playwright need not sell to a producer his entire performance right; he may give live stage rights to one producer and motion picture rights to another. Rights can be carved up geographically and chronologically as well. There is in fact no end to the number of possible subsidiary rights, although some of them are more appropriate to certain kinds of work than to others. And any licensee, such as the motion picture producer, is considered a copyright owner of the work, to the extent of his license, as long as the license is exclusive.[39]

It is important to remember that copyright in a work is separate from the physical object. The person who owns a work of art, for example, does not necessarily own copyright in it.[40] All he owns is the right to display it publicly, to persons present where the object is located. Furthermore, if the object is a movie or other audiovisual work, he can display publicly only one frame at a time.[41]

In short, the author of a work retains copyright even if the embodiment of the work is sold or given away. There is one major gap in this rule, however. Although the author theoretically owns the right to copy the work, nothing in the law requires the owner to give the author access to the actual object. An artist who has sold a canvas may find the right to copy it a rather empty privilege.

To deal with this apparent inequity, one court has fashioned, out of whole cloth, what it calls an "implied easement of necessity." On this basis it has compelled the owner of a work to give the artist sufficient access to enable him to copy the work.[42] This new doctrine, while laudable in many ways, creates peculiar conflicts between copyright and the laws of private property. Whether and how it evolves will be interesting to watch.

Community Property

A special problem of ownership affects those who live in states that treat property acquired during marriage as belonging equally to husband and wife. Is a copyright acquired after a marriage subject to this so-called "community property" rule? One state court, in California, has so held, reasoning that although federal law vests copyright in the author of a work, state law is free to transfer a share of that ownership to the author's spouse. The Fifth Circuit rejected this theory, but held that the nonauthor spouse has a community property interest in the economic fruits of the copyright. This seems the better-reasoned result, but time will tell which view prevails.[43]

Duration of Copyright

Authorship determines not only ownership of a copyright but also its duration. I have provided a quick-reference chart of copyright duration in appendix A, but will discuss the rules in some detail here.

The regular copyright term is life of the author plus 70 years. In the case of a joint work, it is life of the *last joint author to die* plus 70 years. In either case the copyright runs until the end of the calendar year 70 years after the author's death. (Special rules apply to works created before 1978; see chapter 10.) If the joint work was, however, partly created as work for hire, then the work-for-hire duration rules (see below) apply.

Suppose you do not know if or when an author might have died. Does the copyright go on and on forever, sheltered by public ignorance? No; the law provides that if, 95 years after first publication of a work or 120 years after its creation, the records of the Copyright Office contain no information as to the author's being alive or as to when the author died, the author will be presumed to have been dead for 70 years. Anyone who in good faith relies on this presumption may not be held liable as an infringer. The only requirement is that he must obtain from the Copyright Office a certified report that it has no information on the subject. Presumably he will be able to continue using the work even if, after receiving that certified report, he learns the author has not been dead for 70 years, although the statute is not explicit on this point.

Anyone who has a stake in the copyright can file a statement with the Copyright Office, indicating that the author is still alive, or died on such-and-such a date. This may or may not be desirable, of course; it would actually shorten the copyright term if the author died fewer than 45 years after publication of his work or in some cases fewer than 70 years after its creation.

There are exceptions to the life-plus-70 rule. Mask works receive only a 10-year term, measured from the date of registration or from first commercial exploitation, whichever occurs first.[44] The most important exception, however, is that for works made for hire. Copyright in a work made for hire lasts for 95 years from the date of first publication or 120 years from the date of creation, whichever is the shorter period. Suppose, for example, that in 1978 a publisher of a children's story commissioned someone to illustrate it as a work for hire, and the story, complete with illustrations, was published in 1979. The writer has a copyright in the story for her lifetime plus 70 years, but copyright in the illustrations, which are made for hire, lasts for 95 years (that is, through December 31, 2074). However, if the book was not published until 2012, copyright in the illustrations would expire in 2099 (120 years from the date of creation) rather than in 2107 (95 years from the date of publication). These provisions also apply to any joint work if any contribution to it is made for hire.[45] Thus if a freelance journalist collaborated with a consulting company on a research report, the work-for-hire rules would govern.

The term for a work that is authored anonymously or under a pseudonym is much the same as for a work made for hire. If the records of the Copyright Office contain no information as to the true identity of the author, the copyright term, like that of a work made for hire, will be 95 years from first publication or 120 years from creation, whichever period expires first.

At any time up to the expiration of this period, anyone who has a stake in the copyright can file a statement in the Copyright Office revealing the identity of the author.[46] As of that moment the copyright term becomes life plus 70 years (unless of course the work is also a work made for hire). This may not be desirable; if the author died, say, five years after publishing the work, revealing the author's identity will actually cause the copyright term to be shorter than it would have been if he had remained incognito. This situation creates an opportunity for the unscrupulous. Suppose that a movie producer owns the movie rights to a novel written under a pseudonym and has made a film that still, 70 years after the author's death, continues to produce yearly revenues. A rival film company, by buying up some other right in the novel, could obtain a stake in the copyright and be entitled to file a statement revealing the author's identity. The work would then be in the public domain, and the rival would be able to make a film of its own. (A plot for a bad movie?)

There is no way to avoid this result. However, if you are publishing a work under a pseudonym, you should require in every contract by which you transfer any interest in your copyright that the purchaser promises not to reveal your identity unless doing so will lengthen your copyright term. You should also require every purchaser to make the same demand of everyone purchasing from him. In this way you will preserve a right to sue for damages if a statement is filed to your detriment.

The last exception to the basic rules of copyright duration is for architectural works (as distinct from blueprints and drawings protectable as pictorial works). Since these were not eligible for copyright before December of 1990, any earlier architectural work has, as such, no copyright, unless as of December 1, 1990, the work had not been built and existed only in unpublished plans or drawings. In the latter case, copyright expired at the end of 2002 unless the work was constructed before that date, in which event the usual term of copyright (e.g., life of the author plus 70 years) will apply.

TRANSFERS AND LICENSES OF COPYRIGHT

An argument can be made that the word *property* refers not to possession of a thing but only to the right to use or dispose of it. It is this, I think, that underlies our use of the word *property* for so intangible a thing as copyright.

Because copyright is property, it can be sold, given away, donated to charity, bequeathed by will, or rented out on whatever terms the owner desires. And the same is true of any subsidiary right, such as the right to publish, the right to perform, and so on. However, copyright differs from most other kinds of property in two important respects:

First, the property of individual authors (as opposed to corporations that are authors of works made for hire) is immunized in an unusual way from government interference. Until an individual author has made at least one exclusive license or grant of his copyright, or of some part of it—for example, the right to perform the work publicly—no part of that copyright can be expropriated, transferred, or confiscated from the author by any court or other governmental body for any purpose or any reason, except in the context of bankruptcy.[1] This special immunity was originally intended to prevent communist governments from appropriating the U.S. copyrights of dissident authors, but it has possible impact closer to home. Although the issue has not been decided, it seems that this immunity ought to override the power of divorce courts to partition spouses' property. Presumably, also, it insulates copyright in unpublished works from seizure by the tax authorities.

Second, a sale or license that appears to be absolute and irrevocable may be revoked (or "terminated," to use the language of the statute) by the author or by his heirs, provided that certain procedures are followed. This is a statutory right and does not affect any right of termination that the author may have reserved by contract.

Of these two special rules, the second has by far the greater economic consequences. It was enacted to prevent a recurrence in the future of the sad tales we know so well, in which the hero signs away his copyright for a pittance only to see the villain reap enormous profits. It will have little practical value for the average work, however, as will be seen.

Making a Transfer or License

First, a word about nomenclature. The term "license" means a conveyance of copyright rights that is limited in duration, or is subject to being revoked if the licensee fails to make royalty payments or otherwise breaches the contract. A sale or "assignment" of copyright is a transaction in which outright ownership of the copyright—or some right comprised in the copyright—passes from one person to another. The term "transfer" refers to any assignment or exclusive license. The term "grant" includes both transfers and nonexclusive licenses. Nonexclusive licenses tend to be for limited periods of time; for example, a high school theater company needs no more than a nonexclusive license for its spring play. A book publisher, on the other hand, will generally insist on getting at the very least the exclusive publication right in a manuscript in its principal territory.

A nonexclusive license can be as informal as a handshake. It can be inferred from the conduct of those involved. (There is one exception, discussed later in this chapter.) But can it be imposed on someone who would otherwise be merely the buyer of a copy? That is the issue presented by the kind of license often used on software, and on material available on the Internet. This "shrink wrap" (so called because of the kind of plastic wrapping used on the software package) or "click-on" license, or the manner of accepting the transaction terms, changes what would otherwise be the sale of an object into a license of copyright by saying, "By opening this package [or clicking on "I agree"] you will be indicating your consent to the following terms." At the outset the legal validity of this approach was a subject of much debate, but it is now generally acknowledged as enforceable.[2]

An exclusive license or other transfer—be it a mortgage, sale, gift, or bequest—must be in writing and must be signed by the person making it. With regard to unpublished works, this did not use to be so. The old rule was that common law copyrights could be transferred orally or even by implication. The "writing" requirement is satisfied by any "electronic signature" that is recognized for general legal purposes, including electronic "click-on" agreements and the like.[3] The only instance in which an exclusive grant now does not need a signed instrument is where it comes about by what is called "operation of law." For example, if an author dies without a will, the law of the state where she lives will give her copyright to her heirs, and no written instrument is needed.[4]

"Exclusive" is not so broad as it seems. You can give an exclusive license to perform a play in Alaska if you put the agreement in writing and sign it. You can give an exclusive license to perform a play for a limited period of time, say, five years. You can give one person an exclusive license to distribute a work by mail and another person an exclusive license to sell over the counter.

Any limit on a license must be expressly stated.[5] If the license is in writing, the limitation should be as well; if the license is by word of mouth, the limitation must be clearly understood by both parties.

Sometimes, though, even written limitations on a license are less clear than they seem. For example, did a grant of "motion picture rights" back in the 1930s include or exclude television broadcast of the movie? (The source of the contention is that television did not become a standard means or place of showing a movie until a decade or two later.)[6] Cases arising from technologies unforeseen by the contract drafters have gone both ways, depending on minor differences in wording. This and similar problems of interpretation underline the need for careful drafting of licenses. The particular problem of unforeseen technologies can be avoided by a clause something like, "The producer will have the right to perform and display his motion picture in any manner and by any means now known or later developed." But, of course, the licensor is always inclined to resist such a sweeping grant.

The only clear exception to the rule that limitations on a license must be expressly stated is for contributions to collective works. Here the statute reverses the general rule—and standard pre-1978 practice. It provides that if you contribute, say, a poem to an anthology, the owner of the anthology can publish it only in that anthology, revisions of that anthology, or later works in the same series, unless you give a broader license. A contribution to a magazine would be another common example; the publisher is presumed to acquire only the right to publish it in that magazine.[7] Courts have interpreted this to include the right to publish the contribution in electronic versions of the original periodical issue, even in electronic collections of many issues of the periodical. However, the publisher does not acquire the right to include the article in large databases, where the integrity of the original periodical issue essentially disappears.[8]

Can a license be transferred? In other words, can a licensee give someone else part or all of his license? Under the old law, sublicensing, as this is called, was not allowed unless the licensee was clearly given that right.[9] This remains true for nonexclusive licenses. However, because an exclusive license is now treated as a transfer of a part of the copyright, it is generally agreed that an exclusive license can be transferred unless the copyright owner has specified otherwise. However, this is unfortunately not a unanimous view. The Ninth Circuit has opined that an exclusive license cannot be transferred or sublicensed unless the license terms say so.[10] Most observers believe this opinion is a mistake, but until it is corrected, prudent drafters of licenses should specify their intentions. In 2010 an attempt was made to override this Ninth Circuit opinion by legislation, but for some reason did not succeed. One should not infer too much from that failure, however.

Copyright Licenses Distinguished from Sales of Objects

As has been mentioned, copyright in a work exists separately from the tangible forms in which the work may be fixed. Transferring ownership of a painting, therefore, does not transfer copyright in it. And the reverse is also true: transferring copyright does not give the new copyright owner any right to possess the actual painting or other work.

In this respect the law has changed dramatically in favor of authors. Prior to 1978, explicit written instruments were necessary to transfer federal copyright, but not state law rights in unpublished works. Common law copyright could be transferred orally, and state common law would often infer a transfer of copyright from transfers of the physical object, if the work were unpublished.[11] In essence the law assumed that if you were parting with the means of reproduction—be it a painting, photographic negative, in some cases even a manuscript—you intended to empower the new owner to reproduce the work. However, this presumption could be overcome if the circumstances indicated that the parties' intent was to leave copyright with the artist or author.

Now, the parties' intent is irrelevant to the fundamental question of whether a transfer of copyright has occurred. The law requires a written acknowledgment, signed by the transferor. If an artist gave a colleague the means of reproducing an artwork, that could possibly serve as evidence of a nonexclusive license, or of a waiver of rights by the artist, but that would be the extent of it.

A friend of mine in the profession once told me that at cocktail parties—those wonderful clearinghouses of free legal advice—the question he is most often asked is, Who owns copyright in letters? Why does this question seem to trouble so many apparently respectable citizens? Whatever the reason, the answer will comfort them, for it is the writer who owns copyright unless there is some clear indication to the contrary. However, the recipient would have the right to make the letter public if it were necessary for some reason—to his defense against a libel action, or to clearing his character, or something of that sort.[12]

The written instrument necessary for a copyright transfer can come in many shapes and sizes. A written memorandum of the transfer will suffice if it is signed by the transferor. A letter from an author to her mother describing the transfer could satisfy the requirement if a court found it to be adequate evidence. If you are getting a license and are afraid that someone will try to question its existence—for example, if the copyright is likely to be the subject of a family squabble over whether Daddy was competent when he signed it— have the instrument of transfer notarized.[13]

Drafting a Transfer Agreement

The instrument of transfer may be executed at any time. Whether it may be executed retroactively is a muddled issue. Years ago the Second Circuit held that a written confirmation of a previous oral deal to transfer copyright was fine. The Ninth Circuit later ruled that where a license (as distinct from an assignment) is concerned, the written instrument must be signed while the license is still in effect—but in a subsequent opinion seemed to cast doubt on whether that was indeed what it had said. Other circuit courts have disagreed outright with the Ninth Circuit on this issue. The Seventh Circuit has added the fillip—quite reasonably—that a retroactive instrument will not be enforceable against a third party who acted in reasonable reliance on its absence.[14]

Most recently, the Second Circuit held that a co-owner of copyright could not retroactively assign his interest in the copyright, or even make a later written confirmation of an oral deal, at least where doing so would defeat an infringement claim that his co-owner had brought.[15] (The court was surely swayed in part by the facts in this case: the instrument in question was signed after the case had been brought, and on the eve of the defendant's deposition.) The equities of this seem reasonable, but unfortunately the court made several statements that seemed to cast doubt on the validity of *any* retroactive transfer (as distinct from a written confirmation of a previous oral deal). If retroactive transfers were never valid, it would wreak havoc in many industries. In the music business, particularly, companies frequently sign up songwriters retroactively when they learn that the author they first signed may not in fact be the real, or the only, author of a song. For the time being, everyone is simply assuming (read, hoping) that this Second Circuit opinion is limited to situations of egregious fact.

For the benefit of all concerned, any copyright transfer should clearly state, in addition to royalty provisions, warranties, and so on, the answers to the following questions:

1. What rights are being transferred? If the entire copyright is transferred, a clause often used is "X hereby transfers to Y all right, title, and interest, including copyright throughout the world, in and to a certain work entitled *Mud Wrestling for Fun and Profit.*" Otherwise be quite specific; for example: "X hereby transfers to Y the exclusive right to perform publicly a certain work entitled *Mud Wrestling for Fun and Profit*"; or "X hereby licenses to Y the exclusive right to make audiovisual works based on X's work entitled *Mud Wrestling for Fun and Profit.*"

2. How long is the transfer to last? (If for the maximum time, use words such as "for all terms of protection.")

3. What other limitations are there?

4. When, how, and for what reasons can the transfer be terminated? If not at all, nothing needs to be said on this point, but cautious drafters will often add the word "irrevocable." Typical reasons for

revocation are failure to pay royalties, the making of unauthorized alterations, failure to meet agreed sales objectives, and so on. Licensors often try to make the license contingent on compliance with royalty and other terms, so that it automatically terminates if the licensee breaches. This of course means that a licensee who is in breach is also an infringer of the copyright, with all the exposure that that entails. (See chapter 8.) Licensees, naturally, resist this language when they can.

5. Whose name will be placed in the notice on any published copies? Every contract concerning publication should ideally require that the person receiving the grant place proper copyright notice on all published copies.[16] (See chapter 4 for a fuller discussion of copyright notice.)

6. Who will bear the cost of prosecuting any infringement suit?

7. How will damages won in any such suit be apportioned?

8. Who will pay if someone brings an infringement suit against the work? Will that person have to pay for defense even if the suit is without merit?

To keep their dealings with their authors private, many publishers limit their instruments of transfer to a brief description of the transfer and deal with the other issues (points 4 through 8) in a separate contract. Thus when they record with the Copyright Office, they file only a single sheet of paper. This is a practice I recommend to anyone drafting a copyright agreement. If you follow this practice, your separate contract should state, "The instrument of transfer concerning this work is incorporated in this contract by reference and made a part of this contract." Your "short form" transfer should make reference to your contract, but *without* incorporating it by reference. In this way the two documents are tied together for all purposes other than recordation.

Recording the Copyright Grant

The written evidence of a copyright grant—be it a contract, a memorandum, or a letter—may be recorded in the Copyright Office. When recordation has been completed in the Copyright Office, the person who records will receive a certificate of recordation. See http://www.copyright.gov/docs/fees.html for the fees charged by the Copyright Office for these services.

With every document you submit for recordation, you must also submit a "Document Cover Sheet" in duplicate. On this form, which is available at www.copyright.gov/forms, you must state the following information: the parties to the document; the nature of the document; its date of execution and/or effective date; the titles, registration numbers, and author of the works dealt with in the document; and any other identifying information you consider relevant. You must also state whether the document is complete in itself or, in effect, can only be properly understood by reference to other documents or to facts not recited in the document. If the document is not complete in itself, you are not required to supply the missing pieces, but you are obliged to acknowledge the incompleteness. Finally, you must sign an "Affirmation" that the information submitted on the Document Cover Sheet is true and correct.

You need not submit a signed original document, but the Document Cover Sheet requires you to affirm that the copy you are submitting is genuine.

Recordation that clearly identifies the work will give general notice to the world at large of the facts set forth in the recorded document. Other people are presumed to have notice of all the information recorded, regardless of whether they have actually seen the document. For this to be so, however, the work must also be registered (see chapter 5).[17] Recordation of a transfer cannot be used as a substitute for registration of the underlying work.

Copyright owners of computer shareware may also wish to record with the Copyright Office the terms of the general license they give to users. The Copyright Office maintains a separate Computer Shareware Registry, and any document intended for it should be clearly labeled a "Document Pertaining to Computer Shareware." The fee for recording is computed in the same way as other recording fees. Submission of the license document in hard copy is required, but additional PC-compatible copies are encouraged.

Two People Claiming the Same Right

One important effect of recording a transfer is to establish priority of ownership. Suppose that a novelist sells dramatization rights in his novel to Smith on April 1 and then on April 2 sells the same rights to Jones. Smith has a one-month grace period in which to record the transfer (two months if the transfer is executed outside the country). After that time it is a horse race: Jones will be regarded as the legal owner of the copyright if he records before Smith, even though the transfer to him took place later than that to Smith, provided Jones was unaware of the deal with Smith.[18]

But again this is true only if the work has been registered. Thus we see the lengths to which Congress has been willing to go to induce people to register copyright claims. If the work is not registered, or until it is registered, no one has priority over anyone else, and neither Smith nor Jones may sue the other for going about his business. It is therefore in the interest of anyone who is recording a transfer to ensure that the work is registered.

There are two important circumstances under which these rules of priority do not apply. First, if the later transfer is a gift or bequest it cannot take precedence over a sale that preceded it, no matter when the sale is actually recorded.[19] This result seems only fair; it would be hard to justify a law that gave precedence to someone who had paid nothing for a right over someone who had paid. Second, if the person who received the second transfer actually knew of the first transfer, he cannot take precedence over the earlier purchaser by beating him to the Copyright Office. This too seems only fair.

The question of priority occurs not only between one transfer and another but also between a transfer of ownership and a nonexclusive license. Suppose, for instance, that a playwright sells performing rights in her play to a Broadway producer and later in the week gives permission to a local troupe to perform the same play. If the nonexclusive license was taken by the local troupe without knowledge of the prior transfer and before the transfer was recorded, the troupe has the right to perform the work within the limits of its license without regard to the rights of the producer. This is so provided the nonexclusive license itself is in writing, but regardless of whether it is recorded.[20]

Suppose in another instance that the nonexclusive license is given before the sale of rights is made. Here again, the nonexclusive license, if in writing, takes priority over the transfer, regardless of whether or when either of them is recorded. The nonexclusive license in such a case is like a right-of-way over a piece of land: any purchaser of the land is obligated to honor the right-of-way.

In no instance does it matter whether the nonexclusive license was paid for or was a gift or bequest. In this the law with respect to nonexclusive licenses differs fundamentally from the law of transfers.

A special priority rule applies in the case of "security interests" that banks and other lenders demand when lending money to copyright-owning businesses. If the copyrights in question are registered, the security interest must also be registered to be "perfected"; if not registered it is essentially worthless. Ordinary commercial rules, which permit filing of security agreements with state and local authorities, apply to unregistered copyrights.[21]

If you give any public broadcasting station or network a license to perform or display a published musical work or to display a published work of art, whether or not you also give it the right to tape the performance or display, you should ensure that the license is recorded within 30 days. If the license is not recorded, you will be bound by the terms of a compulsory license created by statute (see chapter 7).

Recordation of Licenses for Public Broadcasting

In addition to any termination right an author may reserve in a contract, the author and his heirs have a termination right under the copyright statute. The statutory right of termination, unlike the copyright itself, cannot be contracted away, given away, or bequeathed. No agreement that anyone can persuade an author to sign—in the statutory phrase, "no agreement to the contrary"—will diminish his right or the right of his heirs to terminate a grant of copyright.[22] For this reason a contract clause requiring the author to pay the other party money if he exercises his termination right would almost certainly be invalid. In short, the right to terminate is not a property right but an inalienable privilege under the law.

That phrase, "no agreement to the contrary," is targeted at agreements ginned up to try to circumvent termination, not at every agreement that might lead to

Termination of Grants

a contrary result. Thus, for example, in 1983 the heirs of A. A. Milne entered into a new agreement with the Walt Disney Company, scrapping one that Milne had signed in 1930. Twenty years later another Milne heir who had not been party to the 1930 grant tried to terminate it, but the court held that the 1930 grant could not be terminated because it was no longer in effect, having been superseded by the 1983 agreement. The Milne heir then tried to argue that the 1983 contract was an "agreement to the contrary," but the court did not buy that; by 1983 the prospect of termination was imminent, and the parties had agreed to a much richer deal for the heirs (as identified at that time) rather than wait and go through the mechanics of termination. In other words, the purpose of the termination provision had been accomplished, and the court was not going to give the late-arriving heir a windfall out of literal-mindedness.[23] This case involved the somewhat different termination provisions applicable to pre-1978 grants, but the principle should apply equally to post-1977 grants. If you renegotiate a deal, the old deal no longer exists and so cannot be terminated.

The termination right extends to all grants an author may make, but only to the extent of rights within the United States.[24] Termination of a grant of, for example, "all rights throughout the world," will revert U.S. rights to the author or his heirs but leave foreign rights in the hands of the grantee. Bear in mind, also, that termination affects only copyright grants, not other grants made in the same contract. Thus, if a contract grants trademark rights as well as copyright rights, and if the trademark (for example, the name of a famous cartoon character) stays with the grantee, interesting complications may arise. Just what can the author do with his copyright, if he cannot license use of that trademark as well?

The termination right was created principally for the benefit of individual authors and their families, to allow them to recover rights that an author granted during his lifetime. (Bequests are not terminable.)[25] It does not apply to works made for hire, with one exception: if the for-hire status arose after the work was created, because an individual author agreed retroactively to treat it as a work for hire, that agreement is terminable in the same way as an assignment of copyright.[26] The exclusion of works made for hire almost certainly applies to works that are partly for hire and partly not, although no case has yet addressed the question. For example, suppose a recording artist and a recording studio created a sound recording of the artist performing a song, and jointly conveyed copyright in the recording to a music label. When the time comes for termination, if the recording studio was a sole proprietorship, the assignment would be terminable. If the studio was a corporation, however, then its contribution to the work was made for hire, and the assignment would not be terminable.

After termination, the person who once owned the right or license cannot exploit the work further in any way—with one exception. If someone has made a derivative work under a grant permitting him to do so, he can continue to exploit this work, because the derivative work has a separate copyright. Termination prevents him only from making or authorizing further derivative works. Moreover, any royalty income from that derivative work will continue to be paid as it was before termination, even if this means that an intermediary, rather than the terminating author, receives the benefit.[27]

In the balance of this chapter I am going to focus on the specific mechanics and outcomes of terminating post-1977 grants, meaning grants that became effective after 1977 either because they were made after 1977 or because they were made before 1978 but covered works created after 1977. Please see chapter 10 for the rules applicable to termination of grants covering pre-1978 works.

The statutory termination right is open to authors, their widows or widowers, and their children and grandchildren (whether legitimate or not and whether natural or adopted). If all of these persons are deceased, the author's "executor, administrator, personal representative, or trustee" owns the termination right. This language, added in 1998, creates a fiduciary obligation for those who administer certain authors' estates. The inclusion of "trustee" in the list is presumably intended to give the termination right to trustees who succeed to the bulk of an author's estate. However, the statute gives no guidance for situations where the author has left two or more different trusts with different trustees.

No statutory termination right exists for anyone else. Someone outside the author's line of descent who has received a right from an author, or even the entire copyright, and transferred it to a third person has no termination right.[28]

The right is also limited in time. Termination may be made only in a five-year period beginning 35 years after the date of the grant and ending 40 years after the date of the grant. The only variation from this rule is the case of a publication right. The five-year period in which a grant of a publication right may be terminated can begin at one of two times: either 40 years after the date of the grant or 35 years after the date of first publication, whichever is earlier.[29]

Certain procedures must be followed in exercising this right. These procedures apply whether the original grant or license was exclusive or nonexclusive; even a word-of-mouth license cannot be terminated except by following the rules:[30]

If the work is a joint work, and two or more of the joint authors execute a grant, termination may be made only by a majority of those authors who executed the grant. The law does not require a majority of the interest in the work, only a numerical majority of the authors who made the grant. Because nonexclusive transfers of copyright in a joint work can be made by one joint author without the others' consent, the termination rules focus on who made the grant, not who owns the copyright. In other words, even if one of three joint authors is entitled, by agreement with the others, to 60 percent of the royalties, he cannot single-handedly terminate a grant unless he alone made it. The majority requirement also means that if only two authors executed the grant, they must both join in the termination for it to be effective.

Just what obligations one joint author has to another in this respect is unclear. Co-owners are liable to each other for profits and, in many cases, for loss they may cause to the income-producing ability of what they own. Will joint authors be liable to each other for loss of revenues if the loss is caused by termination of a grant? If a joint author refuses to join in a termination, and thereby causes loss of potential revenue, will he be held liable? My guess in both instances is no, because both are contemplated in the way the statute is constructed, and both involve the exercise of a statutory right.

If an author or joint author is dead, his right to terminate or to join in a termination may be exercised by his surviving spouse (regardless of whether the spouse has remarried) and his children or grandchildren. The spouse controls half of the right and the children or grandchildren the other half. If there are no children or grandchildren, then the spouse controls the entire right, and if there is no spouse, then the children and grandchildren control the entire right. The statute makes no provision for more distant generations, but it does pass the termination right to the author's fiduciaries if there is no surviving spouse, child, or grandchild living.

If children or grandchildren own the termination right, or one-half of it, what they own is to be divided among them in equal shares. This division into shares is a *per stirpes* distribution. This means that if, for example, an author's daughter is living, her children (grandchildren of the author) have no share. But if the daughter is dead but has surviving children, her share belongs to her children and may be exercised only by a majority of them. If all of an author's children are dead, the surviving grandchildren do not take equally; each set of grandchildren takes the share that would belong to their parent if he or she were alive.

The required percentage: The termination right of a deceased author may be exercised only by persons owning, among them, over 50 percent of the termination right. For example, if there are a widow, one child, and three grandchildren of a deceased child, then the widow owns 50 percent of the right, the child owns 25 percent, and the three grandchildren among them own 25 percent, but can exercise their 25 percent only if a majority of them agree. In such a case termination can take place only if the child or two of the grandchildren agree with the widow to terminate. If there are a widower, one child, and two grandchildren, then either the child or both grandchildren must join with the widower. If there is no spouse but there are three children, then two of the children must join together.

Notice of termination must be given in advance. This notice must be in writing and must be signed by the necessary persons or their authorized agents. It must explicitly state that the termination is being made pursuant to Section 203 of the Copyright Act. Notice itself must be given at least two years before the effective date, but not more than 10 years before it.

The notice must be served, in person or by first-class mail, on "the grantee or the grantee's successor in title," that is, on the person who originally received the transfer, or on anyone who has obtained it from him. You are required to carry out a "reasonable investigation" as to the current owners of those rights, and as to their current addresses. The regulations do not suggest what a reasonable investigation would require, insofar as addresses are concerned. Certainly there are many online sources of information for such data, and confirmatory phone calls are always advisable. As for the identity of current owners, the regulations say that a reasonable investigation "includes but is not limited to" a search of the Copyright Office records and, in the case of musical works, a report from whichever performing rights societies (ASCAP, BMI, and/or SESAC) currently license the work. For post-1978 transfers, recorded transfer information is posted on the Copyright Office website at http://www.copyright.gov/records. However, there is sometimes a good bit of lag time between when a transfer is recorded and when the record is posted, so you may want to commission a search-by-hand from the Copyright Office to be absolutely sure you have the right person(s). Also, a thorough Internet search would be advisable, especially if nothing turns up in the Copyright Office database.

The notice must contain certain basic information:

1. The names of all persons whose rights are being terminated and all addresses to which the notice is being sent.

2. The title of the work.

3. The name of the authors of the work. If the work is a joint work, include the names of all authors who signed the grant being terminated.

4. The copyright registration number, if possible. (Finding this may be part of the Copyright Office records search noted above.)

5. A brief statement reasonably identifying the grant you are terminating.

6. The date the grant was executed. *Note*: if you signed a grant before 1978 that covers a work created in 1978 or later, the date of execution as to that work is considered to be the date on which creation of the work was completed.

7. If the grant being terminated includes the right of publication, the date on which the work was first published.

8. The date that termination is to become effective, which of course must be within the appropriate five-year period.

9. If the grant is being terminated by an author's family, a list of all the surviving persons who are entitled to take part in termination (whether they are actually doing so or not) and their relationships to the author. (Remember, those persons include the author's widow or widower, children, and surviving children of any deceased child.) Indicate on the list which persons actually are taking part in the termination and what their percentage shares of the termination right are.

If you are not sure of all the information required under point 9, put down as much as you know, explain why you are uncertain as to the rest, and include a statement that "to the best knowledge and belief of the person or persons signing the notice, the notice has been signed by all persons whose signature is necessary to terminate the grant under section 203 of title 17, U.S.C., or by their duly authorized agents."

The notice must be signed by all persons taking part, or their authorized agents. Agents must indicate on whose behalf they are signing. Each signature should be accompanied by the person's name and address, in typed or hand-printed form.

If you fail to comply with any of these requirements and if your errors or omissions cause other people to be misled to their disadvantage, your notice of termination may be judged legally ineffective.

A copy of the notice must be recorded (for a fee; see http://www.copyright.gov/docs/fees.html) in the Copyright Office before the effective date of termination, or it will be invalid. If you served notices on multiple grantees, a copy of one of them will suffice. You must include with what you record a statement indicating the date on which the notice was served and the manner of service, unless that information is obvious from the notice itself. Where service was made by first-class mail, the date of service is the date you deposited the notice with the United States Postal Service.

Copyright after Termination

As of the date that notice of termination is served, the right or rights that are to terminate become vested in the persons who own the termination right.[31] For example, as of the date that a playwright's widow and children terminate his grant of the performance rights, the performance right vests in them. Vesting means entitlement, not actual possession; what happens is that the rights that will eventually revert, when the termination takes effect, are allocated before that time, and are a limited kind of property interest.

The rights vest in everyone who could have joined in the termination, regardless of who actually did take part in it. If, for example, an author's son did not take part in giving notice of termination, he will still get his proportionate share of the right when it reverts. If the termination is made by the family of a deceased author, the rights vest in the same *per stirpes* manner described previously. In the case of a joint work, nothing vests in an author (or the family of an author) who did not join in the original grant, because he did not own a termination right with respect to that grant.

Making a New Grant Because vesting is less than actual possession, the rule that the rights vest as of the date notice is received does not mean that the new owners can make a new transfer immediately. They cannot make a new grant of any kind, exclusive or nonexclusive, before the date of termination; not even the author can do this. Moreover, with one exception, those in whom the right vests cannot even make a commitment to make a grant before the date of termination. And because selling the right to make a grant is tantamount to making a grant, it is probable that even someone who receives the entire right, when that right vests, cannot sell his right to make a new grant until the date the termination takes effect.

The exception to this rule is that the people terminating may renegotiate a contract with the existing right holder.[32] For example, if a publisher has a license to make and sell reproductions of a photograph, the photographer or her appropriate heirs can give notice of termination and immediately thereafter renegotiate the contract. The renegotiated royalties do not, theoretically, take effect until the date the termination actually occurs, but if the license is lucrative, the publisher may well compromise on this point and pay more royalties in the interim to get a renewal of the grant.

It is important to remember that the right to terminate inheres in the person; it is less like property than like a privilege. It cannot be sold or given away. For example, if an author's widow dies, the termination right that she possessed dies with her, and the entire termination right belongs to the children or grandchildren, if any. However, once notice of termination is given and reversion of the copyright becomes vested in the people who had a right to terminate, we are talking not of a privilege but once again of a property right.

Unlike the right to terminate, this property right does not die with the owner; he can bequeath it in his will to anyone at all, and whoever receives the bequest can take part in any renegotiations or new grants. Presumably, also, the owner can sell or give away his right to receive income from his share of the copyright. But unless he owns the entire copyright, he cannot sell or give away during his life his right to take part in making a new grant, because the law makes very stringent requirements for new grants of terminated rights.

A renegotiation, or a new grant, must be made in the following manner.[33]

Mechanics of Making a New Grant

1. It must be in writing. This requirement applies not only to transfers but also to nonexclusive licenses. (This is the only circumstance in which a nonexclusive license is required to be in writing.)

2. It must be signed by persons representing at least the same proportion of ownership in the right as was involved in the termination.

3. It must be signed by at least the same number of persons as signed the notice of termination.

These requirements concerning number and proportion are difficult to grasp. It may be helpful to take an example. Suppose that an author dies, survived by a wife, one daughter, and two grandsons born of a deceased son. Because termination of the original grant requires participation of over 50 percent of the termination right, in this case it will require the widow's 50 percent, plus another 25 percent from either the living daughter or the deceased son as represented by his children. It will also require at least two signatures.

When the right vests in the author's family upon the giving of notice of termination, it vests 50 percent in the widow, 25 percent in the daughter, and 12½ percent in each of the two grandsons. (Each of these people now owns a separate and distinct interest because the rights are vested.) Suppose the widow then dies, bequeathing her entire share of the right to one of the grandsons, so that he now owns 62½ percent of the right. The law provides that someone who inherits an interest in a right in this way "represents" the person from whom he received it, for purposes of signing a new grant. Thus the grandson represents his grandmother, and he may sign the new grant first on behalf of his grandmother's 50 percent and again on his own behalf, so that in effect there are two signatures on the document. This meets the "number" requirement because there were only two signatures on the notice of termination. However, despite the fact that he now owns over half the right, the grandson cannot single-handedly make a new grant, for the new grant must be agreed to by 75 percent of the ownership—that being the percentage of the ownership that agreed to the termination. Therefore, to make a new grant, this grandson must persuade either his brother or his aunt to join him. If he cannot, no new grant can be made.

Once a new grant or a renegotiation of an old grant has been made, it binds and benefits everyone who had a share of the right to make it, regardless of who actually signs the new grant or renegotiation.[34] In the previous example, if only the widow and the two grandsons join in making the new grant, the daughter is nonetheless treated as if she too had joined in. By "binds" I mean that when the new grant is made, she cannot make a grant of any kind on her own; on the other hand, she is entitled to her share of the proceeds. To take another example, if an author's husband and one of her two children terminate an old grant and then renegotiate it or make a new grant to someone else, the other child cannot go off on his own and arrange a separate sale, but on the other hand he is entitled to a 25 percent share of the profits that the rest of the family has negotiated.

All this talk of deceased authors and their heirs seems to lead naturally to the subject of estate planning for copyrights—the ultimate transfer that any author makes.

Estate Planning

Estate planning has two main components. One has to do with taxes, and the other with how to distribute assets in a way that is best for the family members, charities, or others that will receive the decedent's assets—and, where creative works are concerned, in a way that best preserves the integrity of the assets.

Copyrights like all other assets have value, even if that value is sometimes hard to pin down, and in computing the size of an author's estate it may be necessary to value his or her copyrights to determine whether the estate is taxable, what sort of compensation is due to the executor, and so on. If no one has made an offer to buy those assets, their value has to be determined in some other way, usually by making a plausible projection of the income stream they are likely to generate, and discounting the present value of that income stream.

Given recent changes in federal estate tax law, estate tax planning affects only those with roughly $5 million in assets (or twice that, in the case of married couples). Tax planning is critically important, but it is beyond the remit of this book and I will not delve further into it here.

Taxes aside, the most significant estate planning issue for most authors is how to ensure that their copyrights are properly administered, and that their spouses, children, or other beneficiaries derive the most benefit from the copyrights.

Copyright administration involves making licensing deals, collecting royalties and distributing them to the author's heirs, enforcing rights, pursuing infringements, and also (as you will have seen from the immediately preceding discussion) exercising termination rights where appropriate. This may involve extremely sensitive issues such as who should be brought on board to update a textbook that continues to generate significant royalties, or who should be allowed to make a film of the deceased author's classic novel. Ideally, every author wants his copyrights to be administered by someone who has the same aesthetic sensibility and commitment to the material as he had himself while living.

This brings us to the "literary executor," a mythical creature frequently invoked by authors when they go to a lawyer to prepare their estate plans. A literary executor is imagined as the author's alter ego, exercising taste and judgment in administering the author's artistic legacy for an indeterminate time frame.

State probate laws, which govern decedents' estates, do not recognize any such animal. An executor, in probate law, is someone charged with collecting the assets of a decedent, paying off debts and taxes, and distributing the assets to their ultimate beneficiaries according to the terms of the decedent's will. His tenure is supposed to be short: a few years at most.

This is not to say that an author cannot designate a particular person to be an executor of his estate with special jurisdiction over his copyrights. The problem is that this is not supposed to be a long-term assignment. Probate courts like to wrap up estates and close their files, and that goal is inconsistent with the long-term administration of copyrights.

In truth, an author has two choices. One is to leave his copyrights to his spouse or other heirs and let them thrash things out as best they may, bearing in mind that if there are more than one they are joint owners, with all the complications that arise from joint ownership (see chapter 2). The other is to leave those copyrights in a trust, with one or more trustees having power to administer those rights and with a mechanism for appointing their successors should they die or resign. Unlike estates, trusts are designed for longevity; state laws allow trusts to endure for a length of time as long as, if not longer than, the duration of copyright. A trustee, especially if he or she is competent in the administration of copyrights, is the real-life equivalent of a literary executor. Trusts have the added benefit that they can cope with many of the vicissitudes of life: age, incompetence, and family strife, to name but a few.

If an author decides to leave his or her copyrights in trust, rather than outright to family members, the author has to decide who should be the trustee(s). Here the considerations are essentially those that would apply if there truly were such a thing as a "literary executor"; ideally you want someone who has both aesthetic and business judgment, and a demonstrated commitment to the author's work. If that is not possible, then you want someone who will know his limitations sufficiently to hire others, such as good agents, to do what needs to be done.

Secondly, a trust must explicitly give the trustee(s) sufficient powers to handle all the various tasks that may arise. Under modern probate law trustees are deemed to have a wide array of basic powers, but copyrights require special treatment, and it would be unwise to rely on implied powers for all the issues that may arise over the life of a copyright. In appendix G, I have included trustee powers language that we use in my firm for trusts where the donor is a copyright owner. Similar language should be incorporated in the author's will, for use by the executor(s) of the author's estate.

In planning an author's estate, bear in mind always that the copyrights exist separate and apart from the manuscripts, paintings, or other physical things in which the author's work may be embodied. A good estate plan must ensure that these objects and the copyrights in them are disposed of in ways that complement rather than fight each other.

Open Source, Open Access Recent decades have seen the evolution of numerous new licensing models at odds with traditional copyright norms. While these arrangements have a certain ethos in common, they are conceptually different from one another and need to be carefully understood.

One stems from the "open-source" movement, which was born in the 1980s out of the freemasonry of early software developers. Open-source software has become dominant in certain fields of computer programming, and claims some major products such as the Linux operating system and the Mozilla Firefox web browser. The main idea of the movement is that software developers collaborate, via the Internet, on developing, maintaining, and upgrading software. All participants acknowledge that the software is subject to copyright, and all subscribe to a copyright-based license, but the thrust of the license is to negate copyright in the traditional sense of exclusionary ownership. No one "owns" the code, in the sense of having any material control over it; anyone can use it and work on it so long as he or she signs onto the license that governs it. There are a dizzying array of these licenses, and I decline to get bogged down in the details. Among the most common are the various versions of the GNU General Public License or GPL, the MIT (or X11) License, and the Open Software License. What they have in common is that by agreeing to them, a software developer essentially obtains the right to use and add to the software concerned, while allowing other developers to do the same with what he or she may create.

The success of the open-source movement inspired the birth of the Creative Commons, whose programs and procedures are set forth at www.creativecommons .org. Creative Commons licenses are not recommended for software. Instead, the Creative Commons operates in the more traditional copyright industries, with a particular emphasis on music and scholarly publishing.

A Creative Commons (CC) license basically allows anyone to reproduce and distribute a work at will, without payment to the copyright owner, so long as the original author and source are credited and certain other "metadata" (including any copyright notice) are maintained. For music, the CC license also allows public performance. Beyond that, however, the licensor has a number of choices. A CC license can forbid the making of derivative works (the so-called ND alternative) or permit it (the so-called ShareAlike or SA alternative), and can allow or forbid (the NC option) commercial exploitation by the licensee. As the term ShareAlike suggests, if you make alterations to a work governed by such a license, you must allow others to make the same liberal use of whatever derivative works you create.

Like any other copyright paradigm, the open-source/Creative Commons approach is not without its difficulties. One lies in the sphere of enforcement. So far only one court has entertained a case seeking to enforce an open-source license. The case was brought by one of many contributors to a model railroading program, alleging that the defendant had infringed copyright because it failed to obey the terms of the license. (Among other things, the defendant had failed to give proper attribution to the authors of the original work.) Although the court agreed that the license was enforceable, it denied the copyright owner a prelimi-nary injunction—because the copyright owner had failed to demonstrate that he faced any threat of immi-nent harm from violation of the license.[35] Since dam-ages would be rare in the open-source context, and injunctions are about the only remedy that really mat-ters to those seeking to enforce open-source licenses, this case may discourage people with meritorious claims from seeking redress in court. That would be a pity.

Another difficulty with the Creative Commons licensing scheme, in particular, is the flip side of its simplicity: it comes in only a handful of flavors, and cannot be changed. Thus, if you are willing to allow translations of your work but not any other sort of derivative work, you cannot go into the CC license and tinker with it to achieve that result. Recognizing the rigidity of this, the Creative Commons has recently blessed the concept of a "CC+" license, though discussion of it is not easy to find on their website. Essentially, this involves an add-on that gives the public additional rights beyond what your chosen CC license gives. To take my translation example, to accomplish the result you want you would use a CC ND (no derivatives) license, but then add on a license granting the right to make translations. Creative Commons suggests you post this information on a webpage, for which you can provide a "more permissions URL." If you are offering the CC+ license through analog technology (e.g., in a printed book), however, then presumably you must include the precise terms of your add-on in the front matter of the work. Either way, it seems more complicated than it should be, and may well discourage use of the Creative Commons by some copyright owners.

Finally, there is the problem of context. Although the CC license forbids use in any manner that would suggest endorsement by the original author, there is a large gap between endorsement and mere proximity. The CC license does not and cannot prevent republication in a manner or context that the original author might find offensive, so long as the context does not imply endorsement. If, say, you publish a study under a CC license that casts doubt on the efficacy of certain kinds of gun control, you won't be able to prevent its reappearance on a pro-gun website.

The other main antitraditional copyright paradigm is called "open access." Where open-source was inspired by the idea of massively collaborative undertakings and untrammeled cultural experimentation, open access was inspired (at least in part) by anger at commercial publishers, and its main focus is on free distribution of static content. While open-access content is often made available via one or another Creative Commons license, that is not a necessary feature.[36]

The original impetus for open access was the perception that major scientific, technical, and medical publishers were getting rich off the publication of research that had been funded with public money. It did not help that these publishers continued year after year to raise their prices on scientific journals.

The reaction took two forms. One, from the governmental funders of scientific research, can be boiled down to this: the public has already paid for it; why should it pay again? Proponents have pushed for articles based on publicly funded research to be made freely available for reproduction and distribution after a certain number of months following first publication. As of this writing, this demand was the subject of a tug-of-war on Capitol Hill, but if I were a betting man I would bet on the advocates of open access. Their sound bite is easy to understand. The benefits that publishers bring to the table are complicated to explain and quantify. At the most, publishers are likely to get a 6- or 12-month delay in open-access posting: a short interval in which to recoup their investment.

The other reaction has come from within academia, and focuses more on the contractual relationships between authors and publishers. The *beau idéal* of the academic open-access movement is that universities and their faculty should be able to post on their websites, for free access by all interested scholars, whatever scholarly articles they generate. In support of this some college faculties, such as Harvard University's, have adopted policies that strongly favor faculty either withholding copyright assignments from publishers, or reserving the right to post articles on campus or personal websites. This is called "Open Access Green." (Why "green" I do not know, but it sounds friendly.)

This movement has seen some degree of success, although the data so far suggest that most scholarly research is still being published under the old norms. Also, what scholarly authors may freely post is not always the final, copy-edited, peer-reviewed version of their articles, but sometimes the next previous version, which is of lesser archival and scholarly value.

The open-access movement has been successful in large part because the financial incentives of authors and their publishers are not aligned. The typical author of a scholarly article receives no pay or royalties for it; his or her compensation lies in peer recognition, and in tenure. Thus, the more exposure his or her article receives the better, whether paid for or not. This is in stark contrast to what happens in the textbook industry, which is a source of major revenue for successful academic authors and has not been the subject of any push for change by the academic community. (There has, however, been a push in some states for public funding of open-source textbooks, with notably inconsequential effects.)

As the open-access movement gains momentum, publications that are open-access *ab initio* are increasing in number. Some of these are nonprofit, such as those of the Public Library of Science project; others come from established for-profit publishers. The movement has also been expanding to include full-length monographs, for the most part published by university presses, although the number of open-access books available is so far modest. Some of these projects reach back, for their business model, to a custom that many thought had died forever. In the old days, before selling subscriptions to learned journals became quite profitable, publishers used to make ends meet by levying "page charges" on the authors of journal articles. In essence the author had to pay to have his or her article included in a journal. Open-access journals are now often funded by that model, which is called "Open

Access Gold." A form of Open Access Gold, relying in many cases on subvention by institutions or foundations, also applies to monographs, harking back to the days when books were funded by subscription. Progress can sometimes go in circles.

COPYRIGHT NOTICE

4

Just as much as copyright is property, it is also a bundle of procedures, paperwork, and footwork. These should be followed scrupulously to protect a copyright to the fullest extent.

For purposes of the federal statute, you acquire copyright upon fixation of the work, and at any point before completed fixation you automatically have copyright in as much of the work as you have fixed. Until the United States joined the Berne Convention, a multilateral copyright treaty, on March 1, 1989, another important rite of passage was "publication." Under our pre-Berne law, once a work was published, you acquired federal copyright if you affixed proper notice of copyright to it, and forfeited all copyright if you did not.

This is no longer so. Notice is not required for works published after March 1, 1989. Works published before that date, however, will continue to be governed by the pre-Berne rules. And even though notice is no longer required, it is still advisable, because it deprives an infringer of any defense of innocence.[1] So in applying the rules that follow here it is critical to determine first whether the work in question was published during the period from January 1, 1978, to February 28, 1989, or earlier, or later. If later, then the rules governing copyright notice are advisory only; if during, then they are mandatory. If earlier, then even more stringent rules apply in some respects, and these are discussed in chapter 10.

Publication   The concept of publication has been crucial to copyright law from the beginning. It used to mark the boundary between common law copyright and federal copyright. Until the United States joined the Berne convention, it marked the moment when notice had to be affixed. Even now, it can be critical to determining eligibility for statutory damages and attorney's fees, as discussed in chapter 8.

In determining whether a work has been published, there does not have to be an actual distribution. It is enough that copies have been offered to the public.[2] Actual distribution includes giving copies away to the public. The size of the public is irrelevant; handing out one or two copies can constitute publication.[3] And though performance or display of a work is not publication in and of itself, distributing copies to a group of persons who will themselves perform or display the work does count as publication, unless those persons are your employees or otherwise act under your control.[4]

The sale of one's painting, sculpture, or other unique work of visual art probably constitutes a publication in the eyes of the law, although there is some evidence that Congress did not intend this result.[5]

When is an architectural work "published"? The Copyright Office takes the position that publication occurs when the plans, drawings, photographs, or other pictorial representations of the work are published, but that construction of a building does not itself constitute publication. The latter statement may mean less than it appears to say. Upon construction of a building that is owned by someone other than the copyright owner—as is usually the case—a copy of the architectural work comes into the hands of someone other than the architect, and does so with the architect's permission. To say that this does not constitute publication would contradict the general rules of publication.

Performance and display of a work do not constitute publication. You can perform or display a work as often as you like, to as wide an audience as you like, and you will not be considered to have published it by doing so. (Both "performance" and "display" include broadcasting, film projection, and so on.)[6] Delivering a speech does not publish it.

Nor does circulation of copies within a limited group, for limited purposes, count as publication. However, the persons receiving those copies must understand that they have no right to perform or display them publicly or to make a further distribution outside the group.[7]

Submission of a manuscript to a publisher is a classic example of such "limited publication," as it is called, for which copyright notice is not required. In the academic community there is also a custom of circulating so-called preprints (manuscript copies of forthcoming journal articles) among colleagues for comment and discussion. This too would be a limited publication in most cases. But if you are making what you intend as a limited publication under circumstances where your intent will not be absolutely clear to your audience, you would be well advised to place on the copy either a regular copyright notice or a legend to this effect: "This copy is circulated for comment only and may not be used or distributed in any other manner."

Finally, the filing of copies or phonorecords with a court or other public authority does not constitute publication.[8]

When Should Notice Be Used? In the case of copies from which a work can be "perceived visually," copyright notice should be placed on all copies publicly distributed, whether in the United States or elsewhere. (The only exception is that notice need not be placed on the original of an artwork if no other copies are produced.) It is not necessary that visual perception be possible with the naked eye; it is enough that the copy distributed can be perceived visually with the aid of a machine or device, such as a movie projector. Remember that musical works are regarded as being visually perceived when they are written in musical notation, and the same applies to notation of choreography.

Sound recordings are works that by definition cannot be perceived visually. They are not distributed in the form of "copies" but in the form of "phonorecords." The term "phonorecord" is a hybrid word used, so far as I know, only in copyright law. It includes everything from player-piano rolls to downloadable MP3 files—any method now known or discovered in the future for fixing sounds—but it does not include the soundtracks of audiovisual works; a phonorecord must reproduce only sound.[9] Every phonorecord that is distributed to the public should bear notice of copyright with respect to the sound recording that it embodies. However, no notice of copyright in the underlying music or other work need be affixed to the phonorecord.

An interesting question, which no court has yet faced, concerns the computer programs that embody so-called computer music. These programs, unlike such things as MP3 files, are not a fixation of a performance. They are written to drive the synthesizers that both imitate (or embellish) sounds of more traditional instruments and create entirely new sounds of their own. By the time they enter the synthesizers (which are computers connected to sound-producing mechanisms), they are in object code form. Is such code a phonorecord of a sound recording or a copy of a musical work? Like any more conventional phonorecord, its primary function is to cause a machine to produce sound. On the other hand the program begins life as a series of written notations, which can be likened to ordinary musical notation, and hence constitutes a "copy." Since an object code version of a source code program is a copy of it, not a derivative work, by an equally logical train of thought we can conclude that the file that drives the synthesizer is a copy of the musical work, not a phonorecord.

For now, this conundrum is merely intriguing. But the day may come when there will be a market for computer music among a significant segment of the public. How should the source codes be registered—as musical works or as sound recordings? I think the key point here may be that the code can produce different sounds depending on what synthesizer is used, whereas conceptually a sound recording captures only a single, unique performance. Thus, my instinct is to consider a computer music file a copy of the musical work, not a sound recording.

Notice for Contributors to a Collective Work

A question frequently asked is, What notice should go on a magazine article, or a poem in an anthology, or any other contribution to a collective work? All contributions to a collective work are covered by a general notice affixed to the collective work as a whole, except for advertisements, which should bear separate notice.[10] However, under the pre-Berne rules, if the contributor retained copyright, omission of separate notice might be treated as if notice had been given in the wrong name.[11] It was and still is a good idea to require, if you can, that your contribution to a collective work have its own copyright notice.

Formalities of Copyright Notice

Notice comprises three things:

1. In the case of visually perceived works, the familiar symbol © or, if you prefer, the word *Copyright* or its accepted abbreviation, *Copr.* (In foreign countries, use ©; *Copyright* and *Copr.* do not have international validity.) In the case of sound recordings published in phonorecords, the only symbol to use is ℗ ; © is of no effect. In the case of mask works there are three options: the words *Mask Work,* the symbol *M*, or the symbol Ⓜ.[12]

2. The year of first publication. This date is not necessary where a visual work is reproduced in or on greeting cards, postcards, stationery, jewelry, dolls, toys, or "useful articles" (articles having an intrinsic utilitarian function).[13] A good example of this useful-article exception is the reproduction of a painting on a place mat; in such a case the date when the painting itself was first published would not need to be included in the copyright notice. The date is also optional for mask works.

Bear in mind that the year of first publication of a work may not necessarily be the year in which you first need to affix copyright notice. For example, a musical work is considered to be "published" by the distribution of phonorecords or movie soundtracks embodying it, even though those phonorecords and soundtracks do not need to bear notice as to the musical work. Thus if a piece of music came out on a record in 1994 but not in written form until 1996, 1994 is the proper year to put in the notice.

3. The name of the owner of copyright. This may be abbreviated if the name remains recognizable. If the owner has a generally known trademark, abbreviation, or other symbol, that may be used instead. This term "owner of copyright" is different

from the term "copyright owner" (who may be merely the owner of the exclusive publication right). The owner of copyright is the author or anyone to whom the author has transferred the entire copyright.[14] In the case of a sound recording, notice must be in the name of the owner of the copyright in the recording; the name of the owner of copyright in the musical composition should not be used and may lead to substantial confusion.

There is an additional requirement in the case of works that consist preponderantly of works of the U.S. Government—for example, a collection of public documents edited by a private citizen, or a journal issue including articles by government scientists. Such works are supposed to include in the notice a statement identifying those parts of the work in which copyright is claimed, or those parts that are the product of the U.S. Government and in which copyright is therefore not claimed.

The elements of notice need not appear all together, so long as they are all present on the copy and placed in such a way that a reasonable person would understand them to be parts of a whole.

The location of the notice as a whole is important, although the law's requirements have not, since 1978, been so strict as formerly. In the case of sound recordings, notice must be placed on the surface of the phonorecord, or on the label, or on the container in which the phonorecord is retailed. Its placement must be calculated to give "reasonable notice" to the public. In the case of visually perceived works, the only requirement is that placement be calculated to give reasonable notice to the public. Notice has to be fixed to the copy or phonorecord; the law will not be satisfied by, say, tying to a sculpture a tag with copyright notice written on it, unless no alternative is feasible. The regulations of the Copyright Office, giving examples of acceptable placement of notice, are reproduced in appendix B.

The principle that notice should be "reasonable" has led to some judicial loosening of the rules. For example, it has been held that as long as notice appears on one of a group of items that are sold together, it will cover all those items. Thus it was sufficient to place notice on the cardboard box in which a toy puppy was sold, and not on the puppy itself, because the box was intended to be kept as a "kennel" for the puppy.[15]

As additional protection, it is advisable to place in your notice the statement "All Rights Reserved," to ensure protection in certain Latin American countries that do not recognize *Copyright, Copr.,* or © as proper notice of a claim of rights.

Incomplete or Omitted Notice

If any one of the three principal components of proper notice—name, date, and the symbol, word, or abbreviation for copyright—is omitted, the work will be treated as if notice were omitted entirely.[16] Where the work consists preponderantly of U.S. Government works and the notice does not say so, the work will be treated as if notice were omitted entirely.[17]

Omission of notice, under the *ancien régime,* destroyed copyright, casting the work into the public domain. For works that are wholly or partly of foreign origin, this harsh rule has been nullified (see the discussion in chapter 10). For U.S. works, it continues in effect for works published before March of 1989, with one important qualification: if the work was first published after 1977 and before March of 1989, forfeiture would be avoided if:

- the omission was in violation of an express understanding between the copyright owner and whoever was responsible for publication, or

• the notice was omitted from only a relatively small number of copies that were distributed to the public, or

• the application for registration, complete with fee and the necessary number of copies (see chapter 5), was filed before the date of the publication from which the notice was omitted, or

• the complete application for registration was filed within five years after first publication, and a "reasonable effort" was made to add notice to all copies distributed to the public within the United States after the omission was discovered.

This so-called "cure" procedure remains applicable to works published before Berne accession. In fact, if a work was published without notice before Berne, the obligation to affix notice to copies distributed after discovery of the omission continues for the life of the copyright. By contrast, at least in the view of one court, if a work was published with proper notice before Berne, post-Berne copies need not bear notice.[18]

A few comments on these exceptions to forfeiture are in order. No one knows what a "relatively small number of copies" was or is. Twenty thousand copies of a book with a printing of 100,000 is the same percentage as one bronze casting out of a limited edition of five, yet the latter would have been acceptable and the former probably not. "Relatively," in other words, has only the vaguest of meanings. This is an instance where the law would look to what is fair and just in a particular situation.[19]

Difficult problems may yet arise in cases involving works of fine art. A painting does not need to bear copyright notice when the painter sells it; a unique canvas comes with the exception we are discussing here. But a lithograph in an edition of 200 is a different story. If the artist omitted notice from, say, 40 copies published in the United States in 1986, failed to register his copyright, and failed to make a reasonable effort to correct the omission, and if a purchaser of one of the 40 copies relies on the absence of notice and starts reproducing the work himself, the artist might be out of luck. If a court decides that 40 is a relatively large number of copies in an edition of 200, the work will have entered the public domain in 1991—and copyright, once lost, can never be regained.

What was or is a reasonable effort to correct an omission? Here is another question for ad hoc determination, and one on which the circuit courts have split doctrinally. In the First and Second Circuits one must have made an attempt to affix notice to copies not yet sold at retail, even if they were already in the hands of distributors or wholesalers. The other circuits that have ruled on this are more lenient.[20]

As to what constitutes "discovery" of the omission of notice, there is some dissension among the circuits, but the prevailing answer seems to be that an omission can be "discovered" as late as the time infringement occurs, so long as the original omission did not occur under circumstances where the copyright owner knew or had reason to know that failure to include notice would forfeit copyright and knowingly omitted it.[21]

What happens to a copyright owner who has failed to stipulate in a license agreement that the licensee will be responsible for proper notice? If the licensee's effort to correct notice is later found not to have been reasonable, the copyright owner, though practically powerless to correct the fault, may have lost his copyright.

The total effect of these rules has been to make it virtually impossible at any given moment to know whether a work published between January 1, 1978, and February 28, 1989, without proper copyright notice, is in the public domain or not. The matter is further complicated by the rule that forfeiture of copyright in a derivative work, such as a doll based on a cartoon, does not affect copyright in the original, as long as the forfeiture was not sanctioned by the copyright owner of the original.[22] This whole foggy state of affairs made it easier in the end for Congress to sweep away the notice requirement altogether.

What happens if a notice is facially correct, but information contained in the notice is erroneous? Under pre-Berne law the consequences of erroneous notice could be serious if the copies or phonorecords bearing defective notice were distributed with the copyright owner's permission. Defective notice on unauthorized copies or phonorecords—for example, albums distributed by a record pirate—or on copies or phonorecords distributed in violation of the terms of a contract did not affect the rights of the copyright owner at all.

Defective Notice

    The consequences of a mistake differed depending on the nature of the error. (I am referring to unwitting errors. Fraudulent misrepresentations in a copyright notice could, and still can, bring a fine of up to $2,500.)[23] Bear in mind that the following rules apply only to post-1977, pre-Berne publications.

If the person whose name appeared in the notice was not the real owner of copyright—for example, if a book bearing notice in the name of John Adams was actually the work of his wife Abigail, or if a publisher that had only the publication rights put its own name on the notice, or if a contribution to a collective work did not bear a separate copyright notice—the copyright notice retained some value; the public was put on notice that at least somebody claimed copyright in the work. What if someone in good faith purchased rights in the

Mistake in Name

work from the person named in the notice and proceeded to exploit them? If the copies bearing erroneous notice were published before U.S. accession to Berne, the law states that the purchaser will be considered an innocent infringer if he "begins his undertaking" before the work has been registered in the correct name or before some other document has been recorded with the Copyright Office, signed by the person whose name appears in the notice but revealing the true owner of copyright.[24] This does not mean that the good-faith purchaser actually gets a right in the work; he does not. What he gets is a sort of limited privilege to exploit the right he believed he was buying.

Fairness requires such a result. If the law were otherwise, many unlucky purchasers would find themselves with no way to recoup their investment. Although this exemption by its very terms does not apply to post-Berne works, the principle of fairness within it could still be applied to post-Berne works.

Pre-Berne law provided that this limited privilege not exist until the purchaser "begins his undertaking." Clearly these words mean more than the mere act of purchasing the right, because at that stage the whole problem could be corrected simply by undoing the sale. Only an investment of time and resources in actually exploiting the right will tip the scales in the purchaser's favor. Will setting type be enough? Will hiring extra personnel be enough? As to that, no one knows, for this provision of the law has not been tested. Perhaps it never will be.

And what is the extent of the limited privilege that the purchaser thus obtains? If, for example, he has sunk money into a big Broadway production in reliance on his bogus right, he will probably be permitted to exploit his bogus right at least until he has recovered his investment, perhaps even until he has made a reasonable profit. After that, does his privilege end? Again the law is silent.

From the perspective of the copyright owner whose rights are infringed, the situation is no less fraught with ambiguity. The law provides that he is entitled to receive the profits of the person who sold the bogus right. Suppose the seller has inadvertently sold the rights for a fraction of their true worth? Can the true owner sue anybody for the difference? Probably, but no one knows for certain.

Mistake in Date

If the date written in the notice was earlier than the true date of first publication, in the ordinary case there were no repercussions. But if the work was published anonymously or under a pseudonym or was a work made for hire, so that the copyright term would be computed with reference to the first date of publication, the term would be computed from the date given in the notice, and the copyright owner would lose a year or more of protection.

If the date given in the notice was later than the date of first publication by only a year, there were no repercussions. However, in the case of a work published anonymously or under a pseudonym or in the case of a work made for hire, the date given in the notice would be ignored and the copyright term computed using the correct date.

If the date in the notice was two or more years later than the actual date of first publication, then the pre-Berne statute treated the work as if the date had been omitted altogether.[25]

The Innocent Infringer

In drafting the 1976 act, as Congress wrestled with the need to loosen notice requirements, it also wrestled with the plight of the unwitting infringer. Suppose somebody, seeing no copyright notice on a particular copy published after 1977 (but before Berne accession), decided the work was free to all? To protect this honest wretch proved to be no simple task. In its final form the 1976 act exempted him from liability only if he was "misled" by the absence of notice. If he had reason to believe the work actually was copyrighted, was he under a duty to investigate? If a work that is obviously original lacks copyright notice, the first instinct of any moderately sophisticated person would be to suspect that this omission was an error. Could one who has such a suspicion still be "misled"?

Although this unauthorized user was, technically speaking, infringing the copyright, Congress decided to protect him from some of the penalties of infringement. For example, until it was actually brought to his notice that the work was registered with the Copyright Office, he could continue to publish without fear of liability. He might or might not be required to surrender his profits; that would rest with the discretion of the judge or jury hearing the case. He might or might not be required by the court to stop publication or, if permitted to continue, might or might not be required to pay royalties to the copyright owner. Under no circumstances would he be required to compensate the copyright owner for damages. Damages in this context would include lost sales and injury to an artist's reputation due to the circulation of poor copies of his work; they would also, presumably, include whatever harm might result from the fact that the copies or phonorecords distributed by the infringer bore, themselves, no copyright notice.

The innocent infringer is still with us. The elaborate notice rules I have described continue to apply where copies or phonorecords were published without proper notice before the U.S. accession to Berne, even if the lawsuit is heard now. Post-Berne is another story.

Vestigial references in the statute imply that there may still be an innocent-infringer defense, but who can invoke it and what protection it gives are not entirely clear.[26] One thing we can say for certain: it is as wise now as it was vital before to put proper notice on every published copy of a work.

Notice on Confidential Materials

One question often asked by people in business is, What sort of copyright notice does one place on materials that contain trade secrets—know-how, customer lists, business methods, and so on? It is not an easy question to answer. Now that the law regarding notice has changed, there seems less reason for concern on this point. But for those asserting trade-secret rights, a bare copyright notice has never seemed particularly helpful. It does not warn users against the actions that most worry the owner of the materials.

My suggestion is to place a legend to the following effect on copies distributed on a confidential basis:

> The within material is an unpublished copyrighted work containing trade secret and other proprietary information of XYZ Corporation. This copy has been provided on the basis of strict confidentiality and on the express understanding that it may not be reproduced, or revealed to any person, in whole or in part, without express written permission from XYZ, which is the sole owner of copyright and all other rights therein.

REGISTRATION OF A COPYRIGHT CLAIM

Registration does not affect the existence or validity of a copyright. It is and has been, however, important as a method of protecting one's rights under the copyright, for these reasons:

1. For works of U.S. origin, it is a prerequisite for bringing suit to enforce a copyright. The only exception is that if you have attempted to register in the proper manner but the Copyright Office has rejected your application for any reason, you may still file suit for infringement, but you must give the Copyright Office notice of your suit.[1] Also—although the courts are split on this—in many jurisdictions you can sue even if you have not received a registration, so long as you have filed everything necessary to obtain a registration.[2] Additionally, for some types of works, it is possible to sue prior to registration if you have "preregistered" copyright in your work while it was still in the process of being prepared for commercial distribution. Preregistration is not a substitute for registration, however; if you fail to make full formal registration within certain time limits, your case will be dismissed. These rules,

and the mechanics of preregistration, are discussed further on in this chapter.

2. You cannot, in general, recover your attorney's fees or so-called statutory damages for any infringement that commences before the "effective date" of registration. (The effective date of registration is the date on which the application, fee, and deposit were filed, regardless of when they were finally processed.) Registration, in other words, creates the right to receive these special compensations. In the case of a published work, there is a three-month grace period for registration: if you apply for registration within three months of first publication, you can collect attorney's fees and statutory damages for any infringement that takes place after publication. However, there is no three-month grace period for unpublished works except works first fixed when broadcast.[3]

3. If you are the owner of copyright in a musical work, you are not entitled to royalties under a so-called compulsory license until your identity is a matter of record with the Copyright Office. In practical terms this makes registration a prerequisite to receipt of those royalties. There is no three-month grace period here.

4. If notice of copyright was omitted from copies of a work distributed to the public before March 1, 1989, registration within five years after publication without notice could have been essential to preserving the copyright. The importance of this provision has, of course, somewhat faded.

Who May Register   Anyone who owns or has an exclusive license for any of the rights comprised in the copyright of the work may register the work. It is the work that is being registered, not any of the subsidiary rights that make up the copyright. Registration is of the basic underlying claim in the original work and in the claimant's name.

Who Must Register in Order to Sue?

If you are suing to enforce a moral right (see chapter 6), you need not register your work in order to sue. However, if you are suing to enforce a copyright, you must register the copyright, unless the country of origin of the work is a foreign country that is party to the Berne Convention, the World Trade Organization Agreement, or one of a number of lesser copyright treaties. (In the discussion that follows I will refer to these countries, using the term in the statute, as "treaty parties.") The registration requirement still applies to U.S. works and to works from a few foreign countries. It also applies to mask works regardless of origin.[4]

Determining the "country of origin" is more complicated than the words might suggest. A work is exempt from registration if it passes one of three tests, which I shall call the author test, the country of publication test, and the location test.[5]

The Author Test

If at least one of the authors is a citizen of a treaty party or is domiciled in a treaty party, or has his or her "habitual residence" there, the registration requirement is waived. In the case of a published work, this test is applied as of the date of first publication. In the case of an unpublished work, this test appears to be applied as of the date the suit is brought, although that is unfortunately less than entirely clear. (The alternative would be to apply the test as of the date of creation of the work.) A special rule applies to audiovisual works: if the work is an audiovisual work, any corporation, limited partnership, or other "legal entity" that is the author is considered to be a "national" of a treaty party only if it has its headquarters there, regardless of where it is officially incorporated.[6]

The Country of Publication Test

Even if it fails the author test, a work will avoid the registration requirement if it was first published in a treaty party. However, if the work is first published simultaneously in a treaty party and in the United States—for example, simultaneously in Canada and in the United States—the work will be treated as published abroad, and thus exempt from registration, only if the foreign country's law grants it a shorter term of protection than does U.S. law. For example, in some Berne countries photographs, sound recordings, works of industrial art, computer software, and mask works are protected for much shorter periods than in the United States. These works, if published simultaneously in those countries and in the United States, will be exempt from registration. Publication is "simultaneous" in two countries if no more than 30 days elapse between the two publication dates. Note that simultaneous first publication in a foreign *non*-treaty party does not affect the outcome of this test.

Is a work posted on the Internet "simultaneously" published in every country where it can be viewed (including of course the U.S.)? Very few court cases have addressed this, and they seem to be at odds.[7] I think the right answer is that if a work is downloadable from the Internet, it has been published in every country where a user can download it. If it is merely viewable, then it should not be considered published at all, because copies are not being distributed.

The Location Test

A pictorial, graphic, or sculptural work, regardless of whether it is published and regardless of its author's nationality, will be exempt from registration if it is "incorporated" in a building or structure located in a treaty party. This exemption obviously applies to murals, friezes, and ornamental works that are embedded in the fabric of buildings. It may or may not also include architectural plans (remember that such plans are considered to be pictorial or graphic works) if the plans have been embodied in buildings; the answer depends on what "incorporated" means, and no one knows.

Oddly, there is no such provision for architectural works (remember that an architectural work is separate and distinct from the pictorial work that exists in the blueprints), even though one would have thought such works ideal for a test based on location. Thus, in considering whether an architectural work is a U.S. work or a treaty party work, one must determine whether it has been published. I have discussed in chapter 1 the ambiguities surrounding that question.

Overall, though at the cost of no small intricacy, these rules achieve the goal of encouraging registration for works of U.S. origin. If you ask "Why?" or "So what?" you would not be alone. And yet the Library of Congress depends in large measure on the registration system for the thoroughness of its collections. Moreover, in a country as large as the United States, with such a vast and diverse output of copyrightable works—larger and more diverse than in any other country in the world—it is a benefit to have as complete a public record as possible.

An application for registration has three components: the registration form, the filing fee, and deposit of copies of the work. The effective date of a copyright registration is the first date on which the Copyright Office has all of these in hand. Be warned, though: registration may take months to process, due in part to staffing shortages and in part to a backlog caused by the Copyright Office's painful (though now largely complete) conversion to its new electronic system. (The ultimate cure for this, I believe, lies in further

How Is Registration Accomplished?

automation of the process, but that is a long way off.) If you need to have your registration confirmed quickly, you can pay for "special handling"—see discussion below.

In certain cases it is possible to register a group of works; I discuss those later in this chapter. In general, though, a registration covers only a single copyright. Thus, if two or more authors' creations coexist in a work, each must be separately registered unless the work is a joint work (in which case there is really only one copyright) or copyright in all the elements belongs to the same person or entity (for example, by assignment).

The Form   *Electronic Registration*

Most registrations may be made online through the Copyright Office's eCO (electronic Copyright Office) system, at http://www.copyright.gov/eco. This is a password-protected site, and will store incomplete applications should you need to log off before completing them. Online registration involves filling out a series of fields following prompts from the eCO system. While it is not the world's most user-friendly website, it is quite efficient once you get the hang of it. There are copious help screens along the way.

In mid-2013 the Copyright Office added a stream-lined registration procedure for single works—e.g., one photograph, one short story—that were created, and are still owned, by a single individual. You can register most types of works using this streamlined procedure, but you cannot use it for collective works, databases, or websites. You do not have to be the author/claimant to use this procedure, but if you are acting on behalf of the author/claimant you have to give your own coordinates as the correspondence address on the application. When logging onto the eCO system, you will be asked three questions to determine whether you qualify for this procedure. If you answer "yes" to all three, the system will send you to the streamlined electronic form.

The application system will ask for the following information (note that some of the below will not apply to the streamlined procedure just mentioned):

• Screen 1: Type of work. If the work contains more than one type of authorship—for example, if it is a book that contains both text and artwork—select the type that predominates; if none is predominant, select whichever you prefer. There are two exceptions to this. If your registration includes any sound recording, identify the type of work as "sound recording." For example, a songwriter may simultaneously register both his song and his recording of his song, if he is submitting the recording as his deposit material. He should identify the type of work as "sound recording." If the work you are registering is a motion picture or other audiovisual work, it may well contain many types of works within in, but it should always be identified as a "motion picture."

• Screen 2: Title. The system first asks for the "title type," then the title. You must enter the "title of work being registered." By clicking "save" and then "new" again, you may also enter other information of value, such as a previous or alternative title, the title of a series containing the work, or the title of individual contents (e.g., if the work is a compilation of separately titled components). It is advisable to provide this information if applicable.

• Screen 3: Whether the work has been published or not. If you answer "yes," you will be prompted for the year of completion, date of first publication, and nation of first publication. For literary works there is also the option to enter the ISN number.

• Screen 4: Information concerning the author. If there are multiple authors, enter their names by clicking "new" before clicking "continue." For each author, you must supply his or her nationality and domicile, and you should also indicate whether the work is made for hire, pseudonymous, or anonymous. The author's years of birth and death may be entered here as well. For each author you will then be prompted to state the nature of that author's contribution. For example, for literary works there are specific boxes for "text," "editing," "photographs," "artwork," "translation," "compilation," and "computer program." There is also a box for "other" should the standard offerings not suffice. For example, if the work is one of the performing arts, there is no standard box for "choreography"; you would enter that in the box for "other."

• Screen 5: Name and address of the copyright claimant(s)—again, by repeat clicking of "new" you may enter the names of multiple claimants. Bear in mind that only the author or someone who has acquired the basic, underlying claim from the author by sale, gift, or otherwise can be a "claimant."[8] An owner of any subsidiary right under the copyright is not a "copyright claimant." If the claimant is not the author, you must indicate here how the claimant came to own copyright. "Written agreement" and "inheritance" are the standard options offered in the form, but if you came by your copyright in some other way (say, by gift), there is a space to enter that.

• Screen 6: Limitations on the claim. This screen seeks disclosure of any material in which the claimant does not own copyright, or which is part of a previously published work even if the copyright owner is the same. If the work is a derivative work based on someone else's work, on public domain material, or on the claimant's own previously published work, or if the work for any other reason contains any substantial amount of material that the claimant does not own, this should be disclosed here. But do not disclaim more than you should. While this screen offers a few standard boxes to check, in many cases the right answers for the fields "Material excluded" and "New material included" will be "other," and you will want to supply some detail. However, the "other" box will not always accept your description; pay close attention to the examples given on the help screen in fashioning your information. Finally, if the preexisting material was registered, information concerning that registration must be supplied.

• Screen 7: Rights and permissions contact information. This is a new question that was never asked in the predigital world. It is optional but worth answering. It allows you to supply the name, email address, mailing address, and telephone number of the person whom anyone seeking to obtain reprint permission or any other license in the work should contact.

The rest of the screens one must fill out are basically administrative. Note, however, that on screen 11 you have an opportunity to include any special comments you may wish to communicate to the Copyright Office concerning the application.

Antediluvian Paper Registration

The Copyright Office still accepts registrations using the old forms that were used before the eCO system was up and running. These forms are available only on request, from http://www.copyright.gov/forms/formrequest.html. The fee for registering in this manner is higher and the processing time slower, so there is no reason to use these forms for single copyright claims. They do remain relevant for group registration, however.

If registering in this manner, see "Mail and Courier Requirements" later in this chapter.

The registration form used will vary depending on the type of work being registered. For a nondramatic literary work other than a periodical or serial work, use form TX; for a periodical or serial work, use form SE; for a dramatic work or any other work of the performing arts (including music, dance, and film, among others), use form PA, unless you also own copyright in the sound recording of the work and are simultaneously registering your sound recording copyright, in which case you should use form SR; for a work of the visual arts (not including film or other audiovisual works) or an architectural work, use form VA; for a sound recording, use form SR. (If both the sound recording copyright and the underlying musical copyright are owned by the same person, one form SR may be used to register both. This would be the case, for example, when a songwriter records a performance of his own work.) For a computer program or database use form TX, unless the audiovisual displays are the predominant part of the work, as in a video game: in such a case use form PA. If the work consists of elements in more than one medium, use form PA if there is *any* audiovisual component; if not, use form SR if there is *any* sound recording component.

All forms are available through the following sources:

- by mail, from:

Library of Congress
Copyright Office—COPUBS
101 Independence Ave., SE
Washington, DC 20559;

- by phone at (202) 707-9100.

In addition, though they are not well advertised, forms TX, PA, and VA are available online at http://www.copyright.gov/forms/. As the website is currently set up, you will find these forms under the heading "Group Registration Forms" and the subheadings "Literary," "Performing Arts," and "Visual Arts" if you click on the "GR/CP" link and then scroll to the end.

Finally, ignore all of the above if you are registering a work that has been restored to copyright on account of GATT (see chapter 10); for such works use form GATT, or GATT/GRP for group registration. These forms are available at http://www.copyright.gov/forms/formgatti.pdf.

The various forms just discussed do not vary much in content, but each requests information that is especially important to the type of work it covers. All of the registration forms require certain basic information:[9]

1. The name and address of the copyright claimant. An owner of any subsidiary right under the copyright is not a "copyright claimant"; that term is used only for the author or for someone who has acquired the basic, underlying claim from the author by sale, gift, or inheritance.

2. The name of the author(s), unless the work is published anonymously or under a pseudonym,

and a brief description of each author's contribution to the work. This description can be as simple as "entire text" or "photographic illustrations" or "entire source code."

3. The nationality or domicile of the author(s), even if the work is published anonymously or under a pseudonym.

4. If one or more of the authors is dead, the dates of their deaths.

5. If the copyright claimant is someone other than the author(s), a brief statement of how the claimant came by the copyright (for example: "written transfer of copyright").

6. If the work is a compilation, a statement identifying the preexisting work or works that it incorporates; if it is a derivative work, a statement identifying the work or works on which it is based. These statements should also identify in a general way what material is original with the claimant, because that is all that is covered by the claimant's copyright. They can be as simple as "substantially revised and updated text" or "new modules added."

7. A statement that the work was made for hire, if it was so.

8. The title of the work and, if in its finished state it had any other titles by which it might be identified, those other titles as well. This is particularly important if the work has been published before under a different title, a not infrequent occurrence in the case of books that were first published outside the country. The word *identified* refers to identification by the public; you need not include titles by which the work has been known only to the author or private viewers. In general if the

work you are registering contains material that appeared in a different form under a different title, you would be well advised to make note of this fact when registering.

9. The year in which "creation of the work was completed"—that is, the year in which it was fixed in its final form, disregarding minor editorial changes. Remember that different versions of the work, if they differ substantially, are considered to be separate and distinct works; you should mention previous versions of this type not under this heading but in the space where you are asked if the work is a derivative work.

10. If the work has been published, the date of its first publication and the nation in which that first publication took place. Note that there is some uncertainty as to whether an online database should be regarded as "published." The Copyright Office has pointedly declined to take a position on this issue and will accept the copyright owner's assertion that the database is or is not a published work.

In any of these categories, do not omit any information that may bear on the validity of the copyright claim. If you do so unintentionally, you may suffer much in lost time and money. If you do so intentionally, you run the risk of being fined up to $2,500, and if you have committed a fraud upon the Copyright Office you may find judges decidedly unsympathetic when you seek protection of your copyright in court.[10]

The application form must be accompanied by a fee. *The Fee*
See http://www.copyright.gov/docs/fees.html for the amount of this fee. If registering online, you may pay by credit or debit card or electronic check. Fees can

also be charged to a deposit account at the Copyright Office, if you have established one. Deposit accounts are a good idea if you register works frequently, but not otherwise.

Deposit

The application must be accompanied by deposit of either one or two copies of the work or, in special cases, some other kind of material that will identify the work you are registering. It must be an actual copy of the work; you cannot "reconstruct" a work for which you no longer have a copy.[11]

If you are registering online, you may effect deposit by uploading digital files to the Copyright Office website in the following circumstances: if the work is unpublished; if the work is published only in electronic form; or if the work is one for which the Copyright Office wants "identifying material" rather than actual copies of the work as published. (Those works for which identifying material is required are discussed below.) Otherwise, you must make the deposit by mail or courier (see "Mail and Courier Requirements" later in this chapter). In some cases you may wish to make a hard-copy deposit even if online deposit is available. For example, if you are registering a computer program that is published only online, you may wish to do a paper deposit that conceals all but the required identifying portions of the code (see discussion below).

When depositing by mail or courier in connection with an online registration, you will need to print out a shipping slip from the eCO system.

The rules governing deposit are quite complicated. First of all, although deposit is always made with the Copyright Office, it is intended not only for the purpose of registration but also, for many types of published works, for the archival purposes of the Library of Congress.[12] A single deposit can satisfy both of these requirements, but, for it to do so, it must be made at the same time that the registration application is filed or be accompanied by a letter asking the Copyright Office to hold it until the registration application is filed.[13] If deposit is not made under one of these two circumstances, the Copyright Office will forward it to the Library of Congress, and you will have to make a separate deposit when you register your copyright.

Deposit with the Library of Congress can be required even if you have no desire or intention to register your copyright. If the Librarian of Congress decides that the Library should have a copy or copies of your work, the Register of Copyrights will send you a written demand for deposit. You have three months to comply; if you do not, you will be liable for a fine of $250 and for any expenses incurred by the Library of Congress in acquiring copies of your work. If your failure to comply is willful or repeated, you may also be liable for an additional fine of $2,500.[14]

Library of Congress Deposit

The following rules govern deposit with the Library of Congress:[15]

1. Only published works will be held by the Library. Unpublished works may have to be deposited for registration purposes, but not for purposes of the Library of Congress unless by some special arrangement between the author and the Library.

2. Works published outside the United States become subject to mandatory deposit as soon as the work is distributed in the United States.

3. The following types of published works are *exempt* from deposit with the Library:

• Scientific or technical diagrams and models. Architectural plans, blueprints, and models are covered by this exemption.

• Greeting cards, picture postcards, and stationery.

• Lectures, sermons, speeches, and addresses unless they are published in an anthology or collection. Anthologies and collections are not exempt from deposit, even if all the contents are the work of one person.

• Literary, dramatic, and musical works published only in the form of phonorecords. In other words, if a sound recording is made of a piece of music, for example, but the music itself is never published in print form, the fact that the sound recording is published in the form of phonorecords does not subject the underlying musical work to the deposit requirement.

• Sculptural works.

• Works embodied only in useful articles or in jewelry, dolls, toys, games, or plaques. For example, if a graphic design is published only by being printed on textiles, it is exempt from deposit with the Library of Congress. Maps and globes are not defined as useful articles and do not come within this exemption.

• Advertising material, including labels.

• Tests and answer material for tests, if published separately from other literary works.

• Works that were first published as contributions to collective works. The collective works themselves are not exempt, only the individual contributions.

• Musical or other works that are published only in movie soundtrack form. This exemption is very similar to that concerning literary, dramatic, or musical works published only in phonorecord form. It means that if a musical work, for example, is not published except in a movie soundtrack, no separate deposit requirement applies to it.

• Television programs whose only publication has been by virtue of a license granted to a nonprofit organization, permitting the organization to make videotapes of it.

• Automated databases that are available in the United States only in online form.

4. For published works that are not covered by one of these exemptions, the general rule is that you must deposit two copies of the "best edition." (The current standards for determining what is the "best edition" are in Copyright Office Circular 7b, located at http://www.copyright.gov/circs/circ07b.pdf.) However, there are certain kinds of works for which a single copy of the best edition will suffice, and if the work was first published only outside the United States, either one copy of the best edition or one copy of the work as first published will suffice:

• Two-dimensional visual works, so long as no more than four copies of the work have been published, or, if more than four copies have been, the publication has been in the form of a limited edition of no more than 300, of which every copy is numbered. If your work qualifies for this special one-copy arrangement, you can also satisfy the deposit requirements by depositing photographs or "other identifying material" instead.

• Motion pictures but not other audiovisual works. However, the copy must be accompanied by a separate description of the motion picture's contents, such as a continuity, press book, or synopsis. Also with regard to motion pictures it is possible to enter into a "Motion Picture Agreement" with the Library, permitting you to ask for immediate return of your deposit copy on the stipulation that the Library may demand it back at any time in the following two years.

• Globes, relief maps, and other three-dimensional cartographic works.

• Musical works published only by rental, lease, or lending but not by sale.

• Works published in machine-readable format, including CD-ROMs, if not copy-protected. The copy must be accompanied by the user's guide or other documentation that generally accompanies it.

• Works published in CD-ROM format and copy-protected, if you enter into an agreement with the Library authorizing local area network use by up to five simultaneous users. The copy must be accompanied by the user's guide or other documentation that generally accompanies it.

• Multimedia kits. Multimedia for these purposes means anything involving two or more of the following types of material: printed matter, which might for example be a book (even so humble a book as a user manual), a chart, a poster, or sheet music; audiovisual material; sound recordings; and machine-readable material. Multimedia kits of this type are not to be confused with multimedia works that are embodied entirely in CD-ROM. However, a CD-ROM might be part of a multimedia kit if accompanied by a book.

5. Works published in the form of holograms are covered by special rules. In addition to two copies,

you must deposit two sets of precise instructions for displaying the image and two sets of photographs or other material that will identify the image.

6. If you are depositing copies of a phonorecord, you must deposit with it any label or package on or in which it is usually sold.

7. Periodical issues should preferably be sent in the form of two complimentary subscriptions, addressed to

Library of Congress
Copyright Office
Attn: 407 Deposits
101 Independence Ave., SE
Washington, DC 20559-6000.

8. The Register of Copyrights, in conjunction with the Library of Congress, can grant special absolution from the deposit requirement if you can give persuasive reasons why your work should be exempted. If you wish for such treatment, you must submit your request (and your reasons) in writing to Chief, Acquisitions Division of the Copyright Office. (If you are making your request in connection with registration, see discussion further on.) Any request must be signed by either the owner of the underlying copyright or the owner of the publication right. Thus, for example, the owner of only the performance right in a work right cannot apply on his own to have the work exempted from any deposit requirements.

9. If you would like a receipt for your deposit, you can obtain one for a fee. See http://www.copyright.gov/docs/fees.html for the amount of the fee.

The rules governing deposit for registration purposes are slightly different. For one thing there are no exemptions; and deposit may be a prerequisite for registration. There are differences in the deposit requirements between one type of work and another, and some of these differences are similar to those in the Library of Congress context, but you should be careful not to confuse deposit for registration with deposit for the Library.

Registration Deposit

The rules for registration deposit are as follows:[16]

1. Only one copy is required to register an unpublished work.

2. As with the Library of Congress deposit, the basic rule for published works is that you must submit two copies of the best edition. However, one copy of the best edition—or, at your option, simply one copy of the work as first published, if it was first published only outside the United States—will suffice for the following types of published works (speaking here only of works that are published in traditional format—see below for works published only online):

• Two-dimensional visual works, as long as no more than four copies have been published or, if more than four have been published, as long as publication has been in the form of an edition limited to 300 or fewer, all copies being numbered. Any visual work qualifying for this one-copy arrangement can also be deposited in the form of photographs or other identifying material.

• Motion pictures but not other audiovisual works.

• Globes, relief maps, and other three-dimensional cartographic works.

• Scientific or technical diagrams. Architectural plans and blueprints come under this exception.

• Greeting cards, picture postcards, and stationery.

• Lectures, sermons, and similar material published individually and not as part of a collective work.

• Contributions to a collective work. The deposit for registration of a contribution to a collective work should be of a copy of the collective work as a whole.

• Musical works that have been published in notational form only, or in sound recording form only, but not in both.

• Musical works that have been published both in copies and in phonorecords, if the notational copies have been published only by rental, lease, or lending and not by outright sale.

• Any sculptural work that has been published only in the form of jewelry cast in base metal and measuring no more than four inches in any dimension.

• Literary and dramatic works published not in print but only as embodied in phonorecords or motion pictures.

• Choreographic works and pantomimes that have been published only as embodied in motion pictures.

• Two-dimensional games.

• Decals, and fabric patches or emblems.

• Calendars.

• Needlework and instructions for needlework.

• Craft kits.

• Works reproduced on three-dimensional containers such as boxes, cases, and cartons, if the object can be readily opened out, unfolded, slit at the corners, or in some other way made adaptable for flat storage, and if the copy, when thus flattened, does not exceed 96 inches in any dimension. (If these criteria are not met, you will have to deposit identifying material instead. See point 4.)

• Multimedia kits or any part thereof. If part of the kit is an audiovisual work or is sold in machine-readable form, you must deposit the same kind of identifying matter that you would deposit if that were the only element in your work. (See points 4 and 5.)

• Advertising materials, including labels, other than pictorial advertisements for motion pictures. If an advertisement was published in a magazine or other periodical, it is sufficient to deposit just the page of the periodical on which it appeared, not the entire periodical. If a print or label is physically inseparable from a three-dimensional object—for example, if it is stamped on the base of the object—different rules apply. (See point 4.)

• Tests and answer material for tests, if published separately from other literary works.

• Designs that are published only by being printed on textiles, wallpaper, wrapping paper, and similar merchandise. If the design is repeated on the material, the swatch submitted for deposit must show at least one repetition. However, if the design is published only by the incorporation of the textiles (or what have you) in dresses, furniture, or other three-dimensional articles, different rules apply. (See point 4.)

• Works first published abroad. In such a case the one copy deposited should be a copy of that first foreign edition, not a copy of the best edition.

3. You can make deposit in the form of identifying material rather than in the form of a copy or copies for certain kinds of works:

• Unpublished two-dimensional visual works.

• Published two-dimensional visual works, as long as no more than four copies have been published or, if more than four, as long as publication has been in the form of an edition limited to 300 or fewer, all copies being numbered.

• Unpublished motion pictures (but not other kinds of audiovisual works).[17]

• Unpublished works fixed only in motion picture soundtracks.

• Works that are published only in the form of motion picture soundtracks.

4. For certain kinds of works, the only proper deposit for registration purposes is in the form of "identifying material":

• Three-dimensional sculptural works, including models and maquettes.

• Computer programs and databases, other than databases consisting predominantly of photographs (see appendix C for a fuller discussion).

• Works that are published, or that if unpublished are fixed, only in a machine-readable format, other than (i) computer programs, databases, compilations, statistical compendia, and the like, and (ii) works published or fixed in CD-ROM format. (CD-ROM-format works are instead treated like normal works because the Library of Congress is keen to build up its deposit collection of CD-ROMs.) For these special machine-readable works, identifying material is more complicated than for most. If the underlying work is pictorial or graphic, then you must follow the usual rules for identifying material. If the work is audiovisual, the deposit must consist of either a videotape or a series of photographs and drawings of "representative portions" of the work, plus in all cases a separate synopsis of the work. If the work is musical, include musical notation or a phonorecord of the entire work. If the work is a sound recording, include a phonorecord that can be played on an ordinary device (i.e., not on a computer or synthesizer). If the work is literary, include a transcription of the first and last 25 pages (or equivalent units) and at least five pages that are "indicative" of the remainder.

• Literary works containing both visually perceptible and machine-readable material. (Again, CD-ROM material is not covered by this special rule.) For the machine-readable portion, include a transcription of the first and last 25 pages (or equivalent units) and at least five pages that are indicative of the remainder.

• Unpublished visual works that are fixed only in useful articles, toys, or dolls.

• Published visual works that are fixed only in games, unless the games are packaged and published in a box or similar container with flat sides and with dimensions of no more than 12×24×6 inches.

• Published visual works, if they are published only in useful articles or in toys, dolls, or containers that cannot be flattened (see point 2 above). This category includes visual works that are published only by virtue of the fact that the textile or other material on which they are printed is used in making a three-dimensional article. For example, if a design is printed on fabric used to upholster chairs and the only manner by which the design is published is the sale of chairs upholstered in that material, then deposit must be made in the form of identifying material. Neither this category nor the previous one includes visual works embodied in useful articles that are part of a multimedia educational or instructional kit.

• Works that are published, or if unpublished are fixed, only in items of jewelry, unless the jewelry is cast in base metal and does not exceed four inches in any dimension.

• Works for which the copy deposited would be larger than eight feet in length, width, or height.

• Advertising material that is physically inseparable from a three-dimensional article. For example, if the design of a label is stamped into the base of a lamp, to register the label design don't send in a lamp; deposit identifying material.

5. There is a special additional requirement for motion pictures, whether published or unpublished. If you deposit in the form of a copy or copies, you must also submit a synopsis or some other description of the contents of the motion picture.

6. There are also special benefits given to motion pictures. First, the Library of Congress is given 30 days from the effective date of registration (the date on which registration, deposit, and fee are received) to decide whether it wishes to keep the copy or copies that have been deposited for registration. If it does not make a decision within 30 days or if

it decides it does not want the motion picture for its archives, the copy or copies will be returned to the applicant. Second, as an alternative to this you can enter into a Motion Picture Agreement such as I have described. Third, the Copyright Office will accept motion picture soundtracks as deposits for purposes of registering simultaneously all works contained in them, including music.

7. For works available *only* online—other than computer programs and databases—you have the following options for deposit:

• If you are registering online, you may upload a complete copy.

• If the work contains five pages or less of text or artwork, or three minutes or less of music, sounds, or audiovisual material, you may submit a computer disk or CD-ROM containing the entire work, accompanied by a hard copy of the entire work. For this purpose "hard copy" means printout, audiocassette, or videotape. You must represent that the entire work is being submitted.

• If the work contains more than five pages of text or artwork, or more than three minutes of music, sounds, or audiovisual material, you may submit a computer disk or CD-ROM containing five representative pages or three representative minutes, and the samples you submit must include the title, the author, and the copyright notice if any.

8. In the case of unpublished architectural works, the deposit will vary depending on whether the work has actually been constructed. For unconstructed works, the deposit should consist of one copy of an architectural drawing or blueprint in visually perceptible form showing the overall form

of the building and any interior arrangements of spaces and/or design elements in which you claim copyright. If the building has been constructed, you must also enclose photographic identifying material that "clearly discloses the architectural works being registered"; photographs should show several exterior and interior views. In either case, your deposit should disclose the names of the architect(s) and draftsperson(s) and the building site or, in the case of an unconstructed building, the intended building site. The form of the drawing or blueprint should be one of these, in descending order of preference:

• Original format, or best-quality form of reproduction, including offset or silk screen printing;

• Xerographic or photographic copies on good-quality paper;

• Positive photostat or photodirect positive;

• Blue line copies (diazo or ozalid process).

9. There is a special additional requirement for holograms. For each copy submitted, you must also submit precise instructions for displaying the image and some kind of material clearly showing the image.

10. The Register of Copyrights can permit you to deposit one copy instead of two, or to deposit an incomplete copy or copies, if you can present a convincing reason why you should receive special treatment. A request for special treatment must be signed by the applicant. (This signature rule is less strict than that for the Library of Congress deposit.) To make such a request, write to the Chief of the Examining Division of the Copyright Office. This is a different person from the person to whom you

submit such requests in the Library of Congress context. You can combine the two requests; if you do so, the Chief of the Examining Division is the person to address, and the application must be signed either by the owner of the underlying copyright or by the owner of the publication right.

The identifying material that can be used to satisfy the deposit requirement (except for works in machine-readable form) is a photograph, transparency, drawing, photocopy, or any other two-dimensional reproduction or rendering of the work. For example, a photograph of a limited-edition woodcut or a drawing of a sculptural work will suffice. There are a few special rules.[18]

• Material reproducing two-dimensional visual works must reproduce the actual colors of the work. This is not true of material reproducing sculpture or other three-dimensional works.

• If you submit more than two pieces of material for any one work, all must be the same size.

• Transparencies must be 35 mm and must normally be mounted in cardboard, plastic, or similar materials. All other types of material must be not less than 3×3 inches and not more than 9×12 inches; the preferred maximum size is 8×10 inches.

• Except in the case of transparencies, the image must be at least life-size, except that it can be less than life-size if it is at least four inches in any one dimension.

• At least one piece of identifying material must indicate the title of the work and the exact measurement of at least one of the true dimensions of the work.

• These rules do not apply to unpublished motion pictures or to works that are fixed or published only in the form of a motion picture soundtrack. For unpublished motion pictures, identifying material is composed of a description of the movie, together with either a phonorecord of some kind, reproducing the entire soundtrack, or a set of visual reproductions of single frames—at least one frame from each 10 minutes of footage. The description may be a synopsis, a continuity, or anything of that sort, but it must include the title and also the episode title, if it is an episode; the nature and general content; the date of first fixation; the date of first transmission; if the work was fixed simultaneously with transmission, a statement to that effect; the running time; and the credits appearing on the work.

• Because copyright notice is no longer legally required, deposit materials no longer need to show notice. However, if you are prudent enough to use notice anyway, the identifying material you deposit should show where the notice is placed.

Group Registration

It is possible in some cases to register a group of works for a single fee, using a single application. You can do this if:

• All the works are unpublished, were created by the same author or authors, and are owned by the same claimant or claimants; or

• All the works were first published in the same publication on the same date, and are owned by the same claimant or claimants.[19]

Thus, for example, a songwriter may register a collection of songs that have not yet been published, or a collection of songs that appear on a single CD. When registering a group of published works, you must register them using the title of the collection in which they were published. If you are registering a group of unpublished works, you must assign them a collection title for registration purposes. In either case, the eCO registration process allows you to supply the titles of the individual works as "content titles."

In addition, it is possible to make group registration of works in some more narrowly targeted categories. (All the forms required for these are available at http://www.copyright.gov/forms/.)

First, an individual author may register in a single application, for a single fee, all works he has created that were published in periodicals (including newspapers) in a given 12-month period. This kind of registration is of particular use to freelance journalists and photographers. It has its limitations, though:

- To make this kind of registration, you must be the copyright owner of each contribution, and none of the works can have been originally created as work for hire.

- Each contribution must be of the same type. In other words, if you published a literary work (say, a poem) in one periodical and a work of visual art (a photograph, for example) in another, you cannot register them together.

If you are going back to register works published this way prior to March 1, 1989, each of the works, on the occasion of its first publication, must also have borne a separate copyright notice (separate, that is, from the general copyright notice on the periodical), and each notice must have identified you as author in the same manner (for example, not by name in one issue and by pseudonym in another).

Group registration such as this requires filing two forms: form VA, PA, or TX, depending on the type of work that your contributions happen to be, and in addition a special form called GR/CP. The VA, PA, or TX will contain all information except the titles of the works and the statistics of their publication; these facts will be put on the GR/CP.

Group registration for published photographs is perhaps the most lenient group registration of all. Photographs taken by a single photographer and published within a single calendar year may be registered using a single application form VA, and for a single fee, so long as the copyright claimant for all of them is the same. In the space for "Title of this Work," provide the title of one of the photographs and add "and other photographs." In the space for "Previous or Alternative Title," insert "Group Registration/Photos" and indicate approximately how many photographs are in the group.

If you are registering photographs all of which were published within three months prior to your filing date, you need not provide the publication date for each photograph. However, you can file up to a year's worth of published photographs if you are willing to undertake the work of identifying the date of publication for each photograph.

There are two ways of doing this. The simplest way, but the one which also makes the least information available in the Copyright Office index, is to include the date on each image, or to include a list either as a text file on the CD-ROM or DVD you submit or as a separate document. If you take this route, there is no limit to the number of photographs you can register in such a group.

The alternative is to use continuation sheet form GR/PPh/CON. This presents more information and in a more organized way; it is limited, however, to 750 photographs or 50 continuation sheets.

There is also a procedure, mainly for the benefit of stock photo companies, of using database registration as a way of registering large groups of photographs. Where a database consists primarily of photographs, however, the Copyright Office now requires that not just identifying material but actual files or other copies of all photographs included must be submitted. However, the photographs do not have to be individually identified by author so long as the stock company owns copyright in all of them.[20]

Group registration is also available for multiple issues of periodicals, whether published in paper form or online. (Note, however, that e-journals are not registrable as collective works if published article by article. Possibly, an e-journal of that type could be reclassified as a dynamic database and registered under the rules for such databases.) There are rules for periodicals published weekly or less frequently, and different rules for daily newspapers.[21] For weekly or less frequent periodicals, group registration is available if the following conditions are met:

- The group of issues presented for registration must all have been published within a three-month period, and all within a single calendar year. The purpose of this rule, as of some of the others that follow, is to ensure that each question on the registration form (e.g., "year of publication") can be answered at one stroke for all issues.

- Each issue must have been a work made for hire. The rule that all issues must be made for hire does unfortunately disadvantage those entrepreneurs who publish newsletters that are entirely their own handiwork, unless they have incorporated and are thus working "for hire" for their own corporate alter egos.

• Each issue must have been actually created—i.e., assembled and arranged—within one year preceding the filing of the registration application.

• Each issue must be essentially a new collective work, not a revision or adaptation of a preexisting work. Thus, if an Italian architecture journal is being merely translated for sale in the United States, group registration is not available to it, although it might be available to the Italian original.

• The author(s) and copyright claimant(s) must be the same for all issues. Thus, if a magazine is sold by one publisher to another, the issues submitted as a group cannot straddle the change of ownership.

• Two complimentary subscriptions of the periodical during the three-month period must have been sent to:

Library of Congress
Group Periodicals Registration
Washington, DC 20540-4161,

and a separate letter must have been sent to the same address confirming that the subscriptions have been entered. The letter must identify the first issue in the subscription by publisher, title, volume, number, and issue date.

• The subscriptions just described are for the Library of Congress, and do not suffice for registration deposit. For registration, you must deposit one complete set of the issues being registered.

The form to use is form SE/Group. Although the basis for the registration is the authorship of the issues as collective works, the registration form may also recite that the applicant owns copyright in specified contents of those issues. Note that there is a special fee per issue included in the registration, in lieu of the normal fee. See http://www.copyright.gov/docs/fees.html.

For daily newspapers, the rules are as follows:

• The group of issues must all have been published within a given calendar month.

• The application must be filed within three months after the publication date of the last issue in the group.

• The registration may include early editions as well as final editions of each issue, so long as all editions were published on the same day in a given metropolitan area served by the newspaper.

The form to use is form G/DN. There is a special fee; see http://www.copyright.gov/docs/fees.html for the amount.

Group registration is also available to cover up to three months' worth of updates and revisions to electronic databases. (Ironically, such registration may only be made in hard copy, using Form TX.) The rules are discussed in appendix C.

Mail and Courier Requirements You may submit a copyright registration by hand at the Copyright Office's Public Information Office, located in Room LM-401 at the Office's main address:

James Madison Memorial Building
101 Independence Ave., SE
Washington, DC 20559.

When registering by mail, or sending deposit materials by mail, use the following address:

Library of Congress
Copyright Office
101 Independence Ave., SE
Washington, DC 20559-****.

In this address, add "—TX" after "Copyright Office" when registering a group of electronic databases, or "—SE" when registering a group of periodicals. For "****" substitute one of the following zipcode extensions, as applicable:

- 6222 for literary works,

- 6211 for works of visual art,

- 6233 for works of the performing arts,

- 6238 for motion pictures or other audiovisual works,

- 6237 for sound recordings (including a work for which you are registering the sound recording and the musical work at the same time),

- 6226 for periodicals,

- 6000 for a group of daily newspapers or newsletters.

The same addresses apply to deliveries made by Federal Express or UPS. However, if you are using any other courier or messenger service, there are special rules—see below.

If you are sending any of the following, send them in a box rather than an envelope:

- electronic media such as audiocassettes, videocassettes, CDs, and DVDs,

- microform,

- photographs,

- slick advertisements, color photocopies, and other print items.

Also, the Copyright Office advises that "CDs packaged in standard full-sized jewel boxes are more likely to survive the mail irradiation process than those packaged in slim-line cases." (Yes, irradiation is the Copyright Office's terrorism deterrence plan at work.)

If you want to register or deposit using a courier other than FedEx or UPS, the address is:

Congressional Courier Acceptance Site
2nd and D Streets, NE
Washington, DC.

A courier may deliver up to 10 items at a time. Packages accepted at this site may not exceed 4×14×18 inches in size. A courier attempting to deliver anything larger will be directed to deliver it to the Copyright Office's off-site mail processing center.

Special Handling

The Copyright Office will give your application "special handling" upon payment of an additional fee (see http://www.copyright.gov/docs/fees.html), if you need a registration certificate in connection with:

- pending or prospective litigation,

- a customs matter, such as an effort to seize incoming counterfeit goods,

- a contract or publishing deadline.

The turnaround time for this service is normally 5–10 business days.

You may make a request for special handling in person at the Copyright Office, in which case you will be asked to fill out a special form certifying that one of these applies. Otherwise you must accompany your application with a letter explaining why you need special handling, and certifying that the information provided is correct to the best of your knowledge.

The rules described above for delivering items to the Copyright Office apply to a request for special handling, with one exception: if submitting your request by mail, use the following address:

Special Handling
Copyright RAC Division
PO Box 71380
Washington, DC 20024-1380.

Can You Register More Than Once?

Under certain circumstances, you may wish to make a second registration of a work. In fact, in the case of a work that you first registered when it was still unpublished, you will be well advised to register again when you publish it if you have changed the title. You will also want to make a second registration if the first registration was not made in the name of the true copyright claimant, or if the original registration was for some other reason unauthorized or legally invalid—for example, if it was made by someone not entitled to make it. However, these are the only circumstances in which the same version of a work may be registered more than once. For correction of nonfatal errors, there is a separate procedure, described below.

Appeals of Denial of Registration

Although the Copyright Office rejects a minuscule percentage of the claims that are submitted to it, it does reject applications, usually on the grounds that the work does not appear to be copyrightable.

If you are denied registration of a work, you have three months in which to request that the Examining Division reconsider its denial. If it upholds the decision of the examiner, then you can appeal (again, within a three-month period) to the Copyright Office Review Board.

Appeal from a denial by this Board is the final administrative action, and thus may be taken to federal court under general principles of administrative law.

Both appeals can be mailed or hand-delivered. The mailing address is:

RECONSIDERATION
Copyright RAC Division
P.O. Box 71380
Washington, DC 20024-1380.

The hand-delivery addresses vary depending on who makes the delivery.[22] The first page of each appeal must contain the Copyright Office control number and clearly indicate either "FIRST RECONSIDERATION" or "SECOND RECONSIDERATION," as appropriate, on the subject line.

Be sure to check http://www.copyright.gov/docs/fees.html for the current fee applicable to your appeal.

Correcting an Erroneous or Incomplete Registration

After you have registered, you may wish to correct certain information contained in your registration or to supply additional information. This may be done by filing form CA, the application for supplementary registration, along with the appropriate fee (see http://www.copyright.gov/docs/fees.html). No additional deposit need be made. Supplementary registration does not change the legal validity of the original registration. Because of this, supplementary registration may not be used for adding to a list of works covered by a previously filed group registration. It may not be used to record transfers of copyright ownership. Nor is it an appropriate way to notify the Copyright Office of changes in the content of your work. If the content has changed so much as to constitute a new version, you should make a new registration, and if it has not, your

old registration remains valid. Nor is it the right procedure to use if the original registration was made in the
name of someone who was not the proper copyright
claimant; in such a case a new registration must be
made. Minor errors in the name of the copyright claimant, however, can and should be corrected by supplementary registration. Also, use form CA to bring to the
Copyright Office's attention any prior registrations of
materials incorporated in a registered work.

An application for supplementary registration may
be made by anyone who at the time of filing would be
eligible to make the underlying registration.

Form CA is available at http://www.copyright.
gov/forms/formca.pdf. When completed, it should be
mailed with the necessary fee to:

> Library of Congress
> Copyright Office—RPO
> 101 Independence Ave., SE
> Washington, DC 20559-6200.

Certificate of Registration

When the Register of Copyrights approves your application for registration or for supplementary registration, the Copyright Office will issue you a certificate of
registration or a certificate of supplementary registration. The certificate has no separate legal significance,
but it is useful to have it in your possession in case the
official record of your registration is misplaced by the
Copyright Office. Moreover, in subsequent transfers
and other contracts involving the copyright, it will
prove convenient to refer to the certificate because it
contains, or should contain, the exact description of the
copyright. It will also inform you of the registration
number, to which you should refer when making or
terminating transfers of copyright. (The registration
number will be changed if a supplementary registration is made.) Additional copies of the certificate can

be obtained from the Copyright Office for a fee (see http://www.copyright.gov/docs/fees.html).

Preregistration Preregistration is available only for certain types of works:

- Motion pictures;

- Sound recordings;

- Musical compositions;

- Literary works being prepared for publication in book form;

- Computer programs (including video games); and

- Advertising or marketing photographs.

These types of works are vulnerable to prerelease piracy. Preregistration allows the owners of such works to sue for infringement, and obtain the benefits of timely registration, without having to wait for actual registration. It is, however, only a stopgap.[23]

Preregistration is for works that are in the process of being prepared for commercial distribution. Remember that you can register an unpublished work for as little as $35 (as against $115 for preregistration), and full registration of an unpublished work in final or nearly final form will give you complete, as opposed to merely interim, protection. On the other hand, full registration can encounter delays, which may hinder your ability to react swiftly to prerelease infringement. The decision whether to preregister depends, therefore, largely on your risk assessment.

Preregistration is done online, using electronic form PRE on the Copyright Office website. This form requires very different information from the standard registration form.

You must also state the date on which preparation of the work for commercial distribution began. What that means is:

- For a musical composition, the date the music and/or lyrics began to be fixed in tangible form, by being written down or recorded;

- For a motion picture, the date filming began;

- For a sound recording, the date recording sessions began;

- For a book, the date actual writing of the text began;

- For a computer program, the date the writing of the source code or object code began;

- For a video game, the date the writing of the source code or object code began, or the date the images of the visual aspect of the video game began to be fixed;

- For an advertising or marketing photograph, the date the photograph was taken. If you intend to release a group of photographs simultaneously, and are preregistering them as a group, then the date on which the first of them was taken will suffice.

Both the month and year must be given; the day of the month is optional. If you do not know the exact date, you can give your closest approximation.

You must also state the date on which you expect the work will be in final form for distribution. If the work has already been substantially completed except for final editing, give the anticipated date of final editing. However, for motion pictures you may give the anticipated date when principal photography will be completed. Again, both the month and year must be given; the day can be approximate.

You must also state the date on which you expect commercial distribution to begin. (To be eligible for preregistration, you must have a reasonable expectation that the work will be commercially distributed to the public.) For this, the year must be accurate; the month and day can be approximate.

Finally, you must provide a description of the work, not to exceed 2,000 characters in length (approximately 330 words). The Copyright Office regulations list the elements that your description should include; these are reproduced in appendix D. However, deciding how much information to divulge can be tricky. The regulations say that "in an action for infringement of a preregistered work, the court may evaluate the adequacy of the description to determine whether the preregistration actually describes the work that is alleged to be infringed, taking into account the information available to the applicant at the time of preregistration and taking into account the legitimate interest of the applicant in protecting confidential information." Thus, you want to be accurate and specific enough that a court will agree that your preregistration really covers your final work product; otherwise you will have wasted time and money and be thrown out of court. On the other hand, since preregistration descriptions are available to the public, you do not want to disclose confidential information that might tip off a competitor.

As I have said, preregistration is only a stopgap. If your work is infringed before, or very soon after, it has been released to the public, preregistration allows you to sue for infringement immediately without waiting for registration. However, you cannot simply coast on your preregistration.

In essence, a preregistration is good for the first three months following publication. If an infringement occurs before publication, or within two months following publication, you must register the work within one month after you learn of the infringement—and in no event later than three months following publication—or your preregistration will be null and void, and if you have sued based on your preregistration the court will have to dismiss the suit. If an infringement commences any time later than the third month following publication, preregistration will not get you into court; you must register the work in order to sue. However, the statute is ambiguous as to what happens if the infringement occurs *in the third month* following publication. It says that those who have preregistered must make full registration within three months following publication, but it does not say what happens if they do not. It does not require a court to dismiss a lawsuit filed in the third month if registration is not done. It does, however, explicitly say that if timely registration is not made, the copyright owner will lose any claim to attorney's fees and statutory damages.

RIGHTS IN COPYRIGHTED WORKS

6

One of the many respects in which copyright resembles property in land is divisibility. If you own a parcel of land, you can sell mineral rights to A, water rights to B, and a right of way to C, and still be considered the owner of the underlying property. Copyright too can be exploited in many different ways. It comprises five basic rights, which, along with certain limitations, are set forth in the statute.

The limitations take various forms. One consists of specific exceptions and exemptions, which I will discuss in this chapter along with the rights to which they relate. The second consists of compulsory licenses for the use of certain types of works in certain media; these I discuss in chapter 7. Finally, all rights are subject to fair use, which I discuss in chapter 9.

The right to copy is the right to reproduce the work in copies or phonorecords. Together with the right of distribution, it is the oldest and most fundamental right under copyright. A number of statutory exceptions to this right have accrued over the years. I will discuss the narrowest, targeted ones first, then the larger exemption for libraries and archives.

The Right to Copy

• *Sound recordings.* With regard to sound recordings, this right is limited in several ways. First, anyone else is free to make a recording that blatantly imitates yours; only if he actually lifts sounds from your recording is he infringing. (This rule shows practical wisdom. Two renditions of a piece of music are bound to sound alike; it would stifle artistic competition to require performers to differentiate themselves in unproductive ways.) Second, it is permissible to copy sound recordings in the context of educational programs distributed by or through public broadcasting entities, provided that the resulting copies are not distributed commercially to the general public. Third, certain limited classes of other broadcasters and transmitters may make phonorecords for their own internal use.[1]

• *Computer programs.* The statute also limits to some degree the exclusivity of the right to copy computer programs. It provides that anyone who is an "owner" of a copy of a computer program may make an object code copy of it, so as to be able to use it in a computer. Such a copy may not, however, be transferred unless the original copy is also transferred and unless the owner is also transferring whatever rights he may have in the program. The owner is also permitted to make copies for archival purposes, so long as the archival copies are destroyed if continued possession of the program "should cease to be rightful."[2]

Curiously, the statute does not in so many words require destruction of the object code version when possession of the source code ceases to be rightful, but one can only presume that this was an oversight and that any cessation of rights in the program would cover all copies made, as well as copies originally received.

Although the statute speaks only of an "owner" of the program copy, courts have generally held that the provisions just discussed extend to licensees as well.[3] Of course, a license agreement could forbid such activity, but how that would be enforced is hard to imagine. Software licensees will do what they need to do.

Indeed, it is not clear why these provisions were added to the statute at all. It is hard to believe that the concept of fair use, which I discuss in chapter 9, would not permit anyone in rightful possession of a program to take whatever steps might be necessary to make full use of it.

Another express exception to the reproduction right excuses the copying of a program in an owner/lessee's computer for purposes of system repair or maintenance, provided the copy is erased when the work is finished.[4] The purpose of this exception was to prevent software licensors from monopolizing the market for maintenance services.

• *Reproduction for the print-disabled.* The law contains some significant exemptions for reproduction (and distribution) of works, for the use of persons who are blind or have some other disability that makes it difficult from them to read regular print formats. These exemptions appear in Section 121 of the Copyright Act, often referred to as the "Chafee Amendment," after Senator John Chafee of Rhode Island, who was instrumental in its enactment in 1996.

The Chafee exemption is available to any "authorized entity," namely, any nonprofit organization or governmental agency that has "a primary mission" to provide specialized services relating to "training, education, or adaptive reading or information access needs" of print-disabled individuals. The exemption applies only to published nondramatic literary works, and allows only reproduction in "specialized formats" that are exclusively for the use of print-disabled persons. Such formats include Braille but also such things as electronic files that can be used with text-to-speech software, so that the text is "read" for the user.

Prior to the enactment of the Chafee Amendment, we had bumped along for many years under a system whereby publishers licensed books to companies that specialized in producing Braille or other accessible formats. For these licenses some publishers charged a fee, but most granted permission at no cost. Apparently, this system was not getting accessible formats into the hands of those who needed them, and a fix was needed. The answer, however, should have been some sort of compulsory license, not a law that allowed free taking of copyrighted materials, however worthy the purpose. The potential imposition of the Chafee Amendment on copyright owners is becoming larger as the technology for making specialized formats becomes cheaper and as our understanding of what it means to be print-disabled expands.

Advocates for the blind have also pushed the envelope of what qualifies as an "authorized entity." Until the 2012 *HathiTrust* decision, it was generally assumed that only a few such entities and agencies existed in the United States: organizations such as BookShare and the National Federation for the Blind, whose purpose is to serve the blind. In the *HathiTrust* decision—which I also discuss in the context of fair use in chapter 9—the court held that any university library making digital copies of works available to the university's print-disabled students qualified as an "authorized entity."[5] This, to my mind, violates the intent of Chafee, and its potential implications are enormous. At the moment, the University of Michigan—which runs the HathiTrust Digital Library—is making its digital files available only to its own print-disabled students. We must hope that restraint continues, and that the Second Circuit corrects the mistake made by the District Court in *HathiTrust*.

The friction between copyright and the desire to do good for the blind has become particularly acute in the field of instructional materials (i.e., textbooks and related works). Federal law requires educational institutions from kindergarten through graduate school to be accessible to all individuals regardless of disability. This has put the onus on schools to provide accessible formats to their print-disabled students—but how were they to do so consistent with copyright? At the K–12 level, Congress stepped in with a sort of solution. Rather than specifically require publishers to provide specialized formats—a step that would have raised worrisome Constitutional issues—Congress set up the National Instructional Materials Access Center (NIMAC) and required *schools*, as a condition of receiving federal money, to require *publishers* (by contract) to provide a certain kind of electronic file to NIMAC, which could then be converted into accessible formats.[6]

As a general rule, K–12 schools purchase instructional materials in bulk from publishers, based simply on the number of students in the school system. Thus, publishers end up getting paid for the use of their works by print-disabled students, so everyone benefits. The NIMAC solution may impose some additional transaction costs on copyright owners but should not reduce their income. One cannot rule out some element of risk here, though, if through NIMAC these materials end up in the possession of the special entities that can reproduce them without copyright permission.

At the college and postgraduate level, things are not nearly so organized. The largest textbook publishers have mechanisms in place, including an online clearinghouse, to get accessible formats into the hands of students; so long as they receive the same payment they would have received otherwise, there should be no complaint on either side. However, smaller publishers are not geared up to deal with the problem. Some states have enacted laws purporting to require publishers to provide specialized formats for their students, even including fines for noncompliance. These laws seem to me clearly unconstitutional. I did, however, have the privilege of working on the Wisconsin statute, which takes a very different approach, and which the publishing community and the state hope may serve as a model nationwide.[7]

On the international front, there has been substantial pressure from various quarters to carve out broad exemptions from copyright for the benefit of the print-disabled. Responding to this pressure, on June 27, 2013, the member states of the World Intellectual Property Organization (WIPO) formally adopted, after years of negotiation, the Marrakesh Treaty to Facilitate Access to Published Works for Persons Who Are Blind, Visually Impaired, or Otherwise Print Disabled.[8]

The Marrakesh treaty, if ratified by the U.S. Senate—by no means a sure thing—will have mixed implications for U.S. copyright owners. On one hand, it will require the United States to enact legislation much broader than Chafee. The treaty adopts a wider definition of what is an "authorized entity," does away with the concept that an accessible format must be "specialized" (so long as the copies made are actually used only by print-disabled persons), and would apply to nearly every sort of work (whereas Chafee applies only to nondramatic literary works). On the other hand the treaty does permit—but does not require—participating countries to require remuneration to copyright owners for copies made for the print-disabled: in effect, a sort of compulsory license. It also permits—but does not require—a contracting party to limit the exemption to situations where an appropriate format "cannot be obtained commercially under reasonable terms." These last two qualifications will allow the United States (if it does ratify the treaty) to adopt rules that protect the legitimate expectations of copyright owners, though any such protections remain to be hammered out in the legislative (sausage-making) process.

The implications for the treaty outside U.S. borders are even harder to predict. The treaty allows a lot of leeway in how contracting states implement it, and remuneration to the copyright owner is (as noted) not required. On the other hand, the treaty does contain a general statement that limitations and exceptions should be confined to "special cases which do not conflict with a normal exploitation of the work and do not unreasonably prejudice the legitimate interests of the right holder." Unfortunately, it contains no enforcement mechanisms, so how copyright owners will fare may vary widely from country to country.

Finally, the treaty also encourages but does not require the cross-border provision of accessible formats. This part of the treaty seems largely aspirational, and any implementation a long way off.

The Right to Create Derivative Works

The general concept of "derivative works" has already been discussed. As with the right to copy, this right has also been limited by statute where computer programs are concerned. The "owner" of a copy of a program is entitled to adapt it to his own needs, but may not transfer the adaptation except with the consent of the copyright owner in the original. Again it seems unnecessary to have provided this in the statute, since the concept of fair use is surely broad enough to protect this kind of activity. Also, the limitation of the statute to "owners" ought not to be read as implicitly depriving lessees of a similar right. However, software licenses usually impose specific contractual restrictions on licensees or lessees.

In the case of sound recordings, the only derivative work that is covered by copyright is a rearrangement of the *actual sounds* of the recording.

It is possible to make a derivative work of a derivative work, but, as I have mentioned, anyone doing this should take great care to obtain all necessary permissions. If, for example, a company wishes to make dolls based on a movie character derived from a comic book, it must buy the right to do so not only from the person who owns the movie rights but also from the copyright owner of the comic book.

The most important restrictions on the right to make derivative works affect architectural works embodied in constructed buildings. The copyright owner cannot prevent anyone from making photographs, postcards, drawings, and other "pictorial representations" of a constructed building if the building is located in or "ordinarily visible from" a public place.[9] Some wags have suggested that since the air is public space, and all buildings can be photographed from the air, all buildings are free to be photographed from any angle. This is almost certainly not correct, but it does raise an interesting (and unanswered) question of whether aerial photography of otherwise private buildings is a copyright violation. Lawyers could spend many a happy hour debating the question.

Pictorial representations of publicly visible buildings may be reproduced, distributed, and displayed without liability to the copyright owner. However, the statute does not say they may be performed. Thus the movie industry may (absent a fair use defense) need the same sorts of licenses from architects as it has routinely sought from visual artists and composers of music.

The owner of a building may alter the building without fear of infringing the derivative work right in any architectural work that may be embodied in it. Oddly, the statute also says the owner may destroy the building without liability. One assumes this sprang from an excess of caution: destruction of a copyrighted work has never been considered to create a "derivative work."

The Right to Distribute Copies or Phonorecords to the Public

The distribution right is the second part of the traditional right of "publication," the first part being the right of reproduction. Legally, however, it is a separate right, and can be exercised separately from the right of reproduction. It should be noted, though, that once you part with a particular copy of a work you lose control over its further distribution. The buyer can sell it, rent it, throw it away, or whatever he pleases. The only exceptions to this "first sale" doctrine are for computer software and recordings of musical works.[10]

The distribution right owner also has the right to prevent importation into this country of unauthorized copies.[11] (In the digital context, this should include any transmission of unauthorized digital copies into the United States where the user has the ability to download and keep a copy of the transmission.) For decades, even authorized copies could be kept out of the United States if manufactured abroad; however, in 2013 the Supreme Court threw out that rule and applied the first sale doctrine to authorized goods wherever made.[12] That decision may have far-reaching consequences. Legal importation of copyrighted goods made abroad may result in lower costs for American consumers, but it may have pernicious effects elsewhere. For example, before this Supreme Court decision many publishers sold cheap editions of textbooks in developing countries; they may have to abandon that practice, and the greatest losers may be foreign students. Time will tell.

There are minor exceptions to the importation right. An individual may bring in no more than one copy in his or her personal baggage for personal use. Governments may import copies of audiovisual works for public archival purposes, and copies of other works for governmental purposes other than use in educational institutions. A nonprofit organization may import one copy of an audiovisual work for archival purposes, and up to five copies of any other type of work for library lending or archival purposes, so long as the use is not for "systematic" reproduction (see discussion of "systematic reproduction" in chapter 9).

With respect to computer software, no one may rent, lease, or even lend it to anyone else without permission of the copyright owner.[13] Only certain nonprofit institutions are immune from this restriction, and then only in part. A nonprofit library may rent, lease, or lend software to any person for "nonprofit purposes" if the loan copy bears a warning of copyright. (See appendix E for the proper text of this warning.) A nonprofit educational institution may rent, lease, or lend software for nonprofit purposes without the need of any warning notice. Just what the phrase "nonprofit purposes" includes or excludes is nowhere made clear. From one point of view, *any* revenue generation by a nonprofit institution is for nonprofit purposes. Congress evidently intended, however, that some business enterprises by nonprofit institutions would be viewed as "commercial" and not pass muster, though where the line should be drawn is left ambiguous. Curiously, Congress thought it necessary to specify that any rental, lease, or loan by a nonprofit educational institution to its faculty, staff, or students, or to another nonprofit educational institution, is deemed to be for a nonprofit purpose. I respectfully suggest that this attempt at clarification, while no doubt well-intentioned, in fact confuses the issue. In some minds it may well leave a nagging doubt: if Congress thought that something so obvious needed to be spelled out, what other uses that seem just as obviously nonprofit may be suspect? My own view is that what prompted Congress to this unnecessary clarification was probably an excess of caution, not some hidden meaning of "nonprofit." But that is as much light as I can shed on the matter.

Another unanswered question is what liability, if any, a library has if it lends in good faith for a purpose that turns out to be commercial. A strict reading of the statute would make the library liable, but it is hard to picture any court imposing more than a nominal liability in such a case.

While these rules cover most types of programs, they do not cover all. Programs that are embedded in machines or products, and that cannot be copied during ordinary operation, are still subject to the first sale doctrine and may be lent or rented out (as so embedded) without liability. Common examples of this are your smartphone, the diagnostic software in your office photocopy machine, or the operating system in your computer. Secondly, video games may be freely rented, leased, or lent for use in video game machines, but not in general-purpose computers.

Apart from these statutory rules, courts have upheld the right of software vendors to avoid the first sale doctrine by structuring their transactions as "licenses" rather than sales. (The End User License Agreement that a consumer must accept by clicking "I agree" or the like is a typical example of this.) Not every software license will be considered a true license for purposes of the first sale doctrine, however. Courts will look to the specifics of the agreement to determine whether it is truly a license or simply a sale in license's clothing. What the court looks at is whether the agreement "significantly restricts" the customer's ability to transfer the software to third parties, and imposes "notable" restrictions on the customer's use of the software. If so, then the transaction is a license, and the software will not be subject to the first sale doctrine.[14]

With respect to musical works, no one may rent, lease, or lend phonorecords of such works without the permission of those who own copyright in both the music and the sound recording. As with computer software, nonprofit libraries and educational institutions may rent, lease, or lend phonorecords so long as they do so for nonprofit purposes. There is no requirement that any copyright warning be placed on phonorecords before they go out the door.

The Right to Perform the Work Publicly

"Publicly" in this case means outside the normal circle of family and social acquaintances. "Perform" includes both live performance and indirect performance by means of web streaming and similar processes. (Note, though, that transmitting digital files is distribution, not performance, unless the recipient actually hears the sounds while the download is occurring.)[15] In the case of a movie or other audiovisual work, to perform the work means to show it by means of a projector or other device, or by streaming.

Until late in the twentieth century, the owner of copyright in a sound recording had no right to control public performance of that recording. Only the author of the underlying work would receive royalties from, for example, the playing of a Top 40 track on the radio; the record company (the "label," in industry parlance) would receive nothing, and the performing artist would receive nothing.[16] And this remains true now, with certain exceptions for digital transmission.

What, then, of a videotape, which in theory seems indistinguishable from a sound recording? Alas, there is no logical consistency here. If you permit someone to videotape a performance of your song, the video producer will control public performance of the videotape, as such, although you will continue to control performance of the music. (Anyone who wants to perform the video will thus need permission from both of you.) There is no logical reason for applying this principle to audiovisual derivative works and not to sound recordings. The causes of the inconsistency are more powerful than logic, though; they have their roots in history. The rule is like certain rules of grammar that you can only memorize and should not struggle to understand.

The music recording industry lived quietly if unhappily with the old rules for many decades. But the advent of cheap digital technology was one straw too many. The digital revolution, the industry realized, would enable people who receive transmissions of their favorite recordings to make endless, undegraded copies of what they receive. To prevent this, the industry lobbied hard in the mid-1990s for the right to control digital transmission of their sound recordings.

There were powerful lobbies opposing restrictions, and all the music recording industry got in the end was an exclusive right to control digital transmission by means of interactive services (where the customer sends in an online order for the transmission), most kinds of subscription services, and certain other such arrangements; the performance right does not cover traditional radio or TV broadcasting even where the content is simultaneously streamed over the Internet. Furthermore, the right to control digital transmissions is subject to two compulsory license schemes. (See chapter 7.)

The long and complex negotiations that produced this compromise led to one rather peculiar, and unprecedented, addition to the statute. This addition provides that "no interactive service shall be granted an exclusive license [of the digital performance right in a sound recording] for a period in excess of 12 months."[17] If the interactive service is a small one, with fewer than 1,000 sound recordings in its repertoire, the maximum period is extended to 24 months. The purpose of this restriction on licensing freedom was, apparently, to prevent the recording industry from gaining dominance over public performance of music by forcing digital performance to pass through tollbooths it could control.

Separately from the recording industry, music performers have long lobbied Congress to obtain the right to be paid for performance of their recordings. Such a right would exist independent of copyright in the music performed; indeed, performances of public domain works would be just as entitled to royalties as any other. The Boston Symphony Orchestra would be able to demand performance royalties whenever its recordings were played on public radio, whether the composers have (for example, John Williams) or do not have (for example, Beethoven) any concurrent right.

How might performers in fact be paid? One answer would be to set up a clearinghouse that would handle the licensing of performers' rights on a nationwide basis, as BMI and ASCAP (which are described later in this chapter) do for music copyright, and be able to grant "blanket licenses" covering a performer's entire oeuvre. This would of course mean that, in addition to paying music copyright holders, the owners of bars, discotheques, radio stations, and the like would have to pay another fee to performers. Not surprisingly, the industry groups who represent such businesses lobby hard against the proposal. The music industry, which might be thought more sympathetic, views the proposal with a jaundiced eye, fearful that Congress might protect music users from additional financial burden by forcing copyright owners to share their existing revenue stream with performers, rather than creating a new revenue stream for performers. Given the difficulties of putting such a scheme in place, and the entrenched opposition of both users and copyright owners, it seems unlikely that Congress will ever see its way clear to adopt a performer's right.

The law permits certain types of performances in spite of copyright. These exceptions are elaborately defined.[18]

Special Exceptions to the Performance Right

One exception covers performances by nonprofit educational institutions in the course of face-to-face teaching activities. A performance in a Berlitz classroom, for example, would not benefit from this exception because Berlitz schools are commercial, not nonprofit. Moreover, the exception does not apply to performance of audiovisual works if the person performing the work knows, or has reason to know, that the copy being used is an unlawful copy. Thus, for example, a teacher cannot show a film using a DVD that she suspects was pirated.

Exceptions Applicable to All Works

A related exception covers performance in the context of distance learning. Added to the law by the so-called Technology, Education and Copyright Harmonization Act of 2002 (the TEACH Act), this exception is carefully— many would say, too carefully—defined. Governmental agencies can take advantage of it, as can accredited nonprofit educational institutions. (Note the accreditation requirement, which does not apply to the live classroom performance exception.) It does not apply to works that are designed for mediated distance learning. It does not permit performance by means of a copy or phonorecord that the instructor knows, or has reason to know, was unlawfully made or acquired. However, the TEACH Act does specifically authorize digitization of works for use in distance learning, if no existing digital version is available to the institution or government agency, or is available but is subject to technological protection that makes it impossible for use in the class transmission.[19]

For any work other than a nondramatic literary or musical work, the TEACH Act exception covers use only of "reasonable and limited portions" of the work. The performance must be an integral part of a mediated class session (i.e., a session in which the instructor actually takes part), and the transmission of the work must be made by, at the direction of, or under the actual supervision of the instructor. To the extent technologically feasible, the transmission may reach only students enrolled in the course concerned, or government employees engaged in their official duties.

Where distance learning occurs by digital transmission, further restrictions apply. The transmitting body must make reasonable technological efforts to prevent retransmission, and to prevent retention in accessible form beyond the end of the class session. It must not interfere with any technological measures embedded in the work for those purposes by the copyright owner. And it must "institute policies regarding copyright, [provide] informational materials to faculty, students, and relevant staff members that accurately describe, and promote compliance with, the laws of the United

States relating to copyright, and [provide] notice to students that materials used in connection with the course may be subject to copyright protection."

Most of these rules seem reasonable enough. In their long-winded way, they attempt to ensure that real distance learning is going on, not mere free-for-all digital dissemination, and to ensure that the materials in digital form do not escape into the wider world. But why should performance in the context of distance learning be more restricted in length than performance in a live classroom? If a teacher thinks that performing an entire one-act play in the classroom makes pedagogical sense, why should he have to truncate that performance when giving the class to distance learners, just to squeeze into the protection of the TEACH Act? Most educators have adopted the position that anything that would be permitted in live classroom teaching, under the first exception, is fair use even if not specifically excused by the TEACH Act. I think they are probably right to do so.

A third general exception to the performance right applies to works included in broadcast signals. It covers the cable systems used by hotels and apartment houses which connect all of the rooms or apartments to a common antenna, so long as no direct charge is made to users. Cable systems used by governmental bodies or nonprofit institutions are also exempted, so long as they are not used for any sort of commercial advantage and charge no more than enough to meet expenses.[20]

The fourth exception to the performance right covers the use of radio and television reception in bars, restaurants, shops, and other public places. It exempts all performances occurring in such places by means of a "single receiving apparatus of a kind commonly used in private homes," provided there is no direct charge to patrons for watching or listening to the performance.

When that language was first enacted, most TV sets were rather small. As public taste adapts to larger and larger TV sets, the definition of what is "commonly used" must also have grown, presumably.

Exceptions Applicable to Nondramatic, Nonvisual Works

In a 1998 amendment to the statute, Congress substantially altered the relationship between music copyright owners and the owners of restaurants, hotels, and other establishments. To understand what has happened, it is important to know the history of music licensing.

Decades ago, music publishers, composers, and other copyright owners organized themselves into so-called "performing rights societies"—ASCAP, BMI, and SESAC. Of these, SESAC is the smallest, being primarily European in membership, but still represents a large portfolio of important music. ASCAP and BMI each represent the owners of millions of musical works. These societies have the right, on a nonexclusive basis, to license (for nondramatic performance only) the entire repertoire of their members. They offer what they call "blanket licenses": licenses that entitle a licensee to use all the music in the society's repertoire for a fixed fee. They license the premises where music is performed, not the performers, on the theory that premises are easier to monitor than itinerant musicians. The fee varies depending on the type and size of establishment, whether live or recorded music is used, whether dancing is allowed, and so on. Due to antitrust considerations, the fees charged by the societies have long been subject to the supervision of the federal court in New York.

Premises owners have long complained that they were being gouged by the performing rights societies. In 1998, after years of bitter lobbying and negotiation, Congress passed the so-called "Fairness in Music

Licensing Act," which altered the licensing playing field in two ways. First, it gave certain small business owners the right to bring special lawsuits to challenge societies' fees, solely as applied to their own establishments. (I discuss this in chapter 7.) Second, it exempted certain small establishments from licensing requirements altogether.[21]

The first of these innovations has rarely if ever been invoked. The second, however, has certainly—and unconscionably—impinged on music copyright owners' revenues. The World Trade Organization has ruled that it violates our treaty obligations, yet Congress has taken no steps to undo it. Here are the terms:

The exemption applies to performance of music by means of radio and television reception. It covers:

• any food service or drinking establishment with less than 3,750 square feet of floor space (other than parking space);

• any other establishment—e.g., a shop, a car wash, a bus station—if its total area excluding parking is less than 2,000 square feet;

• any establishment of any kind that uses no more than six loudspeakers, of which no more than four are located in any one room or adjoining outdoor space. If the speakers are connected to "audiovisual devices" (TV sets, video monitors, etc.), there may not be more than four of these and no more than one in any room, and none of them may be bigger than 55 inches.

Any proprietor of an establishment who defends against an infringement claim on the basis that his equipment or his premises fall below one of these thresholds should be careful in doing so. If the court finds that this claim of exemption was not reasonable, he will be liable (in addition to other damages) for a special penalty of twice the fee that he would have paid during the previous three years to ASCAP, BMI, or SESAC for the right to use the music in question.

Other exceptions are created by law for performances of nondramatic literary or musical works. The first is for educational broadcasts. It covers broadcasts whether on the air or by cable, so long as they are a regular part of the educational program of a nonprofit educational institution or a governmental body. A broadcast must be made primarily for reception in classrooms or "similar places normally devoted to instruction" (which, for handicapped persons, may mean their own homes) or on governmental premises. Interestingly, the school or governmental body making any such broadcast is free to make up to 30 copies of the program, so long as all except one archival copy are destroyed within seven years.[22] Just what can be done with the copies is unclear, but it seems fair to say that any educational use within the institution or agency would be permissible.

A performance of such a work is also outside the scope of copyright if not for commercial profit. However, for a performance to fit under this exception, there must be no admission charge—or the profits must go to charity—and no compensation may be paid to any performer, producer, or promoter. Both of these conditions must be met: a charity concert will be a copyright infringement if the performer receives any payment beyond reimbursement of expenses.

The privilege given to charitable benefit performances has one other important qualification. It is still possible for the owner of the exclusive performance right in a work to prevent such a performance, if he gives written notice of objection to the promoters or other persons responsible at least a week in advance.[23]

The notice must comply with two rules, relating to content and to timing.

First, it must be signed by the copyright owner or by the performance right owner, or by someone empowered to act on behalf of one of them, and the signature must be dated and accompanied by the name, address, and telephone number of the signer, printed legibly or typed. If sending such a notice, you must include the following information:

1. Reference to the statutory authority on which you rely. The statute should be cited. It is 17 U.S.C. §110(4).

2. The date and place of the performance that you object to or, if you do not know this information exactly, as much information as you do know about it, as well as your source, unless your source is confidential.

3. The reasons for your objection.

4. Clear identification, by title and at least one author, of the work you do not want performed, or, if you prefer, a blanket identification of a group of works that have something in common, which can be as general as being written by the same author or published by the same publisher. If you choose the blanket-notice route, you must give the name, address, and telephone number of at least two persons from whom the other party can obtain a more specific identification of the works. Also, if your notice does not identify the copyright owner or owners of all the works, you must offer to provide that information, including names and last known addresses.

5. A statement that the persons will be free to go ahead with the performance if no admission charge

is made and if no profit inures to the performers or the promoters, but that otherwise those persons may be liable for copyright infringement.

The second rule is that the notice must be received at least a week before the performance. You can instead give brief notice by telegram or "other similar form of communication," if you get a signed letter with all the above information to the proper party before the performance. The phrase "or other similar form of communication" has not been updated in the Copyright Office regulations. Given that telegrams barely exist anymore, it seems reasonable to assume that a fax or email would qualify.

Exceptions for performances of nondramatic literary or musical works have also been made where the performance takes place as part of a service of religious worship or at a function organized and promoted by a nonprofit veterans' organization or fraternal organization. The latter exception applies only if the general public is not invited to the performance and if the organization uses any proceeds (after paying reasonable production costs) exclusively for charitable purposes. It is designed, in short, to permit the local VFW or Elks or what-have-you to hold a fundraiser for their members without paying royalties. It does not, by the way, extend to college fraternities or sororities unless the performance is held to raise money for charitable purposes that are specified in advance.

Other Special Exceptions   In addition to the above, the law has carved out some even more specialized exceptions. A dramatic musical work (such as an opera or a ballet) may be performed in a religious service. A nondramatic musical work may be performed in a store for purposes of advertising sheet music, phonorecords, or the electronic devices used for performing such works. (Implicitly, the movie on the screens at your local big box electronics store may be an infringement—but who is likely to sue?) And a nondramatic literary work may be broadcast to blind, deaf, or other handicapped persons by a governmental body, a public broadcasting station, a cable system, or a radio subcarrier. The governmental body or public broadcaster can make up to 10 copies of the program and keep them on hand for this purpose or lend them to similar organizations for the same purpose.[24]

The only noneducational exception created for performances of dramatic literary works, such as plays, is in the case of performances for the benefit of people who cannot read normally. Such a performance may not be made for profit, may be made only once by any one group of performers or under the aegis of any one organization, and may be made only of works that were first published at least 10 years previously.

Lastly, if a governmental or nonprofit body sponsors an agricultural or horticultural fair, it will not be liable for unauthorized performance of music at that fair unless it arranges for or is in charge of the performance.

The Right to Display the Work Publicly

Display, like performance, includes broadcasting and other mechanical forms of communication. Where audiovisual works are concerned, display should not be confused with performance: you perform a film by playing it in the usual way; you display a film by projecting isolated frames.

The display right is a significant change from prior law and is of great importance to artists working in the visual arts. Someone who buys a painting has the right to place the work on exhibit in a museum or to display it to the public in any other way, so long as the public are physically present at the place of display. But the buyer has no right, unless he specifically buys the right from the artist, to broadcast an image of the painting or permit anyone else to broadcast it. Moreover, this limited right to display a painting is given only to buyers; people who rent, borrow, or lease works of art have no right to display them in any way outside the circle of their friends and guests.

When it created the display right, Congress was thinking of traditional media. However, the most important (that is, economically important) displays now occur in the digital world. When a computer user visits a web page, the website owner is "displaying" the contents of the page, to the extent that those contents are static or consist of single images that appear sequentially. (A performance would occur if the contents were in video form.) Suddenly, the display right matters not only for works of visual art, as it always did, but also for literary works, for which the display right used to be largely irrelevant.

Like the performance right, the right of a copyright holder to control display of a work does not extend to display in the course of face-to-face nonprofit or governmental teaching.[25] (However, as with performance, this does not give a teacher the right to display a copy of an audiovisual work if he knows or has reason to believe that the copy was unlawfully made.) The TEACH Act (described in detail earlier in this chapter) applies to distance-learning display of works as well as performance, so long as the display is "in an amount comparable to that which is typically displayed in the course of a live classroom session."

Also like the performance right, the right to control display does not extend to display by a hotel proprietor or someone of that sort if all she uses to display the work is an ordinary television set and if she charges nothing to the public for the privilege of seeing the display.

Other exceptions permit unauthorized display in a service of religious worship[26] and display, in an advertisement or a news report, of a useful work—for example, a pillowcase or a place mat—that lawfully incorporates a work of visual art.[27] Thus if a painter licenses a wildlife painting to a maker of plastic place mats, the maker can advertise the place mats without infringing the painter's display right.

In many European countries, and especially in France, the law has long protected artists even beyond the sale of their works, by what are known as the *droit de suite* and *droit moral*. *Droit de suite* is the right to share in the profits of future sales of a work; when a work is sold by one collector to another, the artist gets a portion of the profit made by the seller. *Droit moral* ("moral right") is the right to control alterations of the work and to prevent its destruction, sometimes referred as the "right of integrity," and the right to be acknowledged as its author if one chooses (or when appropriate to disclaim authorship), sometimes referred to as the "right of paternity."

Moral Rights in Visual Works

The Berne Convention requires all its signatories to give some measure of recognition to the moral right. At the time of U.S. accession to Berne it was argued, by those who did not wish to rock the boat, that a U.S. law prohibiting "false designation of origin" on goods in commerce already, in effect, protected the rights of integrity and paternity. This was largely wishful thinking at the time, and the Supreme Court has since ruled that the federal law in question does not apply to false attributions of authorship of copyrighted works.[28] It seems unlikely that more general laws regarding false advertising and unfair competition will really fill the gap. In fact, one court has held that a scientist had no right to object to a colleague's presenting the scientist's research as his own without proper attribution; because the research was not copyrightable, the claim was an impermissible attempt to get copyright-like protection.[29]

In any event, the United States has enacted a very limited moral right scheme for certain works of visual art.[30] The relevant law is the Visual Artists Rights Act or VARA, which added Section 106A to the Copyright Act. By enacting VARA it is generally assumed that we have fulfilled whatever duty we had to our Berne partners. (They have chosen not to argue the point.) Tightly circumscribed as the statute is, I think it unlikely that it will be expanded at any time in the foreseeable future.

Scope of Works Protected

The statute is narrow in two ways. First, it covers a fairly limited range of art objects. The types of works protected are:

> • A painting, drawing, print, sculpture, or art photograph (see discussion below) of which there is only one copy. In most instances this one copy will be the original created by the artist. In the case of a photograph, the artist's signature must be affixed for the work to receive moral right protection. The work need not be completed to qualify for protection.[31]

> • A painting, drawing, print, sculpture, or art photograph that is part of a limited edition of no more than 200 copies consecutively numbered and signed by the artist; in the case of a sculpture, the artist's identifying mark may be used instead of a signature.

A number of things need to be said about these definitions.

First, the statute appears to be inflexible on the subject of numbering and signing. Any print in a limited edition that is not both signed and numbered will be beyond the reach of moral rights. That may seem needlessly draconian, but it is the inescapable meaning. Although the statute could well be read to exclude the entire edition if the artist's signature is accidentally left off one copy, this result is probably too draconian and one suspects that courts will struggle to avoid it.

What of the widespread custom of selling so-called "artist's proofs" of prints? Artists will be well advised to drop the practice, unless the proofs plus all numbered copies total 200 or fewer. The proofs will in any case be unprotected because they are not numbered; the greater damage is that by increasing the size of the edition they may render the entire edition ineligible for moral rights.

The term "print" was almost certainly intended by Congress to be broader than the art world's use of that term. I think it is safe to assume that it includes lithographs, monotypes, and any other work in which an image is applied to paper (or similar medium) by mechanical means. The statutory history makes clear that it was also intended to cover collages.[32] On the other hand, other items of aesthetic merit are excluded: pottery (except those pieces that can be construed as "sculpture" or whose decoration can be construed as "paintings"), textiles, and many "craft" items, to name some obvious examples.

I have used the phrase "art photograph" above as shorthand for the statutory phrase "photographic image produced for exhibition purposes only." The only case so far to analyze this phrase in depth determined that it applies separately to negatives and to positive prints. The case also held, however, that at either stage a given photographic image must have been produced for exhibition purposes only. On this basis the court denied VARA protection to prints that a photographer had made for his then-girlfriend to use as studies for her paintings.[33]

What this seems to mean is that a news photographer's negatives—even the unused ones—would not qualify for VARA protection because they have been produced for nonexhibition purposes. However, if the photographer were to make exhibition prints of those negatives, the prints themselves would qualify because the motive for production fits the statutory requirement.

Does "exhibition" mean public exhibition, or would it include private exhibition in one's house? The case just discussed hints that the latter is the meaning, but it did not address the question directly. There seems no real policy justification for such a narrow interpretation, but until a court directly decides the issue we will not know.

In addition to what is excluded from VARA by omission, there is a long list of things that Congress specifically excluded from the list of protected works. These are:

- posters,

- maps and globes,

- charts,

- models, diagrams, and technical drawings,

- "applied art" (defined as artistic ornamentation incorporated in utilitarian objects other than buildings),[34]

- motion pictures and other audiovisual works,

- books, magazines, newspapers, and periodicals (a curious exclusion, since none of these could ever qualify as a painting, print, etc. anyway),

- databases, electronic information services, electronic publications, and "similar" publications (ditto my comment immediately above),

- merchandising items and advertising, promotional, descriptive, covering, or packaging materials and containers,

- any portion of any of the above,

- works made for hire, even though they might otherwise qualify for protection,

- works not subject to copyright protection—such as, for example, utilitarian works in which design elements are not "physically or conceptually separable."

The phrase "any portion" has odd ramifications. Suppose that an artist issued an illustrated book in a limited edition of 200 copies, signed and numbered: she would not have any moral right in any print in the book. Unfair, but inescapable. Or suppose an artist produces a work consisting of projected images with soundtrack: he has no moral right in any of the images. Would it matter if the images had earlier been exhibited separately? Probably not. Could moral rights be reclaimed if the artist subsequently broke up the work and sold each slide as a separate, self-contained work? It seems they should. Finally, if the work is broken up and sold by the purchaser rather than the artist, would moral rights attach to the components as separately owned? Probably not, for the logical focus of the statute should be the form of the work as sold by the artist.

The narrow literalness of VARA's definition of a "work of visual art" has not discouraged some artists from trying to push the envelope, especially regarding large public installations. One was an artist who had installed a group of related sculptures in a Boston park. When the company that controlled the park redesigned it, and as a part of that redesign removed the sculptures, with no intent to reassemble them elsewhere in the same configuration, the artist sued under VARA.

He argued not only that the sculptures were a unified work, so that dispersing them violated the work's integrity, but also that the entire assemblage was site-specific—i.e., that their location in the landscape and with relation to surrounding buildings and landscape features was inviolable artistic matter. The First Circuit accepted his argument that the various pieces of sculpture constituted an "integrated" work, and that integrated works may be protected as such. However, the court refused to grant protection to those elements of the work that were site-specific, finding site specificity to be outside the scope of VARA because, among other things, it would interfere with the legitimate expectations of real estate ownership.[35]

Another artist—known for painting landscapes and wildflowers—tried to prevent the City of Chicago from altering a wildflower garden he had designed. The Seventh Circuit demurred, noting that while a landscape design drawn on paper might constitute a "work of visual art," the garden itself was almost certainly not a "painting" within the strict definition of VARA. The court did not exactly decide that point, however; it marched further upstream and declared that a garden is not copyrightable because it is insufficiently "fixed," and lacks human "authorship," because it is constantly changing due to forces beyond the artist's control. All this made it unnecessary to address the site-specific aspects of the landscape design, but the Seventh Circuit could not resist taking a swipe at the First Circuit. It stated that while the artist of a site-specific installation might not be able to prevent destruction of that element of his work, at least he should be able to assert a right of attribution in it. This is almost certainly wrong; a work of visual art cannot be entitled to one right under VARA but not other rights. Furthermore, the Seventh Circuit's finding no authorship in a work shaped by nature is inconsistent with finding authorship in a work shaped by the neighbors' buildings.[36]

The other respect in which the U.S. moral rights statute is narrow is in the scope of protection it gives. The two rights granted artists are the right of attribution and the right of integrity.

Right of Attribution

The first of these rights has both a positive and a negative application. In the positive mode, it enables the artist to "claim authorship" of his work. What does this mean? Unquestionably it entitles an artist to prevent removal of his or her name from a work, and to insist on receiving credit whenever the work is displayed. It does not, however, go much beyond this, since it extends only to the particular objects made by the artist and not to the underlying work, the copyrightable image. Thus, the moral right does not entitle an artist who has sold her copyright to object when the copyright owner sells copies or derivative works without attribution.

The negative side of the right of attribution is the artist's right to prevent having his or her name attached to works he or she did not create, and to insist on removal of his or her name from a work of visual art that has been distorted, mutilated, or otherwise modified in a manner that would be "prejudicial to his or her honor or reputation." However, since the statute prevents misattribution only on "works of visual art," it only half-protects the people it ought to help. The moral right will prevent, for example, sale of a fake David Hockney original; it will not prevent sale of a poster of that same fake Hockney. It will entitle David Hockney to remove his name from a defaced canvas, but not from 100,000 copies of a painting altered without his approval by someone who owns the derivative work right in the painting. Perhaps some state laws may fill the void, but they are laws lacking the unusual benefits given to actions under the Copyright Act.

Right of Integrity

An artist has the right to prevent any distortion, mutilation, or other modification of a work of visual art, if the modification is intentional and if it would be prejudicial to the artist's honor or reputation. The requirement of intent is critical; it means that no one will be liable for mistakes, or negligence, or Things That Happen. The accidental nail through the canvas, the mover's bad packing that breaks the nose off your sculpture, the burst pipe that water-stains a painting: these are not actionable. An open question, though, is whether reckless or willful disregard will be construed as intent. One can imagine circumstances where it ought to be. The statute does say that grossly negligent conservation, and grossly negligent exposure to harmful light or similar damaging influences, will violate the artist's right.[37]

The question of what is prejudicial to an artist's honor or reputation sounds complicated in theory but probably is not in practice. When someone has deliberately distorted or mutilated a work of art, no court is going to need much encouragement to find the result prejudicial. The whole moral rights statute is premised on the right of the artist to safeguard his reputation. Who can judge better than the artist whether her unique vision has been compromised? What court is going to say, "We like the altered painting better than the original; you should be grateful for the improvement"? (Although one must acknowledge the story that T. S. Eliot told on himself, of a Dutch admirer who told him that he preferred the Dutch translation of "The Love Song of J. Alfred Prufrock" to the original English. Eliot supposedly answered his admirer with the words, "Yes, I suffer in the original.")

Prejudice to honor or reputation seems to imply public exposure of the modified piece, but here too I suspect the courts will apply the law liberally. A work that may happen to be kept in private hands now may easily be sold or hung in a museum tomorrow, and there is no good reason to postpone enforcement of the artist's right until that day.

The moral right to prevent modification conflicts to some degree with the right to make derivative works. In essence, where a work of visual art is concerned the artist can prevent modification of his or her own original, but control over modified copies lies with whoever owns the derivative work right.

Strange as it may at first seem, the right to prevent modification of a work does not include the right to prevent destruction of the work altogether. Someone seems to have decided that destruction of a work is somehow less prejudicial to an artist's reputation than its preservation in altered form. One might well question such reasoning. In any event, there is a separate right to prevent destruction, but it protects only works of "recognized stature." This unhappy phrase is nowhere defined. In the only case to date that has had cause to interpret it, the judge observed that a plaintiff need not demonstrate that the work is "equal in stature to that created by artists such as Picasso, Chagall, or Giacometti." Rather, the artist must show that the work is "viewed as meritorious" by "art experts, other members of the artistic community, or . . . some cross section of society."[38]

For this category of recognized works, the law prohibits not only intentional destruction but also destruction that is "grossly negligent." In other words, the owner of a work of visual art may be liable for its destruction if he acts with gross negligence in its storage, handling, or conservation. The line between gross and ordinary negligence will be for the courts to draw on a case-by-case basis.

These rights against modification and destruction are subject to special limitations where buildings are concerned.[39] If the owner of a building wishes to remove a work of visual art (such as a mural) that is "incorporated in" or "part of" the building,[40] and if there is a chance that the work can be removed without suffering modification or destruction, the owner must make a diligent, good-faith effort to notify the artist of the intended removal. If such effort fails, there will be no liability to the artist. If the effort to notify succeeds, then the owner must give the artist 90 days to remove the work or pay for its removal. If the artist removes the work or pays for its removal then the artist gets back the title to the work. What will constitute a good-faith effort to notify is somewhat ad hoc, but the Copyright Office has established a Visual Arts Registry for artists whose works are "incorporated in or made part of" buildings, and if the owner attempts notice by registered mail to the address shown in that registry then he will have satisfied his statutory obligation. The owner would be well advised to file a statement of his efforts at compliance in the Visual Arts Registry.[41]

Any statement by the artist for filing in the Registry should be titled "Registry of Visual Arts Incorporated in a Building—Artist's Statement." It should identify the artist by name, address, age, and (if publicly listed) telephone number. It should identify the work by title, dimensions, physical description, and copyright registration number if known. The Copyright Office recommends but does not require further identification in the form of 8×10-inch photographs. Finally, the Artist's Statement should identify the building by name, address, and (if known) the owner's name, and preferably should include 8×10 photographs of the building and of the location of the artist's work in the building.

A statement of compliance by an owner should be entitled "Registry of Visual Arts Incorporated in a Building—Building Owner's Statement." It should identify the owner of the building and give the name of a person who represents the owner and a telephone number if publicly listed. It should identify the work and the building in the same manner as if it were an artist's statement, except that the copyright registration number is unnecessary. It should include copies of any contract between the artist and the owner (or the owner's predecessor in title) regarding the rights of attribution and integrity. Finally, it should state the measures that the owner has taken to notify the artist of the removal or pending removal of the work, and should include photocopies of any relevant correspondence or other documents.

The recording fee for these statements is the same as for other copyright documents. These statements may be updated as needed. Updates should in any case identify the artist, work, building, and building owner.

All this paperwork is a boon for culture, and at the cost of mere nuisance to the building owner, in cases where the owner is tired of the work and wishes to replace it with a nice clock or fountain. But what if the owner loves the work and wants to remove it to another location—perhaps even a better location? Here, it seems to me, the notion that title should revert to an artist who pays for removal of the work seems open to constitutional challenge. If the owner wants to remove the work so as to incorporate it in another building, by what right should the artist get it back for (perhaps) a fraction of its worth? I suggest that this right should survive challenge only where the owner of the building has no intent to keep the work.

What of the situation where removal cannot be achieved without modification or destruction of the work? In such a case, the owner will not be liable if the artist has signed a written acknowledgment that the installation of the work may subject the work, in the event of removal, to modification or destruction. Buyers of buildings beware: failure by the original owner to obtain such an acknowledgment creates a potential for legal liability to the artist.

It should be noted that nothing in the statute addresses the situation where the building itself is torn down and that process leads to the destruction of an installed artwork that cannot be removed. By implication, though, the rules just discussed may apply. *Caveat aedificator.*

Effective Date of the Law

The moral right statute became effective on June 1, 1991. Any work that an artist still owned on that date is covered, as is of course any work created afterward. What counts here is not whether the artist still owned copyright in an existing work on that date, but whether he still owned legal title to the physical object. In no case does the moral right reach back to punish modification or destruction that occurred before June 1, 1991.

Who Can Exercise the Right?

The artist's moral right cannot be transferred. It can be waived, but only by an instrument signed by the artist. Furthermore, any waiver must specify the potentially damaging uses of the work that are permitted, and any modification or destruction that results from a use not specified will still impose liability.

If the work concerned is a joint work, any of the joint authors may enforce or waive the moral right, and a waiver signed by one is binding against all. The statute has thus created the irrational and unfair possibility that an artist who does not want his own name used on a work can permit the owner to remove his coauthors' names as well, or can permit the mutilation or destruction of a work to which he has contributed only fractionally. Furthermore, since all this is specifically sanctioned by the statute, there seems little scope for a suit by an injured coauthor against the artist who did these things, other than for a share of any compensation received for the waiver.[42]

Works of visual art created before June 1, 1991, but which remained the property of their creators on that date, are protected by moral rights for as long as their copyrights last. Works created on or after June 1, 1991, are protected only for the lives of their creators. Why works created before the moral right was even enacted should be given longer protection than new works is a mystery I cannot explain. And since the statute specifically says that moral rights cannot be transferred, what happens to them after the artist's death is an even greater mystery.[43] *Duration of Moral Rights*

As with copyright, where joint authors are concerned the measuring life is the life of the last author to die. Also as with copyright, all terms run to the end of the calendar year in which they would otherwise expire.

Anyone whose moral right has been or will be infringed can sue for damages or the profits of the infringer derived from the infringement, or for statutory damages in lieu of damages and profits, and for injunctive relief, all in the same degree as if the infringement were of the copyright itself. These various remedies are discussed more fully in chapter 8. In addition, although no criminal prosecution is available for infringement of moral rights, the law relating to copyright management information (discussed at the *Remedies for Infringement* end of chapter 8) may provide an avenue for criminal prosecution of the same conduct.

In contrast to copyright suits, registration is not a prerequisite for suit on moral rights or for eligibility for statutory damages or attorney's fees.

State Law Moral Rights

Before Congress enacted the moral rights legislation I have just described, a number of states passed somewhat similar statutes. These laws are now null and void insofar as they give to the same types of works any right that is "equivalent" to any of the federal moral rights. "Equivalent" should probably be interpreted broadly; any state law creating a right of attribution, or preventing modification or destruction of a work, will probably be void as applied to federally protected works even though it may differ in minor respects from the federal scheme.

However, state law can still apply to infringements that predate June 1, 1991, or that occur after the death of the artist. (Yes, this is what the federal law says, even though the federal law can itself apply to some works beyond the artist's death.)

Regrettably, the various state laws are neither uniform nor, on the whole, much better thought out than the federal. For example, Connecticut prohibits intentional alteration or defacement of a work of fine art, and gives an artist the right to claim (but, curiously, not to disclaim) authorship. Maine, New Jersey, New York, and Rhode Island give a full right of attribution and also prohibit the display or publication of a work with attribution to the artist if the work has been "altered, defaced, mutilated, or modified" without the artist's approval, but they do not prohibit the defacement itself. California and Massachusetts give the artist a cause of action for unauthorized modification or destruction; Louisiana and Pennsylvania go so far as to declare that negligent conservation and grossly negligent maintenance are actionable by the artist. This crazy patchwork of laws makes for a most unsatisfactory situation.[44]

The moral right is a highly personal right that aims to protect the artist's honor and reputation, and to preserve our common cultural heritage. The *droit de suite* is often mentioned in the same breath with it, but is really a very different creature.

The *Droit de Suite*

The *droit de suite* is the right of an artist to be paid a royalty on profits made from resale of his or her work. It has long been the rule in France and a few other countries; in the United States only California has ever had such a statute, and it was ruled unconstitutional in 2012 after 34 years of desultory existence.[45] The grounds of unconstitutionality would not prevent the California legislature from enacting a version of it that applied only to sales in California, but the likelihood of the legislature doing so seems remote.

Tellingly, perhaps, the London art market (where until recently no resale royalty applied) has for decades far exceeded that of Paris. But under pressure of an EU directive intended to harmonize the European art market, the UK imposed a resale royalty on the works of living artists in 2006.[46] In early 2012, that was extended to the works of deceased artists. London dealers and auctioneers naturally fear all this will drive sales to New York, Switzerland, and Hong Kong. However, the maximum royalty that may be paid is €12,500—a pittance where major works are concerned—so the effect may be modest.

In the area of rights as in other areas, semiconductor chip masks are subject to special limitations. The copyright owner of a mask has the exclusive right to

Mask Works

reproduce the work by optical, electronic, or other means, and to distribute chips in which the mask work is embodied. The other rights generally afforded copyright owners are denied. Like most other copyright owners, the owner of a mask work loses control of the distribution of chips once they are sold.

THE COMPULSORY LICENSES

7

Implicit in the ownership of property is the privilege of determining who reaps the profits of it and what those profits will be. This is true of copyright no less than of other kinds of property. But in recent decades our laws have tended to make exceptions to this privilege; in the case of copyright these are the so-called compulsory licenses.

The most venerable of the compulsory licenses affects the right to make and distribute phonorecords of non-dramatic musical compositions. In essence, once phonorecords of a piece of music have been distributed to the public in the United States (and remember that a movie soundtrack is not a phonorecord), any other person may make another sound recording of the work and distribute phonorecords of this recording.[1] Moreover, and more important, the artist who records the work under a compulsory license may arrange the music, though not the accompanying words, to suit his own style or interpretation, if he does not change the basic melody or what the statute calls, with admirable complacency, the "fundamental character" of the work. What "fundamental character" means no one

The Phonorecord Licenses

knows, and no one has shown any eagerness to find out in court.

This license is called in the music industry a "mechanical license," reflecting its origins in the early days of recorded music. What inspired it was the concern that a single company was buying up all available rights to make piano rolls of popular music, threatening the creation of a monopoly. Many in the industry and elsewhere believe it has outlived its usefulness, but I see no realistic likelihood of its repeal.

There are two ways to obtain a mechanical license: the statutory route and the private route. To take the former, one must serve notice by registered or certified mail on whoever owns the underlying copyright in the musical work. If there are two or more owners, only one needs to be served.[2] If the records of the Copyright Office do not identify the copyright owner or do not give an address, or if the last known address yields no results, notice may be served instead on the Copyright Office. Except where delivery cannot be made at the last known address, the Copyright Office charges a fee for this filing. (See http://www.copyright.gov/docs/fees.html for the current fee.) The filing can be made in paper form or electronically; if you are interested in the latter, contact the Copyright Office at licensing@loc.gov or at (202) 707-8150.

If the person seeking the compulsory license does not serve notice one way or another before distributing any phonorecords or within 30 days after he makes his first phonorecord, he cannot obtain a compulsory license, and his phonorecords will be copyright infringements.

At the top the notice should bear the caption, "Notice of Intention to Obtain a Compulsory License for Making and Distributing Phonorecords." It should state the title of the work and the names of the author or authors, so far as they are known. It should contain the following information about the person or entity seeking the license:[3]

1. The full legal name. All trade names and stage names used in the record business should also be listed, even if they are not going to be used in connection with this particular work. For example, if Bridget Mahoney, known to the world as Wanda Waverly, intends to take out the license, she should list both her names.

2. The full and complete business address used in the record business. A post office box number or similar address is not sufficient unless there is no street address.

3. A statement of the type of business organization used in connection with the record business—for example, individual proprietorship, partnership, corporation, or charitable foundation. Publicly traded companies must identify themselves as such; other corporations must list their directors and officers and the names of every stockholder owning 25 percent of more of their stock. (The true beneficial owner is what is wanted here; if the stock is held by a trustee for someone else's benefit, the beneficiary's name must be given.) Every noncorporate organization must list the names of every true owner (beneficial owner) of 25 percent or more of the enterprise, and if any of these is itself an organization, it has to be identified in the same way as for actual licensees. Suppose that a private individual forms a joint venture with a corporation to make records. The joint venture is the licensee, but the corporation's officers, directors, and so forth must still be listed.

4. The accounting year. For example, if a company seeking the license keeps its books and pays its taxes on a June 30 fiscal year, that must be stated.

5. Every type of phonorecord that the licensee will publish, such as cassette or compact disc.

6. The intended date of publication.

7. The name of the principal recording artist or group that is or will be involved.

8. The catalog number or numbers that published phonorecords will bear.

The notice has to be signed, and the name of the person signing has to be legibly printed.

If you are the copyright owner in the musical work, you will not receive any royalties under the compulsory license until the copyright has been registered and any other documents necessary to identify you have been recorded. However, these filings are not onerous, and they are all you need to do to receive a compulsory license royalty.

The amount of the royalty to be paid on each phonorecord distributed under a compulsory license—including permanent digital downloads—stood in early 2012 at either $0.091 for each separate work on the phonorecord or $0.0175 per minute of playing time for each separate work, whichever might be larger. The rate for ringtones—a surprisingly lucrative market for music copyright owners—stood much higher, at 24 cents. (These rates are subject to periodic increase to account for inflation, through proceedings before the Copyright Royalty Board, a tribunal organized by the Copyright Office.) There is also a complicated royalty arrangement for downloads that remain available to the user for limited periods of time, including certain kinds of streaming.[4]

Royalties for physical phonorecords, permanent downloads, and ringtones must be paid every month, on or before the twentieth day of the month. Once a year every person making phonorecords under a compulsory license must send to the copyright owner an accounting statement, certified by a certified public accountant, showing how many phonorecords he has distributed and any other relevant information. Failure to pay royalties on a monthly basis and to file accounts when they are due can result in loss of the license.

It is important to remember that royalties are to be paid to the copyright owner. This is the person who owns the sound recording right in the musical work, for that is the right that is being sublicensed here. In almost all cases this will be the composer or someone (the "music publisher," in industry parlance) who has obtained the basic copyright from the composer.

There are several qualifications to the compulsory license:

1. It may be obtained only if the primary purpose of producing phonorecords under it is to distribute them to the public for private use. Phonorecords made primarily for broadcasting or for background music systems cannot be made under a compulsory license. These must be expressly authorized by the copyright owner. However, sale of a phonorecord to a broadcaster, if the phonorecord is available to the general public, would not invalidate the compulsory license.

2. It may be obtained only if phonorecords have already been distributed with the permission of the owner of the underlying copyright in the music. In other words, the music copyright owner has the right to control the first release of a phonorecord; only after that does the compulsory license kick

in. The distribution of a bootlegged phonorecord, being an infringement, does not give rise to a compulsory license in anyone else.

3. The compulsory license does not permit a subsequent producer simply to duplicate a recording made by someone else.

4. Every sound recording made under a compulsory license is copyrightable as a derivative work. But an arrangement of the music, made to suit the style or interpretation of a particular performer, will not be deemed a derivative work and cannot be copyrighted except with the express consent of the music copyright owner.

5. As noted above, the compulsory license may be lost if royalties are not paid on time and if the required monthly and yearly statements of account are not sent to the copyright owner on time. In the case of such a default, the copyright owner may give written notice to the licensee, and if the matter is not remedied within 30 days, the license will terminate. If the license terminates, continuing to make or distribute phonorecords will be regarded as infringement of the copyright.

Here endeth the lesson as regards the statutory mechanical license. It underpins the private mechanical license by setting the basic parameters of royalty etc., but most performers do not go through the complexities of obtaining a compulsory license. Instead, they deal directly with the copyright owner or with the Harry Fox Agency, Inc., a large phonorecord license clearinghouse located in New York City. "Harry Fox licenses," as they are called, are much simpler to obtain and administer, and are generally considered safer for someone who wishes to adapt music to his or her own style.

As noted in chapter 6, the right of sound recording copyright owners to control digital transmission of their works is subject to a compulsory license. It applies to performances by subscription transmitters, who are eligible for the license so long as they offer fixed programming rather than custom programming or programming on demand, and so long as they do not exceed certain ceilings on the amount of material used. This favored class of digital transmitters includes "webcasters," who transmit music on the Internet (and are often referred to as "Internet radio"). It does not include persons who use music as background for other commercial transactions. The rules for this statutory license are complex and will not be examined here; the royalty rates are set by periodic settlements among the interested parties.[5] It is worth noting that in creating this license Congress took the unusual step of specifying exactly how the statutory license fee gets divided, as a result of intensive lobbying and private negotiations. Fifty percent goes to whoever owns the sound record performance right, and 45 percent to the featured artist(s); these royalties are collected and distributed by a nonprofit corporation called SoundExchange.[6] The remaining 5 percent is divided evenly among two funds, one for nonfeatured musicians and one for nonfeatured vocalists; these funds are distributed among all musicians and vocalists who have performed on sound recordings.

Digital Transmission of Sound Recordings

Cable transmission of a broadcast signal is a performance (or with respect to works of art, a display) of the broadcast content. However, some cable transmissions need not obtain a copyright license, others can acquire a compulsory license, and still others must negotiate a license from the content owners.

The Cable Broadcasting License

Cable transmission of a network broadcast signal need not be licensed so long as it complies with three rules. The first rule is that the cable system may not make any change in the given program, or any change in the advertisements that immediately precede or follow the program or are interspersed in the program. The reason such alterations constitute infringement is that a cable system that indulges in them is really playing the role of broadcaster, not simply of transmitter, and also is interfering with the justifiable expectations of advertisers. This rule is not absolute; alteration of advertisements is permitted for the purposes of advertising market research, if the research company doing the alteration has obtained the agreement of the advertiser, the broadcaster, and the cable system itself. Also there are certain circumstances under which the Federal Communications Commission permits or even requires alterations of the content of the signals. These exceptions, however, are of minor importance.

The second rule is that the cable transmission must be "simultaneous"; it may not be recorded and then transmitted at a later time. The only exception is in the case of cable transmissions made in Alaska, Hawaii, or any U.S. possession or protectorate, and this exception is available only if the videotape copy made by the cable system is performed only once and is not changed in any way, and only if the cable system takes steps to ensure that no duplicate is made of its videotape. (The owner or other officers of the cable system must file a public affidavit that those steps have been taken.)

The third rule is that cable transmission must be made available to the general public. Unless required by the FCC, any transmission that is made to a limited group, such as a group of pay-television customers, will infringe copyright unless authorized by the owner of the performance or display right.

A cable transmission that violates any of these three rules is an infringement. Interestingly, it becomes subject to suit not just by the copyright owners affected but by other stakeholders as well. The broadcast station in which the copyrighted work was included can sue, even though it may have only a nonexclusive license. Furthermore, if the cable system has altered the content of a cabled program, the statute gives every broadcaster in the area where the cable system operates the right to sue, regardless of whether the broadcaster has any interest whatsoever in the particular copyright being infringed.[7]

By contrast to this construct for network broadcasts, the transmission of *nonnetwork* programs is subject to a compulsory license, but the license royalties apply only to transmission outside the area served by the broadcaster.

Computation of the compulsory license royalties is extraordinarily complicated. The royalties are paid into the Copyright Office for distribution by the Copyright Royalty Board. Anyone who wishes to assert a claim to such royalties must file the claim during July of any given year.

Every cable system must file a statement with the Copyright Office twice a year, listing all the broadcasting stations whose broadcasts it has transmitted during the previous six months. It is not required to identify the individual works it has transmitted. Thus, a burden of vigilance falls on those who would assert rights to the royalty pot.

Who is entitled to present a claim? The answer to this question depends on who owns the broadcast performance right in the work or the broadcast display right. If an author has written a play, for example, and granted a producer the exclusive right to perform that play by means of broadcasting media, the producer is the person who has the right to present a claim, not the author. If an artist has granted the producer a nonexclusive right to include a painting in the set of the play, the artist is the one who should present the claim related to that painting.

The Public Broadcasting License

This license is for the benefit of PBS, National Public Radio, and other noncommercial broadcasters. It is a fairly narrow license, permitting only the performance of published nondramatic musical works and the display of published works of art.[8] It also permits a public broadcasting station or network to tape a show in which the performance or display occurs and reuse the tape. It is not, however, a license to dramatize a musical work or to make any other kind of derivative work; nor does it extend to display of any *compilation* of works of art.

The license will supersede any privately negotiated license not recorded with the Copyright Office within 30 days of execution. Most affected industry groups have negotiated licenses with the public broadcasting entities.

Every public broadcaster is required to keep cue sheets and other records concerning its uses under the license, and you as a copyright owner have the right to see them. You are not obliged to take any affirmative steps; the broadcaster will forward your royalties to you. However, if you do not register your copyrights, the broadcaster may not know where to find you and after three years will not be obliged to pay you.[9]

The Satellite Transmission License

The counterpart to the cable compulsory license is the compulsory license for satellite transmission of television broadcasts.[10] The license is complicated, and to parse it thoroughly here would be inconsiderate to the reader. The salient points are these:

- For a satellite company retransmitting broadcasts of "superstations," the license applies not only to transmissions directly to home satellite dishes but also to transmissions to intermediary carriers such as local cable companies that capture the signal and deliver it to households.

- For a satellite company that wishes to retransmit network broadcasts, the license applies only where viewers cannot receive network broadcasts directly and do not subscribe to cable.

- As with royalties for the compulsory cable television license, royalties from the satellite license are held in escrow by the Copyright Office and divided up by the Copyright Royalty Board.

- Since 1992, fees have been established by negotiations.

As of this writing, these three broadcast-related compulsory licenses—the cable license, the satellite license, and the public broadcasting license—may be nearing the end of their useful lives. The Copyright Office has issued a lengthy report recommending their elimination. This is no surprise, as the Office has always disapproved of compulsory licenses as a matter of principle. However, the fact that this report was made at the specific request of certain key members of Congress suggests there is now some real momentum in that direction.

The Digital Audiotape License

One of the most heated copyright controversies of the early 1990s was the dispute over digital audio recording technology (DART). The cause of the discord was that DART would permit a consumer to make a tape copy of any digital sound record. Because the recording being copied is in digital form, the copy will be perfect, without the degradation that inevitably occurs in making a conventional analog copy. Understandably, the U.S. recording industry at first viewed the advent of consumer versions of this technology with dread.

Just as politicians speak of the "lessons of Vietnam," the recording industry spoke of the "lessons of the Betamax [home video recording] battle," in which home VCR technology had become widespread by the time a lawsuit to stop it came to fruition. The movie industry lost the public relations battle over VCR technology long before it lost its case in court. The lesson: stop any copying technology before it can establish itself as a public "entitlement."

The recording industry had sufficient lobbying muscle to stop the invasion of DART recorders at the water's edge, so to speak, and it did so. But the electronics manufacturing industry was not without powerful friends, and in the end a legislative compromise was worked out that amounts to something unprecedented in this country: a compulsory license of the right to sell technology that will enable consumers to make copies of copyrighted works.[11]

Manufacturers of digital audio recording equipment and blank recording media (tapes, disks, etc.) are required to give notice to the Copyright Office of each new technology they introduce into the marketplace, and to pay a royalty on sales into the Copyright Office. The royalties thus collected are to be distributed to affected copyright owners, using the same rough justice as already applies to cable royalties and the like. Most important from the consumer's point of view is that though the consumer is now expressly permitted to copy both analog and digital sound recordings for private, noncommercial use, all digital audio recorders must contain a device that will prevent them from copying *copies* of digital recordings. In practical terms, consumers are free to copy digital recordings as legitimately transmitted, and to copy digital recordings sold by the recording industry, but not to copy second-generation copies. And from the tapes and recorders they buy, a cut will go to the copyright owners whose products they are presumed to be copying.

From the point of view of the music industry, this was at the time a major victory, with one possibly bittersweet aspect: for the first time, performers of sound recordings are given a vested financial interest in the revenues from those recordings. Not only the lead performers but also the backup vocalists and musicians are entitled to shares to the kitty formed from the DART compulsory license fund. However, due to changes in the technology of music distribution, royalties have been steadily declining, and will likely continue to do so.

Court-Imposed Licenses

Courts often become involved in interpreting licensing agreements, when disputes arise between the parties over questions such as what technologies were meant to be covered. Rarely, though, do courts attempt to second-guess the pricing of a contract; judges have no training for that sort of thing. Notable exceptions have arisen in cases involving governmental regulation of licenses. In the copyright arena, the most significant of these have been the cases involving the performing rights societies ASCAP and BMI. These societies were sued by the U.S. Department of Justice on antitrust grounds over the validity of the "blanket licenses" they offered to restaurants, hotels, and other public users of music. (I discuss these in more detail in chapter 6.) The government withdrew its claims in return for the societies' agreeing to certain fee structures. Those fee structures are revised periodically, always subject to ongoing oversight by the federal district court located in New York City.

Proprietors of bars, restaurants, and other places where music is performed have the right to challenge the fairness of the societies' fees not in general, but as applied to their particular establishments.[12] Thus, the owner of the Sidetrack Tap in Lake Wobegon, Minnesota, may sue claiming that to charge him, say, $650 a year for the right to use BMI's repertoire is unfair because, although he offers live music in a bar that seats 100 people, he actually has live music on the premises only on Christmas Eve. Jurisdiction over such cases lies not only in the Southern District of New York but also in ten other courts around the country.

This special type of proceeding hands the publican a gun with one bullet. That is to say, a proprietor can sue each performing rights society only once. Furthermore, even if the bullet hits the target, it helps no one but the plaintiff: Congress has also provided that the outcome in any given case cannot be used as precedent in any other. This lack of precedential value creates a risk of inconsistent litigation, especially from region to region. (One may assume that within any of the eleven designated courts there will be a fair degree of consistency.) It appears that the prevailing party in any such action is eligible to recover its attorney's fees, but one cannot say for certain. Given the expense of litigation, and the relatively minor sums at issue, perhaps it is no surprise that as of this writing, there is not a single reported decision of any litigation under this section of the Act.

The idea that courts are qualified to determine the fairness of licensing fees may strike you as odd. If so, it may worry you that Congress seems to have developed a taste for this sort of thing. The United States' GATT-implementing legislation empowers courts to set reasonable royalty rates for ongoing use of specific "existing derivative works" based on specific restored copyrights. (See chapter 10 for a detailed discussion of this.) At the time of enactment this was a highly unusual, if not unprecedented, mandate. Time will tell whether it will prove a model for solving problems of this sort, or an example of what not to do.

INFRINGEMENT   8

If copyright is like property in land, infringement is like moving onto someone's land without permission, chopping down trees, mining coal, and stealing water from the well. But unlike boundaries in land, the boundaries of a copyright are never clearly defined and frequently are not known until the end of a lawsuit. I can give, then, only general guidelines for determining those boundaries ahead of time.

Some cases are relatively easy. If an artist claims that someone has performed or displayed his work or made and sold copies of it without his permission, he has raised a simple question of fact. Either the defendant did these deeds or he did not. The difficult infringement cases are those in which the artist claims that someone else's creation is so like his or her own that it infringes the underlying copyright in his or her work. The legal phrase for non-verbatim copying is "substantial similarity"—a phrase so obviously subjective that one can only pity the judges and juries who must try to apply it, and particularly the judges who must try to squeeze their gut reactions into a rational legal explanation.

In the early days of copyright law, the only theft for which the law took retribution was theft of the exact words of a writing. However, as the literary marketplace grew and new forms of literature emerged, and as the public began to pay more attention to the artist and the demands of the artistic ego, this literalism became untenable.[1] In the past few decades it is doubtful that even five infringement suits out of one hundred have charged the defendant with actually using the plaintiff's language, word for word. Suits now are more likely to allege theft of plot, theft of characters, theft of musical theme, and so on. Necessarily in such cases the courts make judgments that are at least partly intuitive.

How Does a Court Find Infringement?

The following are some of the factors that a court will consider when someone claims copyright infringement:

Did the defendant see or otherwise have knowledge of the plaintiff's work? If not, the defendant will not be regarded as an infringer. This is a corollary of the doctrine of subjective originality, which I have discussed in chapter 1. Knowledge of a prior work, however, does not have to be conscious; the plaintiff will win if he can prove that the defendant must have been exposed to the work, even though the defendant may honestly have forgotten the event entirely. Sometimes that "must have" is proven by similarity so striking that no other explanation is plausible.[2]

Is the plaintiff's work original? This question is closely similar to the previous one, only we are asking now whether the plaintiff himself has a valid copyright on which to sue. If the elements he claims are infringed are things that in fact he took from someone else's work, whether knowingly or not, his copyright claim in those elements is invalid.

Is the copied material expression that can be protected, or is it only the author's ideas, or historical fact, or the like? Like the first two questions, this is a threshold test that, if determined adversely to the plaintiff, will be fatal to his case. As discussed in chapter 1, this analysis can become quite complicated, especially as regards computer programs, in which courts must try to determine what elements are dictated by considerations of efficiency and the like.

When the suit charges theft of a story line in a novel or movie, courts will look at how closely the defendant's details track the plaintiff's. (Also, are the details unusual, or are they the sort that anyone would be likely to choose who set out to write a variation on the same old theme?) One famous copyright judge has suggested that upon any work "a great number of patterns of increasing generality will fit equally well" and that at some level of generality copying must be excused.[3] The same judge once observed that no one ever has reliably defined, or ever will be able to define, the boundary between idea and expression.

A related question is, *Is the similarity between the works dictated by their subject matter?* Remember that where there are only a limited number of ways of expressing an idea, the "merger" doctrine denies copyright to any of them. Even if merger does not apply, where a copyright is "thin" due to the shortage of feasible alternative expressions, courts will not find infringement unless the copying is virtually identical.[4]

Details can be misleading, and to avoid this danger courts will frequently step back some distance and ask, *What is the intent of the two works?* If characters, for example, or sequences of musical notes seem similar in certain particulars but are, taken as a whole, quite different from each other, the court will be less likely to find infringement.

In considering infringement claims, courts will generally shy away from the type of close textual analysis used in doctoral dissertations; they will look at the two works from the standpoint of an ordinary observer.[5] This does not mean that they will ignore copying merely because the offending work contains some original matter. A thief is liable for what he has stolen, even if he has possessions of his own; an infringer is liable for what he has copied, whether or not he has added to it material of his own invention.[6] On the other hand, what has been taken must be more than what the law calls "de minimis," more than slight or trivial.[7]

The "ordinary observer" test is certainly appropriate for most works. It is probably not appropriate for highly technical works such as computer programs, and, as I predicted in an earlier edition of this book, courts are coming increasingly to rely on expert opinions in such fields.[8] Less persuasively, courts have also held that works addressed to a juvenile audience should be judged by how children, not adults, would perceive them.[9] Perhaps this is valid, but I am skeptical that we can reliably determine how children perceive "substantial similarity." Furthermore, we should be wary of fragmenting the audience test, for we then run the risk of having a different standard for every sort of work, and thus becoming dependent on surveys and "experts" to tell us whether infringement has occurred.[10]

Finally, new media technologies have forced courts to ask, in some cases, a new question: *Who is actually doing the copying*? These technologies have blurred the traditional line between the active distributor of programming and the passive customer/recipient. Thus, the Second Circuit had to deal with Cablevision's "Remote Storage-DVR" system, which allocated a small portion of a central server to each of its customers, on which the customer could cause a program to be recorded for later viewing. The broadcasting companies alleged that Cablevision was engaged in unauthorized reproduction, since the reproduction was done on its server using its elaborate technical system. The broadcasters also alleged that, in the aggregate, customers' playbacks amounted to unauthorized public performance. The court disagreed on both counts. Since each Cablevision customer controlled his own little piece of Cablevision's server, Cablevision lacked the necessary "volition" to be found liable for direct infringement. (Plaintiffs had waived their claims for contributory infringement, so the court did not have to reach that issue.) It also held there was no public performance, noting that "each RS-DVR playback transmission is made to a single subscriber using a single unique copy produced by that subscriber."[11] This ruling has encouraged the growth of cloud-based "locker" systems where users can store copies of music for their own use by Internet devices.

Taking this precedent to heart, a start-up company called Aereo created a system that allowed it to sell each customer a small piece of its antenna and server, and made it possible for the customer not only to create a remote personal copy of a broadcast program but also to view the program via Internet streaming in almost real time, with only a few seconds' delay. The court found this legally indistinguishable from the facts in the Cablevision case, because again the consumer had complete control over the reproduction and transmission of the content.[12]

Although the court did not make anything of it, to me it is significant that the Aereo service operated only in the user's home market. It thus made available to its customers only signals that they could receive free on their television set, and which local cable channels would, for the most part, be able to supply to them without a license. A California court, likewise overlooking this fact, came to the opposite (and I believe wrong) result.[13] The Supreme Court will rule on this in 2014.

Infringement in the Visual Arts

Where works of visual art are concerned, certain special problems exist. Many piracies that offend our moral sense are not, strictly speaking, infringements. For example, imitation of style, though frequently egregious and irritating, and possibly a violation of other laws,[14] is not copyright infringement unless concrete elements of previous works are plagiarized. The many famous fakes that have been painted of twentieth-century artists, to the extent that they imitate style—brushwork, use of light, type of subject, and so on—and do not actually replicate elements of pictures by the real artist, are not copyright infringements. The fakers might be sued on other grounds—for example, for fraud—but this is an ordinary action at common law and has nothing to do with copyright.

In the area of visual arts, the problem of subject matter becomes particularly acute. The physical world is of course in the public domain. Any number of artists can paint a face, a harbor, or a street without infringing each other's copyrights. As Justice Oliver Wendell Holmes said, "Others are free to copy the original. They are not free to copy the copy."[15] Does this mean that anyone is free to photograph Yosemite from the same angles as Ansel Adams did, without liability to Adams's estate? Perhaps so, but surely one is not free to copy the special effects Adams achieved through his use of special filters, lenses, and development techniques.

Difficulties multiply when we talk of arranged subjects. In a well-known case involving a posed photograph of Oscar Wilde, it was held that a photographer's copyright covers any arrangement he makes of natural objects to compose his shot.[16] Should the rule foreclose another photographer from shooting the same subject with different filters and special effects? Or in the realm of painting, should an artist who paints a still life of an identical composition but in a radically different style be considered an infringer? My personal belief is that he should not. What would such a rule have done to the great visual dialogues among the impressionists, or between Picasso and Braque? Perhaps fortunately, no case on point has yet arisen.

It is generally agreed that when two works are being compared, all material that is unprotected by copyright should be excluded from the analysis; one should not give the plaintiff any subconscious credit for material he doesn't own.[17] This is fairly easy to do where literary works are concerned, because we perceive such works one word at a time. Where visual works are involved, though, the task is much harder; we tend to perceive such works as totalities. More than one court has gone seriously astray by overlooking this problem, and the proper procedure for judging infringement in visual works remains one of the most perplexing questions in all of copyright law.

Suing the Infringer

An infringer is anyone who violates any of the rights created by law. Suppose you have written a story that someone in Hollywood adapts into a screenplay without your permission. You may sue not only that scriptwriter but also the studio, the film distributors, and the movie theater where the movie is shown ("performed").

Infringement liability extends beyond those who actually participated in the infringing conduct. For example, bars and restaurants often find themselves on the hook for infringing performances on their premises even if they had no role in deciding what music would be performed there. So long as they had the theoretical right and ability to control the performance, and benefited from it financially, they have what is called "vicarious liability" for the infringement. And the performance of music in a commercial setting like a bar or restaurant is presumed to benefit the owner financially. As Justice Holmes once famously remarked, "if music did not pay, it would be given up."[18]

Furthermore, even if the owner of the premises is a corporation, individual officers of that corporation may have personal liability for the infringement if they had the requisite authority and personal financial stake.[19]

Another sort of infringement liability attaches to people who induce or contribute to an infringement without directly taking part in it. Thus, someone who provides architectural plans to a builder who, he knows, intends to use them to build an infringing building would be guilty of what is called "contributory infringement." The purveyors of Grokster software were held liable for inducing infringement because they distributed the software knowing it would be used primarily for illegal sharing of music MP3 files, and indeed promoted that very use in a wink-and-nod sort of way.[20]

A copyright infringement suit must be brought in federal court within three years of the time that the infringement took place, unless the infringement was hidden from view, in which case the statute begins to run from the date the infringement was discovered. However, this three-year limit is a rolling one, because the law regards each separate copy, distribution, performance, and so on as a separate infringement. So if an infringing book was published in 2010 and you bring suit in 2014, you can still receive damages, but only for copies made or distributed from 2011 on.[21]

As is discussed in detail in chapter 5, for most works of U.S. origin it is necessary to register a copyright in order to sue upon it. And for all works, regardless of origin, registration must be made within three months of first publication, or in the case of unpublished works must precede the infringement, for statutory damages and legal fees to be recoverable. The possibility of an attorney's fee award is often a key element in both parties' assessment of a case, and prompt registration is for this reason highly advisable.

Only a person who owns the particular right that has been infringed, or who owns that right jointly with others, or who is entitled to royalties from that right, can sue.[22] Suppose that a playwright has sold stage performance rights in his play to a Broadway producer for $200,000 and has sold the motion picture rights to United Artists for cash plus a share of profits. Suppose someone has surreptitiously videorecorded a performance of the play and posts the video file online. Who can sue? United Artists can, because it owns the movie rights, and the author can, because he is entitled to royalties from the movie rights. However, the Broadway producer cannot bring suit even though he may stand to lose box office revenues, because he has no ownership interest in the particular right—the motion picture right—that has been infringed.

For another example, suppose that a singer sets up a trust for the benefit of her child and transfers to it the right to exploit her sound recordings. In such a case either the trustee or the child can bring suit, because the trustee is the legal owner of the copyright and the child is entitled to the profits.

To return to the example of the play, the fact that the Broadway producer cannot bring suit does not necessarily mean that he will never get into court. Quite the contrary. If his interest is likely to be affected by the outcome of the suit, the law requires that he be given notice of it, and he will then be able, at the court's discretion, to join in the fray. The law requires that notice be given to every person whose interest in the work may be affected, and the court may even require that persons whose claims could not possibly be affected also receive notice. All of these people can join in the lawsuit, if the court permits.[23]

Monetary recovery in an infringement suit may take the form of actual damages and, to the extent that they exceed the plaintiff's lost profits, the profits that the infringer has made.[24] To put it another way, the plaintiff is entitled to recover the damages he has suffered, or the illicit profits the infringer has made, whichever is greater.

Actual damages can include lost profits, compensation for injury to reputation, and compensation for loss of business opportunity (difficult to prove, but valuable if you can prove it). Profits must be actually attributable to the infringement. In a famous illustrative case, the court awarded the plaintiff only a fraction of the profits that had been made by an infringing motion picture, because it found that much of the movie's success was due to the fame of the leading actor and actress.[25] However, the burden of proving which profits did not derive from the infringement lies on the infringer.

If at any time during the lawsuit it appears that you will not be able to prove actual damages or the infringer's profits, or if the amount you can prove seems small relative to the expense of proof or the moral turpitude of the defendant, you should consider electing to receive statutory damages. Statutory damages are in the discretion of the court—or of the jury, in jury cases—and are often set at a goodly sum to punish the wrongdoer. They cannot be less than $200—and that minimum figure will be applied only if the infringer can prove that he had no reason to believe that he was committing an infringement. If he cannot prove this, damages will be not less than $750 and not more than $30,000, unless you in turn can prove that the infringer committed the infringement willfully, in which case you may be awarded as much as $150,000. (For mask works the maximum is $250,000.) These figures are for all infringements of any one work, by each infringer or group of jointly liable infringers.[26] For this purpose all parts of a collective work are treated as a single work, unless they have been published separately prior to being compiled. Thus, a music copyright owner was entitled to only a single award when multiple songs on its album were infringed, because the songs had not been issued separately before the album.[27]

Infringement is willful if carried out with knowing or reckless disregard of the plaintiff's rights. The statute includes a rebuttable presumption of willfulness where the infringement is carried out using (as is common in online piracy) a domain name for which the infringer has provided materially false information to the domain name registrar.[28]

Statutory damages can take on a distinctly punitive character. In the course of the recording industry's campaign against illegal downloads and file sharing, two defendants either failed to take this into account or mistakenly believed that jurors would sympathize with them. The jurors did not, and awarded seven-figure damages. Although the courts subsequently reduced the damages awards, they still ended up in the six figures, and the lesson remains.[29]

In addition to damages and profits, you may be reimbursed by the infringer for your court costs and also for your attorney's fees. On the other hand, if you lose your lawsuit you may be required to pay the other side's costs and attorney's fees.[30] Although legal fee awards for either side are discretionary with the court, the default in recent years has been to reimburse the fees of the prevailing party. Since attorney's fees in copyright cases can be substantial, this risk must be a major factor in both parties' assessment of the case.

Whether or not you receive damages, you may receive injunctive relief, which is to say that the infringer will be prohibited from further acts of infringement. Such an injunction is good only against the defendant you have brought to court and anyone acting in concert with him, although it may also serve as a warning to others.

Injunctions may occur both before a case is tried and after. Copyright plaintiffs frequently seek so-called "preliminary injunctions," that is, injunctions against any further infringing acts by the defendant while the case is in progress. To achieve such an injunction gives the plaintiff enormous leverage for settlement, since the defendant faces immediate loss of revenue and of investment. For that reason courts will not grant such relief lightly. The plaintiff must show not only that he is likely to win the case when it is eventually tried, but also that he will suffer "irreparable harm"—harm that cannot be compensated by any eventual damage award—unless the injunction is granted, and that the harm to him from allowing the defendant to continue exceeds the harm the defendant will suffer from an injunction. The same balancing of harm may apply to a post-trial injunction, but once a plaintiff has definitively won his case a court is likely to decide that the infringement must stop.[31]

The Sovereign Immunity Problem

One rather large group of possible infringers is exempt from any sort of copyright damages, and that group consists of the fifty states. Although Congress enacted legislation specifically subjecting the states to damages for violation of the copyright and patent laws, the Supreme Court, in a patent case, held that Congress had exceeded its authority; the states, it said, are immune from such suits under the Eleventh Amendment to the Constitution. It took no time for a lower court to extend the same reasoning to copyright.[32]

The one exception to state immunity is a suit for injunctive relief. A copyright owner may sue to prevent ongoing or anticipated infringement, but the suit must be brought against individual state officials, not the state as such.[33]

Indian tribes are immune to copyright infringement suits on a different but analogous basis. It is not clear whether the workaround just described—suit for injunctive relief against individual tribal officials—is available. Probably it is, but the one case involving a tribal defendant did not reach that issue.[34]

Imagine you have found a work you want to use, but you cannot identify the copyright owner. It may be a photograph that would perfectly illustrate a point in your new book, or a magazine article from the 1960s that you want to include in an anthology, or a novel you would like to turn into a play. What do you do?

Orphan Works

Welcome to the world of "orphan works."

There is a sizeable and growing body of such material. Works can become "orphans" in many different ways. Some were never formally published but simply circulated among friends and colleagues, and over time the authorship attribution (if it was ever attached) has become separated from the work. Some were ephemera or created for short-term commercial use, and no one ever expected them to have lasting value, so no one bothered to take credit for them, let alone register them. Some were published by companies that have gone out of existence, and there is no trace left of the company that published them—and if you could find some trace of the company, good luck finding what happened to its intellectual property when it gave up the ghost. And then of course there are those for which you have, tantalizingly, an author's name, but who knows where John Smith lived, or died, and who his heirs were?

The problem such works pose has been compounded by the elimination of the renewal requirement for works published after 1963. (See chapter 10.) A work of ephemera from 1965, say, that you could once have confidently assumed would never have been registered, let alone renewed in 1993, must now be assumed to be under copyright, so long as the copy you have meets the formality requirements that applied in 1965, i.e., bears a proper copyright notice.

Everyone agrees this is a big problem, but finding a comprehensive solution has proved exceedingly difficult. In 2008 competing bills were introduced in the House and Senate; the Senate bill passed and it looked for a while as if Congress might actually enact a law, but it was a Presidential election year and Congress recessed before acting on the legislation. Since then it has lain dormant, although in October of 2012 the Copyright Office published a Notice of Inquiry in an effort to revive the project.

A few principles seem to be agreed. First, if you make an objectively reasonable inquiry and cannot find the copyright owner, you should be able to use the work, and if the copyright owner later surfaces, your liability for damages should be limited to paying reasonable compensation—what you would have paid in an arm's-length bargain—and injunctive relief should be disfavored, especially where you have incorporated the orphan work in a derivative work that contains significant new creative material. As a Senator deeply involved in copyright matters said back in 2008, "By providing an incentive to search, in the form of a limitation on remedies, more users will find more owners;

more works otherwise hidden will be used; and more copyright owners will receive compensation."[35]

Second, you must give proper attribution when you use a work, to the extent you can, and include a notice identifying the material as orphan material. Third, there needs to be some consensus, perhaps blessed by the Copyright Office after due deliberation, on what an objectively reasonable inquiry would be for each given type of work. Fourth, we need good databases of information, particularly for works of visual art.

On the details, though, especially as to the third and fourth points, there is much disagreement.

The photographers' guilds have been especially nervous about all this, and have made legislative progress agonizingly slow. Their concern is understandable to some degree, especially when you consider how much photographic material now circulates on the Internet, with or without attribution. And the U.S. copyright registration system does not allow photographs to be economically registered, or if registered to be easily identified, at a granular level. Indeed, since our registration system is searchable primarily by title and author, finding in it the copyright owner of a photograph that has come adrift from its title and creator is well nigh impossible. Yet with the growing sophistication of image identification search tools, it ought to be possible to create a good enough public database that photographers who care about protecting their work from the license-by-default can make their claims known. Many of them would probably make money, in the end, that they would not otherwise make.

A number of other countries have enacted limited orphan works legislation, and the EU has adopted a directive requiring orphan work solutions, though chiefly for the benefit of museums and other nonprofit entities.[36] The U.S. legislative solutions that have been proposed, by contrast, would be comprehensive and set an international benchmark.

The fact that the Copyright Office issued a Notice of Inquiry reflects the keen interest of the current Register, Maria Pallante, in this topic. It also suggests there may be renewed stomach in Congress for dealing with this problem. But one should not assume it will come to anything. In the meantime, what is a good-faith would-be user to do?

I have always advised clients facing this situation that, realistically, the risks they run if they undertake a diligent search and find no one from whom to obtain permission is rather small, though they should be prepared to pay a reasonable fee, or perhaps a bit more, if the owner eventually surfaces. I concede this does not apply to all uses across the board. A Hollywood studio would be taking a materially different risk in basing a movie on an orphan novel than a biographer would take in illustrating her book with an orphan portrait of her subject. Yet in the main, I do not believe that a jury is likely to punish a user who made that effort, or give a windfall to some copyright owner who has allowed his work to fall into complete disuse and then comes out of the woodwork when someone else gives it a moment in the sun. Nor do I believe that Congress's failure, thus far, to legislate a solution has changed this fundamental reality.

But what is a "diligent search"? The 2008 bill did not attempt to define that term, but suggested that the Copyright Office, in coming up with recommendations for best practices, should take into account the records available from the Copyright Office itself (i.e., its registration and assignment records), public and private databases, industry practices, the guidelines of any relevant association or organization, and available technology and expert assistance, with the important caveat that the latter should be adopted as best practices "to the extent that the use of such resources is reasonable for, and relevant to, the scope of the intended use." This caveat acknowledges the fact that it may not be reasonable to require a would-be user to undertake a search whose costs are out of proportion to the value of the work and the use.

One positive development in this regard is that all registration and renewal records of the Copyright Office are now available online at http://archive.org/details/copyrightrecords/, and a more easily searchable database of renewals (though for books only) is available at http://collections.stanford.edu/copyrightrenewals. Unfortunately, the Copyright Office records regarding assignment are still available only through a manual search at the Copyright Office, which may be done through a commercial search firm.

Given the wide variety of orphan works, and of the sort of facts that may be available, it is impossible to predict with any certainty what a court might find was "diligent" under any particular circumstances. Whatever you end up doing, though, be very careful to keep notes and document what you have done, in case a copyright owner does emerge to claim his due.

Criminal Infringement

A willful infringer can be prosecuted by the federal government and, if convicted, can be fined or sent to jail or both. Criminal prosecutions are rare, but when they occur the stakes are high: fines up to $250,000, with up to five years in jail for a first offense and up to 10 years in jail for a second offense. Typically, prosecutions under this statute are aimed at video pirates, smugglers of counterfeited goods, and the like. Any willful reproduction or distribution (including by electronic means), during any 180-day period, of a copy or copies having a total retail value of more than $1,000 can be treated as criminal *whether or not the infringer acted with any motive of financial gain.* This provision of the law, contained in the No Electronic Theft Act of 1997, was overtly aimed at people who distribute unauthorized copies of software over the Internet, sometimes for free and sometimes in barter for other pirated software.[37] Note that only reproduction and distribution can lead to criminal liability; illegal performance and display cannot.

Infringement on the Internet, and Other Digital Offenses

The Internet has greatly increased the opportunities for distribution of copyrighted materials. It is changing fundamentally how the copyright industries conduct their business, how they make their money, and how much money they make. It also, of course, has increased the opportunities for unauthorized distribution. Yet despite breathless pronouncements from *Wired* magazine and the like, the end of copyright is not nigh.

In late 1998, Congress enacted the portentously named the Digital Millennium Copyright Act (DMCA), a sweeping attempt to forestall cyberpiracy of every kind. The DMCA regulates in excruciating detail many of the activities that pose the greatest threat to copyright owners. It protects the sanctity of copyright-related information placed on works by their copyright owners. (See the final section of this chapter.) It prohibits unauthorized decryption of encrypted works. It circumscribes the liability of online service providers, including those in academe as well as in commerce, but at the same time places powerful weapons in the hands of copyright owners policing infringement on the Internet. These are only its most prominent features. Much of it is so complicated that no one but those who wrote it (and I'm not sure about them) can read it easily. In the discussion that follows I have endeavored to translate it into plain English, while sacrificing as few details as I could consistent with that goal.

In the digital world an ounce of prevention, if one could get it, would be worth many pounds of cure and many paragraphs of finger-wagging enactments. The prevention that most interests copyright owners at present is encryption.

Encryption and Decryption

Copyright industries have employed, with varying success, techniques such as digital rights management (DRM) to prevent piracy, or at least police it. (DRM is technology that limits access to a digital work to authorized users.) In some instances market blowback has forced copyright owners to retreat, as when the record industry threw in the towel and agreed to let songs be sold without DRM on iTunes—but such efforts are likely to continue.

Encryption, of course, always inspires decryption; locks inspire lock pickers. To prevent this, the DMCA forbids anyone to "manufacture, import, offer to the public, provide, or otherwise traffic in" anything that is designed or produced *primarily* to circumvent technological measures that effectively control access to copyrighted works or that effectively protect the rights of a copyright owner—for example, by making it impossible to copy a work without permission.[38] Technologies that pass this test—i.e., that are not designed or produced primarily for illicit decryption—will nonetheless be banned if their legitimate uses have only limited *commercial* significance (whatever that means). And finally, even if a technology survives both of these cuts, it is unlawful to *market* it as an anticircumvention measure. The only exception to all of this is for measures whose sole purpose is to prevent the access of minors to certain kinds of material on the Internet.

This anticircumvention law is intended to protect the normal rights of copyright owners, not to stifle markets for compatible products. In this spirit the Federal Circuit quite properly denied an anticircumvention claim brought by the maker of a garage door opener against a company whose products circumvented the lockout code embedded in the opener. The court pointed out that the user of the defendant's device did not view, reproduce, or otherwise make any copyright-type use of the door opener; all he did was get into his own garage.[39] In fact, the Federal Circuit has asserted that violation of the DMCA can only be found if the conduct is part of an act of infringement, or facilitates infringement.[40] On this broader principle there is some disagreement, as a company selling "bots" that could play World of Warcraft automatically for their users found out the hard way. When Blizzard Entertainment, the owner of World of Warcraft, created software designed to prevent the use of those bots, and the crafty bot company redesigned its products to evade detection, the Ninth Circuit found it had violated the DMCA. The reason was not that player use of bots infringed Blizzard's copyright, but that Blizzard's protective software was designed to deny access to World of Warcraft by bots.[41]

In addition to cutting off the flow of products that could defeat encryption measures, the statute also forbids anyone from personally gaining unauthorized access to a work by circumventing any technological measure that effectively controls access to the work. However, the Librarian of Congress and the Register of Copyrights are charged with periodically determining whether there are particular classes of works to which this part of the law should not apply. Any such classes of works will be excluded for a three-year, renewable period. The standard for determining to exclude a class of works is that users will be "adversely affected . . . in their ability to make noninfringing uses" of such works.[42] In other words, the technological protection measures at issue must impede genuinely noninfringing—read fair— use of the works. This is a fairly high hurdle.

Despite pleas from various user groups for wide and deep exclusions, the Librarian and Register have tended to grant only rather narrow ones. For the three-year period that began on October 28, 2012, circumvention is allowed in the following circumstances:

- If a blind or otherwise print-disabled person has obtained a lawful copy of a literary work, for which the publisher was appropriately compensated, and the encryption protecting it prevents its use with a reading-aloud device or other assistive technology;

- If the work is a nondramatic literary work, lawfully obtained and used by an "authorized entity" for the blind pursuant to the Chafee Amendment (discussed in chapter 6), and encryption prevents its use with a reading-aloud device or other assistive technology for print-disabled individuals;

- If circumvention is necessary to allow a cell phone to operate a lawfully obtained app (there was also, for the first three months of the period, an exception for decryption necessary to allow a cell phone user to switch his phone to a different service provider);

- If a motion picture is lawfully obtained via online distribution, or is on a DVD protected by a content-scrambling system, and circumvention is reasonably necessary to obtain a high-quality digital file, where only short portions will be used and the use is for criticism or comment in (i) videos created for noncommercial use, (ii) documentary films, (iii) nonfiction multimedia ebooks offering film analysis; and (iv) film studies or other courses requiring close analysis of film and media excerpts;

• If a motion picture is lawfully obtained via online distribution, or is on a DVD protected by a content-scrambling system, and circumvention is solely to access the "playhead" and other time-coding information, in connection with research and development of captioning technology.

In connection with the fourth of these exemptions, the Register heard a lot of argument about "screen capture" technology. She was undecided as to whether such technology offered true decryption or just simple reproduction; user groups pushed hard, wanting to be reassured that use of such technology was permissible. On the other hand, labeling screen capture software as a decryption device could have adverse consequences for those who sell it, by submitting it to scrutiny under the antitrafficking rules. Unwilling to give it a free pass, she came up with a Solomonic decision that the Librarian of Congress endorsed: use of screen capture technology qualifies for the above exclusion only if it is offered to the public as a *noncircumvention* technology, i.e., as a technology for copying already-decrypted motion pictures.

Thus, at the end of a long and arduous process, with reams of testimony leading to a 166-page report,[43] the only exemptions granted were ones that no reasonable observer could possibly find objectionable. This is not the Register's fault. The fault (if it is such) lies in the statute, which requires the Register every three years to run a gauntlet of highly argumentative industry groups to accomplish a very limited objective.

There are also a few permanent exemptions to the broad sweep of this law. One rather odd one permits

nonprofit libraries, archives, and educational institutions to gain unauthorized access to works "solely in
order to make a good-faith determination of whether
to acquire a copy." What the librarians and educators
thought they were getting by this is hard to say; is any
sane copyright owner going to deny a potential customer the right to look at its wares?

More meaningful exemptions apply to law enforcement, intelligence, and other governmental activities.
Others cover bona fide encryption research and security testing. Yet another exemption permits computer
programmers to circumvent protection so as to reverse-
engineer software, to the extent necessary for achieving interoperability with other programs, and permits
the sale of technologies for this purpose. This exemption does not take a position on whether reverse engineering of any particular sort is permissible; it places
the risk of determining that on the programmer. The
risk is not negligible: to the extent that circumvention
is used to facilitate reverse engineering that infringes
copyright, the circumvention is itself unlawful, with
the effect that the programmer concerned may be pun-
ished twice for the same course of conduct. (As I will
discuss in chapter 9, some cases have blessed some
reverse engineering as fair use; beyond the writ of
those cases, you're on your own.)

On a plane more of interest to most of us, the law
permits circumvention for the sole purpose of disabling a function that collects information on the user.
The purpose here is to protect user privacy. The right
to disable does not apply to encryption mechanisms
that give the user clear warning that personal information will be collected and an opportunity to prevent or
restrict such collection. Where one may disable, however, how is one to do that when the statute prevents
the sale of technologies that would enable the

circumvention? Only geeks capable of writing their own code will benefit from this exemption.

The remedies for violation of this section of the statute include both damages and injunctive relief, and "any person injured" by the violation may sue. Damages may be actual damages or statutory damages; repeat offenders may be subject to treble damages. In addition, the court may award attorneys' fees to the prevailing party in any action brought under this section of the law—which may of course be either the plaintiff or the defendant. The range of statutory damages at first looks lower than for actual infringement of copyright—between \$200 and \$2,500—and this tends to protect the private circumventor from outsized liability. On the other hand, statutory damages can be awarded for each "act of circumvention, device, product, component, offer, or performance of service," rather than for each copyrighted work affected. Thus, a company that sells 1,000 decrypting devices can be liable for up to \$2,500,000. (Courts have tended to limit maximum awards to cases of willfulness.) A defendant that shows it had no reason to believe its acts violated the law can have damages reduced or even waived.[44]

Is fair use (discussed in chapter 9) dead as a result of all this? Theoretically, no; the law as such does not in any way limit the defense of fair use. But in practical terms, by restricting access through technological means the law is narrowing the field in which fair use can occur. There is no fair use defense to the charge of circumvention itself, regardless of a defendant's *bona fides* in terms of the ultimate use of the unlocked material.[45] There is likewise no fair use defense for the manufacture of decrypting technologies.[46] Furthermore, by controlling access, copyright owners can compel their customers to sign contracts in which the customers give up rights of fair use. Unless the courts begin to hold that fair use is a constitutional right—something no court has yet done, but perhaps only because the issue has not been squarely presented—fair use could become a historical artifact of the analog age.

What about works that are outside of copyright? One of the disturbing things about this statutory scheme is that, by focusing on the door rather than what lies behind the door, it does not distinguish in its effect between copyrighted material and public domain material. It may well be, for example, that the owners of databases that do not qualify for copyright will lock up their products inside technologies that are used "primarily" by the owners of valid copyrights. Once that happens, the database is effectively given protection by the copyright law—by this odd new part of the copyright law that attempts to control the flow of allegedly dangerous technology.

I am concerned, in short, by the sweeping breadth of this addition to the copyright law. Its conception and birth took place largely out of the public eye, although the public will be directly impacted by it to a major extent. Granted, there were voices speaking up for users of copyrighted materials, but they were special-interest groups themselves, and in the end were bought off with some exclusions that don't do much for the ordinary citizen. It seems a mistake for Congress to act so preemptively with regard to new technologies whose nature and impact are still largely unknown.

Internet Service Providers

In addition to pushing laws to protect their technological fixes, the copyright industries have attempted to deter piracy through litigation. However, most infringers on the Internet are highly mobile, even fly-by-night, and the copyright industries soon found it impractical if not impossible to pursue them. Instead, they put pressure on a much easier target: the Internet service providers (ISPs), through whose servers nearly all infringing material must pass at some point or other. They argued that ISPs should be treated like publishers, because they are involved in transmitting the material—and publishers are always liable for infringing content they publish, even if they publish it innocently.

Thus began another war of analogies, such as digital technology has repeatedly provoked. The ISPs protested that they were not publishers at all, because they exercised no control over what passed through their systems. Instead, they argued, they should be treated like phone companies, who are not liable for unlawful telephone calls.

This dispute might ultimately have sorted itself out through litigation, albeit at great length and expense. But then Congress began work on the DMCA; seeing their chance, the ISPs lobbied hard for their problem to be dealt with in the Act. They bargained intensively with the copyright industries. The result was, as part of the DMCA, a new section (Section 512) for the Copyright Act, entitled "Limitations on Liability Relating to Material Online."

Section 512 provides, in essence, a safe harbor for ISPs. They may not be held liable for damages, attorney's fees, or any other monetary relief for infringing uses of their systems so long as they meet certain criteria and abide by certain rules. Failure to comply with these criteria and rules, however, does not deprive ISPs of whatever protection from liability they might otherwise have as a matter of general legal doctrine. And while almost all thought, energy, and litigation on this topic have been addressed to the rules of the DMCA, general legal doctrine may be coming back into play for one particular category of work. In 2013 a New

York appellate court held that the DMCA rules do not apply to pre-1972 sound recordings, which—as discussed in chapter 10—are protected by state antipiracy law, not federal copyright law. This ruling is almost certainly correct as a matter of statutory construction, but the policy outcome is most unfortunate: it forces ISPs to monitor the traffic on their websites, the very result the DMCA was intended to avoid. I would not be surprised to see Congress fix this problem by amending Section 512 to include pre-1972 sound recordings.[47]

To be able to enter the safe harbor, an ISP must adopt and "reasonably implement" a policy of terminating subscribers who are repeat infringers, in appropriate circumstances. (The statute does not say what "appropriate circumstances" are, or how one must go about "reasonably implementing" one's policy.) The ISP must inform its subscribers and account holders of this policy. (A prudent ISP will include this policy in its terms of use, "Legal Notices," or the like by link from its home page.) Furthermore, the ISP's system must be compatible with whatever standard technical measures may henceforth be used by copyright owners to identify and protect copyrighted works. Presumably, these measures might include standard forms of encryption and "copyright management information" discussed later in this chapter, as well as technologies such as digital "watermarking." The statute imposes an obligation on ISPs only to honor those measures that are developed "pursuant to a broad consensus of copyright owners and service providers in an open, fair, voluntary, multi-industry standards process," that are available to any person on "reasonable and non-discriminatory terms," and that do not impose substantial costs or burdens on ISPs. In other words, Congress passed the task of filling in the blanks to the ISPs and copyright industries, while not imposing on the ISPs any obligation to agree to anything. To date, no such standards have been agreed.

An ISP that meets these criteria must also follow certain rules to be certain of escaping liability for transmission (including routing and any necessary transient storage), storage, and "system caching" of infringing material on its system. There are separate rules governing each of these activities.

An ISP will be exempt from liability for an infringing transmission if the transmission occurs as part of "an automatic technical process" triggered by instructions from someone other than the ISP itself. The ISP must take no part in selecting or modifying the content of the transmission. It must exercise no say in who receives the transmission.

As regards storage, an ISP will not be liable for innocently allowing others to store infringing material on its system unless it has the right and ability to control infringing use of the material and receives a direct financial benefit from such infringing use. (An example of direct financial benefit would be a per-transaction fee paid to the ISP by the infringer.) The ISP will be considered innocent unless it has actual knowledge of the infringement, or the facts and circumstances that it does know are such that any reasonable person would infer the presence of infringement. Once it has that level of knowledge, it must act "expeditiously" to remove the material or disable access to it.

Third, an ISP will not be liable for referring or linking users to a site that contains infringing material or activity, so long as it meets the same conditions as apply to storage of infringing material. (Congress probably included the safe harbor for linking because it was safer to do that than legislate, back in 1998, whether linking was an infringement. It has since been fairly conclusively held that linking and framing do not constitute infringement, but I have left in the statutory provisions regarding it, just in case.)

In the case of storage and linkage, but not mere transmission, the ISP has to meet a further obligation. It must have a designated agent to whom copyright owners can send notice of infringement that they believe is occurring on the ISP's system. The name, address, phone number, and email address of this person must be posted on the ISP's website and sent to the Copyright Office, which is to maintain a directory of such persons and has the right to charge the ISPs a fee for the privilege. Until the Copyright Office adopts official regulations concerning this directory, you should use the draft forms posted on the Office's website. The form to use initially is called "Interim Designation of Agent to Receive Notice of Claimed Infringement." To amend it, use the "Amended Interim Designation [etc.]" form. Links to these forms are at http://www.copyright.gov/onlinesp/.

If a copyright owner believes that the ISP's system, or a linked site, contains infringing material or activity, the DMCA has choreographed an elaborate dance. The copyright owner starts by sending a written notice to the ISP's designated agent. This notice must contain a physical or electronic signature of the person sending it and give his or her contact information—name, address, phone number, and email address. It must identify the work or works infringed. In the case of multiple works, a representative list of the works infringed will suffice. The notice must also identify the offending site and material, or the offending link or reference. Finally, it must state that the complaining party "has a good faith belief that use of the material in the manner complained of is not authorized by the copyright owner, its agent, or the law." It must state that the information in the notice is accurate. Finally, it must state that the signer of the notice is authorized to act on behalf of the owner of the right infringed, and this last statement must be notarized or otherwise made "under penalty of perjury."

If the notice fails to identify the infringed work or the infringing work, or fails to give adequate contact information for the sender, it is null and void and will not be construed as putting the ISP on notice of any infringement. If, however, it is defective in any other respect, the ISP has an obligation to follow up so as to "assist in the receipt of notification that substantially complies" with the foregoing rules.

Upon receipt of a notice that does comply with the rules, the ISP must "expeditiously" remove or disable access to the site or the link. Also, the sender of a fully compliant notice can get a subpoena compelling the ISP to reveal the identity of the alleged infringer.

And to protect ISPs against breach-of-contract claims by their subscribers, the DMCA provides that an ISP will not be liable to anyone if it removes or disables access to material identified in a valid notice or if the ISP in good faith believes that infringement is apparent, even if it turns out in the end that no infringement has occurred. But of course, in the real world, the ISP has to worry about more than legal liability to its subscribers. It must also worry about their loyalty, and shutting down customers' sites every time third parties claim infringement is not a way to win customer loyalty. The DMCA recognizes this, though in an oddly backhanded way. For at this point, the focus of the dance shifts to the alleged infringer.

The DMCA provides that in order to be immune to contract claims from a subscriber accused of infringement, the ISP must take reasonable steps to notify the subscriber that it has removed or disabled access to the material that the subscriber has stored on the ISP's system. The subscriber then has the right to send a counternotice. (Note: there is no similar counternotice option where the copyright owner is protesting a link provided by the ISP, rather than actual storage of content by the ISP.) The counternotice must identify the material in question and its former electronic address, and must contain the subscriber's name, address, telephone number, and physical or electronic signature. It must state under penalty of perjury that the subscriber in good faith believes the material was removed or disabled as a result of mistake or misidentification of the material. In this counternotice the subscriber must also consent to the jurisdiction of the Federal district court in the district where the subscriber's address is located, or (if the subscriber is outside the United States) in any district where the ISP may be "found" (i.e., sued), and the subscriber must agree to accept service of legal process from the person who gave the original notice of infringement.

Upon receipt of a counternotice that complies with these rules, the ISP must forward it promptly to the person who provided the original infringement notice, and inform that person that it, the ISP, will replace the removed material or cease disabling it, as the case may be, in 10 business days. The ISP is then obligated to replace the removed material or cease disabling it, not less than 10 and not more than 14 business days after receipt of the counternotice, unless the ISP's designated agent first receives notice from the person who submitted the original infringement notice that such person has filed an action seeking a court injunction against the subscriber's infringement on the ISP's system. Here the dance finally ends.

All this is, to say the least, an intricate procedure. It does serve to balance the interests of the copyright owner and the alleged infringer, while keeping the ISP entangled in the middle no longer than necessary. Note, though, that the entire scheme gives a copyright owner the power to obtain, in effect, an injunction shutting down an alleged infringer for several weeks, possibly more, before the owner must finally appear in court, argue its case, and put money at risk.

Such a system could lead to substantial abuse. Anticipating this, Congress built into the law strong incentives to discourage abuse or manipulation. Each party is liable to the other for any knowing and material misrepresentation, in a notice or counternotice, as to whether the material in question is infringing or not infringing. Each party will also be liable to the ISP for damages and attorney's fees resulting from the ISP's reliance on the misrepresentation.

The DMCA also provides immunity to ISPs in the matter of "system caching." System caching is the temporary storage on an ISP's system of material that has already been transmitted. Once material has been transmitted through an ISP's network to one subscriber, the ISP stores it in system cache for delivery to subscribers who make subsequent requests. By eliminating the need to send those subsequent requests back to the original source, the ISP saves bandwidth and provides faster delivery. This procedure does not hurt the original vendor of the material so long as the ISP does not interfere with the vendor's right to update or "refresh" material and to get full and accurate "hit" information back from buyers. To accommodate all these interests, the Act provides that an ISP will not be liable for system caching provided the ISP does not interfere with the rights of the copyright owner to be paid for usage, to receive user information, and so on, and complies with negotiated industry standards (which, as the statute acknowledges, do not yet exist).

Where infringing material in a system cache originated with a subscriber, the rules I have described above concerning storage liability apply, except that the ISP's obligation to remove or disable access to system-cached material arises only if the notice of infringement states that the material has already been, or is under court order to be, removed or disabled at the original source.

All of the above limitations on ISP liability apply to damages and other monetary relief. They do not exempt an ISP from injunctive relief. However, the DMCA does restrict the kinds of injunctions that can be issued. In the context of storage of infringing material, the injunction can force the ISP to deny access to a particular online site, or to shut down specified accounts of a specified individual. In the context of infringing transmission, the injunction may only compel the ISP to terminate specified accounts of a specified individual, or to take reasonable steps to block access to a specified online location outside the United States. These limitations mean that the court cannot by injunction turn the ISP into a police or peace-keeping force.

So how has the DMCA's notice-and-takedown procedure worked in practice? Has it chilled fair use and free speech? Or has it only slightly changed the odds of copyright owners winning the game of whack-a-mole against online infringers? That depends on whom you listen to.

Not surprisingly, a large amount of DMCA activity centers on websites like YouTube that exist to enable people to share material. The variety of material posted on these sites is astonishing. Alas for public morals, some people seem to think it is perfectly fine to post the file of an entire movie or television program. How do they imagine that is legitimate? (Of course, it does have the economic benefit of creating jobs; there are people in the motion picture industry who do nothing but scour the Internet looking for piracy.)

On the other hand, a lot of material posted online shows great amateur creativity. When that amateur creativity involves use of copyrighted material without permission, interesting questions arise. Is an obviously amateur home video infringing because it uses a copyrighted song in its soundtrack? Is it fair use? Should we even bother to care?

The DMCA makes no specific reference to fair use. However, it does say that a copyright owner who "knowingly materially misrepresents" that an infringement has occurred is liable for damages to the alleged infringer. Accusing posted material of infringement, if the accused material is of such a nature that no reasonable person could doubt it is fair use, is a misrepresentation that gives rise to that liability.[48]

In addition to this objective threshold, there may be a subjective one. Since whoever sends a takedown notice must have a "good faith belief that use of the material in the manner complained of is not authorized by . . . the law," it is a misrepresentation to send a notice if one does not have that good-faith belief. One court has held that since "the law" includes fair use, it is a misrepresentation to send a takedown notice if one has not at least considered the possibility that a use is fair. (Whether the fair use section of the law "authorizes" copying or merely excuses it is an interesting question.)

This holding came in a case with facts that should have given the copyright owner pause. On one side was a woman who had posted, for the enjoyment of her friends and family, a 27-second home video of her young children dancing in the kitchen, with Prince's song "Let's Go Crazy" in the background for 20 of those 27 seconds. On the other side was Universal

Music Corp. Luckily for Mom, her plight attracted the interest of various Internet freedom advocacy groups; otherwise she would never have had the resources to fight the case. Five years later, the case was still in pretrial stage, after endless motions back and forth.

The lawsuit was actually brought by Mom, alleging that Universal had committed misrepresentation in sending its DMCA takedown notice, because it had never even considered whether her use was a fair use; thus, she alleged, Universal had not had the requisite good-faith belief that the law did not authorize her use. Very early in the case, the court agreed that she had stated a cause of action.[49]

This ruling has already had some impact, and will have lasting impact if ultimately upheld on appeal. But the burden it imposes is not great. As the court acknowledged, the "good faith" standard in the DMCA is a subjective standard, not an objective one. Universal's exposure came not from its views on fair use but from its failure even to consider the question. So to comply with this ruling, copyright owners need not become soft and empathetic, they need only engage in a fair use analysis before sending a DMCA takedown notice. Still, one hopes that during the required pause and deep breath, they will have second thoughts about the threat posed by such things as 27 seconds of children dancing in their mother's kitchen. They may even stop to consider the blowback from too-aggressive enforcement. Prior to the DMCA notice, Mom's home video had less than 300 hits. After word got around of Universal's attack, it received over half a million.

Indeed, anecdotal evidence indicates that some of the most aggressive senders of takedown demands from the early days of the DMCA have become more tolerant of amateur efforts that do not use overlarge portions of their works. This is good news. It really is hard to descry the market harm posed by most amateur efforts. Better to save one's powder for things that really tip the moral scale, such as (perhaps) a video created with the obvious intention of jump-starting the maker's career in film.

Another case involving YouTube addressed the question, What sort of knowledge will render an ISP liable for infringements posted by its users? The DMCA says an ISP has a duty to remove infringing material when it becomes aware of "facts or circumstances from which infringing activity is apparent." Viacom sued YouTube claiming that YouTube had exactly this so-called "red flag" knowledge of widespread illicit posting of Viacom's movies and television programs. (Viacom's moral ground somewhat eroded when it turned out that numerous videos had been posted by its own marketing staff to create "buzz.") YouTube admitted that it was generally aware that some customers were abusing its service, but with some exceptions there was no evidence that it knew just which postings were illegal. The Second Circuit sided (but for those exceptions) with YouTube, stating that YouTube had no duty to monitor user-generated content. Furthermore, "red flag" knowledge has to relate to *specific* postings for an ISP to have a duty to shut them down: general awareness that one's site is being used for infringement does not create liability. All this was critical to the ISP industry. Any greater burden of inquiry would have completely changed the nature of the game. The only consolation to copyright owners in this opinion was the court's discussion of what might constitute "knowledge." "Willful blindness" to an instance of infringement, the court noted, could in appropriate circumstances equal actual knowledge or red flag knowledge.[50] What exactly is "willful blindness" the court did not say.

This complex decision may, in the end, have more impact on everyone else than on YouTube itself. (Technology has a way of innovating around seemingly portentous court decisions, and the richest technologists have the best odds of doing so.) Shortly after being sued, YouTube unveiled a service called Content ID that obviates the need for DMCA procedures in most cases. A producer can provide YouTube a file of a copyrighted motion picture and ask YouTube to comb its files looking for whole or partial matches to that file. The producer can dictate how any file that Content ID identifies as potentially infringing will be dealt with. The options are to shut it down (without going through the bother of DMCA procedures), monitor it, or initiate a potentially profitable interaction with the user. As for the infringer, one of YouTube's standard procedures is to send an infringer to "Copyright School"—a short animated video followed by some multiple choice questions—to learn better behavior.

Though I have focused largely on public service providers, the statute is not limited to such services. It applies to any online network, including intracompany and educational networks. However, there is a special exemption available to educational institutions that meet certain criteria. Most colleges and universities have developed campuswide electronic networks carrying everything from administrative messages to homework assignments. Often these are linked to the institutions' libraries. Such networks present obvious opportunities for copying and distribution of textbooks, journal articles, and the like without copyright permission.

The educational community argued strenuously that most conduct of this sort is by faculty and graduate teaching assistants acting on their own, without the blessing of the Dean's office. Furthermore they argued, and Congress agreed, that academic freedom requires that institutions forbear from constant monitoring of their faculties' conduct. The compromise they worked out relieves a college or university from liability for infringements committed by its faculty and teaching assistants in the course of genuine teaching and research, if the institution has provided to all users of its system "materials that accurately describe, and promote compliance with," copyright restrictions. In no event does the exemption apply where the professor or teaching assistant puts up on the network anything that he or she recommended or required for any course during the previous three years. (We hear in this an echo of the older rule of "spontaneity" in classroom photocopying.) Furthermore, if the institution receives in any three-year period two or more good-faith notices of infringement, of the type I have described above in the commercial context, with respect to any particular teacher, the institution will be liable for any infringements committed by that teacher in the following three years, even if those notices turn out to have been incorrect.

All in all, this is not much of an exemption. To make matters worse, an institution that takes shelter on these terms from a damage award cannot at the same time invoke the limitations on injunctive relief that are granted to other ISPs. This means, among other things, that an institution may be compelled to do more than simply shut down a particular teacher's access to the system. Any court asked for such an injunction, though, must consider other mitigating factors, such as whether restrictions would unduly burden the institution or interfere with access to noninfringing material by other users, and whether "other less burdensome and comparably effective means of preventing access to the infringing material" are available.

As you will have noticed, the statute seems to take as a given that the posting of material on the school's network can be an infringement even if carried out for genuine teaching or research purposes. In practice, things have not worked out like that, and campus intranets carry more and more copyrighted content without permission.

Online Piracy

The DMCA works reasonably well for amateur, ad hoc infringement. It was not designed to deal with serious, deliberate online piracy.

Serious piracy takes two main forms. One is the pirate website. There are many such, hosted primarily in countries with dodgy or inefficient legal systems, devoted to "free" books, "free" movies, and the like. For some of these, the website operators create PDF files of entire works and post them on these sites. Others allow the posting of files by contributors.

Most notorious of these was The Pirate Bay, established in Sweden by anticopyright zealots who imagined that movies (which of course cost *nothing* to make) should be free for everyone. The technology used was BitTorrent, a highly efficient file-sharing protocol; The Pirate Bay acted as a sort of clearinghouse for BitTorrent sharing of movie and other files. Since Sweden has a good, efficient legal system, in time the founders of The Pirate Bay were thrown in jail and fined, and the mother ship scuttled in deep water. However, fellow travelers of the aforesaid zealots opened up proxy sites in other countries less able to shut them down.

The other main form of piracy occurs through file sharing, chiefly via BitTorrent, that does not operate through fixed websites but rather through widely distributed sharing of computer resources. It is much harder to pin down.

To deal with the first type of piracy, Congress drafted a bill called the Stop Online Piracy Act (SOPA). It would have empowered U.S. law enforcement officers to shut down websites found to be dedicated to piracy, using technological measures. On the verge of its enactment, however, a number of major Internet companies and organizations mounted a huge online campaign against it, claiming that it risked gumming up the operation of the Internet. Faced with an unprecedented barrage of emails, and dramatic gestures such as Wikipedia going black for 24 hours, Congress lost its nerve in early 2012 and indefinitely "suspended" action on SOPA.

I must assume that the opposition of some players such as Google was in good faith and based on some genuine concern. Rather than try to fix the technical problem, though (if there was one), these opponents whipped up a mob and sent them to the barricades. And I am equally sure that many of those who rushed to the barricades had no clue what the bill actually said—because I spoke with some of them, and found out they had never read it. The whole debacle made me think of the remark attributed to Daniel Defoe, that "there were a hundred thousand stout country-fellows in his time ready to fight to the death against popery, without knowing whether popery was a man or a horse."[51]

For the foreseeable future, then, we will see no concerted governmental action against piracy. Meanwhile the private sector is trying to do what it can.

Roughly a year after the "suspension" of SOPA, and after years of development and delay, a private initiative called the Copyright Alert System was launched. By agreement between the Center for Copyright Information (a consortium representing the motion picture and recording industries) and the Internet service providers AT&T, Cablevision, Time

Warner, Verizon, and Comcast, the CAS operates a "six strikes" program. When the CAS monitoring service identifies infringement, the ISP is notified and sends a warning to the subscriber responsible for the illegal file. If the subscriber persists in infringing activity, after the fifth or sixth episode the ISP will take "mitigation measures" such as throttling down the subscriber's Internet access to dial-up speed. There is an anonymous appeal procedure for subscribers who consider themselves wrongly accused.

Whether this initiative—a sort of private DMCA—will be effective remains to be seen. It will not work against dedicated offshore pirates, but it may at least keep the onshore sort under control.

Fear that in the digital world copyrighted works may be stripped of their identity—enabling piracy both witting and unwitting and making it impossible to trace—drove Congress in include in the DMCA unprecedented protection for "copyright management information."[52] As will be seen, the cure goes beyond the ostensible disease.

Copyright Management Information

Copyright management information (CMI) is information that the copyright owner chooses to include on copies of the work. Some of the possible forms of CMI are obvious: the copyright notice placed on a work, and any other information that identifies the work, the author, or the copyright owner. Other possible elements are: the terms and conditions for use of the work (which could include, for example, any Creative Commons or similar designation); if the work is an audiovisual work, any information identifying any writer, performer, or director who is credited in the work; and in the case of any other sort of work (principally sound recordings), information identifying any performer whose performance is fixed in the work. Some of this information is relevant to the performers' rights discussed in chapter 6, but some of it goes beyond that and is responsive to the concern of European countries, many of which give broader rights to film directors and the like than we do. CMI may be in plain English, or it may take the form of "identifying numbers or symbols referring to such information." It may be affixed directly to copies of the work, or it may consist of hyperlinks to the relevant information.

Although protection of CMI arose via the DMCA, it is not limited to digital forms of copyrighted works. (This is not generally appreciated.) It is now unlawful to do any of the following, *whether in digital mode or in any traditional medium:*

- intentionally remove or alter CMI with intent to induce, enable, facilitate, or conceal infringement of any right protected under the Copyright Act (which would include the moral rights discussed in chapter 6);

- knowingly provide false CMI with intent to induce, enable, facilitate, or conceal infringement of any right protected under the Copyright Act;

- knowingly distribute, or import for distribution, any altered, truncated, or false CMI;

- distribute works or copies of works, or import them for distribution, knowing that CMI has been removed or altered without permission and knowing, or having reason to know, that doing so will induce, enable, facilitate, or conceal infringement of any right protected under the Copyright Act;

- publicly perform any work knowing that CMI has been removed or altered without permission on the work itself, or on the copy of the work that one is using for the performance, and knowing, or having reason to know, that doing so will induce, enable, facilitate, or conceal infringement of any right protected under the Copyright Act. (For example, publicly performing a motion picture from which CMI has been removed would violate this prohibition if it met the other criteria just stated.)

There is a carve-out for law enforcement, intelligence, and other activities of any level of government, federal, state, or local. There are also various carve-outs for broadcast and cable transmissions, the most significant of which is that the identity of performers of a sound recording, and the identity of writers, performers, and directors of an audiovisual work, are not considered CMI in the context of radio and television broadcasts.

Ironically, this CMI legislation has greatly expanded the moral right of attribution beyond the very narrow scope of the moral right section of the statute, discussed in chapter 6. (I say "ironically" because only a few years earlier Congress had deliberately passed the narrowest moral right law it could possibly come up with.) Previously the right to be acknowledged as author of a work, or to remove a false attribution to oneself, applied only to an extremely narrow class of works of fine art. Now it applies to any work whatsoever (albeit with the extra requirement that the infringer have wrongful intent to facilitate infringement), and to copies as well as to originals. Furthermore, unlike the express moral right, this *de facto* moral right lasts beyond the life of the author. The statute provides that any person injured by a violation of these provisions may sue for damages and injunctive relief. As with unlawful decryption etc., damages for the removal of CMI or use of false CMI may be actual damages or statutory damages, and the latter may be not less than $2,500 nor more than $25,000 per violation (not per work). Thus, an ongoing series of violations directed at a single work could yield multiple damage awards. Repeat offenders may be subject to treble damages. In addition, the court is empowered to award attorney's fees to the prevailing party, which may of course be either the plaintiff or the defendant.[53]

If the violator was not aware and had no reason to believe that its acts constituted a violation, the court may reduce or eliminate any damage award; if the violator in these circumstances is a nonprofit library, archive, or educational institution, the court is required to eliminate the damage award. This is a catchall provision and probably directed more at the antidecryption provisions of the DMCA than at the CMI provisions, since liability for CMI violations requires a finding of willfulness in the first place.

Although the statute does not say so explicitly, it seems that one may recover damages under this section *in addition to* damages for straight copyright infringement or violation of the attribution moral right. Thus, someone who infringes a work *and* removes CMI or includes false CMI in so doing is exposed to two different types of damage claims.

Apart from civil penalties, a violator of this section of the statute is liable for criminal penalties if the violation is willful and for purposes of commercial advantage or private financial gain. The penalties are as steep as for copyright infringement, and, as with civil damages, appear to be additional to those for copyright infringement.[54]

What does all this do to fair use? Someone making a transformative use of digital material in the digital environment—a parodist, say—is, after all, not likely to retain CMI relevant to the original. I see no cause for alarm here. The good faith implicit in fair use would be inconsistent with the intent to conceal infringement, as is required for a CMI violation. A finding of fair use thus, almost by definition, precludes a finding a CMI liability.

Finally, alteration or removal of CMI is not a violation where permitted "by law." Additionally, CMI requirements may not be enforced in a manner that would conflict with statutes designed to protect the privacy of Internet users. These are both welcome, if rather vague, reassurances.

FAIR USE 9

In infringement suits the two great principles of copyright law almost invariably clash: on one hand the need to protect the financial interests of creators, to make it worth their while to create; on the other hand the need to make each person's addition to the sum of human art and knowledge available for the use of all. From this second principle has evolved the concept of "fair use" of copyrighted material. Fair use, as its name makes no attempt to conceal, is not a fixed navigational point; in any given case much will depend on the judge or jury's instincts.

Underlying the concept of fair use is the problem of economic competition. A use is most likely to be considered permissible if the resulting work does not poach on the commercial value of the original. In this context the quality or nature of the use becomes of primary concern. The Supreme Court has stated that "transformative" uses are more likely to be fair than mere duplicative uses; I will discuss this point further in a moment.

The statute adopts four criteria, developed by courts over the last 150 years, by which a use should be judged fair or unfair:

1. The purpose and character of the use, including whether such use is of a commercial nature or is for nonprofit educational purposes;

2. The nature of the copyrighted work;

3. The amount and substantiality of the portion used in relation to the copyrighted work as a whole;

4. The effect of the use on the potential market for or value of the copyrighted work.[1]

The statute says that these factors are not necessarily exclusive, but in over 30 years the courts have not strayed from them. Nor should they be—though they often are—applied in a lockstep, mechanical manner. Fair use is really a gestalt, as the Supreme Court reminded us in a famous parody decision (which I will discuss momentarily). Indeed, a more elegant formulation may be the one that Justice Joseph Story gave back in 1841, and which Justice Souter quoted with evident approval in 1994: when assessing fair use, judges should "look to the nature and objects of the selections made, the quantity and value of the materials used, and the degree in which the use may prejudice the sale, or diminish the profits, or supersede the objects, of the original work."[2]

Scholarly and Related Use of Text and Images

Scholarly quotation is one of the most ancient forms of fair use, as is news coverage. The law's interest in propagating knowledge requires that critics, news reporters, and similar persons be allowed to quote from works without paying for the privilege. News media should also be allowed to perform small portions of movies, music, and other performable works for purposes of criticism, a common example being the movie reviews on the evening news. Also, news coverage will necessarily perform bits of music or display public art when these are part of the background of the event being covered; think of political conventions with their brass bands and rock stars. Such news coverage is certainly fair use.[3]

In one interesting case the writer of a book on how to win at Pac-Man was permitted to use Pac-Man drawings for instructional purposes in the text but not for promotional purposes on the cover.[4] As this case suggests, at some point a quotation will cease to be merely a functioning part of the critical text and begin to stand by itself—to be, in short, a copy. As a general rule a critic or reporter should not quote at any one point more than two or three paragraphs of a book or journal article, a stanza or two of a poem, or a solitary chart or graph from a technical treatise.

Is it fair use for a scholar to quote someone else's work in support of his own thesis rather than for purposes of criticism? The custom in the publishing industry is to request permission wherever possible in such cases, and this is certainly an honorable approach. However, it is simply not necessary so long as credit is given to the author and the quotation is kept to a minimum.[5] In my view, the publishing industry has become needlessly punctilious in seeking permission to quote short passages. Worthy publishing projects have languished or died as a result. Short quotations are the lifeblood of scholarship and should be presumed lawful except in unusual circumstances.

By the same token, too frequent quotations from any one work or related body of work will not be fair use. For example, a biographer of Stravinsky was found to have infringed by excessive reliance on copyrighted statements of the composer to express certain themes. He claimed he used his subject's "radiant, startlingly expressive phrases to make a richer, better portrait of Stravinsky and to make better reading than a drab paraphrase reduced to bare facts." The court was not impressed.[6]

In the world of scholarly publishing, at least, there is significant movement toward adopting and publicizing fair use policies: guidelines for what a publisher will consider to be fair use of its material, so that any author making use within those boundaries need not request permission or pay any fee. I have worked with two university presses—the University of Chicago Press and the publisher of this book—on such guidelines, which may be found at http://press.uchicago.edu/infoServices/fair use.html and http://mitp-web2.mit.edu/sites/default/files/files/Fair_Use_Guidelines.pdf. The International Association of Scientific, Technical and Medical Publishers (STM) has also adopted guidelines for fair use that are reciprocally binding on all STM members that agree to them. See http://www.stm-assoc.org/2012_01_11_STM_Permission_Guidelines_FAQ.pdf. The standards are lenient in each case. This sort of thing should be strongly encouraged, but may be difficult to replicate outside the scholarly community.

What of the common practice of quoting short passages from poems or other works as epigrams? To my eye, such uses rarely if ever rise to the level of infringement. Leaving aside those few cases where the quotation might be seen as insulting the author (such as quoting religious poetry in an obscene novel), the epigram honors the original author and at the same time sets up a certain resonance between the prior work and the new. This resonance may shed light on both of them. Such uses are, it seems to me, part of the continuum without which our culture would be atomized. Allusion is integral to the evolution of literature—indeed of every art form—and copyright should never choke it off. But of course, at some point the use of epigrams for thematic richness may shade into mere repetition of one's favorite quotations, at which point it becomes clearly impermissible.

The principle of moderation applies equally well to the use of visual works. I have been asked so often to define "moderation," to give guidelines on this topic, that in an effort to respond I will state here what seem to me appropriate rules of thumb, always with the caveat that fair use is an ad hoc matter and can never be reduced to formulae.

First, it seems to me that graphic works that convey factual information are more susceptible to fair use than artistic works. It is important, though, to distinguish between charts and graphs that simply convey data in spatial format, and those that are embellished by artistic elements. Good examples of the latter are the graphs found in the popular press, but any average computer-literate person can, with computer graphics, create a chart or graph that not only conveys information but conveys it in a pictorially interesting way. Those pictorial elements should rarely be used without permission unless the purpose of using them is a scholarly critique of the original.

Before the issue of fair use is even reached, of course, there is a threshold question of whether the spatial arrangement of data is protectable by copyright. As I discussed in chapter 1, the U.S. Supreme Court has held that the white pages of a telephone book lack the necessary creativity, in terms of selection and arrangement of data, to be eligible for copyright. This suggests that some charts, graphs, and tables may be too elemental in their organization to be eligible for copyright.

Be that as it may, where a chart, graph, or table is being reproduced in a critical study of the work from which it is taken, no permission is necessary. For example, an economist seeking to rebut the work of another economist may reproduce a graph from the other's work and then criticize it as misleading, inadequate, etc. It need hardly be added that the reproduction must be entirely accurate. Similarly, it seems to me no sin to reproduce a simple chart, graph, or table (but probably not more than two or three, well spread out) from a given work for any other scholarly purpose: in effect, to "quote" it to buttress an argument of the writer, in the same way that a short passage of text would be quoted. In all of these cases, proper credit to the original is essential.

Different considerations apply to artistic works, photographs, and architectural works. In my view, there is no need for a license to reproduce small portions of such a work, to the extent that you need to do so in order to reinforce or illuminate a critical discussion of the work. For example, if it would assist your discussion of a painter's brushwork to reproduce a portion of one or more of his paintings, that should be acceptable even without permission of the copyright owner. Nor do I see a problem with reproducing the entirety of a work, albeit on a significantly reduced scale, to the extent necessary to reinforce or illuminate a critical discussion of the work, or of any other scholarly point, but for works originally in color the reduced-scale reproduction should be in black and white unless color is critical to the analysis. Furthermore, what is permissible for critical discussion should be equally permissible for political discussion, in those unhappy cases where a visual work has become a political issue.

Where architectural drawings and other utilitarian design works are concerned, entire images, even in reduced scale, should be used sparingly. On the other hand, use without permission is more acceptable where the reproduction eliminates detail that is not germane to the author's critical analysis.

In any case, the images you seek to reproduce under fair use should always be subordinate to your text, rather than your text serving as an accompaniment to the images. An image is subordinate to the text if it directly serves the scholarly purpose of critical analysis and is directly related to a specific portion of the text. The obvious example at the other end of the spectrum is the coffee table art book, in which text is strictly secondary; we buy such books for the pictures, not the words.

In contrast to scholarly uses, therefore, I suggest that you will almost always need permission to reproduce an entire image in full color, to reproduce an entire image in full scale, or to reproduce a full or partial image for any purpose that is not subordinate to the text. For example, use of an image on the cover of a book or journal will require permission except where the image is the object of the book's critical analysis in the book and its use on the cover continues, or at least closely reflects, the dialogue of the text. Permission will almost always be required where the artist is *not* the subject you are writing about. This would apply even to something as basic as a news photograph, and would probably not be affected by how much or how little of the image you propose to use.

Fair Use of Unpublished Works

Should it matter, in a fair use analysis, whether the work reproduced is published or unpublished? Viscerally, we want to respect an author's wishes as to when his work becomes public. (Remember that common law copyright was the "right of first publication.") Sometimes that visceral feeling makes for good policy, sometimes not. In a case involving President Gerald Ford's memoirs, the U.S. Supreme Court found it unfair for *The Nation* to "scoop" *Time* magazine by quoting small excerpts from Ford's memoirs before they were published by *Time*, which had purchased from Ford's publisher the right to be the first magazine to publish excerpts. The Court noted that the use made by *The Nation*, though small, was qualitatively significant, and damaging to Ford's publisher since *Time* backed out of its contract as a result. This was clearly the right outcome. But the Supreme Court also went out of its way to express a special solicitude for unpublished material in general.[7]

Following this lead, the Second Circuit found infringement where an "unofficial" biographer of J. D. Salinger quoted from Salinger's unpublished letters. The court's opinion made much of the fact that the letters were unpublished, even though Salinger's letters were already on deposit in libraries, having been donated by the recipients. The defendant had been using quotations more to spice up his prose than to make scholarly points, and so the nature of the use was less than compelling as a defense.

By contrast, in a case involving an unauthorized (and quite critical) biography of L. Ron Hubbard, the founder of Scientology, the author quoted unpublished materials not to "enliven or improve" his book but to "prove a critical point, or to demonstrate a flaw in the subject's character." Yet here too the Second Circuit found the use unfair, notwithstanding strong evidence that the quotations were necessary to prove deceit and venality on the part of Hubbard.[8]

Many in the copyright bar, in Congress, and on the court itself believed that the Second Circuit had at this point gone overboard in its zeal to protect unpublished works. A broad application of the Hubbard ruling could stifle scholarly use of unpublished materials, even where they are used as source materials and not as mere embellishments to a scholar's prose. Reacting to this danger, Congress amended the law to make clear that use of an unpublished work, while it will be scrutinized perhaps more closely than use of published material, must still be scrutinized according to the time-honored principles of fair use. I should note, though, that the Berne Convention can be read to prohibit application of the fair use doctrine to quotations from unpublished works.[9] To date none of our Berne partners has tried to make an issue of this, but some mischief may yet come of it.

Despite the amendment of Section 107, works whose value depends on secrecy will probably continue to receive special protection. Anyone claiming to make fair use of confidential business documents will have an uphill fight, for our laws give strong protection to trade secrets. Even things like standardized test questions, which are handed out by the millions, are "unpublished" because test-takers are required to surrender them when done. Such works have always found sympathetic courts. In one unusual case, the Seventh Circuit held a teacher liable for infringement who, strongly objecting to the Chicago Board of Education's use of certain standardized tests, published some of them with the purpose of exposing their inadequacy. What made the case unusual was that the court focused not on market harm to the plaintiff, but on a more systemic harm. The tests, once published, could not be reused for purpose of validation, and the court noted that if other critics piled on, disclosing other tests, validation might become impossible, forcing the Board of Education to abandon the use of standardized tests altogether. (The defendant, of course, would have been pleased with that outcome.) How the teacher was supposed to illustrate his point about the tests, without being allowed to reproduce them, the court did not say.[10] The necessity of secrecy in effect trumped standard fair use analysis.

Derivative Works, Parody, and the "Transformative Use" Doctrine

So far our fair use discussion has focused on verbatim copying. Fair use in the area of derivative works presents its own special problems. I cannot help wondering what would have happened had our current copyright regime been in force when Brahms wrote his *Variations on a Theme by Haydn*, with Haydn (or whoever composed the original theme; musicologists have been unable to pin that down) dead less than 70 years. Or rather, I fear I know the answer and it troubles me. Modern courts have specifically said that a musical "homage" may nonetheless be an infringement.[11] If the composer of the theme were litigious, he might well have been able to extract a royalty, and perhaps that is reasonable, but if he were litigious and vindictive he might even have been able to prevent the performance of the *Variations* altogether, however important a work the latter was.

To use another analogy from classical music: suppose that the ditty "Frère Jacques" were under copyright and Mahler were alive today writing his First Symphony. Would his use of that tune in a dirgelike, minor key be an infringement or a fair use?

One time-honored fair use in the derivative-work arena is parody or burlesque. (Perhaps a clever lawyer for Mahler could argue that his use of "Frère Jacques" is a parody—and perhaps indeed it is; Brahms, though, would have no such defense for his *Variations*.) Parodies are by definition criticisms, and so are favored uses. Yet court after court has wrestled with the question of how much a parodist can appropriate from the original work. To draw too tight a boundary will foreclose the possibility of effective parody, but on the other hand parody cannot be an excuse for a free ride.

One case that in its time caused tremendous controversy is that of *Loew's, Inc. v. Columbia Broadcasting System,* in which Jack Benny was sued for his parody of the movie *Gas Light*.[12] The melodramatic mood in *Gas Light* is so splendidly created that it virtually cries out to be parodied. Jack Benny was not one to pass up such an invitation, and his television parody, entitled *Auto Light*, is a grand example of burlesque. The court, however, found Benny's parody to be infringement because the outline of the plot, the characters, the setting, and some dialogue were copied from the original. Well, you may ask, how can someone burlesque a work without copying these things? Who would even know the object of the satire, or be instructed by it, were these things omitted?

Posterity has not taken a kindly view of the decision of this case. Nonetheless we must recognize that the judge had to grapple with a difficult problem, for, as he remarked in another case, "The defense, 'I only burlesqued,'. . . is not per se a defense."[13]

The Supreme Court has more recently brought some clarity to this troubled area of fair use. The case before it involved two unlikely adversaries: the copyright owner of Roy Orbison's famous 1960s song "Oh Pretty Woman" and the rap group called 2 Live Crew, whose song "Pretty Woman" sought, at least in part, to parody the Orbison original.[14]

Justice Souter, writing for the Court, distinguished between parody, which is a particular species of criticism, and satire, which may use a work as a vehicle for criticism that is not directed at the work itself. For example, the troupe known as the Capitol Steps is famous for its songs lambasting politicians, set to well-known tunes from Broadway musicals and the like. Such use is satire, not parody, and as Justice Souter observed, is not inherently a justifiable taking of the original work. Parody is inherently justified so long as it does not take more of the original than is appropriate to its purposes of criticism.

The Court took the occasion of this case to quash two mischievous doctrines that had grown out of over-zealous application by lower courts of certain earlier Supreme Court cases. First, said the Court, commercial use (a term that certainly includes parody such as 2 Live Crew's) is not presumptively unfair, at least where the use is "transformative" as opposed to simply verbatim duplication for commercial purposes. "Transformative" use, as the term implies, is use that builds upon prior material, transforming it into something new, and is generally accepted as the preferred form of fair use. (The term had been popularized by Judge Pierre Leval in an influential law review article.)

Of course, any derivative work is "transformative," which makes this phrase less than optimal. I find it more useful to think in terms of there being a dialectic or tension between the original work and the user's own expression; where that dialectic or tension exists, the commerciality of the second use should count less against it.

The Supreme Court's second corrective action was to decree that the fourth factor—harm to the value or market of the work—is not a consideration overriding all others; its importance will vary depending on the other factors. The opinion shows great sensitivity, in fact, to the interrelated nature of the four fair use factors, which some other courts had tended to treat as separate, watertight compartments.

The Court also had interesting things to say about how to assess a work's impact on the value or market of the copied work. Where a later work is alleged to preempt a market for an earlier work, that market must be one that the copyright owner of the original work either has entered or might reasonably be expected to enter. Parody is categorically neither of these; no one is going to parody his own work, or license others to do so. However, although the distinction drawn by the Court seems unassailable in the context of parody, it may be more difficult to apply in other markets, where it cannot be so clearly said that the copyright owner would or would not be disposed to attempt to exploit his work.

As it happened, the Court remanded the case to the courts below to determine whether 2 Live Crew's song had inflicted any market damage on Roy Orbison's song, other than whatever harm the parody might cause simply by being an effective parody. Because "Pretty Woman" was not purely a parody of "Oh Pretty Woman," the Court thought it legitimate to inquire whether "Pretty Woman" had damaged the potential market for rap versions of the original.

What if the judge or Appeals Court had in fact found serious harm to the market for rap versions of "Oh Pretty Woman"? The Supreme Court gave no guidance on this point. The statute does not expressly permit a Solomonic decision, in which the parody could continue to be performed, subject to a royalty of some kind. But one suspects that courts will be tempted to craft such decisions, with or without the Supreme Court's blessing.

In literary criticism, parody has a fairly narrow definition. But once the law gets hold of such a term, its borders (for legal purposes) tend to swell and become porous, because all litigants thereafter try to seek shelter under the tent erected in previous cases, whether they belong there or not. Thus, the author and publisher of a "sequel" to *Gone with the Wind* called *The Wind Done Gone*, which rewrites the original story from the point of view of a slave girl at Tara, successfully defended their sequel as a "parody." The outcome was correct, but not the rationale. *The Wind Done Gone* was a trenchant criticism of Southern nostalgia for slavery, and it made its point by showing how different reality looked from the point of view of the victims of slavery. That by itself should have supported a fair use defense, without the need to contort it into a "parody."[15]

In the visual arts, parody cases are quite rare, though why this should be is not self-evident. One case of interest involved "Food Chain Barbie," a series of 78 photographs depicting the famous doll in various absurd or sexually suggestive positions with kitchen appliances. The Ninth Circuit found fair use even though the parodist had used the entire copyrighted image of Barbie. With works of visual art, the court noted, such extensive use may be harder to avoid than with works of literature and the like.[16] Another case involved the portrait photographer Annie Leibovitz and the *Naked Gun* movie series.[17] The defendant had copied, in part, Leibovitz's famous *Vanity Fair* nude cover photograph of Demi Moore, eight months pregnant. Defendants had posed a different model so as to replicate the overall impression of the plaintiff's photograph, but had superimposed on it the smirking face of (male) actor Leslie Nielsen, and placed underneath the photo the legend "Due This March." All this was to promote the forthcoming movie *Naked Gun 33⅓: The Final Insult*. The plaintiff argued that the poster was simply taking a free ride on her photograph for commercial, albeit perhaps satiric, purposes. The court, however, found the use to be a parody of Leibovitz's work, notwithstanding its obvious commercial motivation. The court said:

> Like all parodies, it relies for its comic effect on the contrast between the original—a serious portrayal of a beautiful woman taking great pride in the majesty of her pregnant body—and the new work—a ridiculous image of a smirking, foolish-looking

pregnant man. It thus fits squarely within the definition of parody as a "literary or artistic work that imitates the characteristic style of an author or a work for comic effect or ridicule." . . . Because the humorous nature of the Nielsen ad depended on the unique qualities of the Moore photograph and its instant recognizability, it demonstrates the necessary "joinder of reference and ridicule" to qualify as a parody.

The court went on to find that it was unlikely there could be any market substitution of the defendant's work for the plaintiff's, given its transformative and parodic character, and that in any event Leibovitz had failed to present evidence of any injury to her own ability to sell or license her photograph.

This finding on the fourth fair use factor, which the Second Circuit upheld, is questionable. One cannot help wondering if the court, having found that the parody element outweighed the commercial element, then ignored the possibility that the Nielsen ad had damaged Leibovitz's market for *nonparodic* advertising use of her photograph. Would any movie producer want to make use of her photo now that its *advertising* value has already been exploited? If not, then the court may have dismissed Leibovitz's claim too quickly. In any event, the court placed the burden of showing harm on the plaintiff, whereas the Supreme Court had said the burden should be on the defendant to prove the absence of harm.

The genre of so-called "appropriation art" has pushed the idea of "transformative" fair use in a new direction. The groundbreaking decision in this area involved an artist's appropriation of photographer Patrick Cariou's portraits of Rastafarians. The appropriation artist, Richard Prince, made blown-up copies of those photographs and painted over them. For example, one painting took a full-length portrait and painted on it in such a way as to make it appear that the figure was holding a blue guitar.

Prince's paintings were not intended as parodies of the photographs, and did not comment on the photographs in any way. They simply used them as the starting point for the artist's own "crude and jarring" works, as the court put it. That was enough to qualify them as fair use. "Cosmetic" changes would not suffice, but Prince's paintings "have a different character, give Cariou's photographs a new expression, and employ new aesthetics with creative and communicative results distinct from Cariou's."[18]

Along with the Grateful Dead case that I will discuss momentarily, this is one of the great liberating fair use cases of recent times. It acknowledges that culture progresses by creative use of what has gone before. It even gives me hope that Brahms could write his variations without fear of liability to whoever composed that "theme by Haydn."

Cariou v. Prince may also have important ramifications for so-called "intermediate" copying—the reproduction of a work as a step in the artistic process—although it never directly addresses the issue.

In the leading case that explicitly deals with "intermediate copying," the defendant was an animation studio found in possession of unauthorized copies of Disney movies. It claimed that these were for study purposes only, and that it should be judged by its final product, which it claimed would be noninfringing. The court rejected the defense.[19]

This was an easier case for the plaintiff, though, than it should have been. The defendant had been caught *in medias res* (or *in flagrante delicto*, if you will), and the court was not required to believe its protestations of good intent.

But what if the defendant had come out with its noninfringing product before being sued—would the noninfringing end product justify the temporarily infringing means? On this point, alas, the only extant decision goes (to my mind) the wrong way. The case concerned a photograph, which the defendant had scanned into its computer and then manipulated so as to add elements from it into a new image. The court held this to be infringing even though it refused to find that the end product was infringing.[20] This is where *Cariou v. Prince* is an important corrective. Although the court did not expressly address the question of "intermediate" copying, it clearly did not bother the panel of judges that in the process of creating his paintings, the artist had made large-scale reproductions of the photographs.

Intermediate copying is of particular concern in the area of digital art. Digital technology makes possible all kinds of uses of preexisting images that were unimaginable before. When someone takes a digital image and morphs it to look like something altogether different, has an infringement occurred? Holding the end result next to the original, we might not even call it a derivative work unless we knew its ancestry, for nothing of the original can be recognized in it. And yet the second artist has undeniably made use of the first artist's work.

Clearly there is no market harm in such a use. Beyond that, though, *Cariou v. Prince* teaches that we should find infringement, or not, based only on the finished product. With any other approach we risk killing in their cribs useful or important works, or whole unimagined genres.

The question of market harm and the concept of "transformative use" may tend to obscure one of the other defenses that can be raised for some kinds of copying, namely, the right of free speech. Where lies the boundary between copyright and freedom of speech, both of which derive from the Constitution? One's first answer is to say that although a citizen may be free to speak, he is not entitled to speak his mind in the same words as his neighbor. He is free to speak the idea, if you will, but not the expression. A number of courts and pundits have adopted this platitude, without acknowledging its limitations. For, in fact, it has been held to be fair use to reproduce works in their entirety, albeit for a different purpose than that of their authors. If it were true that copyright and First Amendment cohabit because of the idea-expression dichotomy, such cases could not have come out as they did. It is more honest to admit that in some instances our commitment to free speech requires us to allow one speaker to copy another speaker verbatim.

I once came close to having to make this argument. A publisher whom I represent had reprinted two speeches by the Reverend Sun Myung Moon in a book that was a study of Moon's organization and theology. The book, a collection of scholarly pieces by sociologists and students of religion, showed Moon in rather a bad light. Two satellite organizations of Moon's church—The Bicentennial God Bless America Committee and the International Cultural Foundation—sued the publisher, claiming infringement of copyright.

We had a number of technical defenses—prior publication without notice among them—and as our last line of defense, the First Amendment. I never learned the strength of any of them, though, because both plaintiffs settled out of court.

I have often wondered what would have happened had I raised the issue of the First Amendment. The precedents were not favorable. One that particularly worried me was a case involving a group of Catholic priests who went on tour with their own theologically corrected version of *Jesus Christ Superstar*.[21] Among their defenses to an infringement suit was that the original musical was sick and perverted, and that therefore they were within their First Amendment rights in defending the true faith. The court did not agree. Copying verbatim all but a small fraction of a two- or three-hour musical could not be justified in the name of freedom of speech and religion. Furthermore, in our case there was no commentary directly addressed to Moon's speeches; the speeches were simply reprinted, leaving the reader to draw his or her own conclusions. Not that the book itself did not contain much that was critical of Rev. Moon, it was simply that no contributor to the book directly commented on the two speeches included in it.

On the other hand there was the case of Abraham Zapruder's movie of President Kennedy's assassination. Zapruder, a Dallas dress manufacturer, had by sheerest chance been aiming his home movie camera at the President's car when the shooting occurred. He sold his film to *Time* magazine, which later brought suit when someone used various film frames in a book analyzing the assassination. The court in that case held that the use was in the public interest and therefore was a fair use.[22] The book's commentary was addressed not to the footage itself, but to the terrible event that the footage captured. This was not exactly a First Amendment case, but it came close.

Which precedent would have counted for more in the Moon case? I firmly believe that the speeches were of great public importance but, more tellingly, that excerpts or abstracts of them would not have been sufficient. Taken as a whole, the speeches were extraordinary jumbles of disconnected platitudes and logical absurdities, and the essence of what the book's readers deserved to know lay precisely in that. In a sense, allowing the speeches to stand before the public, to be judged on their merits, was the most effective commentary one could make.

No doubt, commentary helps the fair use defense. Cases that have come down since we settled with Rev. Moon have allowed wholesale reproduction where that element of commentary is also present. In one, a police officer had written a "fable" that appeared in the Police Officers' Federation monthly newspaper. A newspaper, in the context of reportage, reprinted the article in its entirety, along with commentary that criticized the "fable" as racist and inappropriate material for a Police Federation publication.[23] This was held to be fair use.

In a similar vein, another court exonerated a reporter who published quotations from a speech in editorials and distributed transcripts of the speech. It weighed heavily with the court that the copying and distribution were for the purpose of validating the reporter's analysis of the speech and its author.[24]

A third case pitted the Rev. Jerry Falwell against Larry Flynt, publisher of *Hustler* magazine. *Hustler* had printed an obscene attack (which was itself a parody, presumably unauthorized, of a Campari ad) on Falwell, accusing him (albeit tongue-in-cheek) of incest with his mother. Falwell photocopied the piece and sent it to all his followers to show what evil deeds *Hustler* was up to, and to raise money for his cause. The court found this to be fair use. Of all the characters in this farce Campari, which seems to have decided to ignore the whole thing, comes off best.[25] Relying on this precedent, a later court allowed the Council on American-Islamic Relations to post on their website an entire four-minute anti-Muslim tirade by a talk radio host, along with detailed criticism of his remarks.[26]

A fourth case involved reproduction *in toto* of photographs of a prospective Miss Puerto Rico. The pictures showed her naked or nearly naked, and rumors of them had created a scandal, raising questions as to her suitability for the honor. A newspaper reprinted the photos in a news story about the kerfuffle, "not just to entice the buying public, but to place its news articles in context," the court found. Indeed, as the trial court had pointed out, "the pictures were the story." The First Circuit held this to be a fair use.[27] On the other hand, as the First Circuit was at pains to point out, there is no per se defense of newsworthiness. Following that lead, the Ninth Circuit denied fair use where a celebrity magazine, "exposing" the secret marriage of two celebrities, published photographs of the wedding, when all that was needed to debunk the plaintiff's claim of celibacy was a photocopy of the marriage certificate. The photographs themselves were not the story; the marriage was the story.[28]

In a sense these cases were easy; but for the reproduction, there could be no meaningful discussion of the works reproduced. A far more important fair use case involved a biography of the Grateful Dead. The Second Circuit upheld as fair use the book's reproduction of entire concert posters, even though the book contained no commentary on the posters as artistic works. This was not a case where the pictures were the story. Rather, the posters were "historical artifacts that could document Grateful Dead concert events and provide a visual context for the accompanying text." This the court found to be a transformative use. It was certainly not a use in competition with the purpose of the originals. Furthermore, the posters were reproduced at significantly less than original size, indeed at "the minimal image size and quality necessary to ensure the reader's recognition of the images as historical artifacts." These considerations outweighed the fact that the copyright owner had been willing to license the reproductions in the book, and had even quoted the publisher a fee (which the publisher found excessive).[29] This opinion should be taken to heart by authors and publishers, freeing them from many threats and levies that copyright owners attempt to impose on uses of their material that are indisputably informational.

The thoughtful and sensible "Statement of Best Practices in Fair Use" promulgated by a consortium of documentary filmmakers' organizations, and available at http://www.cmsimpact.org/fair-use/best-practices/documentary/documentary-filmmakers-statement-best-practices-fair-use, applies these same principles to the use of historical footage and music in documentary films. It is well worth reading.

In a similar vein, the Ninth Circuit held it was fair use for *The Jersey Boys*, a play about the musical group the Four Seasons, to perform a seven-second clip from the Ed Sullivan Show on which the Four Seasons performed. The clip was shown not for its entertainment value, but rather to underscore how the Four Seasons (unlike many domestic American groups) survived the so-called British Invasion launched by the Beatles a few years previous. In fact, said the Ninth Circuit, in a statement that should serve as a cautionary reminder for all eager copyright plaintiffs, the use was so obviously fair that the plaintiff should have known better than to sue, and so the court required it to reimburse the defendant's legal fees.[30] Together with the "Let's Go Crazy" case discussed in chapter 8, the holding in this case underscores the need for copyright owners to consider the possible fair use defense of those who they think are pirating their work. Put yourself in the shoes of the user before you rush to court, and see how you would feel if the tables were turned.

Formulating rules in this area is certainly risky, to be sure. But these cases suggest, and it makes sense, that use of a copyrighted work is fair to the extent that the user could not otherwise convey or demonstrate the facts or ideas that the public needs in order to understand what the author is trying to say. (It behooves the author, of course, to make clear to the reader or viewer how the material he has used illustrates the point he is making.) We may call the use "transformative" since that is the buzzword of the era, but a better way of thinking about such uses, as I have said, is that there is a dialectic or tension between the copyrighted material and the matrix in which it is presented that justifies the use. Such a concept better unifies these cases with the more traditional cases of parody and scholarly quotation.

Fair Use and the Internet

The Internet has yielded fascinating fair use cases that cannot be neatly fit into any of these constructs. Perhaps the most important involved the use of "thumbnail" reproductions by an Internet search engine. The photographer plaintiff, whose work was posted on his own website, alleged that the storage of low-resolution, thumbnail reproductions of his work in the search engine's database infringed his copyright. The Ninth Circuit disagreed, finding that the use for purposes of search was informational and did not compete with, or damage, the photographer's market for the full-size images. Because the thumbnails were low-resolution, no one could recreate valuable full-size versions of the photographs from them.[31] The court claimed that the use was "transformative," indeed that a use can be transformative even if the original work is not changed at all. This is mere Humpty Dumptyism ("When *I* use a word," Humpty Dumpty said, in rather a scornful tone, "it means just what I choose it to mean—neither more nor less") in the service of judicial conformity. Why not simply admit that the use is a socially useful one, and that this should be a category of fair use, rather than pretending to be following Pierre Leval and the Supreme Court? (For my part, I readily acknowledge that the use is not dialectical either; it's simply fair.)

In a similar vein, the Fourth Circuit found "transformative" fair use by the Turnitin Plagiarism Detection Service, which without permission added students' papers to its archive of searchable material, the better to be able to identify future plagiarism by other students. Even though this service was commercial, and could not be used without paying a fee, the court found it fair. Again, the outcome seems right even if the "transformative" rationale is not. How could the student authors possibly be harmed by such a use?[32]

Where does Google Books fit into this fair use construct? In 2004, the Internet search giant made a deal with three major university libraries under which it set out to digitize their entire collections, provide copies to the libraries, and make the whole vast database available for search on the Internet. In 2005, five major publishers under the aegis of the Association of American Publishers brought suit for infringement. Google defended on a number of grounds, including that a user could see only "snippets" of a work unless the copyright owner consented, or the work was in the public domain.

After several years of expensive litigation, the publishers and Google reached a settlement under which

Google could continue as it had been, but would set up a registry that would make payments to copyright owners of the 7 million books already scanned, if and when those copyright owners piped up, at the princely sum of $60 per work (not per copy, per work). In essence, this would have been an opt-out system for copyright owners. It would also have been an end run around the stalled negotiations in Congress over how to deal with "orphan works" (which I discuss in chapter 8).

The Copyright Office objected that opt-out was backward; the presumption should be against copying, not in favor of it. On this and other grounds the Justice Department objected to the settlement, and the settlement collapsed.

A year or so later, the five named publishers settled with Google on private terms that included nothing to affect the rights of any other publisher. This left Google exactly where it wanted to be with respect to all copyright owners other than those five publishers: happily digitizing away, although I hear anecdotally that Google is spending most of its digitizing efforts at present on public domain works.

In a parallel suit, however, the Authors Guild soldiered on, only to be defeated in the District Court, which in November of 2013 ruled that Google's use of copyrighted books was fair use.

If it withstands appeal, this decision blazes new terrain, like so much that Google has touched over the past decade. Google is not an eleemosynary institution, and this project was driven (however indirectly) by considerations of profit. The copying of which I speak is not the copying that Google customers can do: clearly, no copyright owner is damaged by "snippets," and there is no market for snippets. But Google's own copying created a database to enrich the Google user experience; it drives traffic past Google advertising. In other words, for all its stated high-mindedness, this is commercial copying on a scale never seen before.

The court's opinion acknowledges this, although it also emphasizes that there is no direct charge for the use of Google Books. On the other side of the balance sheet, as the opinion points out, Google's use is transformative in the true sense of the term. It transforms text into a "comprehensive word index that helps readers, scholars, researchers, and others find books," and also into data that can used to research such things as "frequency of words and trends in their usage." Likening Google's snippets to "thumbnail" images used for internet search purposes (see discussion above), the court noted that Google Books has become an "important tool for libraries and librarians and cite-checkers," since it helps to identify and find books.[33]

Is the lesson here that a huge land grab is OK so long as some of the land is open as a public park? That is one way to look at this outcome. And yet there is no denying that the park is a great public benefit that could not have occurred but for the land grab.

A related and less ethically challenging case involved the HathiTrust Digital Library (HDL), a service operated by the University of Michigan.[34] When Google digitized the millions of volumes held by this and certain other universities, it gave duplicate sets of the files to the university libraries for their own use. Roughly 73 percent of the volumes copied were estimated to be under copyright. Through the HDL, the University of Michigan allows scholars to search the entire database. For works under copyright, unless otherwise authorized, the search results are limited to the page numbers on which a particular term is found and the number of times the term appears on each page. (Of course, this may change in light of the Google Books opinion.) Such use seems eminently fair, especially as there is no accompanying for-profit operation to complicate the moral picture.

The court also found it fair use for the university to make such files fully available for the use of its print-disabled students. Since this only placed those students on a level with fellow students able to use the library's hard copies, this too seems eminently fair, at least insofar as the books were ones that sighted students were not expected to purchase.

Where the court erred, I believe, was not in these equitable determinations, but in its cavalier treatment of two very specific statutory provisions. The first of these was the definition of an "authorized entity" under the so-called Chafee Amendment (Section 121 of the Copyright Act—see discussion in chapter 6). The court determined, contrary to the clear intent of Chafee, that any university in the country that serves print-disabled students is an "authorized entity." The second bit of cavalier evasion had to do with digital reproduction for preservation purposes. In Section 108 of the Copyright Act, Congress had set out certain quite narrow circumstances in which a library could with immunity digitize a book for purposes of preservation. (I discuss those later in this chapter.) While certain activities beyond this might qualify as fair use, the court simply swept the whole careful statutory regime aside and held (in effect) that all such digitization is fair use. The court also ignored the fact that Google, not the libraries, was the entity actually making the copies; that, it said, was not its problem. And why was Google digitizing library collections at a furious pace? As a *quid pro quo*, of course, to enable it to get hold of the libraries' inventory for its own commercial purposes.

This case was on appeal at the time of this writing, and the Second Circuit may reverse what seem to me the obvious errors of the District Court. If not, expect years of unintended consequences.

Private Use

My remarks thus far have focused on public use. But there is also much copying for private use. Is it lawful? That depends.

Digital technology has made private copying an important issue. In the analog world, things were a bit muddy. It was decided many years ago that an individual could not go into a museum and photograph a work of art without permission of the copyright owner, even if he only intended the copy for his personal archives.[35] The copyright owner has a legitimate expectation of being able to charge museum patrons for copies of a work, and such personal copying interferes with that expectation.

On the other hand, almost from the birth of home recording technology, John Q. Public more or less assumed he had a right to copy music off the air, and to share his recordings with others. That JQP felt this way is fascinating and important; analog broadcast music was in many ways the first hostile encounter between modern technology and copyright.

In part, perhaps, this was but another manifestation of the '60s spirit. It helped that the music in question was broadcast for free, and came into one's living room via the air—the only necessity of life that modern man does not have to pay for. Also, no one attempted to harangue home recorder types or make them feel guilty. (In Europe, lawmakers recognized the harm to copyright owners, but rather than police copying they levied a special tax on recording media, to be parceled out by rough justice among copyright owners. American lawmakers either did not recognize the harm or were unwilling to adopt such a solution.) Moreover, the very existence of the technology seemed to justify its use: a solipsism that has bedeviled copyright increasingly as reproduction technologies proliferate. If all these factors sound familiar and very modern, that is no accident.

Copyright owners did not agree that home recording was fair use, needless to say, but they failed to assert themselves early in the development of off-air taping equipment, and essentially ceded that ground to their customers. Even as it became common for people to swap their tapes of broadcast music, the industry bit its tongue and did nothing, fearful of a backlash and confident that the quality of such tapes was never going to replace the quality of the records they sold. And until the advent of digital recording technology, that was not an unreasonable assumption. Throughout the era of analog technology, sales of music recordings continued to rise.

Photocopying was the next big technology to threaten copyright. By the time the 1976 Act was enacted, this had become cheap and widespread. A case in the early '70s held it was fair use for the National Institutes of Health and the National Library of Medicine to photocopy articles in medical journals for use by physicians and medical researchers in their professional work.[36] This galvanized the publishing industry, which pressed Congress hard to fix what it considered to be bad jurisprudence. (Not surprisingly, the library community pushed back.) In the end Congress came up with a number of fudges to deal with educational and library copying. I deal with those fudges later in this chapter, but note here in passing that Congress implicitly blessed the photocopying of as much as an entire journal article, or a comparable-sized segment of other types of work, so long as the copy would be used for "private study, scholarship, or research." Private copying was otherwise left to fend for itself, and it took a number of decisions over the next 15 years to clarify that photocopying for commercial gain was unfair, even if the ultimate use was private.

First came the *Kinko's* case. Kinko's, at the time an independent national photocopying chain, was successfully sued on its practice of preparing photocopied anthologies of printed works selected by professors and selling them to students.[37] Even though the copying was for personal, educational use by Kinko's customers, the copying was also a commercial endeavor by Kinko's and deprived the copyright owners of significant revenue. Kinko's could not take on the protective coloring of its student customers.

Once sued, twice shy, and FedEx/Kinko's (as it now is named) will not copy anything that looks as if it might be copyrightable. That may be an overreaction. I doubt that nonsystematic, *ad hoc*, small-scale copying for a customer of a copy shop is always and *ipso facto* illegal. What got Kinko's in trouble was systematic, large-scale copying.

(In this regard it may or may not be significant that, when enacting the 1976 Act, Congress unofficially gave a free pass to calligraphers to copy portions of a work, or even an entire short work, for a single customer for profit.[38] Was this motivated by some tolerance of copying for personal use? Or did Congress assume there was no likelihood of a functioning market for such reproductions—or that the labor involved is so extensive as to render the threat to copyright *de minimis*? Perhaps some member of Congress simply had a spouse who was a calligrapher.)

Next came *American Geophysical Union v. Texaco*. It used to be commonplace for a company or firm to take out a single subscription to an expensive newsletter and circulate photocopies through the office. But in a test case, several publishers sued Texaco (at that time a major oil company), which argued strenuously that internal photocopying to assist in scientific research was for the public good and a fair use. The trial court held against Texaco. It found the use, although for scientific research, to be for commercial ends, and damaging to the publishers by depriving them of subscription revenues and photocopying fees.

On appeal, the Second Circuit somewhat criticized the breadth of that opinion. It stated that the court below had placed too much weight on Texaco's being a commercial, for-profit enterprise. The Appeals Court drew a distinction between direct commercial copying and copying, such as Texaco's, that yields at best an indirect commercial advantage. The latter is less disfavored than the former, it said, and some recognition should be made of the potential public good of Texaco's research. Nevertheless, the Second Circuit reached the same result as the lower court, placing considerable weight on the economic harm done to the publishers by depriving them of photocopying license fees.[39]

After this decision it is clear, if it were not already, that any business requiring multiple copies of works on a regular basis should sign on with the Copyright Clearance Center in Salem, Massachusetts. The CCC offers companies an "Annual Copyright License" granting permission for unlimited internal copying and sharing of a wide range of periodicals for a flat yearly fee, computed on the basis of the customer's own self-conducted audit. Indeed, the Texaco decision made a particular point of the availability of this service, as demonstrating that Texaco's activities had interfered with the reasonable income expectations of the publishers, and could have conducted its extensive photocopying under license had it chosen to do so.

No sooner had photocopying become common-place than a third new technology emerged to threaten copyright, in the form of the first off-air videorecord-ing machines. The big movie and TV studios had watched what happened to the music industry, and were determined that their content would not suffer the same fate. Thus came about the famous Betamax case.[40]

The case was brought by Universal Pictures and Walt Disney Productions to prevent Sony from mar-keting its Betamax videocassette player and recorder. (The Betamax technology died an early death to com-petition, but its name lives on thanks to the lawsuit.) To attack Sony, Universal and Disney alleged that by selling these machines Sony was a co-infringer of copy-right because it provided infringers with tools of piracy. This in itself was a rather far-fetched notion. Although it was true that the Betamax was used largely to tape programs off the air, it was also used to play the very videotape cassettes that the plaintiffs had started selling. Moreover, although most television program-ming is under copyright, many old movies are not, and as time goes by, more and more material will enter the public domain. Moreover, as the Supreme Court pointed out on appeal, the copyright owners of a great deal of television programming do not object to taping and may even be said to encourage it.

Nevertheless the District Court chose to decide whether copying by the purchasers of Betamax machines constituted fair use or infringement. To bring this issue before the court, Universal and Disney had also sued William Griffiths, a private user of a Betamax machine. Griffiths was a client of the plaintiffs' law firm, was not represented by counsel, and the plaintiffs

waived all monetary claims against him. These irregu-
larities the court also chose to overlook, believing the
underlying issue to be important and urgent.

The District Court held for the defendants, and on
appeal the Supreme Court, by a 5–4 vote, agreed. In
part the decision relied on the fact that the copyright
owners of television programs and movies were
already compensated by advertising revenues and so
were not necessarily harmed. As the District Court
noted, Griffiths and other television watchers were not
paying a fee for access to the broadcast. Indeed, since
advertising revenues are the financial underpinnings
of commercial television, "time-shifting" (that is,
taping a show so as to be able to watch it at a more
convenient time) would seem to benefit, rather than
harm, the copyright owner. The Supreme Court found
time-shifting to be a fair use and rejected the plaintiffs'
argument that they should be able to deny the privilege to their viewers simply because it was, in "amount
and substantiality," enormous. And since the Betamax
machine had substantial noninfringing uses, the
Supreme Court held, it was essentially a neutral technology and its makers could not be held liable for con-
tributing to whatever infringement might take place.

The advent of the Internet has increased the opportunities for personal copying exponentially, and the
Betamax case has been trotted out again and again to
deal with new technologies that make such copying
possible. Always the question is: Does the technology
have substantial noninfringing use? With regard to
makers of music file-sharing technology such as Napster and Grokster, the answer has largely been "no." Of
course, plenty of music is no longer under copyright,
but very few *sound recordings* that anyone would want
to listen to are in the public domain. Furthermore, the
prophets of file sharing essentially hanged themselves

by overtly promoting the use of their software for sharing contemporary music.[41] In these cases the music industry has won again and again, establishing their legal rights as they failed to do in the old radio days, even as their revenues steadily decline.

Significantly, no court has held it is lawful to download personal copies of music or anything else off the Internet for free. People who have downloaded works from file-sharing services have been hit with large damage awards, especially by juries they hoped would be sympathetic.[42] In the Betamax case the Supreme Court had intimated that "librarying"—recording for permanent retention—might not be fair use, in contrast to "time-shifting." Downloading unauthorized copies of music directly displaces legitimate sales. Such copying, although for personal use, is an infringement.

The Internet continues to challenge traditional copyright and fair use thinking in many ways. It has more or less created a new class of cultural output that is neither private nor commercial. It makes public the very personal output of individuals with no commercial intentions. Should these be fair use?

In a former technological era such uses were largely invisible. If a bunch of kids made a movie with some of their favorite music in the background and shared it with their friends, the record labels neither knew nor cared. No one but their indulgent friends would ever see the results. Now, however, YouTube and other technologies have made such stuff (and more sophisticated efforts as well) available to the world. The record labels are no longer complacent.

Sympathetic as I am to copyright owners, on this topic I think bemused tolerance is the best reaction. If someone posts such material on the Internet with the intention of selling it, or attracting business, that is clearly not fair use and should be licensed or shut down. But amateur creativity is a vital part of our culture, and would probably die if it had to be licensed. I discuss this in chapter 8 in the context of the Digital Millennium Copyright Act (DMCA).

A particularly important question of fair use as applied to computer software is whether a competitor is entitled to copy a program solely for purposes of analysis, so as to be able to design a product that is better than or compatible with the original. In the software industry this is referred to as "reverse engineering." If the resulting product in any way copies protectable source code of the original, the obvious answer is a simple "no." But if the resulting product is noninfringing, what then?

Reverse Engineering

The European Union allows reverse engineering, at least where the goal is to make the new product compatible with the old. In the United States, reverse engineering will be allowed as fair use to the extent that it is necessary to enable the second party to copy the unprotected elements—the ideas, etc.—of the first party's program, which might be for the purpose of interoperability or even of direct competition.[43] However, like all fair use rights, this one can be contracted away, and the typical software license forbids reverse engineering.[44]

Finally we come to the field of nonprofit copying, which has (perhaps surprisingly) seen some of the bitterest legislative and legal battles. The two areas of greatest controversy, the areas where a clear need for public access conflicts with an equally clear need to prevent substantial economic loss to authors, are educational use and library photocopying.

Educational Use

Photocopying of Literary Works and Works of Art

In working on the 1976 law, Congress attempted to establish a code of conduct for educational photocopying. Feelings ran so high on the matter, however, that Congress at last shied away. Instead it gave its unofficial approval, in its report on the statute, to a compromise worked out by the Ad Hoc Committee of Educational Institutions and Organizations on Copyright Law Revision; the Authors League of America, Inc.; and the Association of American Publishers, Inc. The compromise guidelines, often referred to as the "Classroom Guidelines," are excellent so far as they go, but neither Congress nor the negotiators were clairvoyant, and the modern digital techniques for educational copying now steadily erode the utility of all the hard work done back in the 1970s. Be that as it may, the Classroom Guidelines—essentially, safe harbor fair use guidelines—are as follows. (Note that these guidelines do not apply to sheet music, which is governed by a different set of guidelines, discussed below.)

I. *Single Copying for Teachers.* A single copy may be made of any of the following by or for a teacher at his or her individual request for his or her scholarly research or use in teaching or preparation to teach a class:

   A. A chapter from a book;

   B. An article from a periodical or newspaper;

   C. A short story, short essay, or short work;

   D. A chart, graph, diagram, drawing, cartoon, or picture from a book, periodical, or newspaper.

II. *Multiple Copies for Classroom Use.* Multiple copies (not to exceed in any event more than one copy per pupil in a course) may be made by or for the teacher giving the course for classroom use or discussion, provided that

A. The copying meets the tests of brevity and spontaneity as defined below, and

B. Meets the cumulative effect test as defined below, and

C. Each copy includes a notice of copyright.

Definitions

Brevity

   i.   Poetry: (a) A complete poem if less than 250 words and if printed on not more than two pages or, (b) from a longer poem, an excerpt of not more than 250 words.

   ii.   Prose: (a) Either a complete article, story, or essay of less than 2,500 words or (b) an excerpt from any prose work of not more than 1,000 words or 10 percent of the work, whichever is less, but in any event a minimum of 500 words.

      [Each of the numerical limits stated in "i" and "ii" above may be expanded to permit the completion of an unfinished line of a poem or an unfinished prose paragraph.]

   iii.   Illustration: One chart, graph, diagram, drawing, cartoon, or picture per book or per periodical issue.

   iv.   "Special" works: Certain works in poetry, prose, or in poetic prose which often combine language with illustrations and which are intended sometimes for children and at other times for a more general audience fall short of 2,500 words in their entirety. Paragraph "ii" above notwithstanding, such "special works" may not be reproduced in their entirety; however, an excerpt comprising not more than two of the published pages of such special work and containing not more than 10 percent of the words found in the text thereof may be reproduced.

Spontaneity

i.   The copying is at the instance and inspiration of the individual teacher, and

ii. The inspiration and decision to use the work and the moment of its use for maximum teaching effectiveness are so close in time that it would be unreasonable to expect a timely reply to a request for permission.

Cumulative Effect

i.   The copying of the material is for only one course in the school in which the copies are made.

ii. Not more than one short poem, article, story, essay, or two excerpts may be copied from the same author, nor more than three from the same collective work or periodical volume during one class term.

iii. There shall not be more than nine instances of such multiple copying for one course during one class term.

[The limitations stated in "ii" and "iii" above shall not apply to current news periodicals and newspapers and current news sections of other periodicals.]

III. *Prohibitions as to I and II Above.* Notwithstanding any of the above, the following shall be prohibited:

A. Copying shall not be used to create or to replace or substitute for anthologies, compilations, or collective works. Such replacement or substitution may occur whether copies of various works or excerpts therefrom are accumulated or reproduced and used separately.

B. There shall be no copying of or from works intended to be "consumable" in the course of study or of teaching. These include workbooks, exercises, standardized tests, and test booklets and answer sheets and like consumable material.

C. Copying shall not

  a. Substitute for the purchase of books, publishers' reprints, or periodicals;

  b. Be directed by higher authority; or

  c. Be repeated with respect to the same item by the same teacher from term to term.

D. No charge shall be made to the student beyond the actual cost of the photocopying.[45]

The guidelines are intended to be a set of minimum standards rather than maximum standards. If copying for classroom use stays within these guidelines, it will without question be considered fair use. It is conceivable that in a given case a substantial departure from the guidelines might also be considered fair use, by application of the four basic statutory criteria.

Where an anticipated use falls outside the boundaries drawn by the guidelines, it is advisable to seek permission of the copyright owner. One way of doing this is to write directly to whoever is named in the copyright notice on the work, or to whoever appears in the online registration records of the Copyright Office as the owner of the work. (Recent registrations may also include specific contact information for permissions requests.) There will of course be works for which no copyright owner is clearly designated, or for which the owner cannot be located. Such works fall into the general category of "orphan works," discussed in chapter 8.

In general, publishers and authors are fairly accommodating in granting permission for educational uses of their works. However, that permission must be explicit. One is not entitled to rely on silence.

"Spontaneity" as used in the guidelines is a difficult quality to prove or disprove. However, your credibility will decrease, and your liability will increase, if the photocopying that you authorize begins to assume a pattern or if photocopying is "spontaneously" authorized for works that ordinarily would be considered obvious parts of the curriculum.

The requirement that each copy reproduced for classroom use include a notice of copyright should be strictly complied with. Where you are taking an excerpt from a work in such a way that the copyright notice included in the work will not be reproduced, it is your responsibility to ensure that copyright notice in the proper form is put on each copy reproduced. This notice should be identical to that on the work itself. If you are reproducing a previously unpublished work—for example, a friend's manuscript—be certain to obtain his permission for publication. You should put on it proper notice or a legend such as I have suggested for limited publications: "This copy is for private circulation only and may not be used or distributed in any other manner." To be safer yet, you might require that each copy be returned to you at the end of the term.

The guidelines purport to cover single copying for a teacher's personal use. In my opinion they are probably too narrow in this respect, especially as regards section I(D). While it is certainly correct that copying to assist teachers in course preparation or teaching should not substitute for the teacher's purchase of a book, it seems unrealistic to expect that a teacher will need a copy of only one chart or graph, for example. The very act of developing a course may well involve trial and error and sorting through alternatives. It is more important for teachers to understand that their profession does not confer upon them an immunity to copyright, and for them to be sensitive to the economic interests of authors, than to insist on rigid and ungenerous rules.

It is important to remember that these guidelines expressly forbid the unauthorized making of anthologies composed of materials from periodicals and books, even if sold to students at or below cost. They also forbid the copying of consumable items such as workbooks, standardized tests, and answer sheets. Although some flexibility may exist in other parts of the guidelines, no court has tolerated deviation in either of these respects.[46]

One would have thought that digital copying for student use would be subject to similar constraints, but at least according to one federal judge in Georgia this is not so. In a case involving so-called "e-reserves" at Georgia State University, said judge found copying far in excess of the Classroom Guidelines to be fair use.

"E-reserves" are digital copies of published material—chapters from books, articles from journals—posted on a campus intranet and accessible to all students who have legitimate university passwords. The very term reflects a victory by the university library community in the "battle of the analogies." In digital fair use cases each side seeks a supportive analogy in our print past for events in the digital present and future. By calling these posted materials "reserves," librarians invoke the ancient paradigm of copies held at the library front desk, to be checked out by students one at a time. Posted digital files, say librarians, fulfill exactly the same demand and functions, and so should be permissible. Publishers, believing that over time the use of such files cuts down on the purchase of books (because the books never need to be replaced, and duplicates never need be bought to meet demand), beg to disagree. Publishers have also invested heavily to make their materials purchasable on a more granular basis—e.g., a chapter at a time—and at a fee much less than the purchase price of the full book.

The Georgia court did not wade into the analogies battle, but it did agree with Georgia State University that the Classroom Guidelines were excessively constrictive and should have no bearing on e-reserve copying. In their place the court laid down its own bright-line rules, saying that copying that does not exceed 10 percent of a book or one chapter, whichever is smaller, is almost certainly fair use even where there is an easy way (through the Copyright Clearance Center) to license reproduction of such a segment.[47]

Because the Georgia State case is on appeal as of the time of this writing, and may well be modified or overturned, I will limit myself to a few remarks on it.

First, the court made much of the fact that students would not pay (for example) "$146.00 for the entire book for which only 32 of 710 pages were required reading." This of course ignores the impact on sales to the library, but perhaps it is not without some weight if no system exists for buying just the portion that students need. But the court applied this logic even where granular licensing was available, dismissing as insignificant the loss of revenue to the publisher even while acknowledging that "widespread use of similar unlicensed excerpts could cause substantial harm." This strikes me as simply wrong.

The fact is that upholding copyright in these circumstances will not prevent students from reading the material. Posting digital files is a convenience, for both the university and the students. Without that option, though, students would read these materials the way they always used to—by going to the library and picking up the physical book. The latest convenience is not something copyright owners are obliged to provide; it is something that should be paid for.

Second, the court was wrong to brush aside the Classroom Guidelines. True, the guidelines are intended as a safe harbor, not the outer limits of educational fair use. But the concepts of brevity and spontaneity, which everyone back in 1976 agreed should be applied, still have value. The court's opinion ignored both; 10 percent of a book is not brevity, and assigning the same reading year after year is not spontaneity. The court in effect held that Georgia State could maintain the same materials in its e-reserves year after year.

E-reserves are not the only area in which educational use of copyrighted material in digital form poses difficult questions. A group of concerned interest groups attempted back in the late 1990s to reach consensus on sets of guidelines to cover certain kinds of educational digital copying. The negotiating group, which called itself CONFU (Commission on New Fair Uses of Copyrighted Works), issued proposed guidelines covering the creation of digital copies of images for educational use; the inclusion of protected works in educational multimedia projects; and distance learning, defined as "teaching through the use of telecommunications technologies to transmit and receive various materials through voice, video and data." In the end, none of these drafts was adopted, because the parties in one camp or another found them unacceptable. (It appears that the disgruntled were mostly in the educators' camp.) Congress ultimately legislated in the area of distance learning, as discussed in chapter 6. Some educational institutions have adopted as internal policy the draft on educational multimedia projects, and for what they may be worth I include those guidelines in appendix F.

My own view of educational multimedia guidelines is that they are too restrictive. I am also concerned that for the first time the copyright owners' camp thought it necessary to address *student* use of material. I have always believed that student use of material for strictly educational projects of any kind is fair use, and well below any copyright owner's legitimate radar screen. (By "strictly educational" I mean to exclude things such as school plays, which may well have educational value but are also in part simple entertainment.) Finally, I am concerned that while the guidelines are set forth as a safe harbor, in several places they talk about what users "must" do, which runs counter to the spirit of a safe harbor. Are these guidelines, then, better than nothing? The answer probably lies in the eye of the beholder. They do offer an interesting window onto technology's permeation of the classroom. They serve as a useful starting point for analysis of specific factual situations. I would not urge any educator, though, to treat them as more than that.

Why did all the earnest, well-meaning, even strenuous efforts of CONFU come to grief? It is pure speculation on my part, but I suspect one of the reasons was that CONFU tried to grapple with fair use of *visual* materials. Whether analog or digital, visual works present special problems to fair use analysis. By their very nature they may, unlike musical and literary works, be perceived *in toto* all at once. Unlike literary works, they are not easily paraphrased, and it is almost impossible to discuss the "ideas" in them without reproducing the expression. Considering that no one has been able to agree on guidelines for such antiquated activities as making slides of paintings to illustrate lectures, it is little wonder that we are hopelessly at odds where newer, more powerful technology is concerned.

With respect to music in notational form, a compromise similar to that for literary works and works of art was made by the Music Publishers Association of the United States, Inc.; the National Music Publishers Association, Inc.; the Music Teachers National Association; the Music Educators National Conference; the National Association of Schools of Music; and the Ad Hoc Committee on Copyright Law Revision. The guidelines worked out by this group of organizations are as follows. (To date, they have not been revisited in the digital environment.)

Photocopying of Music for Classroom Use

A. *Permissible Uses*

1. Emergency copying to replace purchased copies which for any reason are not available for an imminent performance, provided purchased replacement copies shall be substituted in due course.

2. For academic purposes other than performance, single or multiple copies of excerpts of works may be made, provided that the excerpts do not comprise a part of the whole which would constitute a performable unit such as a section, movement, or aria, but in no case more than 10 percent of the whole

work. The number of copies shall not exceed one copy per pupil.

3.   Printed copies which have been purchased may be edited or simplified provided that the fundamental character of the work is not distorted or the lyrics, if any, altered or lyrics added if none exist.

4.   A single copy of recordings of performances by students may be made for evaluation or rehearsal purposes and may be retained by the educational institution or individual teacher.

5.   A single [phonorecord] of a sound recording . . . of copyrighted music may be made from sound recordings owned by an educational institution or an individual teacher for the purpose of constructing aural exercises or examinations and may be retained by the educational institution or individual teacher. . . . [This guideline deals only with copyright in the music itself and not with copyright in the sound recording; the recording industry was not involved in negotiating these guidelines. However, I believe that the identical standard would apply to the sound recording copyright as well.]

B.   *Prohibitions*

1.   Copying to create or replace or substitute for anthologies, compilations, or collective works.

2.   Copying of or from works intended to be "consumable" in the course of study or of teaching such as workbooks, exercises, standardized tests, and answer sheets and like material.

3. Copying for the purpose of performance, except as in A(1) above.

4. Copying for the purpose of substituting for the purchase of music, except as in A(1) and A(2) above.

5. Copying without inclusion of the copyright notice which appears on the printed copy.[48]

Like the other photocopying guidelines, these are intended to define not the outer limits of fair use but minimum standards within which use may safely be assumed to be fair.

Guideline A(3) should not be understood to prohibit editing a piece of music in one's personal scholarly pursuits or as a classroom exercise. However, no teacher should make substantial revisions of a piece of music and distribute copies of the edited version or cause it to be performed, in class or elsewhere, without the copyright owner's permission.

With respect to guideline A(4), no copyright owner's permission need be sought to sell recordings of student performances if the works performed have been previously recorded for public sale by someone else. The compulsory license for phonorecords would apply here.

The prohibition against the making of anthologies and the requirement that proper copyright notice be placed on each copy made for classroom use apply to sheet music just as to other printed works.

Guidelines have also been developed for off-air videotaping of television programs for use by nonprofit educational institutions.[49] These guidelines do not attempt to define fair use of commercial cable television programming such as Home Box Office, but they do apply to all free programming regardless of whether a

Off-Air Videotaping for Educational Use

particular viewer gets the signal by antenna or by cable service. The term "program" is broad and includes movies as well as works specifically prepared for television.

These guidelines like the others emphasize spontaneity and brevity—in this instance, not brevity of air time but brevity of retention. Programs of any length may be videotaped but may not be retained for more than 45 days. At the end of that period they should be erased or destroyed. They should be made only at the request of, and used only by, individual teachers, and in the spirit of spontaneity should not be regularly recorded in anticipation of requests.

These guidelines forbid recording the same material off-air more than once for any one teacher, although, with seeming inconsistency, they permit making multiple copies of a recording to meet "the legitimate needs of teachers," provided that all copies are used and ultimately erased or destroyed pursuant to the guidelines.

Recordings may be used for teaching programs over any period of 10 consecutive days within the 45-day retention period. During the rest of that 45-day period they should not be performed generally, although they may be viewed for pedagogical purposes by the faculty. In no event should a recording be altered in any way, or combined or merged with other recordings to make any sort of anthology or other compilation.

Like all the fair use guidelines that have been developed, these represent a safe harbor, not the entire universe of fair use. For example, although CNN is commercial programming, I see no reason why a professor at a journalism school who was critiquing for her students the television coverage of the Iraq War should not have been able to tape CNN's news programs off the air and retain the tapes beyond the 45 days. It cannot be too much stressed that fair use is a rule of reason and fairness, not a rigid set of rules.

Copying of Computer Programs

None of the foregoing guidelines applies to copying of computer software. Presumably, copying source code for purposes of analysis and education would be fair use if consistent with the principles discussed above. Copying of object code would almost never be fair use, since that would be copying for use, not analysis, unless perhaps the copies are strictly for archival purposes.

Classroom Performance or Display

For a discussion of this see chapter 6.

Special Exemption: Institutions for the Deaf and Hearing Impaired

In the Conference Committee Report on the 1976 Copyright Act, Congress adopted the view of Congressman Robert Kastenmeier, one of its leading copyright authorities, that fair use covers certain uses of television programs by nonprofit educational institutions for the deaf and hearing impaired. Congressman Kastenmeier had said that such an institution can make an off-the-air copy of a television program, make a captioned version of it, perform that version within the confines of the institution, and lend it to similar institutions for similar use. This use will be fair use only if it is non-commercial in every respect and if its purpose is to contribute to the student's learning environment.[50]

Library Copying

The Copyright Act specifically exempts from liability certain copying done in libraries.[51] (For convenience I use the word *library* to include archives.) Librarians and content owners disagree over whether these library exemptions go beyond what fair use would allow, or whether the fair use defense is available beyond what the statute allows. Depending on which exemption you are discussing, I think each side has a point. One thing is certain: when the 1976 Act was being negotiated, the library community fought hard for these explicit exemptions because they did not want to have to worry about balancing the four fair use factors every time they went to the photocopying machine. Out of deference to that history, and because much of what the statute allows would be considered fair use if the exemptions did not exist, I include the subject in this chapter on fair use.

The library exemptions are limited to circumstances in which the library making the copy owns the work as part of its own collection, only one copy is made, no charge is made for the copy beyond recovery of costs, and the copy made by the library bears the copyright notice that the work itself bears. Subject to these limitations it is permissible for a library to copy works under any of five circumstances:

1. If the work is unpublished and a copy is necessary for purposes of preservation and security. To qualify under this exemption, the copy must be in "facsimile form." The meaning of this phrase is extremely broad—it includes, for example, microfilm—but it does not include putting a work into machine-readable language for storage in an information system. What Congress had in mind when it made this distinction is unclear. A reasonable guess is that facsimile form is any form that stores the work in more or less its given appearance. Microfilm qualifies because it reproduces the printed page; a computer database will not qualify if it stores a work in text format. Might it qualify if it stored pages in bitmapped format? I cannot say.

2. If the work is unpublished and another library requests a copy for its own collection. Here, too, the copy must be in facsimile form.

3. If the work is published and the copy is needed to replace one that has been damaged, lost, or stolen, or is deteriorating. However, the library must first have made a reasonable effort to obtain an unused replacement at a fair price. The effort to find an unused replacement at a fair price would involve resorting to commonly known trade sources in the United States, to the publisher, and to any copyright owner other than the publisher (if the owner can be located at the address listed in any copyright registration that has been made of the work). It will also involve checking with any central photocopying service that is authorized to reproduce the work. Certain additional efforts beyond these may be regarded as reasonable in a particular case but will be unnecessary in most cases. A copy made under this exemption must be a facsimile copy.

4. If the work is in the last 20 years of its copyright, and the copy is needed for preservation, scholarship, or research. This exemption, uniquely, permits not only facsimile copying but also digital copying. It is not available if the work is in print (to use a soon-to-be-antiquated phrase) or otherwise generally obtainable from the copyright owner or its licensee. It is also not available if a copy can be obtained at a reasonable price. Note that this particular exemption does not speak of "reasonable efforts" to find a copy at a "fair price." The reason for this difference in language is obscure. In theory, it would create liability for the library if the copyright owner could prove that a copy was obtainable in some obscure place at a reasonable price, even if the library had been unable, after a reasonable effort, to find one. This seems absurd; one can only assume that in practice a reasonable search will exonerate the poor

librarian. Finally, and most oddly, the statute denies the exception where the copyright owner provides notice that the work is commercially available or that a copy is available at a reasonable price. This makes no sense. If a copy is commercially available, then no notice is needed. If a copy is not commercially available, then a notice is not going to make it so, and a notice saying it is so amounts to fraud. I am truly at a loss to explain what Congress thought it was doing in enacting this language.

5. If the copy has been requested by a user of the library or by another library on behalf of one of its users. A copy made under this exemption must become the property of the user, and the library making the copy must have no reason to believe that it will be used for purposes other than private study, scholarship, or research. The exemption applies only if the library prominently displays a copyright warning notice at the place where patrons order copies and on its order forms.[52] The form and placement of notice are prescribed by regulations, which are reproduced in appendix E.

This copyright warning notice shifts to the patron ordering a copy the burden of determining that his use is a fair use. Library patrons should take it seriously. Unfortunately, it is often abused, especially by companies. A common way for a company to avoid paying copyright fees is to send a "runner" to the local library to get copies of what it needs. The runner, of course, is undeterred by the warning notice, even though it has been clear for 20 years that copyright done for commercial research purposes is not for "private study, scholarship or research."

The exemption for copies made at the library by or for patrons is limited in subject matter; it does not apply to musical works, pictorial or graphic works (except when used as illustrations of literary works), sculptural works, or motion pictures or other audiovisual works. Nor does it apply to any more than a small part of a work (meaning, in the case of a periodical or other collective work, one solitary contribution), unless a copy of the work cannot be obtained at a fair price after a reasonable effort of the type I have described above. Furthermore, this exemption does not apply if the library is systematically distributing photocopies of copyrighted material, except where copies are not obtainable in the market at a fair price.

What is "systematic" copying? No one knows; it has never been tested in court. Some libraries have gotten into the habit of making copies for anyone who can log onto their computer services, no matter from how far away (and thus no matter how unlike true "patrons"). In my view this is "systematic" and infringes copyright, as will not surprise librarian readers with whom I have had "frank exchanges of views" on this topic. Other libraries have recognized the problems with this anything-goes approach, and limited their services to people who are their true constituents.

Where interlibrary loan (ILL) is concerned, we do have some guidance as to what "systematic" copying means. (The terms "interlibrary loan" and "ILL" are commonly used even where a library is making a copy of material and sending it to another library, rather than actually lending the physical material.) ILL copying is systematic if it is so great or continuous as to substitute, in practical effect, for a purchase or subscription. The National Commission on New Technological Uses for Copyrighted Works (CONTU, whose history I discuss briefly in chapter 1) developed a set of specific guidelines to give flesh to this rather bare definition.[53] These guidelines, which have the unofficial blessing of Congress, may be summarized briefly:

- With respect to periodical issues less than five years old, one library may obtain through ILL no more than five copies of material from any given periodical—as opposed to any given issue of a periodical—in any given calendar year, in the aggregate.

- The guidelines do not speak to periodical issues more than five years old. Some interpret this as implying that all such materials may be copied at will; a more reasonable interpretation is that materials of that vintage may be much more freely copied though still within the bounds of fairness.

- With respect to material other than periodicals, one library may obtain through ILL no more than five copies of or from any given work in any one calendar year.

- If the requesting library has on order or in its collection the item that it wants copied, but does not have the item in its possession at the time and cannot reasonably repossess it at the time, the copy made at its request will not count toward the maximum number of permissible copies. For example, if a library has a book out at the binder, it can request a copy from another library without using up any of its five-copy allowance.

- A library cannot satisfy a request unless the requesting library represents that the request conforms with these guidelines, if these guidelines apply.

- Every library must keep on file for three years each request it makes to other libraries.

None of these library exemptions applies if a library has reason to believe that its copying is, or is part of, a concerted reproduction or distribution of multiple copies of the same material. A "related and concerted" reproduction can take place over a period of time and need not involve one single user, but can be with respect to a number of different users; it can also be found where a copy is requested by a group for the separate use of its various members.

None of the numerical restrictions on the library exemption applies to videotape copies of news programs. A library may tape news broadcasts off the air and lend them to scholars and researchers for research purposes. Presumably it may also lend to other libraries for the same purposes. However, the term "news programs" is fairly narrow. It does not apply to documentaries (except "documentary programs involving news reporting") or to magazine-format shows or other public affairs broadcasts dealing with subjects of general interest.[54] For example, the special same-day reports prepared by the major networks on the downing of a Pan Am jet over Lockerbie, Scotland, were "news programs"; segments of *60 Minutes* devoted to discussion of terrorism are not.

None of these exemptions either restricts or expands the rights of fair use. It is conceivable that in particular instances the library would be safe in going beyond the limitations described here if, in its considered judgment, the activity it contemplated was a fair use. On the other hand, the fact that a library may be exempt from liability in no way relieves an individual user who requests a copy from the library if the making of that copy would not be a fair use. In short these exemptions are for the benefit of the library and its personnel, not for persons making use of the library.

None of these exemptions overrules any contractual understanding a library may have with a copyright owner.

Finally, libraries are not liable for wrongful copying done on public machines if they have placed on the machines a warning against copyright infringement. (See appendix E.)[55] Here too, library patrons should take their responsibilities seriously, though I fear they often do not.

So far I have dealt with the law that applies to works created in 1978 or thereafter. In all respects but one it is also the law that applies to works created but neither published, nor registered with the Copyright Office as unpublished works, before 1978. (The previous federal statute permitted registration of certain works of the performing and visual arts prior to publication.) The one difference has to do with duration of the copyright term. For works in this category, no copyright could expire before December 31, 2002, and if the work was published before that date, its copyright will not expire before December 31, 2047.

Works published or registered before 1978 are governed by a different set of rules. Although in many respects the new law applies to those works, several fundamental provisions of the old system that have otherwise been discarded also apply. Since these works are a substantial percentage of works in existence and will be for many years to come, it is important to know those portions of the old law that are still of concern.

Chief among the basic premises of the old copyright system was the division between statutory copyright and common law copyright, a division based on the concept of publication. Common law copyright was, in

Publication and Notice under the Old Law

essence, the right of "first publication"; it entitled its owner to exploit his work exclusively and in almost any manner for an unlimited period of time, so long as he did not publish it, and it entitled him to be the first to publish the work. Beyond that the common law would not go; once you published your work, you either assumed the mantle of federal statutory copyright or, if you did not properly protect yourself, you forfeited your work to the public domain.

At the moment of first publication within the United States, notice became crucial. (I am speaking here of general publication, not "limited publication," a concept discussed in chapter 4.) If you affixed proper notice to the work, you automatically secured statutory copyright. If you failed to affix proper notice, your work went into the public domain. For purposes of this rite of passage, the law generally ignored distinctions between an underlying work and a derivative work: anything that had not been published already was subject to the rule, whether derivative or original, so long as publication was authorized. Thus, for example, release of a motion picture would be deemed to "publish" all material in it, such as the screenplay, that might have been subject to a common law copyright: when the motion picture entered the public domain, so did those preexisting works. If, however, the underlying work had been published, or registered with the Copyright Office, loss of copyright in the movie would have no impact on copyright in the original. This disparate treatment shows the federal law's bias against common law copyrights, which were potentially eternal in duration.[1] (As noted below, however, an exception has been made for musical and other works incorporated in pre-1972 sound recordings.)

First publication with proper U.S. notice would also secure a U.S copyright if it occurred outside the

United States. You might assume, then, that the reverse is true: that a work first published abroad before 1978 *without* proper notice would forfeit U.S. copyright. (Lack of notice would generally have no effect on foreign copyright protection, notice being a peculiarly American formality.) And that is in fact the case for works of U.S. authors. Where works of foreign authors are concerned, the situation is muddled. The Ninth Circuit has held, bizarrely, that foreign publication of a foreign work without notice neither secured nor forfeited U.S. copyright: only U.S. publication would initiate U.S. copyright, and if a foreign work were not published here before 1978, it would receive the benefit of the duration rules that I have described in chapter 2. The Second Circuit holds to the contrary, and the Copyright Office has opined to the contrary; where their view holds sway (and I suspect most other courts would follow their lead) copyright is subject to the restoration rules described further on in this chapter. But something as basic as the duration of copyright should not depend on where a lawsuit is brought. One must hope that Congress or the Supreme Court at some point straightens this mess out.[2]

Requirements for Notice under the Old Law

Notice requirements under the old law[3] were much the same as they are today (as described in chapter 4), with certain important differences:

1. The date of first publication was not required except on printed copies of literary, musical, or dramatic works, and on phonorecords (called "reproductions" in the old law) of sound recordings.

2. On the first publication, only the name of the copyright proprietor could be used. Thus on first publication the person whose name appeared in the notice had to be the owner of the entire copyright.

3. The full name of the copyright owner had to be used except on visual works and sound recordings; abbreviations, trademarks, and other symbols were not acceptable. If the name given in the notice on a visual work was in fact a trademark or other symbol, the full and proper name had to appear somewhere, even if only on the bottom or back of the work.

4. Placement of the notice was strictly regulated. In the case of any printed work other than a periodical, notice had to be placed on the title page or the page immediately following. In the case of a periodical, it had to be placed on the title page or on the first page of text of each separate issue or under the title heading. In the case of sheet music or other printed musical work, it went on the title page or the first page of music. And in the case of phonorecords and visual works, it went in some "reasonable" place. ("Reasonable" had basically the same meaning as under the 1976 Act.)

5. Any defect in the notice, including omission of any part of proper notice, caused the work to be treated as if notice had been omitted entirely. There were only two exceptions. If, by accident or mistake, the year given in the notice was earlier than the true year of first publication, the copyright term simply began in the earlier year, and if, by accident or mistake, the year given was later than the true year by no more than a year, the fault was overlooked, at least where no innocent person, relying on the faulty notice, had begun to exploit the work thinking it to be in the public domain.[4] (This charitable approach to notices defective by only one year was a comparatively recent development.)

Under the old law, if notice was omitted or given improperly, copyright was lost. There were not all the special indulgences provided in the new law for registration within five years, and so on; what was done could not be undone. There were only two exceptions. First, omission of proper notice had no effect if the copies or phonorecords were distributed without the authority of the copyright owner. Second, omission from a very small number of copies, if caused by accident or mistake (other than mistake as to what the law required), did not affect the copyright; however, an innocent person acting in the belief that the work was in the public domain (having been misled by the lack of notice) would not be liable for damages and could be enjoined from further infringement only if the copyright proprietor agreed to reimburse him for his out-of-pocket expenses.

Notice under Current Law for Works First Published before 1978

Works first published before 1978 may continue to abide by the old formalities of notice. Any new copies or phonorecords of those works can bear either the notice that was acceptable under the old law or notice that conforms to current law (which of course is optional). However, the 1976 Act did not attempt to reach back and legitimate notice that was insufficient at the time it was used. If copies or phonorecords distributed before 1978 did not carry notice that was proper at the time, the consequences will be governed by the old law, even though the notice might be permissible by post-1977 standards.

"Restoration" of Foreign Copyrights

As part of U.S. adherence to the North American Free Trade Agreement (NAFTA), and later the General Agreement on Tariffs and Trade (GATT), Congress added a new Section 104A to the Copyright Act. This section grants or restores U.S. copyright to large classes of foreign works. It was billed as solely a restoration of previously lost copyrights, but in many cases it actually creates rights that were never lost because they never existed in the first place. Whether the euphemism of "restoration" was a sop to European pride—for the Europeans pressed hardest for this change in our law—or a sugar coating for domestic political consumption, who can say? The bottom line is that the United States has made a major change in its treatment of foreign works.

What Copyrights Are Restored? The first version of Section 104A, enacted in compliance with NAFTA, restored to copyright a very narrow class of Mexican and Canadian works: films (and any new works, such as original musical scores, incorporated in those films) that were first published on or after January 1, 1978, and before March 1, 1989, and that lost U.S. copyright through omission of proper copyright notice. Restoration was contingent on the copyright owner's filing a statement with the U.S. Copyright Office during 1994, and became effective on January 1, 1995.

With U.S. adherence to GATT, this rather narrow statute has been replaced with one of much greater breadth and depth—although, as will be seen, much greater textual problems.

The classes of works that are "restored" to copyright under GATT, or at least eligible for restoration, are these:

> • Foreign works that forfeited U.S. copyright by failure to use proper notice. (See discussion earlier in this chapter.) Since in most cases such works were never published in the United States, copyright was often forfeited through sheer ignorance of U.S. law on the part of foreign publishers. In this respect restoration seems only fair. However, the broad sweep of restoration will no doubt benefit some

foreign works that were published in the United States with inadequate notice, and such works will be granted benefits for which U.S. works with the same defects are not eligible.

• Foreign works that forfeited U.S. copyright by failure to renew in the 28th year following first publication abroad.[5] Here the moral case for restoration seems weaker, since we are speaking of authors who secured proper U.S. copyright in the first term but failed to follow U.S. procedure for the renewal term. Nevertheless their works are restored to copyright where those of U.S. authors who committed the same error are left in the public domain.

• Foreign sound recordings fixed before February 15, 1972. U.S. domestic sound recordings of identical vintage are still denied U.S. copyright, though they may qualify for state law protection. Here is the most extreme example of a whole new grant of rights masquerading as a "restoration."

• Works created in countries that at the time of creation were not parties to any copyright treaty with the United States. Here again are new, not "restored," rights.

All this was, quite explicitly, the price that the United States had to pay to obtain support from other Berne Convention countries for inserting tough intellectual property standards into GATT. What the United States got in return was international commitment to copyright protection of computer programs and databases; recognition of a rental right for computer programs and sound recordings; protection abroad of existing U.S. sound recordings; a minimum of 50 years' protection for sound recordings; and a minimum of 50 years' protection for motion pictures and other corpo-rate-authored works.

If you are concerned with the copyright status of a work that potentially falls into one of the above catego-ries of restored works, you need to ask the following questions to ascertain if restoration is in fact available:

Who is the author? The simplicity of this question is deceptive. The question must be answered by referring to the law of the "source country" of the work, not to U.S. law. Identifying the source country of a work has its own pitfalls, as will be seen shortly, but so long as the United States is not the "source country" restora-tion may be available.

If the source country takes a narrower view of work made for hire, for example, than American law, the person entitled to the restored U.S. copyright may be the creative employee, not the employer to whom American law would normally have attributed the right. Or if the source country grants joint authorship only to works where the two authors' contributions are truly inseparable (as is the rule in most countries other than the United States), rather than merely interdepen-dent, there will be two copyrights to deal with, not one.

The one exception to the above lies in the case of sound recordings. Where the work is a sound record-ing, one should ask not "Who is the author?" but *Who is the right holder?* The "right holder" of a sound record-ing is whoever first makes an authorized fixation of the sound recording in tangible form, or whoever now owns the rights that that person had. Under American law that person might well also qualify as the "author" of the sound recording, but the statute is deliberately worded to avoid any argument that under foreign law some other person might be regarded as author. Thus, in most cases, we are looking for the recording com-pany or its successor. For convenience, I am going to use the word "author" throughout this analysis, but read "right holder" for "author" wherever a sound recording is concerned.

What is the source country of the work? The answer to this depends in large measure on whether the work is "published" or not. The GATT legislation does not define "publication," so presumably we should apply the normal criteria of U.S. domestic law to ascertain if a work is published. Whether the work is published or not, the source country must be a signatory of one of several copyright treaties, or be subject to a special Presidential proclamation. The treaties are Berne, the World Trade Organization founding agreement, the World Intellectual Property Organization Copyright Treaty, and the World Intellectual Property Organization Performances and Phonograms Treaty. Most if not all countries that belong to one of the latter two will also belong to Berne or the WTO, and few of those that do not belong will be significant sources of copyrightable works with any value in the American market. But for the sake of completeness I will refer to all foreign countries that fall into any of the above categories as "treaty parties."

If a work is published, then the "source country" of the work is the country where first publication occurred. If the work was first published in two countries (neither being the United States) within 30 days of each other, and each is a treaty party, the country having the most significant connection with the work is the source country. If the work was first published in a treaty party but was then published in the United States within 30 days thereafter, the work is not eligible for restoration.

If, on the other hand, the work is unpublished, its source country is the nation of which the author is a citizen regardless of where the work might have been created and regardless of what the author's citizenship might have been at that time. In the case of a corporation or other business entity, read "domicile" (legal situs) for citizenship.

If an unpublished work has multiple authors who are citizens of or domiciled in more than one country, the source country is whichever of the eligible countries is connected to the majority of authors, unless the majority are U.S. authors, in which case the source country is the country other than the United States having the most significant connection with the work. The statute does not say what would happen if there were no majority to be found—for example, if there were only two authors, each from a different Berne country. Presumably, one would seek to identify the country with the most significant connection to the work.

A circularity is embedded in this regime: the author of an unpublished work is determined under the law of the source country, but the source country is determined by the identity of the author. Fortunately, few restored works are likely to present this difficulty. Although the evidence is only anecdotal, it seems likely that most works eligible for restoration are published works that lost copyright protection due to noncompliance with U.S. formalities.

What was the citizenship or domicile of the author(s) at the time the work was created? Unless at least one of the countries you identify in answer to this question is a treaty party, the work will not be eligible for restoration, even if the source country of the work itself meets all eligibility criteria. This requirement seems to have been designed largely to exclude from restoration the oeuvre of American authors first published abroad—a small but culturally significant body of work.

Is the work still subject to copyright in its source country? If not, it is not eligible for restoration.

Assuming one has passed these threshold tests of restoration, one turns next to the mechanics of restoration.

Restoration took effect on January 1, 1996, or on whatever later date the source country became a treaty party. For most countries' works, January 1, 1996, is the operative date.

When Does Restoration of Copyright Occur?

Restoration is not retroactive. The copyright owner of a restored work cannot sue for uses of the work that occurred before the restoration date. Even an act of infringement that occurs now may be beyond reach if the infringement was "commenced" before the date of restoration, or if certain other conditions (which I will discuss presently) are met.

The copyright in a restored work vests originally in the author or the initial right holder. This vesting rule is significant. The statute in effect ignores the intervening history of the restored copyright, and looks all the way back to the time of its birth. Congress evidently wished to give the windfall of a restored U.S. copyright to the author of the work, regardless of who might be the current copyright owner. However, this will not prevent the law of the source country, or the relevant contracts among the interested parties, from reallocating the restored right to the author's heirs or assignees. In fact, the limited statutory history suggests that the drafters of the statute expected the rights to be reallocated from the author or first right holder in this manner to whoever would be their present owner had no forfeiture ever taken place.[6]

Who Gets the Restored Copyright?

Among the interesting anomalies that this vesting rule creates is that the whole elaborate statutory scheme governing who succeeds to the second term of U.S. copyright, where a work is renewed after the author's death, counts for nothing in the case of a restored work. (That scheme is discussed later in this chapter.) The copyright term of a restored work is treated as a unitary whole, of life plus 50 (now 70) years in most cases, not two terms of 28 years and 67 years, respectively. Here again, Congress has chosen to apply a set of rules to restored foreign works quite different from what applies to the works of U.S. authors, and even to the works of foreign authors who played by U.S. rules and renewed their copyrights.

What Happens to People Who Have Been Exploiting Restored Works in the United States?

The prospect of old copyrights arising from the grave is naturally terrifying to those who have, like the suitors of Odysseus's wife, caroused at the supposedly departed's table. In a partial attempt to address the legitimate interests of such persons, Congress created a complex, and not altogether comprehensible, transitional scheme. Part of this scheme involves a new legal character known as a "reliance party."

A reliance party is one who:

• Engaged in acts that would constitute infringement of a since-restored copyright, prior to December 8, 1994 (or whatever later date the source country of the work becomes a treaty party),[7] and continues to engage in these acts after that date,[8] or

• Prior to that date acquired a copy or phonorecord of the work, or

• Is a successor in business of such a person, or

• Acquired "significant assets" from such a person by assignment or license. The statute does not define "significant assets." The phrase seems designed to protect, for example, a publisher that acquired a whole list of titles from another publisher. An isolated sale or license of a particular work probably will not qualify. This means, among other things, that a licensee of a reliance party is not necessarily itself a reliance party.

To assert a restored copyright against a reliance party, the owner of all rights or any exclusive right in the work must prepare a "notice of intent to enforce the restored copyright." This notice may be served on a reliance party at any time after restoration. Alternatively, it could be made effective against all reliance parties if filed with the U.S. Copyright Office within two years after the date of restoration of the copyright (i.e., in most cases, before January 1, 1998). The notice must contain, at a minimum, the title of work with an English translation, any other titles known to the owner by which the restored work may be identified (which would presumably include, for example, English title translations used by reliance parties), the name of the owner of the right(s) concerned, and an address and telephone number where that owner can be reached. The notice must be signed by the owner. The owner's agent may sign the notice if authorized in writing to do so. The notice may cover multiple works by the same author. If filed with the Copyright Office, it should be sent to:

URAA/GATT, NIEs
P.O. Box 72400
Southwest Station
Washington, DC 20024.

Publication of the notice by the Copyright Office in the Federal Register, or service of the notice by the copyright owner on the reliance party, begins the running of a 12-month grace period.[9] During this grace period the reliance party may not make any copies of the work but is otherwise free to make use of the work without liability. After the grace period, any new or continuing use will be an infringement, with one exception. A reliance party may continue to exploit an "existing derivative work" for the duration of copyright so long as it pays a reasonable royalty for the use.

An "existing derivative work" is a derivative work created before (i) December 8, 1994, if the source country of the underlying work was a treaty party on that date, or (ii) in other cases, before the United States has either Berne or WTO treaty relations with the source country of the underlying work.[10] But what if the derivative work has not been completed by the cutoff date: is the derivative work's author entitled to finish it according to plan? Does it matter how near completion it is on the cutoff date? There may be room for argument.

Another concern raised by the restoration of copyrights that had been considered dead and gone is the status of contractual commitments regarding the affected works. Those commitments typically include promises by licensees to exploit works, and warranties by licensors of their right to license. To deal with such concerns, Section 104A specifically provides that no one who made a commitment before January 1, 1995, to exploit a work that is now restored to copyright can be held to his promise if that would force him to infringe the copyright. On the other side of the coin, no one who gave a warranty of noninfringement before January 1, 1995, may be held liable under that warranty if it proves false because of the restoration of a copyright. For example, if an author warranted to a publisher in a 1994 contract that her use of old English photographs is noninfringing, she may not now be held to account under that warranty if the copyright in the photographs is restored. Nor, on the other hand, may the publisher be compelled to publish those photographs.

One last quirk of this restoration statute should be noted in passing. It concerns statutory damages. The general rule, discussed in chapter 8, is that a plaintiff in an infringement suit may elect to recover statutory damages, which are to be determined in the court's discretion, rather than actual damages, which must be proved to the jury. This election may be made so long as the work, if unpublished, has been registered before infringement begins, or, if published, has been registered either before infringement begins or within a grace period of three months after the first publication. With regard to restored works, the statute provides that an infringement by a reliance party will be deemed to have preceded registration—making the copyright owner ineligible for statutory damages—if the unauthorized use of material from a restored work precedes the date of restoration.

In most instances this provision would be redundant. But it would make a difference if, for example, a foreign work had been registered but had fallen into the public domain through failure to use proper copyright notice. In such a case the earlier registration would be disregarded and the work would be ineligible for statutory damages.

As noted above, the act provides that a reliance party who uses an "existing derivative work" must pay a reasonable royalty. When the reliance party and the copyright owner of the restored underlying work cannot agree on a license fee or royalty terms, the matter may be taken before a federal district judge. How is a judge to be guided in awarding compensation to the copyright owner? The statute says that the compensation—be it a royalty, a one-time fee, or anything else—must "reflect any harm to the actual or potential market for or value of the restored work . . . as well as the relative contributions *of expression* of the author of the restored works and the reliance party" (my emphasis). This phrase "relative contributions of expression" is an invitation to endless argument. Courts have grown used, in awarding copyright damages, to assessing the contribution made by an infringer to the commercial value of the infringer's product. In one famous case, no less a judge than Learned Hand (who was no friend of Hollywood) gave Hollywood its due by holding that much of the profits of an infringing movie were due to the stars who played the roles, and similar factors, rather than to the material stolen from the plaintiff's play, and denied the plaintiff that share of profits.[11] But the phrase "contributions of expression" seems to contemplate something very different from contributions of *value*. It threatens to embroil the judge in literary criticism rather than simple market analysis. In fact, it does not appear to permit the court even to consider the economic realities that Learned Hand observed.

Most disconcerting about this provision of the statute is that it does not appear to give any deference to industry custom. A court cannot simply say: standard industry royalties are X percent of gross, so henceforth the reliance party will pay the copyright owner X percent of gross. Perhaps the court will get to that result, but only after beating around the bush weighing "harm to the market" and so on. The best hope is that both parties, contemplating the mysteries of this judicial process, will be moved to settle their differences before submitting to it.

I mentioned above that one type of "reliance party" is a person who made or acquired a copy of a work prior to January 1, 1995 (or the earliest later date that the United States and the source country of the work have treaty relations). A reliance party is free to sell any such copy for a period of 12 months after publication or actual receipt of the copyright owner's "notice of intent to enforce" the copyright. Surprisingly, the prohibition on sale of copies after the 12-month grace period is binding not only on the reliance party but on persons downstream in the chain of title as well. The "first sale" doctrine, which in general permits endless resale of lawfully acquired copies, does not apply, after the 12-month grace period, to copies that were made before the publication or service of the copyright owner's notice. In theory, a second-hand bookseller could be infringing copyright by reselling a copy that had not been authorized. It is hard to believe that the drafters of the statute intended such a thing, but that is what they have written.[12]

Copyright Ownership under the Old Law

The problem of notice brought into play another important principle of the old law, one that the new law has gone to great lengths to eliminate: that copyright ownership was indivisible. You could give other people licenses to use your work in one way or another, but you could not sell them any absolute right under the copyright; the only absolute transfer you could make was of the entire copyright as an undivided whole. This concept caused particular difficulties in the area of notice because the old statute specifically stated that notice at the time of first publication had to be in the name of the copyright owner or it would be considered to be no notice at all, and the work would go into the public domain. Thus if you gave a magazine permission to make first publication of a story, but neither transferred copyright ownership to the magazine nor insisted that separate notice be inserted in your own name, copyright notice in the name of the magazine would not protect your copyright.

Indivisibility and the Periodicals Problem

Over the course of time courts made many inroads in this rather rigid formalism, primarily by finding that an author had in fact conveyed all of his rights to the magazine, but that the magazine held them in trust for him, with a promise to reconvey them after publication. In 1970 the Second Circuit Court of Appeals (generally a bellwether court in copyright matters) simply abandoned the whole doctrine of indivisibility, so far as notice was concerned, at least where the author had shown no intention of abandoning his copyright.[13] Thus if you made any sale or license of magazine rights after 1970, the chances are great, even though a court will be obliged to apply the old law to your case, that you will be protected by whatever notice was put on the magazine as a whole. Indeed in most cases the Second Circuit's view could probably be applied to pre-1970 situations as well.

Presumably this 1970 opinion swept away another old doctrine as applied to periodicals: that if a publisher, having secured copyright in its own name, conveyed its rights to someone else, the name in any copyright notice on the work could not be changed until the conveyance had been recorded with the Copyright Office.[14]

Not only was copyright indivisible in itself; before first publication or federal registration it generally traveled with the tangible object in which the work was fixed, assuming that object was the unique fixation of the work. Sale of an unpublished manuscript or painting, for example, carried with it the sale of common law copyright in the work unless the seller expressed some clear intent to the contrary.[15] This rule was reversed by statute (at least as to works of fine art, though not as to manuscripts) in New York in 1966 and in California in 1976.[16] ("Fine art" in the New York law meant paintings, sculpture, drawings, or graphic art. In California it meant any kind of visual art.) It is not clear, however, what would happen if the case were to arise now concerning a sale carried out in either of those states before their laws were changed or in any state other than California and New York before 1978. Perhaps the old rule would be ignored, but I can offer no guarantee.

The old law was much looser than current law in its approach to works made for hire. Whether a work fell under the rule depended entirely on the intent of the persons involved. This meant that most commissioned works were regarded as works made for hire, but it meant also that an employer and employee could agree to waive the rule and could do so either orally or in writing.

Works Made for Hire

There was some disagreement in the case of a commissioned work as to whether the commissioning party was to be treated as the author or only as the owner of the first-term copyright. The latter seems to be the prevailing view.[17] However, since the intent of the persons involved is a factor here as well, the question is open to litigation.

Whether a work was made for hire, and whether in the case of a commissioned work the hirer got the entire copyright or only the first-term copyright, will be particularly important questions in the context of termination rights. They will also continue to affect the ownership of renewal rights.

In most respects the old law governing joint works does not differ from current law. However, the 1976 Act rejected one doctrine that still has validity for pre-1978 works. This doctrine, first stated in what is known as the "12th Street Rag" case, is that intent to create a joint work can arise after one of the joint authors has already completed his part of the work.[18] Euday L. Bowman had composed "12th Street Rag" as an

Joint Works

instrumental piano solo and then assigned his rights to a publisher. The publisher commissioned lyrics for it. Bowman had no notion of setting words to his music; it was entirely the publisher's idea; nonetheless the court held that the resulting song was a joint work, giving the lyricist copyright in the music as well as the lyrics.

The court stressed that what mattered was the intent of whoever owned the copyright at the time the contributions were brought together, not the intent of either author at the time of creation. Effectively it permitted someone to trade exclusive rights in a work for joint ownership in a larger work. The doctrine would not extend, for example, to someone who sold movie rights in a novel to a producer, for in that case the seller does not intend that the novel will become merely a part of a movie.

Limited as it may be, this "12th Street Rag" doctrine will continue to affect royalty rights and renewal rights even under present law, and will also have repercussions for the termination rights created by the 1976 Act. It should therefore be taken into account whenever you are dealing with a pre-1978 work that can be interpreted as a joint work.

Special Rules for Pre-1978 Sound Recordings and Phonorecords

The copyright status of sound recordings under the 1909 Act presented thorny questions for decades. Just before enactment of the 1909 Act, the Supreme Court had issued an opinion holding that player piano rolls could not be considered infringing "copies" of a musical work because the musical work could not be perceived visually from them.[19] From this it followed, more or less logically, that the original piano rolls—and by extension, in the following decades, vinyl albums and cassette tapes—were themselves not copyrightable because they embodied no work that could be visually perceived from them.

Congress had little incentive, in those early days, to wade into this issue, so it said nothing about sound recordings in the original version of the 1909 Act. It was left to the states to pass record piracy laws, and many of them did.[20] However, as of February 15, 1972, federal law was amended so as to apply to sound recordings published on or after that date. The 1976 Act largely carries this forward, with certain changes in the terms of the compulsory license. But sound recordings made before February 15, 1972, will continue to be protected by state antipiracy laws until February 15, 2067, after which date they will be in the public domain.[21]

For pre-1972 sound recordings, copyrightability was not the only question. A related concern was whether sale of phonorecords (as they are now called) of those sound recordings could be said to "publish" the underlying musical work, with all the consequences that entailed. The prevailing view for decades was that it could not, and accordingly that no copyright notice regarding the music should be placed on phonorecords. But in 1995 the Ninth Circuit ruled to the contrary. Since this ruling, if carried through, would have plunged a good many valuable musical works into the public domain, the music industry lobbied strenuously to have it overturned. Ultimately, in 1998, the Copyright Act was amended specifically to overturn the Ninth Circuit opinion, and in 2010 it was amended again to cast a wider net of protection. Thus, the rule is now clear that pre-1972 phonorecords did not "publish" their underlying musical works, dramatic works, or literary works.[22]

Copyright Term for Pre-1978 Works

The rules of copyright duration for pre-1978 works are summarized in the chart in appendix A, but require no small amount of explanation to be truly understood.

Under the old law, copyright lasted for a 28-year term but could be "renewed" for a second 28-year term. Thus, for example, a copyright secured on May 12, 1932, would have run through May 11, 1960. If a copyright was not renewed in the last year of its first term, it went into the public domain. If it was renewed, it went into the public domain at the end of the second term. However, during the years that Congress was deliberating over the 1976 Act, the expiration of second-term copyright was repeatedly postponed. Any work still in its renewal term on September 19, 1962, remained covered as of January 1, 1978. On January 1, 1978, the renewal term of any work then under copyright was extended from 28 years to 47 years, with ramifications I will discuss presently. And in 1998, the renewal term was extended by a further 20 years, for those works published in 1923 or later, for a total protected term of 95 years. (The 20-year extension does not apply to works whose 47-year renewal term had expired before 1998.)

The law governing the mechanics of renewal were also substantially changed, effective January 1, 1992, and thus applicable to works whose federal copyright began in 1964 or later. Depending on when a work first came under federal copyright protection, the method and the impact of renewal varies substantially. I will describe the old regime first, then how it has changed—and not changed.

Renewal before 1992

Renewal of copyright was accomplished by filing an application for renewal with the Copyright Office in the last year of the original 28-year copyright term. This application could be filed by anyone, or on behalf of anyone, who was or might be entitled to the renewal term. Whether the person entitled had to be alive on the day that the renewal term was to begin, or merely to survive long enough to file for renewal in the 28th year of the first term, was a matter of dispute between the courts—a dispute that the 1976 Act did nothing to resolve.[23] Whichever might be the magic date, if the person entitled to the renewal did not live to see that date the renewal copyright would go to someone else. The right to renew was thus a mongrel sort of creation—rather like the termination right created by the new law—possessed only as long as you lived. If you died before your renewal right vested, the right to renew your copyright might pass to your heirs, and someone who had purchased the renewal copyright from you would be out of luck.

The provision for renewal, like that for termination under the new law, was designed to protect artists from themselves—and from the impossibility of knowing the true value of a work when it is first created—by giving them a chance to regain their copyrights after 28 years. Unfortunately this noble purpose never was fulfilled. Those who wished to exploit artists, and those artists who preferred a dollar in hand to an uncertain hope of future riches, began to arrange sales and licenses of the renewal term in advance. (Generally these sales had to be explicit to be enforceable. A sale by an author of "all my right, title, and interest" in a work was usually interpreted not to include a sale of the renewal copyright.)[24] Moreover, because the sale would be worthless if the artist died before having a chance to renew his copyright, it became common for spouses and children of artists to make ends meet by selling in advance whatever rights they might get if the artist died prematurely.[25]

Sales by authors and their families of the renewal term copyright have not always been upheld. If the seller can show that the sale was made under "such coercion of circumstances that enforcement would be unconscionable," a court will not enforce the bargain.[26] This reflects a tendency on the part of courts to invalidate unconscionable contracts of all kinds, and is not strictly a doctrine of copyright law.

The question of who was entitled to the renewal copyright was rather complicated. If an author died before applying for renewal—or, in the view of some courts, before the renewal term actually began—the right to renew went to his surviving spouse and children, or as many of them as were living, as a group. Any one of them or all of them could then apply for renewal, and the copyright would belong to as many of the family as were alive at the critical time. (The surviving spouse retained the renewal right regardless of remarriage.)[27] Surprisingly, no court ever ruled on how the copyright would be split between surviving spouse and children until 2005; in that year, the Sixth Circuit decided that the spouse should take half and the children the other half *per capita*.[28] For example, if a novelist died before renewal, leaving a husband and two children, any one of those three persons could apply for renewal and the husband would take 50 percent and each child 25 percent of the new copyright. The owners of these various shares were regarded as tenants in common. Each of them could make a transfer of the copyright, but would have to account to the other owners for a fair share of the profits.

The law spoke only of children; more remote descendants were not mentioned. (Whether illegitimate children could take advantage of the statute used to depend on state law regarding the rights of illegitimate children, but it appears that illegitimate children can renew under the 1976 Act.)[29] The omission of more remote descendants meant that if the novelist in the example died leaving no family except grandchildren, the renewal copyright would go to the executor of her estate, who would then pass it on to whoever was entitled to receive it by the terms of her will.[30] If the novelist left no will, the copyright would go to her next of kin, who in this case would be the grandchildren. If, however, the novelist was survived only by her husband and her grandchildren, the husband would get the entire copyright, and the grandchildren would get nothing. If she was survived by a child and by children of a deceased child, those grandchildren would not even take a *per stirpes* share. The rule seems harsh, but it has never been changed.

Because an application for renewal could be made "on behalf of" the person or corporation entitled to renewal, anyone who wished to could apply for renewal, as long as he did so in the name of the person entitled by law to renew. For example, if the author had sold his right to the renewal term, he was still entitled by law to file the claim for renewal, but people who purchased the renewal copyright from an author rarely relied on the author to make the renewal claim; instead they filed the claim themselves on his behalf. Thus also a magazine contributor whose contribution had been registered only as part of a magazine issue could still apply for renewal, as long as he did so in the name of the owner of copyright in the magazine.[31] In this manner he could protect his renewal copyright without having to depend on the publisher.

In the case of a joint work, any one of the authors could file for renewal, and the general rule has been to give all of the joint authors full ownership of the renewal term.[32]

There were four exceptions to the rule that an author or his surviving family, or his estate, or his heirs, were entitled to the renewal copyright. For four categories of works, ownership of the original copyright brought with it entitlement to the renewal copyright as well.

The first category was that of so-called posthumous works. What was a posthumous work? For a long time it was believed that a posthumous work was one not published before the author's death. However, though this definition fit in with familiar usage and conventional wisdom, it had the effect of disinheriting the author's spouse and children, for it meant that if an author before his death sold his copyright to someone else and died before publication, the purchaser would own the renewal right without having paid a dime for it. Responding to this clear inequity, the Second Circuit in 1975 decreed that henceforth it would regard as posthumous only works in which the author had not, during his life, made any contract for exploitation of his copyright by publication, performance, or otherwise.[33] This meant that the only person who would have the right to renew copyright in a posthumous work would be the person who inherited the copyright from the author. That of course still left it open to the author to bequeath his common law copyright by will to some unrelated person, but the practical effect of the rule has generally been a real benefit to the families of authors. This definition of posthumous works has been adopted by Congress for all renewals made after January 1, 1978.[34]

The second category was of works published without separate notice in a magazine or other "composite work." The author of the contribution did not possess the renewal right unless his work bore a separate copyright notice.[35] However, the practical significance of this was minimal, because if the publisher held the original copyright in trust for the author, as courts have tended to declare, it would also hold the renewal copyright in trust.

The third and fourth categories were closely related. The third comprised works made for hire. As noted above, though, where such works were *commissioned,* some courts have awarded the renewal term to the creator. The fourth comprised works in which copyright originally belonged to a corporate body (for example, a company, a board of trustees, or a charitable society). Since this would not be so if the corporate body was not itself the author of the work, in most cases this fourth exception simply overlapped with the work-made-for-hire exception.

If you wish to know whether a pre-1992 work has been renewed, there is only one definitive source of information, and that is the records of the Copyright Office. Most renewal records have still not been added to the Office's online database, and it will be some time before they all are. A manual search of the paper records is always an option, and can be either done oneself or commissioned from the Office. Renewal records are also available online at www.archive.org. Another good, but not definitive, source of renewal information is the Stanford Copyright Renewal Database, available at http://collections.stanford.edu/copyrightrenewals. This database, however, applies only to book copyrights.

Renewal in 1992 and Thereafter

The requirement that renewal had to be actively sought, through registration, created a trap for the unwary. Authors and their families were often ignorant of the law; publishers and production houses might know the law but lose track of a work after 28 years, or go out of business. For example, copyright in the movie *It's a Wonderful Life* expired after 28 years because the movie company that owned it had gone bankrupt and the residual copyright interest had gotten lost in the shuffle.

Congress has now largely deactivated this trap. As discussed earlier in this chapter, foreign works that fell into the public domain for failure to renew have been restored to copyright. And for both U.S. and foreign works due to be renewed in 1992 or thereafter—i.e., for works that first came under federal copyright between January 1, 1964, and December 31, 1977—renewal is now automatic. No application for renewal need be filed; indeed, the work does not even need to have been registered in its first term to be renewed for a second.[36]

Should no one bother, then, to apply for renewal? Not so. To encourage copyright owners to apply "proactively," so to speak, the rules create several compelling incentives. First, if you apply for renewal instead of waiting for it to happen, your renewal will vest at the time you apply; but if you let renewal occur automatically, the renewal right will vest in the person(s) who could have applied on the last day of the first term. Thus, if an author actually renews his copyright and then dies during the last year of the first term, the copyright is his to license or bequeath as he wishes. But if he dies in that last year without having applied for renewal, the renewal term will pass to those of his wife and children who are living at the end of the year. (If there are none it will pass to his heirs by will or intestacy.)

The second incentive to apply for renewal is that it gives your registration for the renewal term the same *prima facie* evidentiary value as a first-term registration. If you let things simply take their course, any registration you make thereafter (for example, to be able to sue an infringer) will have only such weight as a court may choose to give it.

The third and perhaps the greatest incentive is that unless you actively apply for renewal, any licensee who has made a derivative work during the first term of copyright will be entitled to continue exploiting that derivative work—although not to make any new derivative work—during the second term of copyright. This is a significant departure from prior law, which held that a derivative-work licensee had no rights in the renewal term unless he had obtained a license from whoever actually came to own the renewal term copyright.[37] To understand what this may mean in practice, consider the case of a work of fiction that has been made into a famous movie. If the novelist applies for renewal, the owner of the movie will be unable to show the movie in the renewal term without obtaining a new license, probably on terms much more favorable than the novelist got the first time around. If by contrast nature is allowed to take its course, the novel copyright will be automatically renewed but so will the movie owner's rights. If the first two incentives for proactive renewal are sticks, this can be a carrot of major dimensions.

If you miss the 28th-year deadline for renewal and your work was not registered during the first copyright term, it is still advisable to file a late renewal registration, which the law permits you to do, so as to be eligible for attorney's fees and statutory damages in a suit against a subsequent infringer.[38]

Mechanics of Applying for Renewal

The application form for renewal is form RE. (See http://www.copyright.gov/docs/fees.html for the amount of the fee.) If the work has not previously been registered, an Addendum to form RE must be submitted, setting forth much of the same information as would have been required for registration, and deposit of the same type as for normal registration must be made. If a minor error is made, it can be corrected by filing a supplemental registration at any time. Major errors, however, such as errors in identifying the renewal claimant or the basis for the renewal claim, generally cannot be corrected once the renewal term has begun, unless you can convince the Copyright Office that the error was inadvertent. If you are not allowed to correct the error, the copyright will be treated as if not timely renewed, with all the consequences that that entails.[39]

Renewing a Group of Works

As I have mentioned, since 1978 it has been possible for an author to register a number of contributions to collective works on the same form. Since 1978 there has been a similar provision where renewal is concerned. In the case of the works of an individual author, renewal registration may be made on a single form and for a single fee if these conditions are met:

- The renewal claimant or claimants are the same for each work. For example, if a magazine owns two of the renewal rights and the author's family own the other two, the same registration form cannot be used for all four works.

- The basis of the claim is the same for each work. This will be the case in all but a very few circumstances. An example to the contrary would be if the publisher is entitled to renew some works because their renewal terms were assigned to it by the author and entitled to renew others because they were works made for hire; in both cases the publisher is the proper renewal claimant, but it cannot use the same form to renew all of these works.

- The works were all copyrighted at the time of their first publication, either by separate notice and registration or by virtue of a copyright notice having been affixed to the periodical issue as a whole, regardless of whether that issue was registered.

- All the works were first published in the same calendar year.

- The application identifies each work and states the name and date of the periodical issue in which it was first published.[40]

As I mentioned earlier, the renewal term for pre-1978 works now runs for a total of 67 years.[41] It might seem unfair that authors of works copyrighted before 1978 should not get the benefit of the life-plus-50 (now life-plus-70) term, but Congress felt that altering the structure of existing copyrights to that extent would upset the financial expectations of people who had invested in them and would cause numerous other difficulties and contradictions. Instead Congress added to the renewal term of copyright for works in their first term as of January 1, 1978: originally 19 years, later augmented by a further 20 years. Those works, if renewed, are now protected for a total of 95 years from the year of first publication.

Length of Renewal Term

The renewal term for works that were already in their second term when the new law went into effect, or for which a timely renewal application was still pending on December 31, 1977, has also been lengthened by 39 years. Those works too will thus be protected for a total of 95 years from the year of first publication.

In all cases the copyright term for pre-1978 works that were still under copyright on January 1, 1978, runs through the end of the *calendar* year in which it would otherwise expire. This is a great improvement over prior law.

The extension of the renewal term is intended to benefit authors, not the people to whom they may have sold their rights. To ensure that this will in fact be the result, the law has adopted a procedure for terminating renewal term grants, and that includes not only grants of the renewal right but also any grant or license that applies to the renewal term. The procedure is similar in most respects to that for terminating transfers of post-1977 copyrights (discussed in chapter 3).

Terminating Pre-1978 Renewal Rights

The right to terminate transfers of renewal copyright[42] applies only to transfers made before January 1, 1978, of copyright in works published before that date. No grant or license concerning the renewal term made after December 31, 1977, can be terminated, nor can any grant made before 1978 of a work that was not under federal copyright as of December 31, 1977. The right is not available for works made for hire, and it does not affect grants made by will or grants of rights in foreign countries. Furthermore it affects only the extension period, not the basic 28-year renewal term. As with termination of post-1977 grants, the renewal right overrides any agreement that may have been made to the contrary, including an agreement post-creation to treat a work as made for hire.

Grants Made by Persons Other Than the Author

It is now possible for an author's spouse or children to terminate grants of renewal rights that they have made. It is also possible for them to terminate any grant that takes effect during the renewal term. Termination must be made by all of the grantors who are still alive. Thus if three children joined in making a grant of renewal rights and two of them die, the remaining child can effect termination all by himself. But if all three children are still alive, all three must join in making the termination. The heirs of a deceased grantor other than the author have no termination rights. Thus, in my example, if two children die before having a chance to take part in the termination, the remaining child is the only person who can effect termination; a deceased child's children have no rights in this respect. Nor do they have any rights once termination has been carried out. However, from the moment that the copyright reverts to the persons who terminated the grant, which it does on the date the termination becomes effective, it becomes property; it is no longer personal to the grantor but can be inherited. Thus if a child dies after taking part in the termination, his heirs will get an equal share of the copyright. This distinction seems unfair, but it is nonetheless the law.

Termination of grants of renewal rights made by the author may be made by him alone, if he is living. If the author is dead, the termination right is owned and may be exercised by his family. His spouse has the entire right if there are no children or grandchildren; his children and grandchildren have the entire right if there is no spouse; if there are both a spouse and children or grandchildren, the spouse has half the termination right and the children and grandchildren have the other half, divided among them in equal shares *per stirpes*. The share of a deceased child can be exercised only by a majority of his children. And if neither the author nor any of these family members is living, the author's "executor, administrator, personal representative, or trustee" owns the termination right. In short, apportionment of the termination rights is identical to that provided for grants of copyright in post-1977 works.

Grants Made by the Author

Any author who joined in a grant of rights regarding the renewal term may terminate the grant to the extent of his share of the rights. (If he is dead, his termination right may be exercised by his family.) This provision for joint works differs substantially from the rule covering grants of copyright in post-1977 works. The rule

Grants of Renewal in Joint Works

in the latter case is that a majority of authors who signed the original grant must join in giving notice of termination; but in the case of renewal term grants made before January 1, 1978, each of the joint authors can terminate his own individual share of the grant. This may lead to inequitable results. If one of the joint owners pulls out, he can make a grant to someone else; is the person who has the original grant stuck paying royalties to the other joint authors but without any longer having an exclusive license, or is he free at that point to cancel the contract, leaving the other joint authors by the roadside?

Ownership of Copyright after Termination

When a grant is terminated, the copyright reverts on the date termination becomes effective. However, the ownership of the rights that are to revert becomes fixed ("vested," in the legal phrase) on the date the notice of termination is given. The reverting right goes to those persons who could have signed the termination notice. Thus, if the author made the grant and is terminating it, the right (or whatever share of the right the author owned) reverts to the author. If the author made the grant and someone else is terminating it, the reversion goes to the author's surviving family, in the same *per stirpes* shares as they owned the termination right. If the grant was made by someone other than the author, the right reverts to as many of the grantors as are living on the date the notice is sent. Note that the reversion goes to whoever could have signed the notice, whether they did so or not. For example, a deceased author's child who did not sign the termination notice still receives a proportionate share of the copyright when it reverts.

Once the reversion has vested, the expectancy interest in the copyright becomes ordinary property that may be bequeathed or given within the family. However, no new grant of the reverting right may be made until after the effective date of the termination. Where an author's grant has been terminated, any new grant is valid only if it is signed by at least the same number of persons, and by persons representing at least the same proportion of ownership, as were required to carry out termination. This is so whether the new grant is exclusive or nonexclusive. A new grant of a right originally granted by persons other than the author does not have to meet these requirements.

An example may help to demonstrate these rules. Suppose that termination rights in a work are owned 50 percent by the author's widow and 25 percent by each of two daughters. Termination would have to be carried out by at least two persons (the widow and at least one daughter). At the time of notice the right to reversion of the copyright vests in the widow and daughters in the same proportions. Suppose that one of the daughters then dies, leaving her share of the copyright to her alma mater. (She was able to make this bequest because ownership of the copyright had vested in her.) For a new grant of the copyright to be valid, it must be signed by at least two persons, who must represent at least the same percentage of the right as was required for termination. But they need not be the same persons who terminated the original grant. Thus the statute is satisfied if the grant is signed by the widow and the college.

The new grant binds and benefits even those who did not participate in it. Thus the daughter who does not sign the new grant is still legally bound by it, and the buyer is obligated to pay her a share of the royalties.

Mechanics for Terminating a Renewal Term Grant

The following rules apply to all terminations of renewal right grants, whether the grants were made by the author or by his family:[43]

1. In most cases, termination may take effect at any time during the five-year period beginning 56 years after the date copyright was first obtained (normally, the actual date the work was first published, or any earlier date on which it was registered.) That remains the case. However, when Congress extended the renewal term by a further 20 years, in October 1998, it recognized that some persons might have missed their opportunity to terminate and that the 20-year extension would prove a windfall to their licensees. Accordingly, the Act provides that if, back before the 20-year extension of copyright was enacted, you missed the deadline for termination, you may terminate as to the new 20-year extension at any time in the first five years after the 75th anniversary of the date copyright was first secured.

2. Notice of termination, which must be in writing and signed by all persons whose consent is required for termination, must be given not more than 10 years and not fewer than two years before the date termination is to take effect.

3. A copy of the notice must be recorded in the Copyright Office before the date of termination, or the termination becomes null and void. See http://www.copyright.gov/docs/fees.html for the recording fees.

4. As with the termination of grants of post-1977 copyrights, no new grant, and no agreement to make a new grant, can be made until the date termination becomes effective, except that renegotiation of an existing grant may be made as soon as notice is

given. Rights under a renegotiated contract do not ripen until termination takes effect.

5. As with the termination of post-1977 copyrights, termination of renewal grants does not affect the ongoing use of any derivative work prepared by a grantee prior to termination. For example, if a novelist terminates a grant to a film producer, that will only prevent the producer from making a new film of the same story, not from exploiting a film already made.

A notice of termination must state whether you are terminating as to the entire 39-year extension (in which case, refer to "the renewal term extension provided by 17 U.S.C. 304(c)") or only as to the last 20 years of that term (in which case, refer to "the renewal term extension provided by 17 U.S.C. 304(d)"). If the latter, the notice must also explicitly state that no termination of the grant under Section 304(c) has been made.

The notice must be delivered by hand or by first-class mail to each of the original grantees of the rights concerned, or their respective successors. You are required to carry out a "reasonable investigation" as to the current owners of those rights, and as to their current addresses. See chapter 3 for a discussion of what a "reasonable investigation" requires, but with this caveat: until such time as the Copyright Office has uploaded all of its renewal and recordation records from before 1978, you will need to commission a search from the Copyright Office. (See http://www.copyright.gov/docs/fees.html for search fees.) You cannot rely on any third-party source such as the Stanford database discussed above.

The notice must contain certain basic information:

1. The names of all persons whose rights are being terminated and all addresses to which the notice is being sent.

2. The title of the work.

3. The name of at least one author of the work.

4. The date on which copyright was secured. (This will be either the date of first publication or, if the work was registered before publication, the registration date.)

5. The copyright registration number, if possible. (Finding this may be part of the Copyright Office records search noted above.)

6. A brief statement reasonably identifying the grant you are terminating.

7. The date on which termination is to become effective.

8. If the grant was made by someone other than the author, a list of all persons who made the original grant and who are still alive.

9. If the grant was made by the author, but is being terminated by his family, a list of all the surviving persons who are entitled to take part in termination (whether they are actually doing so or not) and their relationships to the author. (Remember, those persons include the author's widow or widower, children, and surviving children of any deceased child.) Indicate on the list which persons actually are taking part in the termination and what their percentage shares of the termination right are.

If you are not sure of all the information required under points 8 or 9, put down as much as you know and explain why you are uncertain as to the rest, and include a statement that "to the best knowledge and belief of the person or persons signing the notice, the notice has been signed by all persons whose signature is necessary to terminate the grant under section 304 of title 17, U.S.C., or by their duly authorized agents."

The notice must be signed by all persons taking part, or their authorized agents. Agents must indicate on whose behalf they are signing. Each signature should be accompanied by the person's name and address, in typed or hand-printed form.

If you fail to comply with any of these requirements and if your errors or omissions cause other people to be misled to their disadvantage, your notice of termination may be judged legally ineffective.

As mentioned, a copy of the notice must be recorded (see http://www.copyright.gov/docs/fees.html for the amount) in the Copyright Office before its effective date. If you served notices on multiple grantees, a copy of one will suffice. What you record must be accompanied by a statement indicating the date on which the notice was served and the manner of service, unless that information is obvious from the notice itself. Where service was made by first-class mail, the date of service is the date you deposited the notice with the United States Postal Service.

TAX TREATMENT OF COPYRIGHTS

Authors generally have two tax problems: how to report their income and how to deduct their expenses. Other copyright owners have similar problems but from a different perspective. For them the problems are not much different from those of someone who buys a machine or farm. For an author, though, Congress has created a veritable funhouse of rules.

The author's trouble arises principally from governmental ambivalence as to whether a copyright is a capital asset in the hands of its creator. In many respects an author is like someone who builds houses rather than like someone who buys them: his profit is taxed as ordinary income, with the signal exception of songwriters, who in 2006 managed to persuade Congress to treat "self-created music works" differently from all other copyrighted works in this respect. A composer, or someone who has received copyright in a musical work by gift or inheritance from the composer, can elect to have the proceeds of sale of that copyright treated as capital gain.[1] This special treatment applies only to outright sales, not to royalty deals.

The Author as Owner: When Is an Asset Not an Asset?

Nonetheless, if an author is a professional author he must treat some of his expenses as capital investments, and if he is not he must treat them all as capital investments. When and how those expenses can later be deducted also depends on whether the author is a professional.

As you can see, this is not an area where common sense or logic will necessarily be of help. The thing to have is a map and a rulebook, and I hope what follows will serve. Please note that what I say here does not necessarily apply to software, which as in so many other respects occupies its own microclimate.

The Amateur An amateur author cannot deduct any of the expenses of his hobby unless and until he sells the work.[2] An amateur author is one who is not engaged in the trade or business of creating copyrighted works. For example, someone who paints for recreation is an amateur for tax purposes, however good the paintings may be.

The question that decides whether someone is an amateur or a professional is whether the activity is carried on primarily for livelihood or profit or primarily for recreation. Dim hopes of future glory will not convert a hobby into a trade. On the other hand financial failure does not brand one as an amateur, if one has made a genuine effort to sell one's creations.[3] Nor is it necessary that the activity be one's sole pursuit in life: painting on weekends may still be a profession if you are actively trying to sell the results. The regularity with which you pursue an activity will help determine whether you are a professional or an amateur.[4] The tortoise is more professional than the hare.

The Professional Generally, if you are a professional author, costs relating to your title in a copyright cannot be deducted in the year you incur them. Instead they have to be capitalized—that is, treated as investments—and depreciated over the useful life of a copyright. Other expenses, such as travel, secretarial help, or supplies, may be deducted in the year they are incurred. The basic principles are the following.

Costs Relating to Title

This phrase covers the cost of copyright registration, including legal fees. It also covers all expenses, including legal fees, that you may incur in defending your copyright against someone who accuses you of infringing, or in suing an infringer yourself. However, it does not include expenses incurred or damages won in defending or asserting a right to income. By the same token, damages that are in the form of profits are taxed as ordinary income. Damages that relate to title are not taxable as income, but the amount of them must be subtracted from the capital basis on which you compute depreciation.

This is the sort of hairsplitting that has earned the Internal Revenue Code a bad name. Suppose you become involved in a complicated infringement suit, where not only the basic title to copyright but also the right to royalties is at stake. How do you decide where title ends and the right to royalties begins? The best you can do is to ask the court to apportion the damages it awards you between the two and apply the same ratio to your legal costs and to the damages you win. Sometimes your attorney will be able to give you an itemized bill, but this method of allocating legal costs runs a risk of being overruled by the IRS.

The foregoing applies only if you win. If the court decides your claimed copyright is invalid and you lose, all of your expenses will be deductible in the year the decision is handed down, and you will also be able to deduct the dollar value of the title you have lost (but not the value of projected income) in the year the decision is handed down. Expenses that arise from litigation over income will be deductible when paid.

Other Expenses

The deductibility of expenses incurred in creating a work is subject to complex rules. For a brief period Congress tried to subject all authors' expenses to the so-called uniform capitalization rules, so that all of these expenses would have to be capitalized rather than deducted. In response to an outcry from authors' groups, Congress quickly retreated, but left in place the following:

- In general, no current deduction is allowed unless you are self-employed.

- Writers, composers, photographers, and artists are allowed to deduct most expenses in the year incurred, but it appears, somewhat ambiguously, that this is not allowed to filmmakers.

- Expenses relating to printing, photographic plates, motion picture films, videotapes, or similar items are not deductible but must be capitalized. Just what are "similar items" is unclear, but judging by the items listed one would have to extend this rule to, say, the costs a sculptor incurs in casting in bronze.

- No current deduction is allowed to an artist—as distinct from an author or photographer—unless the individual is "engaged in the business of being an artist." In this seemingly redundant provision a troublesome value judgment lurks: Congress does not regard anyone as an "artist" for tax purposes unless the aesthetic value of the work produced "predominates" over the utilitarian value. Thus, for example, says the legislative report accompanying the statute, "an expense that is incurred in producing jewelry, silverware, pottery, furniture, or other similar household items generally is not considered as being paid or incurred in the business of an individual being an artist." This presumptuous generalization practically invites litigation.

• Artists who do not qualify for current deduction treatment are given a "safe harbor"; they can deduct 50 percent of their expenses in the year incurred and 25 percent in each of the next two years.[5]

Depreciation

The tax laws permit an author to take a deduction each year for a portion of the capital value of a copyright, until it is reduced almost to zero. Depreciation should be taken over the useful life of the copyright. The presumption is that copyright will retain its value for its entire duration: life plus 70 years, or whatever the applicable term is. However, if you can prove that your copyright has a market life of only a few years, you can speed up your depreciation. Thus if you have written a textbook with a predictable market life of only six years, you can deduct one-sixth of your capital costs in each of those six years, starting with the year of first publication.[6] The general rule for depreciation is that it cannot begin until the asset is "placed in service." With works that are not published but are exploited by performance or display, depreciation would begin when exploitation begins. An interesting question, to which no one has the answer, is whether an unpublished work is "placed in service" when derivative works based upon it are published. I tend to think it should be so treated.

I use the phrase "almost to zero" because until you dispose of your copyright you cannot depreciate it below what is termed "salvage value."[7] Salvage value is, basically, what you could get for the copyright, even after income has dwindled away, by selling it to some optimistic buyer who hopes for a backswing in the pendulum of public taste or who wants to be able to use parts of your work without threat of suit. In most cases salvage value will be negligible. If your copyright is valuable, though, salvage may be a factor. You should consult your tax advisor on this point as on many of the other points noted here.

Matching Depreciation to Income

If you sell your copyright for a flat fee, you can deduct the remaining balance of your capital value in the year of sale. However, if you sell on a royalty basis, you should take your depreciation deductions against royalty income. In such a case the rules differ depending on whether you can predict your income flow. If you can, you should adjust your depreciation accordingly. For example, if you can predict that income will be $20,000 in the first year, $10,000 in the second year, $5,000 in the third, and zero in the fourth, for a total of $35,000, you can deduct $20/35$ of your capital value in the first year, $10/35$ in the second, and the remaining $5/35$ in the third (always, of course, allowing for salvage value).[8] If you cannot predict your income flow, you can deduct for depreciation in any given year only up to the amount of income you receive.[9]

Deduction for Loss

If you abandon or forfeit your copyright, if it is taken away from you in a lawsuit, or if it becomes valueless, you can deduct the remaining balance of your capital value in the year the loss occurs.[10]

Special Problems for Sculpture, Paintings, and Plates

This discussion has so far dealt with the copyright itself, an intangible property right. A sculptor or painter, however, produces something tangible as well, quite apart from the copyright in the work. So does a printmaker or photographer. So too does a publisher.

The physical object has a value quite separate from that of the copyright. It is a capital-type asset. Because of this, the costs of the materials and so on that go into it must be capitalized, even though they might otherwise be regarded as business expenses. Sometimes this will lead to allocation problems. For example, if you weld steel sculptures in your garage, what part of your electricity costs has to be attributed to the object? Your guess is probably as good as the IRS's so long as you guess in good faith. Depreciation cannot be taken unless the object is likely to deteriorate noticeably in the owner's lifetime. Sale of the object by the author will produce ordinary income, against which the author can deduct any remaining capital basis.

Where there are two or more joint authors, the depreciation basis must be divided among them in the same proportions as their ownership. Unless there is an agreement to the contrary, each joint author will take an equal share of the basis. *Joint Authors*

When an author makes a private gift of a copyright, it is valued for gift tax purposes not at its capital basis value but at its fair market value. It may have a basis of only $200, but if its market value (based on projected income) is $20,000, the author is treated as making a gift of $20,000. However, a gift to *charity* will be valued *Gift and Estate Taxes* not at fair market value but at the author's capital value.

Whether a gift other than to charity will actually incur gift tax depends on the number of donees, whether the author's spouse joins in making the gift, and whether the author has used up his "unified credit against gift and estate taxes." These are complex questions and outside the scope of this book. If you are making a gift to any one person of a copyright with a probable market value exceeding the limit on tax-free gifts in any given year—you should consult a tax advisor. In 2013 that limit was $14,000 per donor, per donee, but the amount is subject to periodic adjustment to take account of inflation.

A gift of royalty interest will not circumvent this rule. Indeed, a gift of a royalty interest, without any transfer of ownership, will not even suffice to make the income taxable to the donee rather than the author, although it will nonetheless be taxed as a gift.[11] This problem is frequently encountered by authors who wish to shift the future income stream of a work to their children, or to trusts for their children. The usual solution is to assign all copyright interest to the donee and, if the work is under contract for publication, to assign the *entire* contract, not merely the right to royalties.

Although unified with the gift tax laws in some respects, the estate tax laws as they apply to copyrights differ from the scheme I have described for gifts. A copyright is valued in the author's estate at its market value, no matter whether it is left to private persons or to charity. Thus if a copyright is left to charity—for example, as Shaw left his copyrights to the National Gallery of Ireland—the estate reports the full value in its inventory and receives as an offset a charitable deduction for the full value.

Copyright in a film or other work produced by a large corporation, whose creative staff are paid a salary and have no financial stake in the corporation, in many cases will be treated as a capital asset if the corporation is in the trade or business of exploiting it rather than of selling or brokering it.[12] Corporations are also entitled to certain very favorable deductions for charitable gifts of copyrights, too complicated to be dealt with here.

Special Rules for Corporations

A different set of rules applies to a person to whom the author gives, bequeaths, or sells his copyright. The basis for such a person depends on which type of transfer occurs.

Copyright as Capital Asset: Persons Other Than the Author

Donees

Basis in an Acquired Copyright

Basis in a gift is determined by looking at what lawyers call the owner's "chain of title." If you obtain a copyright by gift, your basis depends on who gave it to you. If you got it from the author, your basis is the author's basis, less any depreciation already taken before it reaches you. The same is true if you got it from someone who was given it by the author. There can be any number of gifts, but if the chain began with the author, the author's basis (as adjusted along the way) will be the basis for every owner in the chain. However, if someone in the chain of title purchased or inherited the copyright, the basis you get is that purchase price, or the estate value, less any depreciation taken on it since then. Each purchase or inheritance in a chain of title establishes a new basis for the copyright.

Inheritors

The tax laws give a break to someone who receives a copyright by inheritance. Basis is "stepped up" to the value of the copyright in the author's estate. Admittedly this makes a strange distinction between, say, a child of an author who is given a copyright and a child who gets it by inheritance. This distinction is sometimes overlooked by well-meaning parents; here, again, it is wise to seek the advice of a tax lawyer.

Purchasers

If you purchase a copyright, your basis will be what you paid for it. However, for there to have been a purchase, there has to have been a sale. The term "sale," as used in the tax laws, has special meaning. Because a copyright is a bundle of distinct rights, there can be a sale of one of those rights even if the others are retained. For example, you can have a sale of the publication right alone. However, if the transferor retains too much control over the right, there is no sale even though, for purposes of the copyright law, there has been an exclusive transfer.

The only controls that a seller can safely retain without running afoul of this rule are the right to sue for infringement and the right to rescind the transfer for failure to make royalty payments or because the transferee has gone bankrupt, or because the transferee fails to market the property. The general principle here is that a transfer is a sale so long as rescission can occur only because of some event that is not in the seller's control.[13] The statutory right to terminate a transfer (see chapters 3 and 10) does not affect the status of a "sale."

A transfer may be limited in geographical scope. If it is, it should be paid for not on a royalty basis but in a lump sum, or it will be treated as a license and not a sale. Conversely, if paid for on a royalty basis it will be considered a sale only if the exclusive rights given are without geographical limitation.[14] And all of this is without regard to whether the arrangement would be called a transfer of ownership for copyright purposes.

In many cases, a purchaser will want to have a transfer characterized as a license so that he can deduct his payments as a cost of doing business instead of capitalizing them. The seller is just as likely to want the opposite. When the transaction is ambiguous, this will be an important bargaining point for both sides.

A donee or inheritor of a copyright can take depreciation only if a copyright is producing income. A purchaser of a copyright, assuming that the purchaser has acquired the property for investment purposes and not as a broker or trader in copyrights, can take depreciation regardless of whether income is being received. A broker or trader in copyrights holds the copyrights as inventory and cannot take depreciation at all. *Depreciation*

The depreciation rules for someone who receives a copyright by gift or inheritance are generally the same as for an author: depreciation may be taken against income in any of the ways discussed. A purchaser of a copyright must also follow these rules if he holds the copyright for investment purposes, except that he can take a deduction in a year of no income. All three types of persons can take a deduction for loss or forfeiture.

Where a copyright is acquired as part of the acquisition of a business, it must be depreciated over a 14-year period.[15]

INTERNATIONAL COPYRIGHT PROTECTION   **12**

If you know something of the life of Charles Dickens, you know something also of the chaos that existed in the early days of bulk printing, when, in the view of the U.S. Government, copyrights stopped at the borders of an author's native land. Dickens and other popular English writers suffered wholesale piracy of their works by American printers, until at last the U.S. Senate, against strong domestic pressure, agreed by treaty to recognize English copyrights.

Copyright is intrinsically a creature of national law. However, there are now few countries that do not have treaty arrangements for the international protection of copyrights. Most of these countries are members of either or both of the two great conventions, as they are called: the Berne Convention and the Universal Copyright Convention (UCC). These conventions are essentially multilateral agreements to give certain recognition to copyrights that arise in other member countries. Neither of these conventions requires a member nation to protect copyright in sound recordings. There is a separate treaty on this subject: the Convention for the Protection of Producers of Phonograms Against Unauthorized Duplication of Their Phonograms. However, the membership of this phonogram convention is comparatively small.

The United States was one of the founding members of the UCC in the early 1950s, but did not join Berne until 1989. The United States pushed for the formation of the UCC as an alternative to Berne; it declined for decades to join Berne out of a reluctance to abandon the notice requirement and certain other formalities and to extend copyright duration to meet Berne standards. It has finally succumbed, with the results I have described in preceding chapters.

Nearly every country in the world belongs to one of the two conventions; most belong to both. A few holdouts remain, but the trend is toward wider membership, and through this and other methods copyright piracy has been substantially reduced. Most of our major trading partners belong to Berne. Even China, Russia, and some other former Communist bloc countries have now joined Berne. Berne membership has widened to the point that the UCC will most likely soon die of irrelevance.[1]

Both Berne and the UCC live largely by two key precepts: "national treatment" and the setting of minimum standards of protection by which all treaty members must abide. National treatment requires that every member nation extend the protection of its laws to works that originate in other member nations. Thus an American sculptor must receive in Italy the same copyright treatment as an Italian sculptor, and the Italian must receive in the United States the same treatment as her American counterpart.

There are two qualifications to this. The first is the "rule of the shorter term," which is, in practice, more an exception than a rule. It permits the United States to protect foreign photographs, for example, only for as long as they would be protected in their countries of origin. To some this seems perverse, like denying Babe Ruth a homer to left in Wrigley Field if the ball wouldn't have cleared the wall at Fenway Park. To others it seems eminently fair; after all, if the author's own government doesn't care to protect him, why should any other?

Under Berne the rule of the shorter term can be applied on a case-by-case basis. Thus, for example, if an American film has gone into the public domain because of failure to renew, other countries will not be obliged to protect it thereafter. (Most will anyway.) Under the UCC the rule can be invoked only if the foreign work belongs to a *class* of works that receives shorter protection in the country of origin.[2] In some countries the situation is further complicated by bilateral treaties with the United States that apply somewhat different rules in cases not governed by Berne or the UCC.[3]

The United States has never invoked the rule, even as to works where it could easily have done so. For many years it protected photographs and sound recordings, for example, much longer than many Berne countries, but it always gave such countries' authors the same treatment as its own. This generosity was not always reciprocated. The disparity continues despite earnest talk of harmonization. When the European Union countries extended their copyright terms to life of the author plus 70 years, Congress followed suit. But in Europe, this extension applies only to literary, dramatic, musical, and artistic works, and (with some minor modification) to motion pictures. In the United States, it applies to all works.

Of course, the rule of the shorter term infallibly works in reverse: in other words, no country will protect a foreign work for any longer period than it will protect native works of the same type.

The other qualification to national treatment favors developing countries. Both Berne and the UCC give these countries the right to reproduce foreign works for teaching purposes, on a sort of compulsory license basis, if no edition is generally available in those countries at a "reasonable price." Both also give some developing countries the right to publish unauthorized translations. The conditions that must be met for either of these rights to be invoked are complicated,[4] and I will not explicate them here. I will allow myself the observation that though the purpose of these provisions is laudable, the method seems unfair. Steel companies are not told that they must sell their steel at a discount to developing countries; if they do so, one government or the other subsidizes them. Why should copyright owners bear a different burden?

National treatment governs fundamental issues of copyrightability. For example, a foreign country must grant copyright to an American factual compilation that, under the *Feist* doctrine, is not eligible for U.S. copyright, if that compilation would be protectable if created by one of its own citizens. Conversely, an American court will not protect such a work created by a foreign author, regardless of its protectability in its country of origin.

However, national treatment does not govern issues of ownership. When it comes to ownership, our courts will in general defer to the law of the place where the work was created.[5] Thus, if a work is regarded in its country of origin as a joint work, our courts will treat the authors as being the joint owners of copyright within our borders, even though the relationship between the authors might be one that we would consider a work-for-hire relationship if the parties were U.S. citizens. The reason for this rule is that, since the work was not created here, the United States has little interest in regulating the relationship between the parties; the country of origin has a much greater interest in that. And even though the United States does have an interest in regulating the duration of copyrights, our courts would probably, for the sake of consistency, look to the country of origin in determining whether a work should have a joint-author term (longest life plus 70 years) or a work-for-hire term (95 years from first publication, etc.).

These issues involve a legal doctrine called "conflicts of laws," and the courts of various nations do not necessarily agree on how to determine which country's law to apply in such situations. Furthermore, different legal systems are built on different concepts, and it may be asking too much to ask a foreign court to apply our concepts, or vice versa. For example, in European countries a work may be considered a "joint work" only if the authors' contributions are truly inseparable. The idea that a lyricist and a composer may be joint authors of a song is alien to them, because the lyrics and the music are capable of existing independent of each other. Would an English court, then, treat an American song as a joint work, or as a collective work? To do the former might create problems in administering the copyright within England. Nor is this the only point of disagreement over joint works. Most if not all European countries require any license, even a nonexclusive license, of a joint work to be signed by both authors. Would a French court honor a license signed by just our lyricist? The answer in that particular case seems to be no: French courts will treat any such license as invalid, to the extent that it purports to give publication rights in France, even if the work is a U.S. work and the license is executed in the United States.[6] Would other European countries follow suit? I hesitate to say. Would a U.S. court honor a nonexclusive license signed in France by just one of two French authors? If tit-for-tat is the rule, then the answer is no, and yet there would seem to be no good reason not to honor such a license, at least within our borders.

How all this will shake out as the Internet promotes cross-border collaborations, as multinational companies increasingly create and traffic in copyrightable works, will be interesting to watch. For example, if an American and a German collaborate on a work, under circumstances that U.S. law would categorize as a work-for-hire relationship but German law would categorize as a joint-author relationship, who wins? No one knows. In this particular example, the problem can be avoided if the two individuals reduce their understanding to writing, and choose the law by which they wish to be governed, for most countries will give great weight to any contractual choice of law. Where contract conflicts with a perceived public policy, though, this relative certainty disappears.

An example of such a public policy lies in regulation of contracts. In some countries rights of reversion are given to authors on moral grounds, rights that U.S. law does not give. Such a country might well insist on enforcing the reversion, at least within its borders, no matter what the contract says—especially if the author were one of its own citizens and the assignee an American. Our own law has rights of termination that are inalienable; the case has not arisen, but I would not be surprised to see an American court enforce the termination within our borders even if the country where the contract was signed has no such provision. Or to take another example: in the United States, one may grant rights in future technologies by referring to "all media now known or hereafter discovered." In some countries, however, a grant of rights will not be extended to cover technologies that did not exist at the time of the grant, no matter how the grant is worded.

Here, too, a court might perceive a public policy needing to be enforced.

Or take the matter of renewal. In the case of, say, a work by a deceased English author, there is really no good reason why the ownership of copyright within the United States should revert to his widow after 28 years while ownership elsewhere in the world remains with his publisher—but our courts would very likely enforce such a result. Indeed, it is hard to see how they could avoid it.

These anomalies complicate international dealings in copyright. One is reminded of the early days of railroads, when rail gauges were not uniform across borders. There have always been differences among nations in economic regulation. But when such differences impede commerce, which, like the railroads, is designed for travel across borders, they are difficult to justify. Copyright is an area where justification runs particularly thin. The Internet makes possible simultaneous worldwide exploitation of rights. That exploitation ought not to be subject to a hundred different legal standards, however reasonable any of them might be in isolation.

Although it might not seem so in light of the preceding discussion, the second key concept of Berne and the UCC is, as I mentioned, the setting of standards. Berne requires longer terms of protection and eschews formalities; Berne is also more broadly favorable to authors in the area of moral rights. The UCC, though it does not encourage formalities, is more tolerant. In particular, although it does not require copyright notice, it establishes "© [name] [year of first publication]" as a sort of international form of copyright notice for those who wish to use it. It is therefore prudent, when using copyright notice, to use this particular form.

One area in which standards may never be set is that of fair use. American law is uniquely strong in its protection of fair use, perhaps because of its uniquely broad protection for freedom of speech, exceeding that of even our closest allies. Even Canada, whose laws (for reasons of cross-border trade) tend to mirror ours more than do the laws of other English-speaking countries, let alone civil law countries, recognizes only a fairly narrow band of activities as what it calls "fair dealing." Our fair use doctrine is largely judge-made, based on the generalities of Section 107 of our Copyright Act. By contrast, Canadian law acknowledges as fair dealing only certain activities specifically enumerated in its statute, though within those activities Canadian courts have tended to be quite generous to users. English law, which you might expect would be much like ours, gives much narrower scope for "fair dealing." In 2011 a special study undertaken for Parliament concluded that England could not adopt a fair use policy similar to America's because to do so would violate Britain's EU treaty obligations.[7]

The setting of standards is an ongoing process—and sometimes a frustrating one for those who believe deeply in it. Treaties are the mechanism for standard-setting on an international level. They may be agreed on in Geneva or Marrakesh or some other venue where the representatives of nations meet and hammer out terms. That does not ensure that the treaties will ever actually be adopted, which in the United States requires ratification by the Senate. (This syndrome is not exclusive to copyright, be it noted; treaties on many subjects die of neglect in the U.S. Senate.) And of course, even if a treaty is formally approved by the Senate, this does not necessarily ensure that the enabling legislation to comply with the treaty will be enacted swiftly or without disputation.

The experience of recent decades has been mixed. In 1996, the United States and other members of the Berne Convention agreed on the text of two treaties expanding and clarifying the treatment of certain copyrights. One of these, the Treaty on Certain Questions Concerning the Protection of Literary and Artistic Works, could be characterized as a victory for U.S. and other "first world" copyright interests. It required all Berne countries to do certain things that the United States had already done: ensure that copyright owners of computer programs and sound recordings can control the rental of their works; protect computer programs as literary works; and protect copyright in photographs for the same term as other types of works (Berne at present requires only 25 years' protection). It made clear that copyright owners control the right to disseminate their works electronically. It contained important provisions concerning technological anti-infringement devices. These have been enacted, in the Digital Millennium Copyright Act, as have the provisions regarding "rights management information."

Another possibly noteworthy provision of this treaty was one requiring signatory nations to give copyright owners of cinematographic works (i.e., movies) the right to control commercial rental of their works. However, the treaty said that this right does not have to be enacted unless commercial rental of movies has "led to widespread copying of such works materially impairing the exclusive right of reproduction." This escape clause has in effect been used by Congress, which shows no greater inclination than previously to give movie producers a video rental right.

The second 1996 treaty concerned sound recordings. It required all parties to recognize the rights of reproduction and distribution of sound recordings that U.S. law has long recognized. If fully implemented, however, it would involve two changes in our law, one of them quite dramatic in its impact. As a result, this treaty has gone exactly nowhere so far as U.S. law is concerned.

The most important of these changes would be the creation of a performance right for sound recordings. The United States already recognizes such a right, subject to limitations, where digital transmission is concerned. The treaty, though, applies to both analog and digital performance. In essence, performers of music would be treated the same way as the copyright owners of music: they would receive "equitable remuneration" from radio stations, discotheques, and others who perform their recordings publicly. The treaty does not make this mandatory, however; any nation can choose to opt out of this particular requirement.[8]

This treaty would also require the United States to enact federal law preventing unauthorized fixation of aural performances. This requirement goes beyond GATT, which (as noted in chapter 1) required such legislation as to musical performances but not all aural performances generally.

The treaty would further require the United States to create moral rights for aural performers. In essence, performers would have the right, at least during their lifetimes, to be identified when their performances are used "except where omission is dictated by the manner of use of the performance" (whatever that means), and to prevent any distortion, mutilation, or other modification of their performances that would be prejudicial to their reputations.

If the U.S. Senate were ever to ratify this treaty—which seems highly unlikely—Congress would have to grapple with issues such as: (1) Where performers perform as a group, are these rights collective or still individual? For example, can an orchestra conductor grant waivers of moral rights on behalf of the entire orchestra? Does each second violinist have to be identified by name on every album, or is it enough to say "Boston Symphony Orchestra"? (2) Does the moral right in a sound recording trump the derivative-work right, or vice versa, if the owners of the two rights are at odds? Our present moral rights law avoids this problem by being limited to the specific art objects that an artist creates; the artist may object to alteration of these but not to the creation of derivative works that may distort the image. No such fudge is available for sound recordings.

For some reason, the treaty specifically includes dancers among the performers whose rights it seeks to protect, though it is hard to imagine any value in the sound of a dancer's feet hitting the floor.

A more recent, equally well-intentioned treaty likely to languish in oblivion is the Beijing WIPO [World International Property Organization] Treaty on Audiovisual Performances, signed by the United States and some 50 other nations in 2012, but so far not ratified by the Senate. It aims to give audiovisual performers a right to control fixation of their performances or an equitable right of remuneration for the use of their performances, and moral rights in their performances.

Regardless of the fate of these particular treaties, the trend toward wider membership in copyright conventions, enhanced standards of protection, greater uniformity of law (for the most part), and less piracy is likely to continue. Overall we now operate in an international system that ensures American copyright owners reasonably predictable and uniform protection throughout most of the world. GATT has reinforced this system, openly acknowledging the link between copyright and free trade. By this and other agreements, nations have been compelled to honor copyright as a cost of access to markets. As international trade in copyrights becomes more and more valuable—in science, software, and entertainment—this system will likely prove to have been not merely fair-minded but foresighted as well.

COPYRIGHT AND THE INFORMATION SOCIETY: A FEW PARTING THOUGHTS, AND A GLIMPSE INTO THE FUTURE

Information is power, as we are often told. But like most other kinds of power, it has no value except in use. We as a society benefit from that use and so we encourage authors as best we know how, realizing, as Samuel Johnson once put it, that "nobody but a blockhead ever wrote except for money."

In 1909, when the predecessor to our current Copyright Act was passed, few if any foresaw the development of radio, television, or sound recording. Yet these three media have radically changed our culture, and for many people they have greater importance than the printed word. By the time the 1976 Act was passed, photocopying had become widespread, but few if any foresaw the advent of digital technology, which has in two decades completely changed our terms of cultural reference. As each new technology challenged copyright, courts and lawyers and their clients found themselves having to discuss new concepts in an old language, with Congress always playing catch-up in adapting the statute itself. The results have been uneven, but copyright has survived.

Indeed I would say, perhaps to the horror of some of my colleagues, that we have cleared the great jagged technological mountains that loomed ahead of us, and are now flying in fairly calm air over fairly level ground. Twenty years ago the arguments over digital technology and copyright were existential; now, fights erupt over such questions as whether a user's allocated piece of an antenna or server permits a customized delivery of digital content over the Internet.

Looking back at the corresponding chapter in the previous edition of this book, I am struck by the things I got right and the things I got wrong. In the latter category, I worried needlessly (it now seems) that digital technology would heighten tensions between the rich world and the developing world over copyright. That problem seems to be diminishing, as developing economies mature and move toward the norms of the developed world. Indeed, the cheapness of digital technology has accelerated that maturing process. I foresaw at least in part the growth of granular digital delivery and payment systems, but placed too much hope in watermarking and similar technologies, which so far have not won wide acceptance.

At a more general level, I said the following:

> Pricing will have to be reasonable; people will be far less tempted to steal if they can buy conveniently and at what they consider a fair price. Finally, education will have to instill in the public a greater understanding of why we have a copyright system, and how the public benefits from the incentives it provides to authors.

Well, I was right about the first. Apple's iTunes and similar services have delivered quality copyrighted content at a price that makes piracy unattractive to most users. The money may not be as good as it was, certainly for the average songwriter or recording artist, but at least the hemorrhaging seems to have stopped.

(Music industry people will tell you, though, that the decline in income from sound recording sales has irrevocably altered the industry and not for the better.) As to the second, I was right in the diagnosis, but the cure has not arrived. In fact, public understanding of the importance of copyright may even have declined over the last 10 years. The bizarre public outcry over the Stop Online Piracy Act has put paid to any idea that the general public cares about protecting copyright owners from thieves and vandals.

Ironically, the copyright industries, whose livelihood depends on telling good stories well, have done a very poor job of telling their own story to the public. Suits by the record labels against grandmothers and teenagers for illicit file sharing were certainly "educational" in a sense, but if there was any real effort to explain to the country why they were necessary (and they may, alas, have been necessary), I missed it and probably you did too.

The fact is that copyright has never been more important: it permeates our lives more than at any time in history. The average American spends several hours a day being entertained by sports or creative programming, delivered on television or via the Internet. All that programming depends on copyright for its existence. The average American listens to a lot of music, whether by iPod or phone or tablet; all that music too depends on copyright—both for the content and for the software that delivers it. The tools we use at work and the toys we use to stay connected are more and more the creatures of copyright in one way or another. The word on this needs to get out.

Readers of this book will, I hope, be in the enlightened minority—and contribute to an informed debate about where we go from here.

We do need an informed debate, for a number of issues have languished too long and ought to be addressed. They are not high jagged mountain ranges, at least conceptually, and they can be worked into our flight plan with just a modicum of good sense and good will.

Register of Copyrights Maria Pallante has called for the "next great Copyright Act,"[1] and some members of Congress have picked up on that idea. I have enormous respect for Ms. Pallante, who has shown great leadership and wisdom. But the call to greatness seems excessive. (Perhaps it is simply her way of inspiring people to do the right thing: no mean feat in Washington these days.) What needs fixing is not of existential proportions, and much of it has been known for some time.

The orphan works problem (discussed in chapter 8) ranks high on her list, and on the lists of many others. The orphan works bill that passed the Senate back in 2008 sought to address another serious problem as well: the lack of a small claims process for copyright. Most copyright owners do not have the resources to pursue legal action against infringers, even if they stand a good chance of recovering their legal fees at the end of the fight. And frankly, their damages often do not justify either the private expense or the public expense (in court resources) that a full-bore copyright lawsuit entails. We need some mechanism for handling these claims quickly and cheaply. In late 2013 the Copyright Office issued a proposal for a small claims system, but it is far too early to tell whether it, or anything like it, will be enacted.

Another issue concerns the 20-year extension of the copyright term from life-plus-50 to life-plus-70. At the time it was enacted, many even in the copyright bar (myself included) thought the extension a mistake. Some in academe took such umbrage at it that they sued to have it declared unconstitutional. Their case went all the way to the Supreme Court, which (probably rightly) refused to second-guess Congress.[2] Some would like Congress, as part of a broader revision, to roll back the 20-year extension, but that is not going to happen. However, momentum is building for an adjustment. Register Pallante has thrown her support behind the idea of making the 20-year extension dependent on some sort of filing in the Copyright Office. Because the extra 20 years go beyond the requirements of Berne, imposing formalities as a condition of the extended protection would not violate our treaty obligations. It would go a long way toward reducing the scope of the orphan works problem, and it would free a lot of material for productive reuse. It would also partly assuage the fears of some that the copyright flag has become permanently captured by the owners' team.

Some technical problems also need cleaning up. Chief among those would be the term of copyright for foreign works first published abroad. (See discussion in chapter 10.) There is simply no excuse for the duration of any copyright depending on which Circuit you live in.

Finally, in a rational world, the Copyright Office would be better funded, so it could improve service to its constituency. With dedicated and hard-working people, the Office has made enormous efforts to bring its records into the twenty-first century, but a lot of work on this remains to be done. It is scandalous that, in a system dependent on the filing of registrations and the recordation of assignments and other transactions, those records are not fully available online. This is not a matter for revision of the Copyright Act but for improvement of the budgetary process. Still, if Congress turns its full attention to the copyright system, this might get fixed along with other problems.

My fear, though, is that if Congress really opens the door to a wide-ranging revision of the Copyright Act, sensible provisions such as these, which command broad support (or in the case of technical corrections, offend almost no one), may be held hostage to a lot of other demands that don't. For example, the Register has suggested that the time may be ripe for creating a performance right for sound recordings, and many consider this an issue of fundamental fairness. However, the push for it has been stymied for decades by powerful lobbies, and those lobbies have not disappeared. Other people have suggested we need to overhaul the statutory damages provisions of the Act, but that is likely to lead to an epic battle. Yet others will try to get Congress to reverse the result of cases that went against them; sometimes justice will be on their side, but in the aggregate such initiatives could seriously bog things down.

However this pans out, Congress could use the input of an educated public. When the 20-year copyright term extension passed, quickly and with barely a breath of opposition, a number of copyright scholars decried the fact that no one was speaking in Congress for the interests of the ordinary citizen in copyright matters. This was a fair criticism, but did the fault lie solely with Congress? In other fields *vox populi* has made itself heard, and why should copyright be any different?

Vox populi, though, needs to speak knowledgably. My main purpose in writing this book has been to acquaint you with the law as it is. However, if information really is power, what I have said may help you to contribute to the growth and orderly change of that law. That would be a benefit to all of us.

APPENDIX A: DURATION CHART

Date of Creation/ Publication	U.S. or Non-U.S. Work	Type of Authorship	Term of Protection
Created after 1977	Either	Single author—individual	Life plus 70 years
"	"	Two or more individual authors	Life of last to die plus 70 years
"	"	Work made for hire	95 years from first publication, or 120 years from creation, whichever expires first
"	"	Pseudonymous	95 years from first publication, or 120 years from creation, unless identity is filed with Copyright Office
"	"	Anonymous	95 years from first publication, or 120 years from creation, unless identity is filed with Copyright Office

Date of Creation/ Publication	U.S. or Non-U.S. Work	Type of Authorship	Term of Protection
Created before 1978 but not published before 2003	"	Same as any of above	Same as corresponding term above
Created before 1978 but published after 1977 and before 2003	"	Same as any of above	Same as corresponding term above or until December 31, 1947, whichever is later
Published or registered between January 1, 1964 and December 31, 1977	"	Same as any of above	95 years from first publication
Published or registered between January 1, 1923 and December 31, 1963	U.S.	Same as any of above	95 years from first publication, if copyright was renewed in 28th year, otherwise now in public domain
Published in the U.S. between January 1, 1923 and December 31, 1963	Non-U.S.	Same as any of above	95 years from first publication
Published abroad between January 1, 1923 and December 31, 1963	Non-U.S.	Same as any of above	95 years from first publication*
Published anywhere before 1923	Either	Same as any of above	Public domain*

* This rule does not apply in the Ninth Circuit. There, foreign works published before 1978 do not start their U.S. copyright term until publication in the United States.

Also note the following special rules for special media; these rules supersede all the above except as noted:

Mask works: 10 years from registration or from first commercial exploitation, whichever occurs first.

Architectural works: Same as in chart above unless (i) constructed or published before 1990, in which case not under copyright, or (ii) created but neither constructed nor published before 1990, in which case same as in chart above but only if constructed before January 1, 2003, otherwise now in public domain.

Sound recordings made before February 15, 1972: Protected by state antipiracy laws only, until February 15, 2067, after which date they will be in the public domain.

APPENDIX B: METHODS OF AFFIXATION AND POSITIONS OF THE COPYRIGHT NOTICE ON VARIOUS TYPES OF WORKS

[From 37 C.F.R. Ch. II §201.20.]

(a) *General.*

(1) This section specifies examples of methods of affixation and positions of the copyright notice on various types of works that will satisfy the notice requirement of section 401(c) of title 17 of the United States Code, as amended by Pub. L. 94-553. A notice considered "acceptable" under this regulation shall be considered to satisfy the requirement of that section that it be "affixed to the copies in such manner and location as to give reasonable notice of the claim of copyright." As provided by that section, the examples specified in this regulation shall not be considered exhaustive of methods of affixation and positions giving reasonable notice of the claim of copyright.

(2) The provisions of this section are applicable to copies publicly distributed on or after December 1, 1981. This section does not establish any rules concerning the form of the notice or the legal sufficiency of particular notices, except with respect to methods of affixation and positions of notice. The adequacy or legal sufficiency of a copyright notice is determined by the law in effect at the time of first publication of the work.

(b) *Definitions.* For the purposes of this section:

(1) The terms *audiovisual works, collective works, copies, device, fixed, machine, motion picture, pictorial, graphic, and sculptural works,* and their variant forms, have the meanings given to them in section 101 of title 17.

(2) *Title 17* means title 17 of the United States Code, as amended by Pub. L. 94-553.

(3) In the case of a work consisting preponderantly of leaves on which the work is printed or otherwise reproduced on both sides, a "page" is one side of a leaf; where the preponderance of the leaves are printed on one side only, the terms "page" and "leaf" mean the same.

(4) A work is published in *book form* if the copies embodying it consist of multiple leaves bound, fastened, or assembled in a predetermined order, as, for example, a volume, booklet, pamphlet, or multipage folder. For the purpose of this section, a work need not consist of textual matter in order to be considered published in "book form."

(5) A *title page* is a page, or two consecutive pages facing each other, appearing at or near the front of the copies of a work published in book form, on which the complete title of the work is prominently stated and on which the names of the author or authors, the name of the publisher, the place of publication, or some combination of them, are given.

(6) The meaning of the terms *front, back, first, last,* and *following,* when used in connection with works published in book form, will vary in relation to the physical form of the copies, depending upon the particular language in which the work is written.

(7) In the case of a work published in book form with a hard or soft cover, the *front page* and *back page* of the copies are the outsides of the front and back covers;

where there is no cover, the "front page" and "back page" are the pages visible at the front and back of the copies before they are opened.

(8) A *masthead* is a body of information appearing in approximately the same location in most issues of a newspaper, magazine, journal, review, or other periodical or serial, typically containing the title of the periodical or serial, information about the staff, periodicity of issues, operation, and subscription and editorial policies, of the publication.

(9) A *single-leaf work* is a work published in copies consisting of a single leaf, including copies on which the work is printed or otherwise reproduced on either one side or on both sides of the leaf, and also folders which, without cutting or tearing the copies, can be opened out to form a single leaf. For the purpose of this section, a work need not consist of textual matter in order to be considered a "single-leaf work."

(c) *Manner of affixation and position generally.*

(1) In all cases dealt with in this section, the acceptability of a notice depends upon its being permanently legible to an ordinary user of the work under normal conditions of use, and affixed to the copies in such manner and position that, when affixed, it is not concealed from view upon reasonable examination.

(2) Where, in a particular case, a notice does not appear in one of the precise locations prescribed in this section but a person looking in one of those locations would be reasonably certain to find a notice in another somewhat different location, that notice will be acceptable under this section.

(d) *Works published in book form.* In the case of works published in book form, a notice reproduced on the copies in any of the following positions is acceptable:

(1) The title page, if any;

(2) The page immediately following the title page, if any;

(3) Either side of the front cover, if any; or, if there is no front cover, either side of the front leaf of the copies;

(4) Either side of the back cover, if any; or, if there is no back cover, either side of the back leaf of the copies;

(5) The first page of the main body of the work;

(6) The last page of the main body of the work;

(7) Any page between the front page and the first page of the main body of the work, if:

(i) There are no more than ten pages between the front page and the first page of the main body of the work; and

(ii) The notice is reproduced prominently and is set apart from other matter on the page where it appears;

(8) Any page between the last page of the main body of the work and back page, if:

(i) There are no more than ten pages between the last page of the main body of the work and the back page; and

(ii) The notice is reproduced prominently and is set apart from the other matter on the page where it appears.

(9) In the case of a work published as an issue of a periodical or serial, in addition to any of the locations listed in paragraphs (d) (1) through (8) of this section, a notice is acceptable if it is located:

(i) As a part of, or adjacent to, the masthead;

(ii) On the page containing the masthead if the notice is reproduced prominently and is set apart from the other matter appearing on the page; or

(iii) Adjacent to a prominent heading, appearing at or near the front of the issue, containing the title of the periodical or serial and any combination of the volume and issue number and date of the issue.

(10) In the case of a musical work, in addition to any of the locations listed in paragraphs (d) (1) through (9) of this section, a notice is acceptable if it is located on the first page of music.

(e) *Single-leaf works.* In the case of single-leaf works, a notice reproduced on the copies anywhere on the front or back of the leaf is acceptable.

(f) *Contributions to collective works.* For a separate contribution to a collective work to be considered to "bear its own notice of copyright," as provided by 17 U.S.C. 404, a notice reproduced on the copies in any of the following positions is acceptable:

(1) Where the separate contribution is reproduced on a single page, a notice is acceptable if it appears:

(i) Under the title of the contribution on that page;

(ii) Adjacent to the contribution; or

(iii) On the same page if, through format, wording, or both, the application of the notice to the particular contribution is made clear;

(2) Where the separate contribution is reproduced on more than one page of the collective work, a notice is acceptable if it appears:

(i) Under a title appearing at or near the beginning of the contribution;

(ii) On the first page of the main body of the contribution;

(iii) Immediately following the end of the contribution; or

(iv) On any of the pages where the contribution appears, if:

(A) The contribution is reproduced on no more than twenty pages of the collective work;

(B) The notice is reproduced prominently and is set apart from other matter on the page where it appears; and

(C) Through format, wording, or both, the application of the notice to the particular contribution is made clear;

(3) Where the separate contribution is a musical work, in addition to any of the locations listed in paragraphs (f) (1) and (2) of this section, a notice is acceptable if it is located on the first page of music of the contribution;

(4) As an alternative to placing the notice on one of the pages where a separate contribution itself appears, the contribution is considered to "bear its own notice" if the notice appears clearly in juxtaposition with a separate listing of the contribution by title, or if the contribution is untitled, by a description reasonably identifying the contribution:

(i) On the page bearing the copyright notice for the collective work as a whole, if any; or

(ii) In a clearly identified and readily-accessible table of contents or listing of acknowledgments appearing near the front or back of the collective work as a whole.

(g) *Works reproduced in machine-readable copies.* For works reproduced in machine-readable copies (such as magnetic tapes or disks, punched cards, or the like), from which the work cannot ordinarily be visually perceived except with the aid of a machine or device,[1] each of the following constitute examples of acceptable methods of affixation and position of notice:

---

1. Works published in a form requiring the use of a machine or device for purposes of optical enlargement (such as film, filmstrips, slide films, and works published in any variety of microform) and works published in visually perceptible form but used in connection with optical scanning devices, are not within this category.

(1) A notice embodied in the copies in machine-readable form in such a manner that on visually perceptible printouts it appears either with or near the title, or at the end of the work;

(2) A notice that is displayed at the user's terminal at sign on;

(3) A notice that is continuously on terminal display; or

(4) A legible notice reproduced durably, so as to withstand normal use, on a gummed or other label securely affixed to the copies or to a box, reel, cartridge, cassette, or other container used as a permanent receptacle for the copies.

(h) *Motion pictures and other audiovisual works.*

(1) The following constitute examples of acceptable methods of affixation and positions of the copyright notice on motion pictures and other audiovisual works: A notice that is embodied in the copies by a photomechanical or electronic process, in such a position that it ordinarily would appear whenever the work is performed in its entirety, and that is located:

(i) With or near the title;

(ii) With the cast, credits, and similar information;

(iii) At or immediately following the beginning of the work; or

(iv) At or immediately preceding the end of the work.

(2) In the case of an untitled motion picture or other audiovisual work whose duration is sixty seconds or less, in addition to any of the locations listed in paragraph (h)(1) of this section, a notice that is embodied in the copies by a photomechanical or electronic process, in such a position that it ordinarily would appear to the projectionist or broadcaster when preparing the work for performance, is acceptable if it is located on the leader of the film or tape immediately preceding the beginning of the work.

(3) In the case of a motion picture or other audio-visual work that is distributed to the public for private use, the notice may be affixed, in addition to the locations specified in paragraph (h)(1) of this section, on the housing or container, if it is a permanent receptacle for the work.

(i) *Pictorial, graphic, and sculptural works.* The following constitute examples of acceptable methods of affixation and positions of the copyright notice on various forms of pictorial, graphic, and sculptural works:

(1) Where a work is reproduced in two-dimensional copies, a notice affixed directly or by means of a label cemented, sewn, or otherwise attached durably, so as to withstand normal use, [to] the front or back of the copies, or to any backing, mounting, matting, framing, or other material to which the copies are durably attached, so as to withstand normal use, or in which they are permanently housed, is acceptable.

(2) Where a work is reproduced in three-dimensional copies, a notice affixed directly or by means of a label cemented, sewn, or otherwise attached durably, so as to withstand normal use, to any visible portion of the work, or to any base, mounting, framing, or other material on which the copies are durably attached, so as to withstand normal use, or in which they are permanently housed, is acceptable.

(3) Where, because of the size or physical characteristics of the material in which the work is reproduced in copies, it is impossible or extremely impracticable to affix a notice to the copies directly or by means of a durable label, a notice is acceptable if it appears on a tag that is of durable material, so as to withstand normal use, and that is attached to the copy with sufficient durability that it will remain with the copy while it is passing through its normal channels of commerce.

(4) Where a work is reproduced in copies consisting of sheet-like or strip material bearing multiple or continuous reproductions of the work, the notice may be applied:

(i) To the reproduction itself;

(ii) To the margin, selvage, or reverse side of the material at frequent and regular intervals; or

(iii) If the material contains neither a selvage nor a reverse side, to tags or labels, attached to the copies and to any spools, reels, or containers housing them in such a way that a notice is visible while the copies are passing through their normal channels of commerce.

(5) If the work is permanently housed in a container, such as a game or puzzle box, a notice reproduced on the permanent container is acceptable.

APPENDIX C: REGISTRATION OF COMPUTER PROGRAMS AND DATABASES

The general rule and accepted practice in registering computer programs and databases is to deposit "identifying material"—source code or data entries sufficient to give the flavor of what you are registering without disclosing too much. If you are registering a computer program published in CD-ROM format, you should submit for deposit the entire CD-ROM package, including a complete copy of any accompanying operating software and instructional manual, plus "identifying material" for the program itself. If you have questions about what to do, you can reach a Copyright Office information specialist at (202) 707-3000.

Computer Programs

1. In the case of a program, the general rule is to deposit the first 25 pages or equivalent units and the last 25 pages or equivalent units, in visually perceptible form, along with, if the work is published, the page or other unit containing the copyright notice (if any). "Visually perceptible form" means on paper or microform.

2. If the program comes with a printed user manual, your deposit of the user manual will generally need to be in hard copy form.

3. As a rule of thumb, always identify the program as a "literary work" in the appropriate space or prompt screen. Where the code is really just an embodiment of a visual work or audiovisual work, you can (but need not) identify it as such, in which event the code itself may arguably not be protected by your registration. It would be a very rare instance where you would want to go this route.

4. Contrary to some early cases,[1] the Copyright Office takes the position—correctly, I believe—that registration of a program covers not only the code but also the visual displays that the program will create when used. However, you can if you want identify the work as "computer program, including text of screen displays," or "computer program including audiovisual material," or "computer program including artwork on screen displays," and this is probably a good idea in the case of a video game or other program in which what the user sees on the screen is the heart of the work. If you do make reference to the screen content, you need to deposit identifying material for it unless the screens are shown in the user manual. Identifying materal means an electronic file, a printout, or (in the case of audiovisual material) a DVD or CD-ROM.

5. If the program you are depositing is a revision of a preexisting program, the deposit must be representative of the revisions that have been made. If the first 25 and the last 25 pages are not, then you should deposit any 50 representative pages.

6. If the program you are registering contains trade-secret information—as most do—you can take advantage of certain special exceptions:

a. You can block out the trade-secret portions, so long as the blocked-out portions are "proportionately less" than what remains and an "appreciable amount of original computer code" is visible.

b. You can deposit the first 10 and last 10 pages with nothing blocked out.

c. You can deposit the first 25 and last 25 pages, with portions blocked out, plus 10 pages with nothing blocked out.

d. If the program is a revised version, and the first 25 and last 25 pages are not representative of the new material, you can deposit 20 pages with nothing blocked out or 50 pages with block-outs, so long as in either case the pages contain revisions and, if you use block-outs, the material that remains is proportionately more than what you have blocked out and contains an appreciable amount of original code.

7. If the above strategies are undesirable for some good reason, you can apply to the Copyright Office for "special relief," in other words, a special dispensation from these requirements.

8. As an alternative to the above methods in trade-secret situations, you can deposit the first and last 25 pages of binary code rather than source code. The problem with this is that your registration is then made under the "rule of doubt." This means that the Copyright Office, in granting registration, is expressing no opinion on whether the binary code actually embodies the work being registered. The registration is thus more open to attack than one for which identifying material has been deposited.

Databases   The deposit requirements for databases in electronic format are these:

1. For a database on any single subject, the first 25 and last 25 pages or equivalent units, in visually perceptible form, are sufficient. Where the work is a revised version, the rule requires 50 pages that are representative of the revisions made.

2. For a database made up of data files covering two or more separate and distinct subjects, you must deposit either 50 complete data records from each file or the entire file, whichever is less, in visually perceptible form. A "data file" for these purposes is any group of data records, regardless of their size, that pertain to a common subject matter. You must also submit a descriptive statement, typed or printed, containing this information:

- the title of the database;

- a subtitle, date of creation or publication, or other information that will distinguish any separate or distinct data file for cataloguing purposes;

- the name and address of the copyright claimant;

- the name and content of each separate file, including subject matter, origin of the data (if the file is a revised version), and the approximate number of records in the file;

- if the work is published, an exact description of the copyright notice (if any) that is put on the work and the manner or frequency with which it is displayed—for example, at the user's terminal only at sign-on, or on printouts, or whatever.

A procedure has been made available for registration of so-called dynamic databases—those that are updated frequently. The procedure permits registration of all revisions to the database that occur over any three consecutive months in one calendar year, for a single fee and using a single TX form. Special instructions are available from the Copyright Office for the completion of the form. As of this writing, the precise rules were under review, so you much check with the Copyright Office for up-to-date guidance. The prior rules (which will likely be carried forward with minor adjustments) were as follows:

1. You can register up to three months' worth of updates and revisions. The three-month period must fall within a single calendar year. All the updates or revisions must:

   • have been first published, or if unpublished must have been created, within that three-month period (note that you cannot mix published and unpublished material in this group registration),

   • be published only in machine-readable form, or if unpublished must have been created only in machine-readable form,

   • be owned by the same copyright claimant,

   • have the same general title,

   • be similar in their general content, including their subject, and

   • be similar in their organization.

2. The required deposit material consists of 50 pages or records, whichever is less, in hardcopy form. All must have been published on the same date or, if unpublished, must have been

created on the same date, and the date must be "representative" (whatever that means) of dates on which the database was updated or revised. The deposit must comprise:

> • 50 pages or records (whichever is less) marked to disclose copyrightable revisions/ updates from one representative publication date (if published) or one representative creation date (if unpublished) (note that it is not necessary to identify all revisions/updates; the requirement is to identify sufficient revisions/ updates to establish that the work submitted for registration is an original work of authorship);

or

> • 50 pages or records (whichever is less) comprised entirely of revisions/updates from one representative publication date (if published) or one representative creation date (if unpublished); you should confirm in a cover letter that the entire unmarked deposit represents revisions/updates added to the database on the representative date.

Note that the representative date you choose for the deposit is also the date you must list as the publication date, in the case of a published database. However, as noted in the text, the Copyright Office is agnostic as to whether an online database is "published" or not.

APPENDIX D: DESCRIPTION OF WORKS FOR PREREGISTRATION

[From Interim Regulation, 37 C.F.R. Ch. II §202.16(c) (6).]

(i) For motion pictures, such a description should include the following information to the extent known at the time of filing: the subject matter, a summary or outline, the director, the primary actors, the principal location of filming, and any other information that would assist in identifying the particular work being preregistered.

(ii) For sound recordings, the identifying description should include the following information to the extent known at the time of filing: the subject matter of the work or works recorded, the performer or performing group, the genre of the work recorded (e.g., classical, pop, musical comedy, soft rock, heavy metal, gospel, rap, hip-hop, blues, jazz), the titles of the musical compositions being recorded, the principal recording location, the composer(s) of the recorded musical compositions embodied on the sound recording, and any other information that would assist in identifying the particular work being preregistered.

(iii) For musical compositions, the identifying description should include the following information to the extent known at the time of filing: the subject matter of the lyrics, if any, the genre of the work (for example, classical, pop, musical comedy, soft rock, heavy metal, gospel, rap, hip-hop, blues, jazz), the performer, principal recording location, record label, motion picture, or other information relating to any sound recordings or motion pictures that are being prepared for commercial distribution and will include the musical composition, and any other detail or characteristic that may assist in identifying the particular musical composition.

(iv) For literary works in book form, the identifying description should include to the extent known at the time of filing: the genre of the book, e.g., biography, novel, history, etc., and should include a brief summary of the work including, the subject matter (e.g., a biography of President Bush, a history of the war in Iraq, a fantasy novel); a description (where applicable) of the plot, primary characters, events, or other key elements of the content of the work; and any other salient characteristics of the book, e.g., whether it is a later edition or revision of a previous work, as well as any other detail which may assist in identifying the literary work in book form.

(v) For computer programs (including videogames), the identifying description should include to the extent known at the time of filing, the nature, purpose and function of the computer program, including the programming language in which it is written; any particular organization or structure in which the program has been created; the form in which it is expected to be published, e.g., as an online-only product; whether there have been previous versions (and identification of such previous versions); the identities of persons involved in the creation of the computer program; and, if the work is a videogame, also describe the subject matter of the videogame and the overall object, goal or purpose of the game, its characters, if any, and the general setting and surrounding found in the game.

(vi) For advertising or marketing photographs, the description should include the subject matter depicted in the photograph or photographs, including information such as the particular product, event, public figure, or other item or occurrence which the photograph is intended to advertise or market. To the extent possible and applicable, the description for photographs should give additional details which will assist in identifying the particular photographs, such as the party for whom such advertising photographs are taken; the approximate time periods during which the photographs are taken; the approximate number of photos which may be included in the grouping; any events associated with the photographs; and the location and physical setting or surrounding depicted in the photographs. The description may also explain the general presentation, e.g., the lighting, background scenery, positioning of elements of the subject matter as it is seen in the photographs, and should provide any locations and events, if applicable, associated with the photographs.

APPENDIX E: WARNINGS OF COPYRIGHT FOR USE BY CERTAIN LIBRARIES AND ARCHIVES

[From 37 C.F.R. Ch. II §201.24.]

(a) *Definitions.*

(1) A "Display Warning of Copyright" is a notice under paragraphs (d)(2) and (e)(2) of section 108 of Title 17 of the United States Code as amended by Pub. L. 94-553. As required by those sections the "Display Warning of Copyright" is to be displayed at the place where orders for copies or phonorecords are accepted at certain libraries and archives.

(2) An "Order Warning of Copyright" is a notice under paragraphs (d)(2) and (e)(2) of section 108 of Title 17 of the United States Code as amended by Pub. L. 94-553. As required by those sections the "Order Warning of Copyright" is to be included on printed forms supplied by certain libraries and archives and used by their patrons for ordering copies or phonorecords.

(b) *Contents.* A Display Warning of Copyright and an Order Warning of Copyright shall consist of a verbatim reproduction of the following notice, printed in such size and form and displayed in such manner as to comply with paragraph (c) of this section:

NOTICE

WARNING CONCERNING COPYRIGHT
RESTRICTIONS

The copyright law of the United States (Title 17,
United States Code) governs the making of photocopies or other reproductions of copyrighted
material.

Under certain conditions specified in the law,
libraries and archives are authorized to furnish a
photocopy or other reproduction. One of these
specified conditions is that the photocopy or reproduction is not to be "used for any purpose other
than private study, scholarship, or research." If a
user makes a request for, or later uses, a photocopy
or a reproduction for purposes in excess of "fair
use," that user may be liable for copyright
infringement.

This institution reserves the right to refuse to
accept a copying order if, in its judgment, fulfillment of the order would involve violation of copyright law.

(c) *Form and Manner of Use.*
(1) A Display Warning of Copyright shall be
printed on heavy paper or other durable material in
type at least 18 points in size, and shall be displayed
prominently, in such manner and location as to be
clearly visible, legible, and comprehensible to a casual
observer within the immediate vicinity of the place
where orders are accepted.
(2) An Order Warning of Copyright shall be
printed within a box located prominently on the order
form itself, either on the front side of the form or immediately adjacent to the space calling for the name or

signature of the person using the form. The notice shall be printed in type size no smaller than that used predominantly throughout the form, and in no case shall the type size be smaller than 8 points. The notice shall be printed in such manner as to be clearly legible, comprehensible, and readily apparent to a casual reader of the form.

[Condensed from 37 C.F.R. Ch. II §201.24.]
Whenever a nonprofit library lends a copy of a computer program the copy must have the following notice affixed to its packaging:

Warning of Copyright for Software Lending by Nonprofit Libraries

NOTICE

WARNING OF COPYRIGHT RESTRICTIONS

The copyright law of the United States (Title 17, United States Code) governs the reproduction, distribution, adaptation, public performance, and public display of copyrighted materials.

Under certain conditions specified in law, nonprofit libraries are authorized to lend, lease, or rent copies of computer programs to patrons on a nonprofit basis and for nonprofit purposes. Any person who makes an unauthorized copy or adaptation of the computer program, or redistributes the loan copy or publicly performs or displays the computer program, except as permitted by Title 17 of the United States Code, may be liable for copyright infringement.

This institution reserves the right to refuse to fulfill a loan request if, in its judgment, fulfillment of the request would lead to violation of the copyright law.

This Warning of Copyright Restrictions must be affixed to the packaging that contains the copy of the computer program, by means of a label cemented, gummed, or otherwise durably attached to the copies or to a box, reel, cartridge, cassette, or other container used as a permanent receptacle for the copy of the computer program. The notice must be printed in such manner as to be clearly legible, comprehensible, and readily apparent to a casual user of the computer program.

For any sort of database, if you affix a visually perceptible notice to the work or to the container in which you publish it, you should include a sample of that notice with your deposit. This is mandatory for registrations of multifile databases and for group registrations and is strongly advised, if not actually mandatory, for all others.

APPENDIX F: DIGEST OF CONFU
DRAFT ON FAIR USE GUIDELINES

The full text of the draft guidelines can be found in *BNA's Patent, Trademark & Copyright Journal* vol. 53, December 19, 1996, pp. 125–137.

The Inclusion of Protected Works in Educational Multimedia Projects

The guidelines under this heading apply to the use, without permission, of portions of lawfully acquired copyrighted works in educational multimedia projects created by educators or students "as part of a systematic learning activity by nonprofit educational institutions." The term "educational multimedia projects" refers to work that "incorporate[s] students' or educators' original material, such as course notes or commentary, together with various copyrighted media formats including, but not limited to, motion picture media, music, text material, graphics, illustrations, photographs and digital software which are combined into an integrated presentation." The term "systematic learning activities" includes use in connection with "non-commercial curriculum-based learning and teaching activities" at nonprofit educational institutions. Just what sort of thing the phrase "curriculum-based" is meant to exclude is not clear.

One of the interesting and novel things about these particular guidelines is that for the first time copyright owners have attempted to place implicit limits on what students can do; previous fair use guidelines have been focused exclusively on the activities of teachers and institutions. The guidelines say:

> [2.1] Students may incorporate portions of lawfully acquired copyrighted works when producing their own educational multimedia projects for a specific course.

And

> [3.1] Students may perform and display their own educational multimedia projects created under Section 2 of these guidelines for educational uses in the course for which they were created and may use them in their own portfolios as examples of their academic work for later personal uses such as job and graduate school interviews.

It seems remarkable that anyone thought it necessary to reassure anyone on these points. Not surprisingly, though, most of the guidelines are aimed at teacher activities.

> [2.2] Educators may incorporate portions of lawfully acquired copyrighted works when producing their own educational multimedia projects for their own teaching tools in support of curriculum-based instructional activities at educational institutions.

Other excerpts follow.

> 3.2 Educator Use for Curriculum-Based Instruction. Educators may perform and display their own educational multimedia projects created

under Section 2 for curriculum-based instruction to students in the following situations:

3.2.1 for face-to-face instruction,

3.2.2 assigned to students for directed self-study,

3.2.3 for remote instruction to students enrolled in curriculum-based courses and located at remote sites, provided over the educational institution's secure electronic network in real-time, or for after class review or directed self-study, provided there are technological limitations on access to the network and educational multimedia project (such as a password or PIN) and provided further that the technology prevents the making of copies of copyrighted material.

If the educational institution's network or technology used to access [a lawfully made educational multimedia project] cannot prevent duplication of copyrighted material, students or educators may use the multimedia educational projects over an otherwise secure network for a period of only 15 days after its initial real-time remote use in the course of instruction or 15 days after its assignment for directed self-study. After that period, one of the two use copies of the educational multimedia project may be placed on reserve in a learning resource center, library or similar facility for on-site use by students enrolled in the course. Students shall be advised that they are not permitted to make their own copies of the educational multimedia project.

3.3 Educator Use for Peer Conferences. Educators may perform or display their own educational multimedia projects created under Section 2 of these guidelines in presentations to their peers, for example, at workshops and conferences.

3.4 Educator Use for Professional Portfolio. Educators may retain educational multimedia projects

. . . in their personal portfolios for later personal uses such as tenure review or job interviews.

4 Limitations: Time, Portion, Copying and Distribution

The preparation of educational multimedia projects incorporating copyrighted works . . . [is] subject to the limitations noted below.

4.1 Time Limitations. Educators may use their educational multimedia projects . . . for a period of up to two years after the first instructional use with a class. Use beyond that time period, even for educational purposes, requires permission for each copyrighted portion incorporated in the production. . . .

4.2 Portion Limitations. . . . These limitations apply cumulatively to each educator's or student's multimedia project(s) for the same academic semester, cycle or term. All students should be instructed about the reasons for copyright protection and the need to follow these guidelines. It is understood, however, that students in kindergarten through grade six may not be able to adhere rigidly to the portion limitations in this section in their independent development of educational multimedia projects. In any event, each such project retained under Sections 3.1 and 4.3 should comply with the portion limitations in this section. . . .

4.2.4 Illustrations and photographs. The reproduction or incorporation of photographs and illustrations is more difficult to define with regard to fair use because fair use usually precludes the use of an entire work. Under these guidelines a photograph or illustration may be used in its entirety but no more than 5 images by an artist or photographer may be reproduced or otherwise incorporated as part of an educational multimedia project created under Section 2. When using photographs and illustrations from a published collective work, not more than 10% or 15 images, whichever is less, may be reproduced or otherwise incorporated as part of an educational multimedia project created under Section 2.

4.3 Copying and Distribution Limitations. Only a limited number of copies, including the original, may be made of an educator's educational multimedia project. For all of the uses permitted by Section 3, there may be no more than two use copies only one of which may be placed on reserve as described in Section 3.2.3. An additional copy may be made for preservation purposes but may only be used or copied to replace a use copy that has been lost, stolen, or damaged. In the case of a jointly created educational multimedia project, each principal creator may retain one copy but only for the purposes described in Sections 3.3 and 3.4 for educators and in Section 3.1 for students. . . .

5.2 Duplication of Multimedia Projects beyond Limitations Listed in These Guidelines. Even for educational uses, educators and students must seek individual permissions for all copyrighted works incorporated in their personally created educational multimedia projects before replicating or distributing beyond the limitations listed in Section 4.3. [Note: the use of the word "must" here, and at certain other places in the excerpts that follow, is somewhat at odds with the general intent that these guidelines are "safe harbor" guidelines, not the last word on the topic.] . . .

6.2 Attribution and Acknowledgment. Educators and students are reminded to credit the sources and display the copyright notice and copyright ownership information if this is shown in the original source, for all works incorporated as part of educational multimedia projects prepared by educators and students, including those prepared under fair use. . . .

The credit and copyright notice information may be combined and shown in a separate section of the educational multimedia project (e.g. credit section) except for images incorporated into the project for the uses described in Section 3.2.3. In such cases, the copyright notice and the name of the creator of the image must be incorporated into the image when, and to the extent, such information is reasonably available; credit and copyright notice information is considered "incorporated" if it is attached to the image file and appears on the screen when the image is viewed. In those cases when displaying source credits and copyright ownership information on the screen with the image would be mutually exclusive with an instructional objective (e.g. during examinations in which the source credits and/or copyright information would be relevant to the examination questions), those images may be displayed without such information being simultaneously displayed on the screen. In such cases, this information should be linked to the image in a manner compatible with such instructional objectives.

6.3 Notice of Use Restrictions. Educators and students are advised that they must include on the opening screen of their multimedia project and any accompanying print material a notice that certain materials are included under the fair use exception of the U.S. Copyright Law and have been prepared according to the educational multimedia fair use guidelines and are restricted from further use. . . .

6.5 Integrity of Copyrighted Works: Alterations. Educators and students may make alterations in the portions of the copyrighted works they incorporate as part of an educational multimedia project only if the alterations support specific instructional objectives. Educators and students are advised to note that alterations have been made.

APPENDIX G: STANDARD FIDUCIARY COPYRIGHT POWERS

Intellectual Property: Upon such terms and conditions as the Trustees deem suitable, to exercise or grant waivers with respect to, and to assign or license to others the right to exercise or grant waivers with respect to, (i) all rights, powers and discretions in all copyrights and interests in copyrights that come into the possession of the Trustees; (ii) all rights of termination accruing to the Trustees as a matter of law under Section 203 or 304 of the Copyright Act or otherwise; (iii) all so-called "moral rights," including without limitation all rights of attribution and integrity, and resale royalty rights, which the Trustees may be entitled to exercise as a matter of law in any jurisdiction, it being understood that the Trustees shall be entitled to exercise all moral rights in works in which tangible ownership, or copyright, comes into the Trustees' possession, except as other disposition of moral rights is expressly made elsewhere; (iv) all rights in characters, titles, and the like, contained in works in which copyright comes into the Trustees' possession, including without limitation all rights to use any artistic work (or any character, title, etc. relating thereto) as the basis for trademarks or trade names for other products; (v) all other rights accruing to the owner of intellectual property that comes into the Trustees' possession, including but not limited to the right to prevent the removal of "copyright management information" under Section 1202 of the Copyright Act, and (vi) all so-called "neighboring rights," arising out of or relating to any audiovisual, pictorial, graphic, sculptural, or multimedia work, or any other work protected under the copyright laws or neighboring rights laws of any country. The Trustees shall be entitled and empowered to take such actions (including legal actions) as the Trustees deem suitable to enforce any right described herein against any suspected infringer of such right. The Trustees shall have the care and possession of all paintings, prints, sculptures, manuscripts, computer-readable media, and any and all other tangible personal property embodying any work or other property hereinabove described, to the extent the same comes into their possession. The Trustees shall have no obligation to exercise any right described above unless they determine in their sole discretion that the likely proceeds will exceed the likely expense of such exercise. If they determine not to exercise any right they may in their discretion, and to the extent permitted by law, assign the same to another person for that purpose.

NOTES

Chapter 1

1. 17 U.S.C. §102(a).

2. 17 U.S.C. §301.

3. *See, e.g.,* Hoehling v. Universal City Studios, Inc., 618 F.2d 972 (2d Cir. 1980), *cert. denied*, 449 U.S. 841 (1980); Miller v. Universal City Studios, Inc., 650 F.2d 1365 (5th Cir. 1981).

4. Sheldon v. Metro-Goldwyn Pictures Corp., 81 F.2d 49, 54 (2d Cir. 1936).

5. 17 U.S.C. §101.

6. 17 U.S.C. §103(b).

7. Curiously, an Israeli court granted copyright to a scholar's reconstruction of the Dead Sea Scrolls. This would not happen in the United States. *See* D. Nimmer, "Copyright in the Dead Sea Scrolls: Authorship and Originality," 38 *Houston Law Rev.* 1 (2001).

8. Schrock v. Learning Curve Int'l, Inc., 586 F.3d 513, 521 (7th Cir. 2009).

9. Durham Industries, Inc. v. Tomy Corp., 630 F.2d 905 (2d Cir. 1980); L. Batlin & Son, Inc. v. Snyder, 536 F.2d 436 (2d Cir. 1976).

10. Alfred Bell & Co. v. Catalda Fine Arts, Inc., 191 F.2d 99 (2d Cir. 1951), *aff'g* 74 F.Supp. 973 (S.D.N.Y. 1947); Alva Studios, Inc. v. Winninger, 177 F.Supp. 265 (S.D.N.Y. 1959). One case has held that affixing an art print to a ceramic tile creates a derivative work, but this is almost certainly an aberration.

Mirage Editions, Inc. v. Albuquerque A.R.T. Co., 856 F.2d 1341 (9th Cir. 1988).

11. Bridgeman Art Library v. Corel Corp., 36 F.Supp.2d 191 (S.D.N.Y. 1999).

12. Gilliam v. American Broadcasting Companies, Inc., 538 F.2d 14 (2d Cir. 1976).

13. 111 S.Ct. 1282 (1991).

14. I discuss this issue in detail in "Database Protection after Feist v. Rural Telephone Co.," 42 *Jrnl. Copr. Soc.* 1 (1994).

15. Silverstein v. Penguin Putnam, Inc., 522 F.Supp.2d 579 (S.D.N.Y. 2007).

16. Peter Pan Fabrics, Inc. v. Martin Weiner Corp., 274 F.2d 487, 489 (2d Cir. 1960).

17. Satava v. Lowry, 323 F.3d 805 (9th Cir. 2003).

18. *Compare* Oriental Art Printing, Inc. v. Goldstar Printing Corp., 175 F.Supp.2d 542 (S.D.N.Y. 2001), *aff'd on other grounds*, 34 Fed.Appx. 401, 2002 U.S. App. LEXIS 5754 (2d Cir. N.Y. 2002), *with* Latimer v. Roaring Toyz, Inc., 601 F.3d 1224 (11th Cir. Fla. 2010).

19. Dyer v. Napier, 2006 U.S. Dist. LEXIS 68990 (D.Ariz. Sept. 25, 2006).

20. 101 U.S. 99 (1880).

21. Harcourt, Brace & World Inc. v. Graphic Controls Corp., 329 F.Supp. 517 (S.D.N.Y. 1971); Manpower, Inc. v. Temporary Help of Harrisburg, Inc., 246 F.Supp. 788 (E.D.Pa. 1965).

22. Morrissey v. Procter & Gamble Co., 379 F.2d 675 (1st Cir. 1967).

23. Montz v. Pilgrim Films & TV, Inc., 649 F.3d 975 (9th Cir. 2011).

24. 17 U.S.C. §102(a).

25. Leon v. Pacific Tel. & Tel. Co., 91 F.2d 484 (9th Cir. 1937); Amsterdam v. Triangle Publications, Inc., 189 F.2d 104 (3rd Cir. 1951).

26. *See, e.g.,* Becker v. Loew's, Inc., 133 F.2d 889 (7th Cir. 1943); CCM Cable Rep. Inc. v. Ocean Coast Properties, Inc., 97 F.3d 1513, 1519 (1st Cir. 1996); *compare* John Muller & Co. v. New York Arrows Soccer Team, Inc., 231 U.S.P.Q. 319 (8th

Cir. 1986), *with* Reader's Digest Association, Inc. v. Conservative Digest, Inc., 821 F.2d 800 (D.C. Cir. 1987).

27. Paramore v. Mack Sennett, 9 F.2d 66 (S.D.Cal. 1925); *cf.* Duff v. Kansas City Star Co., 229 F.2d 320 (8th Cir. 1962). The scope of the law on unfair competition has been severely limited in recent years. Federal copyright law now preempts state laws in the field, to the extent that they purport to protect rights equivalent to rights under copyright in works fixed in tangible form, whether or not they are copyrightable. 17 U.S.C. §301; H.R. Rep. No. 94-1476, 94th Cong., 2d Sess., at pp. 130–133 (1976). (This, the House of Representatives Report for the Copyright Act of 1976, will be referred to hereafter as "H. Rep.") This does not apply quite so broadly to causes of action arising before 1978. There is no reason to feel it would restrict protection of titles, because titles are regarded as trademarks under federal law, not as works of authorship.

28. H. Rep., pp. 53–54.

29. The leading toy case is Gay Toys, Inc. v. Buddy L Corp., 703 F.2d 970 (6th Cir. 1983). The slipper and Halloween cases are Animal Fair, Inc. v. AMFESCO Industries, Inc., 620 F.Supp. 175, 177 (D.Minn. 1985), *aff'd without op.*, 794 F.2d 678 (8th Cir. 1986), and National Theme Productions, Inc. v. Jerry B. Beck, Inc., 696 F.Supp. 1348 (S.D.Cal. 1988). The Copyright Office position is stated at 56 Fed.Reg. 56530. The bad case is Whimsicality Inc. v. Battat, 27 F.Supp.2d 456 (S.D.N.Y. 1998).

30. H. Rep., p. 55.

31. Brandir International, Inc. v. Cascade Pacific Lumber Co., 834 F.2d 1142, 1145 (2d Cir. 1987). Note that "useful article" has been expanded to include buildings. Leicester v. Warner Bros., 232 F.3d 1212 (9th Cir. 2000).

32. *Ibid.*; 17 U.S.C. §§101, 113(b); H. Rep., p. 105.

33. H. Rep., p. 55.

34. Kelley v. Chicago Park District, 635 F.3d 290 (7th Cir. 2011). The holding is also questionable because our law has upheld copyright in other materials where random variation is guided by human creativity, at least in the field of works created using software.

35. H.R. Rep. No. 101-735, 101st Cong., 2d Sess., at pp. 20–21.

36. 17 U.S.C. §101.

37. H.R. Rep. No. 101-735, 101st Cong., 2d Sess., p. 20.

38. 37 C.F.R. Ch. II §202.11. One court has also held that a structure must be freestanding to be a building: a store inside a mall, even if it looks like a building, is not one. The Yankee Candle Company, Inc. v. New England Candle Co., 14 F.Supp.2d 154 (D.Mass. 1998). However, this judgment was ultimately vacated by consent and so its force as precedent is somewhat weakened. 1998 U.S. Dist. LEXIS 21434.

39. 37 C.F.R. Ch. II §202.11.

40. *See, e.g.,* Nichols v. Universal Pictures Corp., 45 F.2d 119 (1930), *cert. denied*, 282 U.S. 902 (1931).

41. Warner Bros. Pictures, Inc. v. Columbia Broadcasting System, Inc., 216 F.2d 945 (9th Cir. 1954); *see* Borroughs v. Metro-Goldwyn-Mayer, Inc., 683 F.2d 610 (2d Cir. 1982).

42. Fleischer Studios, Inc. v. A.V.E.L.A., Inc., 654 F.3d 958 (9th Cir. 2011).

43. Reader's Digest Assoc. v. Conservative Digest, 821 F.2d 800 (D.C. Cir. 1987).

44. Williams Electronics, Inc. v. Artic International, Inc., 685 F.2d 870 (3rd Cir. 1982); Apple Computer, Inc. v. Franklin Computer Corp., 714 F.2d 1240 (3rd Cir. 1983), *cert. denied*, 464 U.S. 1033 (1984); Apple Computer, Inc. v. Formula International Inc., 562 F.Supp. 775 (N.D.Cal. 1983).

45. Final Report of the National Commission on New Technological Uses of Copyrighted Works (CONTU) (1978), pp. 9–38; available at http://digital-law-online.info/CONTU/. Prior law had held that if a work was not intelligible, even with magnification, to the human eye, it neither infringed copyright nor was entitled to copyright. White-Smith Music Publishing Co. v. Apollo Co., 209 U.S. 1 (1908); Corcoran v. Montgomery Ward & Co., Inc., 121 F.2d 572 (9th Cir. 1941). At first it was thought that this doctrine might apply to object code. Data Cash Systems, Inc. v. JS&A Group, Inc., 480 F.Supp. 1063 (N.D.Ill. 1979), *aff'd on other grounds*, 628 F.2d 1038 (7th Cir. 1980). *See* Stern, "Another Look at Copyright Protection of Software: Did the 1980 Act Do Anything for Object Code?," 3 *Computer Law Jrnl.* 1 (1981).

46. Final Report of CONTU, at pp. 19–21.

47. Chamberlin v. Uris Sales Corp., 150 F.2d 512 (2d Cir. 1945); *see* Brief English Systems v. Owen, 48 F.2d 555 (2d Cir. 1931), and Universal Athletic Sales Co. v. Salkeld, 511 F.2d 904 (3rd Cir. 1975); *cf.* the factually ambiguous case of Runge v. Lee, 441 F.2d 479 (9th Cir. 1971) and Justice Douglas's dissent to the denial of certiorari thereon, 404 U.S. 887 (1971).

48. 797 F.2d 1222 (3d Cir. 1986).

49. Computer Associates Int'l Inc. v. Altai Inc., 982 F.2d 693 (2d Cir. 1992).

50. Diamond v. Diehr, 450 U.S. 175 (1981); *see also* Diamond v. Bradley, 600 F.2d 807 (C.C.P.A. 1979), *aff'd by an equally divided court*, 450 U.S. 381 (1981).

51. This and several other patented algorithms are described in a story in the *New York Times*, February 15, 1989, p. D1. Indeed, the scope of patent protection for software continues to grow, because the courts have given their blessing to patent claims for software where a "machine" (i.e., a computer) is identified as a component. On this basis, for example, a patent was recently upheld for algorithms used in running a hub-and-spoke mutual fund arrangement. State Street Bank & Trust Co. v. Signature Financial Group, 149 F.3d 1368 (Fed. Cir. 1998).

52. Lotus Development Corp. v. Paperbook Software Int'l, 740 F.Supp. 37 (D.Mass. 1990).

53. 53 Fed.Reg. 21817–21820 (6/10/88); Clarity Software, LLC v. Allianz Life Ins. Co., 2006 U.S. Dist. LEXIS 56217 (W.D.Pa. Aug. 11, 2006).

54. Manufacturers Technologies, Inc. v. Cams, Inc., 706 F.Supp. 984 (D.Conn. 1989).

55. Tetris Holding, LLC v. Xio Interactive, Inc., 863 F.Supp.2d 394 (D.N.J. 2012).

56. Lotus Development Corp. v. Borland International, Inc., 49 F.3d 807 (1st Cir. 1995), *aff'd by an equally divided court*, 116 S.Ct. 804 (1996). The statutory reference is to 17 U.S.C. §102.

57. Oracle America, Inc. v. Google Inc., 872 F.Supp.2d 974, 999–1000 (N.D.Cal. 2012).

58. For interesting analyses of this topic, see Clifford, "Intellectual Property in the Era of the Creative Computer

Program: Will the True Creator Please Stand Up?," 17 *Tulane L. Rev.* 1675 (1997); Miller, "Computers and Copyright Protection," 106 *Harv. L. Rev.* 977 (1993).

59. 17 U.S.C. §901 *et seq.*

60. 17 U.S.C. §906(a). Brooktree Corp. v. Advanced Micro Devices, Inc., 705 F.Supp. 491 (S.D.Cal. 1988).

61. 17 U.S.C. §1101. For state law to the same effect see, *e.g.*, Metropolitan Opera Association, Inc. v. Wagner-Nichols Recorder Corp., 199 Misc. 786, 101 N.Y.S.2d 483 (1950), *aff'd*, 279 App.Div. 632, 107 N.Y.S.2d 795 (1951). The new §1101 expressly does not preempt state laws.

62. 18 U.S.C. Ch. 113, §2319A.

63. United States v. Martignon, 492 F.3d 140 (2d Cir. 2007). I am informed by Marybeth Peters, the former Register of Copyrights, that a definite term of protection was supposed to have been included in the statute but was overlooked by the drafters. As time goes by, hope dwindles that this omission may be cured by remedial legislation.

64. Midler v. Ford Motor Co., 849 F.2d 460 (9th Cir. 1988). *See* Lennon v. Pulsebeat News, Inc., 143 U.S.P.Q. 309 (N.Y. Sup. Ct. 1964); Sinatra v. Goodyear Tire & Rubber Co., 435 F.2d 711 (9th Cir. 1979); Booth v. Colgate-Palmolive Co., 362 F.Supp. 343 (S.D.N.Y. 1973).

65. Estate of Hemingway v. Random House, Inc., 244 N.E.2d 250, 255–256 (N.Y. 1968).

66. Pacific & Southern Co. v. Duncan, 792 F.2d 1013 (11th Cir. 1986).

67. *See* Swatch Group Mgmt. Services v. Bloomberg L.P., 808 F.Supp.2d 634 (S.D.N.Y. 2011), and cases cited therein.

Chapter 2

1. 17 U.S.C. §101.

2. Shapiro, Bernstein & Co. v. Jerry Vogel Music Co., Inc., 161 F.2d 406, 410 (2d Cir. 1946, 1947), *cert. denied*, 331 U.S. 820 (1942).

3. H. Rep., p. 120.

4. Childress v. Taylor, 945 F.2d 500 (2d Cir. 1991).

5. Thomson v. Larson, 147 F.3d 195 (2d Cir. 1998).

6. Erickson v. Trinity Theater, 13 F.3d 1061 (7th Cir. 1994).

7. Janky v. Lake County Convention & Visitors Bureau, 576 F.3d 356, 362 (7th Cir. Ind. 2009).

8. Aalmuhammed v. Lee, 202 F.3d 1227 (9th Cir. 2000).

9. Childress v. Taylor, *supra*; Ashton-Tate Corp. v. Ross, 916 F.2d 516 (9th Cir. 1990); Erickson v. Trinity Theater Inc., 13 F.3d 1061 (7th Cir. 1994). *See* Andrien v. Southern Ocean County Chamber of Commerce, 927 F.2d 132 (3d Cir. 1991), for a perhaps more expansive view of what it means to "contribute" copyrightable expression.

10. Sweet Music, Inc. v. Melrose Music Corp., 189 F.Supp. 655, 659 (S.D.Cal. 1960).

11. Melville B. Nimmer, *Nimmer on Copyright* (New York: Matthew Bender, 1980), §6.10[C].

12. Marshall v. Miles Laboratories, Inc., 647 F.Supp. 1326, 1330 (N.D.Ind. 1986). *See generally* Avtec Systems Inc. v. Peiffer, 30 U.S.P.Q.2d 1365 (4th Cir. 1994).

13. Hays v. Sony Corp. of America, 847 F.2d 412 (7th Cir. 1988).

14. *See* Avedon v. Exstein, 141 F.Supp. 278 (S.D.N.Y. 1956); Lumiere v. Pathe Exchange, 275 Fed. 428 (2d Cir. 1921).

15. Brattleboro Publishing Co. v. Winmill Publishing Corp., 369 F.2d 565 (2d Cir. 1966); May v. Morganelli-Heumann & Associates, 618 F.2d 1363, 1368 (9th Cir. 1980).

16. Aldon Accessories Ltd. v. Spiegel, Inc., 738 F.2d 548 (2d Cir. 1984); *accord*, Brunswick Beacon, Inc. v. Schock-Hopchas Publishing Co., 810 F.2d 410 (4th Cir. 1987); Evans Newton, Inc. v. Chicago Systems Software, 793 F.2d 889 (7th Cir. 1986), *cert. denied*, 107 S.Ct. 434 (1986).

17. Town of Clarkstown v. Reeder, 566 F.Supp. 137 (S.D.N.Y. 1983).

18. 815 F.2d 323 (5th Cir. 1987).

19. Community for Creative Non-Violence v. Reid, 846 F.2d 1485 (D.C. Cir. 1988).

20. Dumas v. Gommerman, 865 F.2d 1093 (9th Cir. 1989).

21. Community for Creative Non-Violence v. Reid, 490 U.S. 730 (1989).

22. Aymes v. Bonelli, 980 F.2d 857 (2d Cir. 1992).

23. *Ibid*.

24. Marco v. Accent Publishing Co., 969 F.2d 1547 (3d Cir. 1992).

25. 17 U.S.C. §109(c).

26. *See* Asset Mktg. Sys. v. Gagnon, 542 F.3d 748 (9th Cir. 2008). The architectural counterexample is Nelson-Salabes, Inc. v. Morningside Dev., 284 F.3d 505 (4th Cir. 2002).

27. *See* 17 U.S.C. §301(a).

28. 17 U.S.C. §201(b).

29. Playboy Enterprises, Inc. v. Dumas, 53 F.3d 549 (2d Cir. 1995), *cert. denied*, 116 S.Ct. 567 (1995). *But see* Armento v. The Laser Image, Inc., 40 U.S.P.Q.2d 1874 (W.D.N.C. 1996).

30. 17 U.S.C. §201(b).

31. *See* Lulirama Ltd. Inc. v. Axxess Broadcast Services, Inc., 128 F.3d 872 (5th Cir. 1997).

32. Schiller & Schmidt, Inc. v. Nordisco Corp., 969 F.2d 410 (7th Cir. 1992).

33. Playboy Enterprises, Inc. v. Dumas, *supra*. At least one court has expressly sided with the Second Circuit and against the Seventh. Looney Ricks Kiss Architects, Inc. v. Bryan, 2010 U.S. Dist. LEXIS 110100 (W.D.La. Oct. 14, 2010), *rev'd on other grounds*, 677 F.3d 250 (5th Cir. 2012).

34. Oddo v. Ries, 743 F.2d 630 (9th Cir. 1984). One court has held that for a partnership agreement to create co-ownership of copyright, it must be in writing. Konigsberg International Inc. v. Rice, 16 F.2d 355 (9th Cir. 1994). This is in keeping with the general rule, discussed in chapter 3, that an assignment of an interest in copyright must be in writing. In essence, the author is assigning copyright to the partnership of which she is a member, and that assignment must be in writing.

35. 17 U.S.C. §101.

36. *See* Ringer and Flacks, "Applicability of the Universal Copyright Convention to Certain Works in the Public Domain of Their Country of Origin," 27 *Bull. Copr. Society* 3 (1980).

37. *See, e.g.,* Public Affairs Associates, Inc. v. Rickover, 268 F.Supp. 444 (D.D.C. 1967); Bell v. Combined Registry Co., 536 F.2d 164 (7th Cir. 1976).

38. 17 U.S.C. §103(a).

39. 17 U.S.C. §201(d)(2).

40. 17 U.S.C. §202.

41. 17 U.S.C. §109(b).

42. This was the holding of the trial court in Community for Creative Non-Violence v. Reid. The issue was not discussed at the appellate or Supreme Court levels (see notes 15 and 17 above).

43. *In re* Marriage of Worth, 4 U.S.P.Q.2d 1730 (Cal. Ct. App. 1987); Rodrigue v. Rodrigue, 218 F.3d 432 (5th Cir. 2000).

44. 17 U.S.C. §904.

45. 17 U.S.C. §302(b).

46. 17 U.S.C. §302(c).

Chapter 3

1. 17 U.S.C. §201(e).

2. ProCD, Inc. v. Zeidenberg, 86 F.3d 1447 (7th Cir. 1996). *Compare* Vault Corporation v. Quaid Software, Ltd., 847 F.2d 255 (5th Cir. 1988).

3. David Grossman Designs, Inc. v. Bortin, 347 F.Supp. 1150 (N.D.Ill. 1972); Gerlach-Barklow Co. v. Morris & Bendien, 23 F.2d 159 (2d Cir. 1927). The recent case on electronic signatures is Metro. Reg'l Info. Sys. v. Am. Home Realty Network, Inc., 722 F.3d 591 (4th Cir. 2013).

4. 17 U.S.C. §204(a).

5. *See, e.g.,* with regard to time limitations, 17 U.S.C. §203(b) (6); Viacom Int'l, Inc. v. Tandem Productions, Inc., 368 F.Supp. 1264 (S.D.N.Y. 1974), *aff'd,* 526 F.2d 593 (2d Cir. 1975).

6. *See, e.g.,* Bartsch v. Metro-Goldwyn-Mayer, Inc., 391 F.2d 150 (2d Cir. 1968); Ettore v. Philco Television Broadcasting Corp., 229 F.2d 481 (3rd Cir. 1956). The Nimmer treatise lists many more of these cases at Nimmer, *op. cit.,* §10.10[B].

7. 17 U.S.C. §201(c).

8. New York Times Co. v. Tasini, 533 U.S. 483 (2001); Greenberg v. Nat'l Geographic Society, 533 F.3d 1244 (11th Cir. 2008).

9. Mills Music v. Cromwell Music, 126 F.Supp. 54 (S.D.N.Y. 1954); *cf.* Viacom Int'l, Inc. v. Tandem Productions, Inc., *supra*.

10. Gardner v. Nike, Inc., 279 F.3d 774, 780 (9th Cir. 2002).

11. Nimmer, *op. cit.*, §10.09. See further discussion in chapter 10.

12. Folsom v. Marsh, 9 Fed.Cas. 342, No. 4901 (C.C.Mass. 1841).

13. 17 U.S.C. §204(b).

14. 17 U.S.C. §204(a). Eden Toys v. Florelee, 697 F.2d 27 (2d Cir. 1982); Konigsberg International Inc. v. Rice, 16 F.2d 355 (9th Cir. 1994); Magnuson v. Video Yesteryear, 85 F.3d 1424 (9th Cir. 1996); Barefoot Architect, Inc. v. Bunge, 632 F.3d 822 (3d Cir. 2011). For the third-party reliance exception see Schiller & Schmidt, Inc. v. Nordisco Corp., 969 F.2d 410 (7th Cir. 1992) (which is otherwise out of step with prevailing opinion) and Billy-Bob Teeth v. Novelty, Inc., 329 F.3d 586 (7th Cir. 2003).

15. Davis v. Blige, 505 F.3d 908 (2d Cir. 2007); *cert. denied*, 555 U.S. 822 (2008).

16. 17 U.S.C. §405(a)(3).

17. 17 U.S.C. §205(c).

18. 17 U.S.C. §205(e).

19. *Ibid.*

20. 17 U.S.C. §205(f).

21. Aerocon Engineering, Inc. v. Silicon Valley Bank (*in re* World Aux. Power Co.), 303 F.3d 1120, 1126 (9th Cir. 2002).

22. 17 U.S.C. §203(a)(5).

23. Milne v. Stephen Slesinger, Inc., 430 F.3d 1036 (9th Cir. 2005); *see also* Penguin Group (USA) Inc. v. Steinbeck, 537 F.3d 193 (2d Cir. 2008).

24. 17 U.S.C. §§203(a), 203(b)(5).

25. 17 U.S.C. §§203(a), 203(b)(5).

26. Marvel Characters v. Simon, 310 F.3d 280 (2d Cir. 2002).

27. 17 U.S.C. §203(b)(1); Mills Music, Inc. v. Snyder, 469 U.S. 153 (1985).

28. 17 U.S.C. §§101, 203(a).

29. 17 U.S.C. §203(a)(3).

30. *See generally* 17 U.S.C. §203.

31. 17 U.S.C. §203(b).

32. 17 U.S.C. §203(b)(4).

33. 17 U.S.C. §203(b)(3).

34. *Ibid.*

35. Jacobsen v. Katzer, 609 F.Supp.2d 925, 937–938 (N.D.Cal. 2009).

36. The *eminence grise* of the open-access movement is Peter Suber, whose lapidary *Open Access* was published in 2012 by the publisher of this book, the MIT Press. Here again, proximity does not equal endorsement, but anyone wishing to understand the open-access movement would do well to read Suber's book.

Chapter 4

1. 17 U.S.C. §401(d), added by P.L. 100-568, 102 Stat. 2853.

2. 17 U.S.C. §101; Jewelers' Mercantile Agency, Ltd. v. Jewelers' Weekly Pub. Co., 155 N.Y. 241, 49 N.E. 872 (1897).

3. Gottsberger v. Aldine Book Pub. Co., 33 Fed. 381 (C.C.D.Mass. 1887); Bobbs-Merrill Co. v. Straus, 147 Fed. 15 (2d Cir. 1906), *aff'd*, 210 U.S. 339 (1908).

4. 17 U.S.C. §101.

5. Grandma Moses Properties, Inc. v. This Week Magazine, 117 F.Supp. 348 (S.D.N.Y. 1953); *cf.* remarks of Rep. Kastenmeier, 122 Cong. Rec. No. 10, 874–875 (daily ed. Sept. 22, 1976).

6. 17 U.S.C. §101.

7. 17 U.S.C. §101; White v. Kimmell, 193 F.2d 744 (9th Cir. 1952).

8. Marvin Worth Prods. v. Superior Films Corp., 319 F.Supp. 1269 (S.D.N.Y. 1970); *see generally* Nimmer, *op. cit.*, §4.10.

9. 17 U.S.C. §101.

10. 17 U.S.C. §404(a). This does not apply to ads inserted on behalf of the copyright owner of the collective work.

11. 17 U.S.C. §404(b).

12. 17 U.S.C. §909(b).

13. 17 U.S.C. §§401(b)(2), 909(b).

14. "Owner of copyright" is defined in 37 C.F.R. Ch. II, §202.3.

15. Tonka Corp. v. Tsaisun, Inc., 1 U.S.P.Q.2d 1387 (D.Minn. 1986); *see also* Koontz v. Jaffarian, 787 F.2d 906 (4th Cir. 1986).

16. 17 U.S.C. §406(a).

17. Russell v. Price, 448 F.Supp. 303 (C.D.Cal. 1977).

18. Charles Garnier, Paris v. Andin International Inc., 36 F.3d 1214 (1st Cir. 1994), *aff'g* 30 U.S.P.Q.2d 1612 (D.R.I. 1994). The not entirely convincing proposition that works properly published before Berne need not bear notice after Berne is found in Encore Shoes v. Bennett Industries Inc., 18 U.S.P.Q.2d 1874 (D.Mass. 1991).

19. It has been held that omission from 1 percent of 40,000 copies was permissible, whereas omission from 22 to 37 percent of 1,335 copies was not. Original Appalachian Artworks, Inc. v. The Toy Loft, Inc., 684 F.2d 821 (11th Cir. 1982); King v. Burnett, CCH Copr.L.Dec. ¶25,489 (D.D.C. 1982).

20. *Compare* Charles Garnier, Paris v. Andin International Inc., note 18 above, and Shapiro & Son Bedspread Corp. v. Royal Mills Associates, 764 F.2d 69 (2d Cir. 1985), *with* Forry, Inc. v. Neundorfer, Inc., 837 F.2d 259 (6th Cir. 1988) and cases cited therein. *See also* Neimark v. Ronai & Ronai, LLP, 500 F.Supp.2d 338 (S.D.N.Y. 2007).

21. Charles Garnier, Paris v. Andin International Inc., note 18 above.

22. 17 U.S.C. §103(b); Grove Press, Inc. v. Greenleaf Publishing Co., 247 F.Supp. 518 (S.D.N.Y. 1965); Russell v. Price, 612 F.2d 1123 (9th Cir. 1979), *cert. denied*, 446 U.S. 952 (1980).

23. 17 U.S.C. §506(c).

24. 17 U.S.C. §406(a).

25. 17 U.S.C. §406(b).

26. Note the negative implication of 17 U.S.C. §402(d). If this merely refers to the innocence defenses under §§405(b) and 406(a), it is simply redundant. One Fifth Circuit case suggests that if lawfully published copies of a work bearing notice are in the marketplace and thus accessible to the defendant, it is no defense that an unlawful copy from which the defendant actually copied bore no notice. Maverick Recording Co. v. Harper, 598 F.3d 193 (5th Cir.), *cert. denied*, 131 S.Ct. 590, 178 L.Ed.2d 511 (2010).

Chapter 5

1. 17 U.S.C. §411(a).

2. *See, e.g.*, Alicea v. Machete Music, 2012 U.S. Dist. LEXIS 22596 (D.Mass. Feb. 23, 2012), and cases cited therein. In some circuits that have not spoken on the issue, there is even disagreement among the trial courts.

3. 17 U.S.C. §412. The special exemption for films first fixed at time of broadcast is only available if advance notice is given to an infringer. 17 U.S.C. §411(b), 37 C.F.R. Ch. II §201.22.

4. 17 U.S.C. §910.

5. The tests described below are embodied in the definitions of the "Berne Convention work" and "country of origin" in 17 U.S.C. §101, as amended by P.L. 100-568, 102 Stat. 2853.

6. The statute is poorly drafted in this respect. Interpreted literally, it would waive registration for any unpublished audiovisual work of which not all authors are legal entities headquartered in the United States; in other words, even if all authors are U.S. citizens, it would waive registration because the authors are not "legal entities." This is clearly not the statutory intent, however.

7. Rogers v. Better Business Bureau of Metropolitan Houston, Inc., 887 F.Supp.2d 722 (S.D.Tex. 2012).

8. Morris v. Business Concepts, Inc., 259 F.3d 65 (2d Cir. 2001).

9. 17 U.S.C. §409.

10. 17 U.S.C. §506(e). *See* Ashton-Tate Corp. v. Fox Software Inc., 760 F.Supp. 831 (C.D.Cal. 1990), rescinded by Order dated Apr. 18, 1991, 1991 U.S. Dist. LEXIS 6577. *See also*

Whimsicality, Inc. v. Rubie's Costumes Co. Inc., 891 F.2d 452 (2d Cir. 1989).

11. Torres-Negron v. J & N Records, LLC, 504 F.3d 151 (1st Cir. 2007).

12. 17 U.S.C. §407.

13. 37 C.F.R. Ch. II §202.19(f).

14. 17 U.S.C. §407(d).

15. 37 C.F.R. Ch. II §202.19.

16. 37 C.F.R. Ch. II §202.20.

17. A motion picture is not considered to be published for these purposes merely because a nonprofit institution has been given a license to make a fixation of it. For example, if a school is given permission to videotape a television broadcast, the television program is still unpublished for deposit purposes though not for other purposes.

18. 37 C.F.R. Ch. II §202.21.

19. 37 C.F.R. Ch. II §202.3(b)(4); Kay Berry, Inc. v. Taylor Gifts, Inc., 421 F.3d 199 (3d Cir. 2005).

20. 77 Fed. Reg. 40,268; Panoramic Stock Images, Ltd. v. John Wiley & Sons, Inc., 2013 U.S. Dist. LEXIS 122218 (N.D. Ill. Aug. 28, 2013).

21. 37 C.F.R. Ch. II §202.3(b).

22. If hand-delivered by a commercial, nongovernment courier or messenger, a request for reconsideration must be delivered between 8:30 a.m. and 4 p.m. to: Congressional Courier Acceptance Site, located at Second and D Streets, NE, Washington, DC. If hand-delivered by a private party, a request for reconsideration must be delivered between 8:30 a.m. and 5 p.m. to: Room 401 of the James Madison Memorial Building, located at 101 Independence Avenue, SE, Washington, DC.

23. The statutory provision is 17 U.S.C. §408(f). The Copyright Office has issued an interim regulation, 37 C.F.R. Ch. II §202.16, regarding the preregistration process. This may be found at http://www.copyright.gov/fedreg/2005/70fr61905.html.

Chapter 6

1. The first two of these three limitations are contained in 17 U.S.C. §114(d); the third is in 17 U.S.C. §112. Under §112, those transmitters who transmit sound recordings to business establishments (for background music, basically) must pay a compulsory license fee to exercise this right. Note also that in the case of *digital* transmitters who have rights under §112, copyright owners are supposed to supply decryption technology to them for purposes of making lawful copies, "if it is technologically feasible and economically reasonable" for the copyright owners to do so. If they do not, then the transmitters are released from that part of the statute which makes it illegal to decrypt copyrighted material. The topic of decryption is treated in chapter 8.

2. 17 U.S.C. §117.

3. *See* Krause v. Titleserv, Inc., 402 F.3d 119 (2d Cir. 2005).

4. Storage Tech. Corp. v. Custom Hardware Engineering & Consulting, Inc., 421 F.3d 1307 (Fed. Cir. 2005).

5. Authors Guild, Inc. v. HathiTrust, 902 F. Supp. 2d 445 (S.D.N.Y. 2012).

6. For information, see http://www.nimac.us/faq_general.html.

7. Wis. Stat. 106.57.

8. For the text, see http://www.wipo.int/meetings/en/doc_details.jsp?doc_id=241683.

9. 17 U.S.C. §120.

10. 17 U.S.C. §109.

11. 17 U.S.C. §602.

12. Kirtsaeng v. John Wiley & Sons, Inc., 133 S.Ct. 1351 (2013).

13. Technically, the restrictions regarding software apply to anyone in possession of a copy of a program, not just the "owner" of a copy. It is odd that Congress thought it necessary to state this, since the first sale doctrine of §109(a) explicitly applies only to copies of which *ownership* has passed from the copyright owner. Despite the appearances this may create, no negative inference should be drawn from the wording of §109(b): the first sale doctrine exempts rental,

lease, and lending *only* where title to the object has passed to the lessor or lender.

14. Vernor v. Autodesk, Inc., 621 F.3d 1102 (9th Cir. 2010), *cert. denied*, 132 S.Ct. 105 (2011). In that case the "notable" restrictions imposed were stated in the license agreement as follows:

> YOU MAY NOT: (1) modify, translate, reverse-engineer, decompile, or disassemble the Software . . . (3) remove any proprietary notices, labels, or marks from the Software or Documentation; (4) use . . . the Software outside of the Western Hemisphere; (5) utilize any computer software or hardware designed to defeat any hardware copy-protection device, should the software you have licensed be equipped with such protection; or (6) use the Software for commercial or other revenue-generating purposes if the Software has been licensed or labeled for educational use only.

15. Ass'n for Info. Media & Equip. v. Regents of the Univ. of Cal., 2011 U.S. Dist. LEXIS 154011 (C.D.Cal. Oct. 3, 2011); United States v. American Society of Composers, Authors and Publishers, 627 F.3d 64 (2d Cir. 2010). In this, the United States is unusual. Most countries treat a download as a performance.

16. 17 U.S.C. §114(a). In addition to the exceptions discussed below, Congress has specifically provided that one who owns a lawfully made copy of a video game has the right to perform the game publicly without the copyright owner's permission. This presumptive right does not apply to works incorporated in the visual part of the game unless those works are owned by the same copyright owner. 17 U.S.C. §109.

17. 17 U.S.C. §§106(6), 114(d).

18. All exceptions under this heading are in 17 U.S.C. §110 unless otherwise noted.

19. 17 U.S.C. §112(f).

20. 17 U.S.C. §111(a).

21. See 17 U.S.C. §§110(5), 504(d), and 513.

22. 17 U.S.C. §112(b).

23. 37 C.F.R. Ch. II §201.13.

24. 17 U.S.C. §112(d).

25. All exceptions under this heading are in 17 U.S.C. §110 unless otherwise noted. As with the performance right, the display right for video games is not effective against owners of lawfully made copies.

26. 17 U.S.C. §110(3).

27. 17 U.S.C. §113(c).

28. Dastar Corp. v. Twentieth Century Fox Film Corp., 539 U.S. 23 (2003).

29. Seng-Tiong Ho v. Taflove, 648 F.3d 489 (7th Cir. 2011).

30. 17 U.S.C. §106A.

31. Mass. Museum of Contemporary Art Found., Inc. v. Buchel, 593 F.3d 38 (1st Cir. 2010)—a case otherwise worth reading as a "how-not-to" for museums and artists.

32. Carter v. Helmsley-Spear, 71 F.3d 77, 85 (2d Cir. N.Y. 1995).

33. Lilley v. Stout, 384 F.Supp.2d 83, 88 (D.D.C. 2005).

34. Carter v. Helmsley-Spear, *supra*, 71 F.3d at 84–85.

35. Phillips v. Pembroke Real Estate, Inc., 459 F.3d 128 (1st Cir. 2006).

36. Kelley v. Chicago Park District, 635 F.3d 290 (7th Cir. 2011).

37. 17 U.S.C. §106A(c)(2). This provision is quite illogical, since intent is clearly required for actionable modification, and the statute specifically distinguishes between intent and gross negligence. See §106A(a)(3)(A) and (B). Nevertheless, we are obliged to take it seriously. The statutory history loses sight of the limitation, further muddying the waters. See H.R. Rep. No. 101-514 at p. 16, under the heading "State of Mind."

38. Carter v. Helmsley-Spear Inc., *supra*.

39. 17 U.S.C. §113(d).

40. In this sentence, I am deviating somewhat from the statutory language, as I believe the statute intends to say more than it does and is poorly drafted. My departure is to speak here of works "incorporated in" a building. Technically, this part of the statute, §113(d)(2), addresses only works that are "part of" buildings, a term that purports to be different from

"incorporated in" (see §113(d)(1)(A)). But the distinction (if there is one) seems contrary to the intent of the statute; furthermore, the section of the statute that provides a registry for artists' names for purposes of notice under §113(d)(2)—namely, §113(d)(3)—speaks of works "incorporated in or made part of" buildings.

41. 37 C.F.R. Ch. II §201.25.

42. See H.R. Rep. No. 101-514 at p. 19; Karlin, "Joint Ownership of Moral Rights," 38 *Jrnl. Copr. Soc.* 4 (1991).

43. Both of these problems appear to have been created by floor amendments to the bill. Compare the statute as enacted with H.R. Rep. No. 101-514 at p. 19.

44. For the state laws just referred to, see: Gen. Stat. of Conn., Title 42 §42-116s *et seq.*; La. Rev. Stat. §51:2151c *et seq.*; 27 Maine Rev. Stat. §303; Mass. Gen. Laws Ch. 231 §85S; N.J. Stat. Title 2A, Ch. 24A; N.Y. General Business Law, Art. 12-J, §228 m–q; 73 Penn. Stat. §§2101–2110; and Gen. Laws of R.I., Title 5, Ch. 62.

45. Estate of Graham v. Sotheby's Inc., 860 F.Supp.2d 1117 (C.D.Cal. 2012). According the court, in 34 years only $328,000 of royalties had been distributed to roughly 400 artists.

46. See EU Directive 2001/84/EC and the UK Artist's Resale Right (Amendment) Regulations.

Chapter 7

1. 17 U.S.C. §115. For the royalty rates see 37 C.F.R. Ch. III §307.3.

2. 37 C.F.R. Ch. II §201.18.

3. *Ibid.*

4. 37 C.F.R. Ch. III §385.10–17.

5. 17 U.S.C. §114(d),(e),(f); see also information at www.soundexchange.com. Note that webcasters are also eligible for a special statutory license entitling them to create, and maintain for short durations, phonorecords of sound recordings as needed for their transmissions. See 17 U.S.C. §112.

6. The license is at 17 U.S.C. §111. SoundExchange has a great deal of information on its website concerning this

statutory license. See www.soundexchange.com. The royalty rates are found at 37 C.F.R. Ch. III §308.2. The license is not available to satellite carriers, even if they are passive retransmitters. Satellite Broadcasting and Communications Association of America v. Oman, 17 F.3d 344 (11th Cir. 1994). The license was extended to "wireless" television by P.L. 103-369.

7. 17 U.S.C. §501(b),(c),(d).

8. 17 U.S.C. §118.

9. 37 C.F.R. Ch. III §304.

10. 17 U.S.C. §119.

11. 17 U.S.C. Ch. 10.

12. 17 U.S.C. §513.

Chapter 8

1. A stimulating discussion of this is Professor Benjamin Kaplan's book, *An Unhurried View of Copyright* (New York: Columbia University Press, 1967).

2. See discussion in Bouchat v. Baltimore Ravens, Inc., 241 F.3d 350, 355–356 (4th Cir. 2001).

3. Judge Learned Hand, writing in Nichols v. Universal Pictures Corp., 45 F.2d 119 (2d Cir. 1930), *cert. denied*, 282 U.S. 902 (1931).

4. Mattel, Inc. v. MGA Entertainment, Inc., 616 F.3d 904, 908 (9th Cir. Cal. 2010).

5. *See, e.g.,* Harold Lloyd Corp. v. Witwer, 65 F.2d 1 (9th Cir. 1933); Twentieth Century Fox-Film Corp. v. Stonesifer, 140 F.2d 579 (9th Cir. 1944).

6. Sheldon v. Metro-Goldwyn Pictures Corp., 81 F.2d 49 (2d Cir. 1936).

7. The Sixth Circuit has held that this does not apply to "sampling" of sound recordings, but its holding has been roundly criticized and is unlikely to hold sway elsewhere. See Bridgeport Music, Inc. v. Dimension Films, 410 F.3d 792 (6th Cir. 2005); EMI Records Limited v. Premise Media Corp. L.P., 2008 N.Y. Misc. LEXIS 8213 (N.Y. Sup. Ct. Aug. 8, 2008).

8. *See, e.g.,* Computer Associates Inc. v. Altai Inc., 982 F.2d 693 (2d Cir. 1992). In Kohus v. Mariol, 328 F.3d 848 (6th Cir. 2003), the court held that the target audience should be taken into account whenever appreciating a work requires "specialized expertise," such as (in that case) technical drawings for mechanical parts.

9. Sid & Marty Krofft Television Prods., Inc. v. McDonald's Corp., 562 F.2d 1157 (9th Cir. 1977).

10. For cases where these evils have arisen, see Dawson v. Hinshaw Music, Inc., 905 F.2d 731 (4th Cir. 1990), in which the court finds that music sold only to choral directors should be judged by what a choral director would perceive, never bothering to inquire what the ultimate audience might perceive; and Original Appalachian Artworks, Inc. v. Blue Box Factory (USA) Ltd., 577 F.Supp. 625 (S.D.N.Y. 1983), in which Dr. Joyce Brothers was allowed to opine on how the works in question would be perceived by juvenile customers.

11. Cartoon Network LP, LLLP v. CSC Holdings, Inc., 536 F.3d 121, 139 (2d Cir. 2008), *cert. denied*, 557 U.S. 946 (2009).

12. WNET v. Aereo, Inc., 2013 U.S. App. LEXIS 6578 (2d Cir. N.Y. Apr. 1, 2013).

13. Fox Television Stations v. Barrydriller Content Sys., 2012 U.S. Dist. LEXIS 184209 (C.D.Cal. Dec. 27, 2012).

14. Romm Art Creations Ltd. v. Simcha Int'l Arts Inc., 786 F.Supp. 1126 (E.D.N.Y. 1992).

15. Bleistein v. Donaldson Lithographing Co., 188 U.S. 239 (1903).

16. Burrow-Giles Lithographic Co. v. Sarony, 111 U.S. 53 (1884).

17. Concrete Machinery Co., Inc. v. Classic Lawn Ornaments, Inc., 843 F.2d 600 (1st Cir. 1988).

18. Herbert v. Shanley Co., 242 U.S. 591 (1917).

19. Shapiro, Bernstein & Co. v. H. L. Green Co., 316 F.2d 304 (2d Cir. 1963).

20. Demetriades v. Kaufmann, 690 F.Supp. 289, 291 (S.D.N.Y. 1988); MGM Studios Inc. v. Grokster, Ltd., 545 U.S. 913 (2005).

21. Merchant v. Levy, 92 F.3d 51 (2d Cir. 1996), *cert. denied*, 136 L.Ed.2d 833 (1997).

22. 17 U.S.C. §501(b).

23. *Ibid*.

24. 17 U.S.C. §504(b).

25. Sheldon v. Metro-Goldwyn Pictures, 106 F.2d 45 (2d Cir. 1939).

26. 17 U.S.C. §504(c). Note that a compilation is considered to be a single work for these purposes, even if its components are capable of being protected as separate works. The right to a jury trial in statutory damage cases was established by Feltner v. Columbia Pictures Television, Inc., 523 U.S. 340 (1998). In a bench trial, one may elect statutory damages at any time up until actual entry of judgment. Branch v. Ogilvy & Mather, 772 F.Supp. 1359 (S.D.N.Y. 1991); Oboler v. Goldin, 714 F.2d 211 (2d Cir. 1983). However, in a jury trial, the election would presumably have to be made before the jury returned with a verdict.

27. Bryant v. Media Right Prods., 603 F.3d 135 (2d Cir. 2010), *cert. denied*, 131 S.Ct. 656 (2010).

28. N.A.S. Import, Corp. v. Chenson Enterprises, Inc., 968 F.2d 250 (2d Cir. 1992);17 U.S.C. §504(c)(3).

29. Sony BMG Music Entertainment v. Tenenbaum, 660 F.3d 487 (1st Cir. 2011), 2013 U.S. App. LEXIS 12968 (1st Cir. June 25, 2013); Capitol Records, Inc. v. Thomas-Rasset, 692 F.3d 899 (8th Cir. 2012), *cert. denied*, 2013 U.S. LEXIS 2340 (U.S. Mar. 18, 2013).

30. 17 U.S.C. §505; Fogerty v. Fantasy Inc., 510 U.S. 517 (1994).

31. eBay Inc. v. MercExchange, L.L.C., 547 U.S. 388 (U.S. 2006); Salinger v. Colting, 607 F.3d 68 (2d Cir. 2010).

32. Florida Prepaid Postsecondary Educ. Expense Bd. v. College Sav. Bank, 527 U.S. 627 (1999); Chavez v. Arte Publico Press, 204 F.3d 601, 603 (5th Cir. 2000).

33. Cambridge Univ. Press v. Becker, 863 F.Supp.2d 1190 (N.D.Ga. 2012).

34. Ingrassia v. Chicken Ranch Bingo & Casino, 676 F.Supp.2d 953 (E.D.Cal. 2009).

35. 154 Cong. Rec. S9867-03 (daily ed. Sept. 26, 2008) (statement of Sen. Patrick Leahy).

36. The Copyright Office Notice of Inquiry contains a brief survey of the international field. See http://www.copyright.gov/fedreg/2012/77fr64555.pdf.

37. 17 U.S.C. §506(a), as amended by P.L. 105-145. The fines are found in 18 U.S.C. §3571, and it should be noted that the fine can be greater: up to twice the defendant's pecuniary gain or twice the copyright owner's pecuniary loss. It should also be noted that copyright infringement has been brought within the scope of the Racketeering and Corrupt Practices Act, which exposes a defendant to yet greater penalties: 18 U.S.C. §1961.

38. 17 U.S.C. §1201. See Universal City Studios v. Corley, 273 F.3d 429 (2d Cir. 2001).

39. Chamberlain Group, Inc. v. Skylink Technologies, Inc., 381 F.3d 1178 (Fed. Cir. 2004); *see also* Lexmark v. Static Control, 387 F.3d 522 (6th Cir. 2004).

40. Storage Tech. Corp. v. Custom Hardware Eng'g & Consulting, Inc., 421 F.3d 1307 (Fed. Cir. 2005).

41. MDY Indus., LLC v. Blizzard Entertainment, Inc., 629 F.3d 928 (9th Cir. 2010).

42. 17 U.S.C. §1201(a)(1)(B).

43. The report is available at http://www.copyright.gov/fedreg/2012/77fr65260.pdf.

44. 17 U.S.C. §1203; TracFone Wireless, Inc. v. Pak China Group Co., 843 F.Supp.2d 1284 (S.D.Fla. 2012).

45. Universal City Studios v. Corley, 273 F.3d 429 (2d Cir. 2001).

46. Macrovision v. Sima Prods. Corp., 2006 U.S. Dist. LEXIS 22106 (S.D.N.Y. Apr. 20, 2006).

47. UMG Recs., Inc. v. Escape Media Group, Inc., 2013 N.Y. App. Div. LEXIS 2642 (N.Y. App. Div. 1st Dep't Apr. 23, 2013).

48. Online Policy Group v. Diebold, Inc., 337 F.Supp.2d 1195 (N.D.Cal. 2004).

49. Lenz v. Universal Music Corp., 572 F.Supp.2d 1150 (N.D.Cal. 2008).

50. Viacom Int'l, Inc. v. YouTube, Inc., 676 F.3d 19 (2d Cir. 2012).

51. William Hazlitt, "On Prejudice." I have not found the source in Defoe himself of this wonderful remark.

52. 17 U.S.C. §1202.

53. 17 U.S.C. §1203.

54. 17 U.S.C. §1204.

Chapter 9

1. 17 U.S.C. §107.

2. This passage from Folsom v. Marsh, 9 F.Cas. 342 (No. 4,901) (C.C.D. Mass. 1841), is quoted by the Supreme Court in Campbell v. Acuff-Rose Music, 510 U.S. 569, 576 (1994).

3. 17 U.S.C. §113(c); Italian Book Corp. v. American Broadcasting Companies, Inc., 458 F.Supp. 65 (S.D.N.Y. 1978).

4. Publications Int'l Ltd. v. Bally Mfg. Corp., 215 U.S.P.Q. 861 (N.D.Ill. 1982).

5. *See* Meredith Corp. v. Harper & Row, Publishers, Inc., 378 F.Supp. 686 (S.D.N.Y. 1974), *aff'd*, 500 F.2d 1221 (2d Cir. 1974).

6. Craft v. Kobler, 667 F.Supp. 120 (S.D.N.Y. 1987).

7. Harper & Row, Publishers, Inc. v. The Nation Enterprises, 471 U.S. 539, 105 S.Ct. 2218 (1985).

8. Salinger v. Random House, Inc., 811 F.2d 90 (2d Cir. 1987), *cert. denied*, 108 S.Ct. 213 (1987); New ERA Publications International, ApS v. Henry Holt & Co., 10 U.S.P.Q.2d 1561 (2d Cir. 1989), *rev'g* 695 F.Supp. 1493 (S.D.N.Y. 1988).

9. Berne Convention, Paris Text, Art. 10.

10. Chicago Board of Education v. Substance, Inc., 354 F.3d 624 (7th Cir. 2003).

11. Bridgeport Music, Inc. v. UMG Recordings, Inc., 585 F.3d 267, 277 (6th Cir. 2009).

12. 131 F.Supp. 165 (S.D.Cal. 1955), *aff'd sub nom.* Benny v. Loew's, Inc., 239 F.2d 532 (9th Cir. 1956).

13. Columbia Pictures Corp. v. National Broadcasting Co., 137 F.Supp. 348, 350 (S.D.Cal. 1955).

14. Campbell v. Acuff-Rose Music, Inc., 510 U.S. 569, 114 S.Ct. 1164 (1994).

15. SunTrust Bank v. Houghton Mifflin Co., 268 F.3d 1257 (11th Cir. 2001).

16. Mattel v. Walking Mountain Productions, 353 F.3d 792 (9th Cir. 2003).

17. Leibovitz v. Paramount Pictures Corp., 948 F.Supp. 1214 (S.D.N.Y. 1996), *aff'd*, 137 F.3d 109 (2d Cir. 1998).

18. Cariou v. Prince, 2013 U.S. App. LEXIS 8380 (2d Cir. Apr. 25, 2013).

19. Walt Disney Productions v. Filmation Associates, 628 F.Supp. 871 (C.D.Cal. 1986).

20. Tiffany Design v. Reno-Tahoe Specialty, Inc., 55 F.Supp.2d 1113 (D.Nev. 1999).

21. Robert Stigwood Group, Ltd. v. O'Reilly, 346 F.Supp. 376 (D.Conn. 1972).

22. Time, Inc. v. Bernard Geis Associates, 293 F.Supp. 130 (S.D.N.Y. 1968).

23. Belmore v. City Pages, Inc., 8880 F.Supp. 673 (D.Minn. 1995).

24. Robart v. J. R. O'Dwyer Co., Inc., 34 U.S.P.Q.2d 1085 (S.D.N.Y. 1995).

25. Falwell v. Penthouse Int'l Ltd., 521 F.Supp. 1204 (W.D.Va. 1981).

26. Savage v. Council on American-Islamic Rels., Inc., 2008 U.S. Dist. LEXIS 60545 (N.D.Cal. July 25, 2008).

27. Nunez v. Caribbean Int'l News Corp., 235 F.3d 18 (1st Cir. 2000).

28. Monge v. Maya Magazines, Inc., 688 F.3d 1164 (9th Cir. 2012).

29. Bill Graham Archives v. Dorling Kindersley Ltd., 448 F.3d 605 (2d Cir. 2006).

30. Sofa Entertainment, Inc. v. Dodger Productions, 709 F.3d 1273 (9th Cir. 2013).

31. Kelly v. Arriba Soft Corp., 336 F.3d 811 (9th Cir. 2003).

32. A.V. v. iParadigms, LLC, 562 F.3d 630 (4th Cir. 2009).

33. Authors Guild, Inc. v. Google Inc., 2013 U.S. Dist. LEXIS 162198 (S.D.N.Y. Nov. 14, 2013).

34. Authors Guild, Inc. v. HathiTrust, 902 F.Supp.2d 445, 449 (S.D.N.Y. 2012).

35. Scherr v. Universal Match Corp., 297 F.Supp. 102 (S.D.N.Y. 1967).

36. Williams & Wilkins Co. v. United States, 487 F.2d 134 (Ct. Cl. 1973), *aff'd by an equally divided court*, 420 U.S. 376 (1975).

37. Basic Books, Inc. v. Kinko's Graphics Corp., 785 F.Supp. 1522 (S.D.N.Y. 1991).

38. H. Rep., p. 74.

39. American Geophysical Union v. Texaco, Inc., 60 F.3d 913 (2d Cir. 1994), *aff'g* 802 F.Supp. 1 (S.D.N.Y. 1992).

40. Sony Corporation of America v. Universal City Studios, Inc., 464 U.S. 417 (1984).

41. MGM Studios Inc. v. Grokster, Ltd., 545 U.S. 913 (U.S. 2005); In re Aimster Copyright Litig., 334 F.3d 643 (7th Cir. 2003); A&M Records v. Napster, Inc., 239 F.3d 1004 (9th Cir. 2001).

42. *See* Capitol Records, Inc. v. Thomas-Rasset, 692 F.3d 899 (8th Cir. 2012); Sony BMG Music Entm't v. Tenenbaum, 660 F.3d 487 (1st Cir. 2011).

43. Sega Enterprises, Ltd. v. Accolade, Inc., 977 F.2d 1510 (9th Cir. 1993); Atari Games Corp. v. Nintendo of America, Inc., 975 F.2d 832 (Fed. Cir. 1992). *Cf.* Vault Corp. v. Quaid Software Ltd., 847 F.2d 255 (5th Cir. 1988).

44. Davidson & Assocs. v. Jung, 422 F.3d 630 (8th Cir. 2005).

45. H. Rep., pp. 68–70.

46. Princeton Univ. Press v. Michigan Document Services, Inc., 99 F.3d 1381 (6th Cir. 1996).

47. Cambridge Univ. Press v. Becker, 863 F.Supp.2d 1190 (N.D.Ga. 2012).

48. H. Rep., pp. 70–71. The text as reprinted here, however, reflects a change in A.2 that was made after the House Report was printed. See remarks of Rep. Kastenmeier in the House Congressional Record for September 22, 1976, at p. 31980.

49. Library of Congress, Circular 21, "Reproduction of Copyrighted Works by Educators and Librarians," p. 26.

50. H.R. Conf. Rep. No. 94-1733, 2d Sess. 70, 1976 U.S. Code Cong. & Ad. News 5659, 5811.

51. 17 U.S.C. §108.

52. 17 U.S.C. §108(d).

53. Final Report of CONTU, pp. 54–55.

54. H. Rep., p. 77.

55. 17 U.S.C. §108(f)(1).

Chapter 10

1. Maljack Productions, Inc. v. GoodTimes Home Video Corp., 81 F.3d 881 (9th Cir. 1996); Batjac Productions, Inc. v. GoodTimes Video Corp., 160 F.3d 1223 (9th Cir. 1998); Shoptalk Ltd. v. Concorde-New Horizons Corp., 49 U.S.P.Q.2d 1599 (2d Cir. 1999).

2. See discussion in William F. Patry, *Patry on Copyright* (Thomson Reuters/West, 2009), at §§6:44 and 7:24.50. The Ninth Circuit blew its chance to correct itself when it decided Societe Civile Succession Richard Guino v. Renoir, 549 F.3d 1182 (9th Cir. 2008), *reh. denied,* 2009 U.S. App. LEXIS 6872 (9th Cir. Apr. 1, 2009), finding sculptures first published in 1917 to be still under U.S. copyright, a result at odds with what had been a universal assumption that anything published anywhere before 1923 is in the public domain in the United States.

3. Former Title 17 of the U.S. Code, §§19, 21.

4. L & L White Metal Casting Corp. v. Cornell Metal Specialties Corp., 353 F.Supp. 1170 (E.D.N.Y. 1972), *aff'd,* 177 U.S.P.Q. 673 (2d Cir. 1973); First American Artificial Flowers, Inc. v. Joseph Markovits, Inc., 342 F.Supp. 178 (S.D.N.Y. 1972).

5. Hoepker v. Kruger, 200 F.Supp.2d 340 (S.D.N.Y. 2002).

6. The Statement of Administrative Action prepared by the U.S. Trade Representative, and explicitly approved in the statute (see P.L. 103-465 §101(a)(2)), states at §B.1(c)(2) that transfers by authors or original right holders are to be given effect according to their terms, "taking into account the

expectations of the parties and relevant laws (including those concerning copyright, neighboring rights, contracts, descent and distribution, estates, and conflicts of law)."

7. The statute is so opaquely drafted that it could be read to impose a much earlier cutoff date where the source country is a Berne country. See §§104A(h)(3) and 104A(h)(4)(b). Such a result can hardly have been intended, however.

8. Discontinuance for any appreciable period of time vitiates the defense of "reliance party" status. Troll Co. v. Uneeda Doll Co., 483 F.3d 150, 158 (2d Cir. 2007).

9. The drafters of the GATT implementing legislation neglected to repeal or qualify §405(b) of the Copyright Act, which could be read to provide a much broader defense to someone who relied on the absence of notice in a pre-1989 foreign work than is available to a reliance party who has received a "notice of intent to enforce." However, it is clear from the context that the new §104A was intended to override any such defense.

10. There is a theoretical gap here, of little practical consequence. The statute assumes that no country would join Berne or the WTO between December 8, 1994, and January 1, 1995. See §§104A(d)(3)(A) and 104A(h)(1).

11. Sheldon v. Metro-Goldwyn Pictures Corp., 81 F.2d 49 (2d Cir. 1946).

12. 17 U.S.C. §109(a), as amended by §514(b) of the Uruguay Round Agreements Act, P.L. 103-465, 108 Stat. 4809.

13. Goodis v. United Artists Television, Inc., 425 F.2d 397 (2d Cir. 1970). *See* Sanga Music, Inc. v. EMI Blackwood Music, Inc., 55 F.3d 756 (2d Cir. 1995), for an odd exception to *Goodis*.

14. Group Publishers v. Winchell, 86 F.Supp. 573, 576 (S.D.N.Y. 1952). However, this recordation requirement might well apply still to other types of works; see former Title 17 of the U.S. Code, §32.

15. Pushman v. New York Graphic Society, Inc., 287 N.Y. 302, 39 N.E.2d 249 (1942); Chamberlain v. Feldman, 300 N.Y. 135, 89 N.E.2d 863 (1949).

16. N.Y. Laws 1966, Ch. 688, §3; Calif. Civil Code §982(e).

17. Picture Music, Inc. v. Bourne, Inc., 457 F.2d 1213 (2d Cir. 1972). *Cf.* Shapiro, Bernstein & Co., Inc. v. Jerry Vogel Music Co., Inc., 221 F.2d 569 (2d Cir. 1955), *mod. on other grounds on rehearing*, 223 F.2d 252 (2d Cir. 1955).

18. Shapiro, Bernstein & Co., Inc. v. Jerry Vogel Music Co., Inc., *supra;* Donna v. Dodd, Mead & Co., Inc., 374 F.Supp. 429 (S.D.N.Y. 1974).

19. White-Smith Music Publishing Co. v. Apollo Co., 209 U.S. 1 (1908).

20. *See generally* Nimmer, *op. cit.,* §2.10.

21. 17 U.S.C. §§301(c), 303; Capitol Records, Inc. v. Naxos of America, Inc., 4 N.Y.3d 540 (N.Y. 2005).

22. The Ninth Circuit case was La Cienega Music Co. v. ZZ Top, 53 F.3d 950 (9th Cir. 1995). The statute is 17 U.S.C. §303(b) as revised.

23. *Compare* Frederick Music Co. v. Sickler, 708 F.Supp. 587 (S.D.N.Y. 1989) *with* Marascalco v. Fantasy, Inc., 17 U.S.P.Q.2d 1409 (C.D.Cal. 1990).

24. Epoch Producing Corp. v. Killiam Shows, Inc., 522 F.2d 737 (2d Cir. 1975).

25. Miller Music Company v. Chas. N. Daniels, Inc., 362 U.S. 373 (1960).

26. Fred Fisher Music Co. v. M. Witmark & Sons, 318 U.S. 643 (1943).

27. Marks Music Corp. v. Borst Music Pub. Co., 110 F.Supp. 923 (D.N.J. 1953). For an excellent discussion of these rules and their many quirks, see Nevins, "The Magic Kingdom of Will-Bumping: Where Estates Law and Copyright Law Collide," 35 *Jrnl. Copr. Soc.* 2 (1988).

28. Broadcast Music, Inc. v. Roger Miller Music, Inc., 396 F.3d 762 (6th Cir. 2005).

29. De Sylva v. Ballentine, 351 U.S. 570 (1956); 17 U.S.C. §§304(a), 101.

30. Copyright Office regulations deal with the complicated problem of an author who leaves a will but has no executor actively serving: 37 C.F.R. Ch. II §202.17(f)(3).

31. Rose v. Bourne, Inc., 279 F.2d 79 (2d Cir. 1960).

32. Edward B. Marks Music Corp. v. Jerry Vogel Music Company, 140 F.2d 266 (2nd Cir. 1944); *but see* Nimmer, *op. cit.,* §9.05[E].

33. Bartok v. Boosey & Hawkes, Inc., 523 F.2d 941 (2d Cir. 1975). For the mechanics of renewal of posthumous works, see 37 C.F.R. Ch. II §202.17(f)(2).

34. H. Rep., p. 139.

35. Former Title 17 of the U.S. Code, §24; *see* Shapiro, Bernstein & Co. v. Bryan, 123 F.2d 1697 (2d Cir. 1941).

36. 17 U.S.C. §304(a), as amended by Copyright Amendments Act of 1992.

37. Stewart v. Abend, 110 S.Ct. 1750 (1990).

38. 37 C.F.R. Ch. II §202.17.

39. *Ibid.*

40. 17 U.S.C. §408(c)(3).

41. 17 U.S.C. §304.

42. 17 U.S.C. §304(c).

43. *Ibid.*; 37 C.F.R. Ch. II §201.10.

Chapter 11

1. 26 U.S.C. 1221(b)(3).

2. Rev. Rul. 68-194, 1968-1 C.B. 87.

3. C. W. Churchman, 68 T.C. 696 (1977).

4. Reg. §1.183-2.

5. Rev. Rul. 73-395, 1972-2 C.B. 87, as affected by P.L. 94-455, §2119. *See* Stern v. U.S.A., 1971-1 U.S.T.C. ¶86,491 (C.D.Cal. 1971).

6. Reg. §1.167(a)-1(b).

7. Rev. Rul. 60-358, 1960-2 C.B. 68.

8. *Ibid.*

9. Rev. Rul. 68-194, 1968-1 C.B. 87.

10. Reg. §1.167(a)-6(a); Rev. Rul. 73-395, 1973-2 C.B. 87, as affected by P.L. 94-455, §2119.

11. Heim v. Fitzpatrick, 262 F.2d 887 (2d Cir. 1959).

12. Rev. Rul. 55-706, 1955-2 C.B. 300.

13. This is by analogy to patents. See Reg. §1.1235-2(b)(2)(ii).

14. Cory v. Commissioner of Internal Revenue, 230 F.2d 941 (2d Cir. 1956), *cert. denied*, 35 U.S. 828 (1956); for a patent analogy *see* Marco (1955), 25 T.C. 544.

15. I.R.C. §197, as amended by P.L. 103-66.

Chapter 12

1. For a compendium of U.S. copyright relations with foreign countries, see Copyright Office Circular 38a.

2. Berne Convention, Paris Text, Art. 7(8). For a detailed discussion of this, particularly as it affects works of the U.S. Government, *see* Ringer and Flacks, *op. cit.,* at pp. 157–204.

3. See, e.g., Nordemann, "The Term of Protection for Works by U.S.-American Authors in Germany," 44 *Jrnl. Copr. Soc.* 1 (1996).

4. Berne Convention, Paris Text, Appendix; U.C.C. Articles Vter, V quater.

5. Itar-Tass Russian News Agency v. Russian Kurier, Inc., 153 F.3d 82 (2d Cir. 1998).

6. Nimmer, *op. cit.,* §17.07[B].

7. *See* 82 *PTCJ* 2017 (5/27/11), at p. 120.

8. This is the WIPO Performances and Phonograms Treaty (WPPT).

Chapter 13

1. Her talk on this subject can be read at http://www.copyright .gov/docs/next_great_copyright_act.pdf.

2. Eldred v. Ashcroft, 537 U.S. 186 (2003).

Appendix C

1. E.g., Atari Games Corp. v. Oman, 888 F.2d 878, 885–886 (D.C. Cir. 1989).

INDEX